Beyond Nationalism?

GLOBAL ENCOUNTERS: STUDIES IN COMPARATIVE POLITICAL THEORY
Series Editor: Fred Dallmayr, University of Notre Dame

This series seeks to inaugurate a new field of inquiry and intellectual concern: that of comparative political theory as an inquiry proceeding not from the citadel of a global hegemony but through cross-cultural dialogue and critical interaction. By opening the discourse of political theory—today largely dominated by American and European intellectuals—to voices from across the global spectrum, we hope to contribute to a richer, multifaceted mode of theorizing as well as to a deeper, cross-cultural awareness of the requirements of global justice.

INTERNATIONAL ADVISORY BOARD

Border Crossings: Toward a Comparative Political Theory, edited by Fred Dallmayr
Race and Reconciliation in South Africa: A Multicultural Dialogue in Comparative Perspective, edited by William E. Van Vugt and G. Daan Cloete
Gandhi, Freedom, and Self-Rule, edited by Anthony J. Parel
Beyond Nationalism? Sovereignity and Citizenship, edited by Fred Dallmayr and José M. Rosales

Beyond Nationalism?

Sovereignty and Citizenship

Edited by
Fred Dallmayr and José M. Rosales

LEXINGTON BOOKS
Lanham • Boulder • New York • Oxford

LEXINGTON BOOKS

Published in the United States of America
by Lexington Books
4720 Boston Way, Lanham, Maryland 20706

12 Hid's Copse Road
Cumnor Hill, Oxford OX2 9JJ, England

British Library Cataloguing in Publication Information Available

Library of Congress Cataloging-in-Publication Data

Beyond nationalism? : sovereignty and citizenship / [edited by] Fred R. Dallmayr and
José M. Rosales.
    p. cm. — (Global encounters)
    Includes bibliographical references and index.
    ISBN 0-7391-0224-9 (cloth: alk. paper) — ISBN 0-7391-0225-7 (pbk. : alk. paper)
        1.   Sovereignty. 2. Nationalism. I. Dallmayr, Fred R. (Fred Reinhard), 1928-
II. Rosales, José María. III. Series

    JC327 .B574 2001
    320.1'5—dc21   00-047803

Printed in the United States of America

♾™ The paper used in this publication meets the minimum requirements of American
National Standard for Information Sciences—Permanence of Paper for Printed Library
Materials, ANSI/NISO Z39.48–1992.

To the memory of
RICHARD ASHCRAFT

AND TO PEOPLE EVERYWHERE
COMMITTED TO JUSTICE AND PEACE

Contents

Part III
Citizenship in a Global World

Foreword

Benjamin R. Barber

The balanced and thoughtful collection of essays brought together in this volume to address the challenges of nationalism in an age of globalization has a delightfully mischievous and provocative history, which helps explain its existence and legitimize its theme. The scholars represented here comprise members who have been part of our international conversations for decades, like Alan Gilbert, Eero Loone, Iván Vitányi, and Paul Thomas, as well as a superb group of younger scholars who have been part of our deliberations for only a few years—including our host in Málaga, José María Rosales, and Matteo Gianni of Italy (both of whom have been guest fellows at the Walt Whitman Center at Rutgers).

Those who have written for these pages, along with many others, including our current chairman, Percy Lehning of Holland, and our former chairman and cofounder, Bhikhu Parekh, are bound together not merely by their common interest in exploring the ways in which postnational global markets have changed how we think about multiculturalism, nationalism, and civic identity—what has globalization done to citizenship?—but by the common history they share as members of the International Political Science Association's Research Committee on Political Philosophy. This, on the face of it, appears as a patent oxymoron. Social scientists trying to imitate hard scientists by imitating American positivists imitating natural scientists? Making room for critical political theorists who insist that the human sciences are value-laden and history-embedded and cannot be reduced to behavioral mechanics in a longer association seemingly defined by the study of behavior? My colleagues Fred R. Dallmayr and José María Rosales will introduce the essays thematically, but I am charged with introducing them contextually and historically by briefly retelling the story of how this lively group of political theorists came together, courtesy of various internal contradictions in the world political science organization known as the International Political Science Association (IPSA).

The authors of the splendid, thematically linked essays assembled here are,

as is immediately evident from the titles of their contributions, political philosophers not in the sense that they are *not* political scientists, but in the sense that they
recognize that political science—if it is not to be what the historian Alfred Cobban
once said was an excuse for avoiding politics without achieving science—must be
rooted in normative theory and critical analysis. The occasion for the common
work that led to this collection was a meeting of our IPSA Research Committee in
Málaga, Spain, in the spring of 1999—a meeting that was but one in a remarkable
series of nearly twenty annual meetings and roundtables that have been taking
place since 1979 with the same core cast of characters and an evolving group of
new, younger participants. As these essays embody our belief that political
philosophy has a great deal to contribute to political science and politics, so the
Research Committee on Political Philosophy embodies our belief that the IPSA
benefits by being deepened and enriched through the contributions of political
philosophers.

It has not always been so. Founded in 1949 with the help of the United
Nations Educational, Scientific and Cultural Organization (UNESCO) as part of
an effort to create vehicles for international research, intellectual exchange, and
cooperative scholarship in social science as part of a campaign to reconstitute
democracy in the postwar world, the IPSA almost immediately became an
institution specializing in an American variety of positivist social science in which
theory and philosophy were marginalized if not invisible. With American political
science as the model at a moment when empirical and descriptive paradigms were
just becoming dominant, political scientists from around the world created a
triennial forum in which those paradigms prevailed.

Hence, when I attended my first IPSA meeting in 1976 in Edinburgh (I was
program cochair of the American Political Science Aassociation National Meeting
that year and had been invited by its President James MacGregor Burns), I was
not surprised, though certainly more than a little downcast, to discover that there
were almost no theory sessions and few political philosophers or social historians
present, even as panelists in the political science sessions. Political science was
being internationalized in the total absence of its theoretical and normative
foundations. It was as if America was exporting architecture by sending trailer
homes around the world. If the IPSA was short on political philosophy, there was
plenty of politics! Carl Friedrich (one of my teachers at Harvard in the early
1960s) had been president of IPSA just a few years earlier, and there was little
chance that another American could be elected for another twenty years, especially
since IPSA politics tends to track UN politics, Cold War and all, so that the
Russians were sure to veto any American campaign for another shot at the
presidency out of turn. Still, Karl Deutsch wanted the job badly. On the other
hand, the Russians wanted the IPSA Congress to be held in Moscow in 1979
badly. So I watched in astonished admiration as my friend, Pulitzer Prize winning
historian James MacGregor Burns negotiated with Russian delegates to secure

Deutsch's election. MacGregor, who had run for Congress from the Berkshires earlier and had by his own admission failed miserably against the formidable Silvio Conte, had nonetheless developed some daunting political skills of his own. We got Deutsch, they got the 1979 IPSA Congress, and I got a trip to Moscow. What America and Russia agreed to, no other delegation dared in those days to dissent from.

I determined then and there that I would go to Moscow in the company of the small band of theorists already present in Edinburgh, and others we would round up for the occasion, and that we would try to establish a beachhead for political theory in future IPSA congresses. Our litle band showed up at Moscow State University in the summer of 1979. It included Bhikhu Parekh, the eminent Indian/British political theorist who in time would become vice-chancellor of Baroda University in India, chairman of Britain's Congress of Racial Equality, a life peer in Tony Blair's House of Lords, and our first chairperson. Also in our ensemble were the great Locke historian Richard Ashcraft, who was a staunch supporter of our work right up until his premature death in 1997; Alan Gilbert, the Marxist political theorist; Preston King, the notable political philosopher from England; and a small handful of others who over the years grew to include Paul Thomas and Fred Dallmayr from the United States, Ernst Vollrath from Germany, Jean Leca from France, Shlomo Avineri from Israel, and Iván Vitányi from Hungary. But back in 1979, we were but a handful of zealots. We played frisbee in the quad of Moscow State and conspired not only to get recognized as an official study group of IPSA but also to infiltrate the regular program and find ways to get theory represented more amply there as well.

By the time we returned to the next World Congress of IPSA in Rio de Janeiro, where we were welcomed by the *generalissimo* of the new Brazilian military junta (political science never seemed to worry too much about the politics of where it met!) and invited to drink and dance till dawn at Rio's poshest waterside yacht club, we managed to establish ourselves as an official IPSA "Study Group." Three years later in Paris, the *generalissimo* had become Parisian mayor Chirac, who welcomed us at the Hotel de Ville rather more sedately than had the junta, and we transmogrified from a "Study Group" with few privileges to a "Research Group" with quite a few more (for example, deserving of two sessions rather than one at World Congresses and eligible for a very modest handout). From then until today we have met every third year at World Congresses in Buenos Aires, Berlin, Washington, and Quebec, as well as at roundtables in the years between in places from Baroda to Zimbabwe, from Budapest to Bonn and London, from Paris to Rotterdam and Málaga.

This Málaga collection is an extremely inviting volume from the Research Committee, but it is by no means the first. We have published a number of articles from our proceedings in the past, notably, a volume on "Comparative Political Philosophy: East and West" that emerged from the Baroda meeting under Bhikhu Parekh's leadership. We plan another volume to coincide with our twentieth aniversary following our next two roundtables in 2001 and 2002, which will be in London and Paris, prior to the next World Congress of IPSA in South Africa in 2003. (We have so many dates for the various stages by which we were established and recognized that we anticipate being able to celebrate our "twentieth anniversary" for six or seven years starting in 2001 and ending in 2006.)

It has been our conceit to pretend that our international research committee is primarily a vehicle for global travel by a group of scholars who are as addicted to rich food as to enriching talk and as committed to vintage wine as to vintage debate. After all, if you scrutinize the cosmopolitan places we have met and the truly global nature of our membership, you might indeed conclude that among our members IPSA stands for something akin to the "International Pleasure Seekers Alliance." Yet there is in fact some serious truth in the claim that the precious civility and intellectual bonhomie our committee has cultivated and displayed over twenty years through its ongoing collaboration have been the indispensable conditions for our serious scholarly work, and that it is the human face of our work together that has permitted us to be so intellectually productive.

Beyond the invigorating debates that hold together this collection of essays then, is a common spirit of global discourse and effortless civility that not only define the nature of our Research Committee but also drive the common concerns of our evolving discourse. Welcome to the Research Committee on Political Philosophy: every reader is a potential member. We trust we will see you and, over a glass of wine in Tuscany or a plate of sushi in Kyoto or a shot of vodka in St. Petersburg, we will continue the conversation for which this volume serves only as a delicious prelude.

Acknowledgments

This book grew out of a conference held at the University of Málaga in June 1999 under the title *Beyond Nationalism? Sovereignty, Governance and Compliance*. It contains a selection of the papers presented in two of the conference's main topical areas. The editors wish to thank the financial support given by the University of Málaga, through its Commissions of Research, International Relations and Culture. From the project's very beginnings in 1998, Professor Adelaida de la Calle, the University's vice rector for research, endorsed it—a decision that entailed a considerable effort for a young, fast-growing university.

We also wish to thank the Autonomous Government of Andalusia and the IPSA Research Committee on Political Philosophy for their financial backing. The Committee invested a generous part of its modest budget, proving once again its enduring support of young scholars. For about a year the research committee's executive worked out the conference program, coordinated with both the 1998 conference in Rotterdam on *Markets and Democracy,* and the 2000 Research Committee's sessions on *Democracy versus the Corporate Millenium* at IPSA World Congress in Québec.

During the preparatory procedures we counted on the support of many people in Málaga, especially the colleagues of the University's Area of Moral and Political Philosophy and the conference's secretarial staff. The diligent organizational work of Victoria González during the process turned out to be indispensable, as we faced times of mounting costs and diminishing resources.

Right after the conference we planned to compile and edit a book based upon its proceedings—the project firmly backed by Serena Leigh of Lexington Books and expertly edited by her team. We had to select the chapters among a series of notably high quality papers. At the conference we greatly benefited from the contributions of H. Johansen, Q. Brugué, R. Gomà and J. Subirats, A. Esmark, A. Messaoudi, M. A. Parejo, X. Etxeberria, I. Räsänen, G. Girod, E. Boggio, K. Palonen, C. Closa, I. Levömaki, P. Springborg, M. Mosher, T. Alekseeva, B. Trencsényi, I. Pohjantammi, M. Ilyin, A. Rivero, E. Cantarino and F. Mertens de Wilmars, S. Langenberg, C. Schnitzer and A. Klestadt, L. Beyers and R. Langenberg, E. Martínez, D. Alvarez, C. José, E. Meleshkina, A. Sorokin, O. Krasnynch, P. King, M. Greven, F. de la Torre, R. Bhargava, J. M. Díaz, and J. M. Panea.

Finally, and above all, we wish to acknowledge the generous contribution of all participants, some seventy scholars from nineteen countries, who made it a lively and engaging interdisciplinary conference.

Introduction

Fred R. Dallmayr and José M. Rosales

Nationalism stands at a crossroads today; the same goes for such corollary terms as nation-state, national sovereignty, and national citizenship. Crossroads here means ambivalence; it signals an undecided (though not necessarily undecidable) condition fraught with dangers on all sides. Our historical situation reveals conflicting and even opposite tendencies: on the one hand, a powerful and relentless momentum pointing toward globalization; on the other, an equally powerful upsurge of nationalistic (or ethnic-national) sentiments sometimes culminating in chauvinistic frenzy and destructiveness. [1]

The title of this volume, *Beyond Nationalism?*, thus carries a question mark. Actually, the title encapsulates a host of questions. What is the meaning of nationalism? Is there only one or are there possibly multiple types of nationalism (so that one might differentiate, for example, between political, ethnic, and cultural nationalisms)? What does it mean to move "beyond" nationalism? Does it involve a straightforward exit or exodus, or a more moderate transformation? In the first case, does one exchange nationalism for a global uniformity without differences? Can one safely abandon nationalism and the nation-state—especially if the latter is the haven of the rule of law and a firm statute of citizenship? After all, who knows what lies "beyond." Is it an arena of international anarchy where the strong coerce the weak, and the rich, the poor—or is it an arena of global comity, civility, and cooperation? And how will the latter be brought about?

As can readily be seen, these questions have institutional connotations, involving the redesign of public institutions throughout the world. But they also have "existential" implications for people living in our time: their well-being, legal safety and protection, and frequently also their sense of identity are at stake. This is an aspect that social scientists—preoccupied with institutional and comparative analytical issues—sometimes tend to slight or forget, to their detriment. Political theorists surely cannot neglect this dimension as long as they remain faithful to their enterprise. As classical texts in this field (taken from several cultures) teach, politics has to do not only with structures and impersonal procedures but also with ways of living or ways of being human; in the view of Aristotle, politics has to do with "living well" or living a "good life," in accordance with standards of goodness.

As Aristotle (joined by Confucius) also teaches, living well requires some kind of community or frame of reference in which individuals can find a degree of purpose and intelligibility. Destruction or sharp rupture of this frame of reference is liable to lead to *anomie* or disorientation. When young people leave their parents' home to venture out into the "world," they usually experience for a time a sense of lostness, coupled with alienation and homesickness, until the wider society emerges as a new and meaningful frame of reference. In our time, millions of people around the world are pulled or pushed by the force of media and markets out of their traditional ethnic, national, and religious communities and into a globalizing arena that they often barely comprehend and that they have no particular reason to trust or welcome. Their agonies are compounded by the haughty conceit of westernized elites disdaining the "unwashed multitudes" and by the impact of globalizing corporate interests undermining their traditional sources of livelihood.

At the crossroads of these countervailing forces today stands nationalism, for good or ill. At this point, it seems appropriate to introduce some defining distinctions. Above all, is the necessity to differentiate between the semantic meanings of the following terms: nation or nationhood; nation-state; and nation-alism. While "nation" or "nationhood" refers to a community of people joined together by common ethnic origins and/or shared historical experiences, "nation-state" designates a political and legal structure erected on the basis of a common, or at least dominant, nation or nationality. Among the characteristic features of the modern nation-state are a constitutional framework, a certain distribution of public powers, and the rule of law (including provisions for a statute of citizenship). The term "nationalism," finally, points to a strategic program or agenda whereby a given nation or nationality seeks to promote its autonomy, freedom, cultural priorities, prosperity, and (sometimes) sheer power.[2]

Seen against this background, there may be nations or nationalities without active nationalistic agendas; and even if there are such agendas, the latter may be limited to cultural priorities and a measure of political and economic autonomy while steering clear of an aggressive or chauvinistic kind of nationalism. These considerations also make clear that there may be nations or nationalities functioning below the threshold of the nation-state or else beyond its lim-its—demonstrating that nation and nation-state do not necessarily coincide (a good example being the so-called first nations in North America and indigenous peoples elsewhere). The situation of subnationalities or national minorities vis-à-vis the nation-state is in many ways analogous to the status of dominant nationalities and nation-states vis-à-vis the emerging global "community." In both cases, the crucial question is whether the more localized or subordinate groups or collectivities can find recognition, safety, and a degree of well-being in the larger (state or global) frame of reference. This, again, is both a structural-institutional and an existential question for the people involved.[3]

As one can gather from these comments, the ambivalence of nationalism carries not only pragmatic but also strongly normative connotations. In a simplified manner, one might say that nationalism is Janus-faced, showing both "positive," or constructive, and "negative," or destructive, features. The more constructive features emerge when the focus is placed on the desire for autonomy and for the removal of invidious forms of domination and abuse. In modern and recent times, this desire was powerfully manifested in the struggles for national independence or "liberation" directed against Western (and sometimes non-Western) types of colonialism and imperialism.

In this respect, India's struggle for independence has been prototypical and emblematic for a host of similar national endeavors to cast off the shackles of foreign bondage or tutelage. In a similar vein, one may also mention the struggles of many subnationalities for greater recognition and autonomy within and beyond the confines of existing nation-states. In this connection, one need also to recall some of the "positive" qualities of nation-states (whose passing away is sometimes prematurely celebrated). In a world arena marked by glaring military, technological, and economic disparities, the legal structures of the nation-state are sometimes the only available institutions guaranteeing a measure of justice and equity, especially to the underprivileged and marginalized (whether these be national minorities or economic underclasses).

On the other hand, one can surely not ignore the grave dangers inherent in unbridled and aggressive types of nationalism or chauvinism. The twentieth century stands as a massive testimonial to these dangers, issuing a wholesome warning to people everywhere (including moderate nationalists). The warning teaches us to moderate and limit—though not to abandon—political strivings and hopes and, above all, to subordinate at all times the desire for power to the dictates of justice and goodness (as Gandhi did in his struggles). In this way, nationalism is a metaphor or parable for the "human condition" or the condition of humanity—which deserves to be praised for its artistic, cultural, and scientific achievements but also to be chastized and rebuked for its horrendous excesses, its Promethean gesture of unlimited mastery and self-sufficiency.

Organization of the Volume

The collection of essays has been divided into three parts. Each one describes from a different, though complementary, angle the crossroads of the debate on nationalism. The first part explores the semantic field of nationalist doctrines, while the second and third parts focus on the national question in light of the novel conditions of sovereignty and citizenship raised by a postnational reconfiguration of the world order and a cosmopolitan transformation of the civil condition in liberal societies. Yet, as indicated, our aim is not only descriptive. It is also normative, as the chapters recast the terms of the debate by advancing in their analyses a reasoned anticipation of the future of nationalism. Basically, the different arguments presented endeavor to ponder the meaning and cogency of the national question in the contemporary context. Proceeding in this manner, the essays address the theoretical and institutional limits of nationalism in a world already preparing the foundations of a postnational order. This approach affects the interpretation of the global scene, which can no longer be exclusively defined in terms of national sovereignty. Likewise, citizenship has begun to lose its older connotation as the legal and political status associated with nationality. These changes and developments highlight the book's three interconnected issues: nationalism, sovereignty, and the civil condition.

Part 1, *Nationalism and Beyond*, reviews some of the central theoretical and analytical issues of nationalist thought. Among other things, the chapters in this part explore the factors contributing to the formation of political identity, the possibility of constructing a typology of national identities, the fortunes and hazards involved in typological thinking, the relation between nations and subnationalities or national minorities, and the complex nexus between nationalism and political self-determination. In their combination, the chapters seek to clear the road to a theoretical and conceptual clarification of problems that are often consigned to hazy ambiguity.

In the chapters in part 2, *Globalization and Sovereignty*, the nationalist controversies are placed within the constellation of prospects generated by the recasting of the international community after the end of the Cold War. Since 1989, the world of opposed blocs has become a polycentric arena, whose geostrategic equilibrium has turned more and more unstable. In addition, political conflicts in any part of the world tend to follow a logic of transnational interconnectivity. The antecedents to this novel architecture can be traced back some decades, when capital movements across frontiers initiated the globalization of financial markets. The chapters offer an interdisciplinary discussion of the challenges posed by globalization for the model of national sovereignty. Although each analysis has a different emphasis, the essays share two critical points. First, the change in the world order challenges the normative assumptions of the model of national sovereignty. Second, the accumulated experience of nationalist conflicts in the world suggests the need to reformulate the rules of the international community.

The change of coordinates also affects the social and civil condition of people in the world. The "rise and decline of nations" (Olson), the peace or war among the states, are but metaphors of the prosperity or misery, the peace or war, among nations and peoples. In the third part of the book, *Citizenship in a Global World*, the changing meanings of the civil condition in response to the effects of globalization are pictured. Today, we recognize the achievements of modern citizenship; but, we also note the precarious character of the universalization of liberal citizenship. The recognition suggests a legitimate aspiration to globalize the humanizing aspects of citizenship as an egalitarian and universalist legal condition. However this trend, which already envisages the features of a cosmopolitan citizenship, stands in contrast to the traditional statute of liberal citizenship, closely tied to the notions of nationality and national identity. In the third part, the inner tensions of the model are explored against the background of challenges and opportunities opened up by the globalization of both immigration and the recognition of human rights. The controversy over citizenship testifies to the intercultural, interethnic, and multinational transformation of states, liberal and nonliberal; but it also points up the opportunity to reform the conditions for membership in the political community worldwide.

About the Chapters

The first chapter, "Modalities of Consent, Compliance and Non-Compliance: *Exit, Voice, and Loyalty* Reconsidered," opens with a reassessment of citizenship as the key feature of political community. In his chapter, Paul Thomas examines the different dimensions of political identity, persuasively criticizing the widely accepted division between civic and ethnic dimensions—a division translated into two opposed types of political identity: civic identity and national identity. This construct simplifies the complexity of a concept that actually operates in practice as a "relational concept."

Accordingly, for Thomas, citizenship is neither a fixed nor a polarized category, but a relational institution comprising the civic and other no less relevant dimensions. This change of view allows us to appreciate the gradual disappearance of limits between state and civil society. Their growing interrelation proves, above all, the transformation of the political realm. In that sphere of civil society, which is closely tied to state institutions, social movements and civil associations provide an experimental domain for political participation. Their membership, participation, and exit conditions, Thomas argues, represent a considerable improvement (in terms of civic integration and performance) over the model of liberal citizenship in the traditional sense.

This line of theoretical argument is further pursued in the second chapter, "Does a Homogeneous Conception of Nation Exist? A Typology of National Identities," which studies the temporal and thematic structure of the liberal conception of nation. While recognizing common elements, Iván Vitányi elaborates a typology of national identities and national political behaviors. The national question thus emerges as a question diversified in time and space, against the traditional assumption that tends to present it as a universally identical problem. As Vitányi points out, the diachronic composition of national conceptions still keeps their incommensurable specificity. But even within each nation we find not a single synthesis of historical, cultural, and political elements, but a "compound" structured into different levels of national identification, each with a distinct political significance. Hence the inner tensions and contradictions of the nation, which in the end influence the civic networks of society, cannot be solved in isolation, but only in the context of a review of its entire structure. Finally, Vitányi holds that only if we make more flexible its structure of civil mobility, namely, participation and integration in, or dissociation from, the community (in a way similar to "open societies"), will we be able to deal *politically* with the national question.

The third chapter also aims to clarify the usage of conceptual categories in the study of nationalism. In "Nationalism and Typological Thinking," Manuel Toscano-Méndez adapts a conceptual distinction of evolutionary biology, between "typological" and "population" thinking, to characterize the "social ontology of nationalism." In that way, he shows how the nationalist imaginary has tended to assume the classification of identities as natural, substantive attachments, free from any conventional determination. The essay focuses on the methodological consequences of typological thinking, as it is developed not only in nationalist discourses but even in nonnationalist ones. This common theoretical stance influences the outcomes of any study of nationalism. This is true not only in political theory but also in the domain of institutions and public policies, where it is not difficult to find that public common resources get distributed along nationalist criteria. The chapter gives an analysis of the national question and its political implications that goes "beyond" the conceptual framework of nationalism. Thus, to focus the national question within a "post-nationalist scenario," as Toscano-Méndez argues, entails more than a compelling theoretical suggestion. It is also a necessary exercise of political pragmatism.

Still at the level of conceptual analysis, chapter 4, "Nations within Nations—Nationalism and Identity Politics," represents an extension of the theoretical perspective on the varieties of nationalism and on the political role of collective identities. Tuija Pulkkinen studies the internal composition of nation-states in terms of identity groups. She underlines how some communities develop, together with a capacity for self-organization, a capacity for effective participation in the political community. What is most revealing in Pulkkinen's research is her interest in the growing diversification of groups along identity patterns. In other words, she demonstrates that the extension of pluralism follows to a significant extent a constructive logic of identity politics. This widening of the civil domain does not mean the enhancement of nationalism as a pattern of growth in the political community. On the contrary, as long as group identities are created by the individuals themselves, it highlights the constructive, non-natural dimension of this *second* national identity.

The fifth chapter concludes this series of essays in conceptual revision. In "Self-Determination without Nationalism," Omar Dahbour defends a view of the principle of self-determination not legitimized by nationalist reasons: namely, one "disaggregated" from the idea of national identity. Indeed, the aggregation of both notions has been a view legitimized, even by critics of nationalism, to the point that in the domain of democratic theory the principles of self-government and national self-determination have been taken as identical. This happens despite the fact that in multinational states the constitutional order carefully distinguishes both concepts. Furthermore, international law recognizes the principle of self-determination under a series of conditions that hardly qualify in modern constitutional and multinational states.

After examining the reasons offered in defense of the principle of self-determination, Dahbour points out how international law has developed alternatives that sufficiently cover the demands of self-government and political autonomy entailed by the principle itself. The demands are treated specifically as "rights" of the people, which are rights that meet the normative expectations of self-determination without implying an argumentative move toward national independence—a circumstance that is envisaged by international law when other alternatives of self-government and political autonomy are inadequately recognized.

Therefore, according to a non-nationalist interpretation of the principle, it can be applied to overcome situations of "discriminatory redistribution" (Buchanan) of resources and entitlements among the different regions of a state. In this sense, it would work as a decentralizing or limiting principle of the central power of a state in favor of its regions or constituent political units. Instead of aiming at "the acquisition of state power," a reformed principle of self-determination, according to Dahbour, would aim "at a more equitable rearrangement of relations within existing states." That way, it would contribute to strengthening the political autonomy of the constituent units of a state, keeping intact balancing devices among their self-government competences.

This discussion leads into the second part of the volume, dealing with the interrelation of nationalism and sovereignty. From different standpoints, the chapters here focus on the liberal model of citizenship—an institution in crisis due to the challenges posed by the postnationalist reframing of the international community and the process of globalization. Nationalism and globalization act as opposing forces in the making of the new world order. Both define a conflictual relation of reactions and counterreactions, of homogenizing and integrating patterns set against movements of differentiation and disintegration in the economic, cultural, and political spheres. What is most revealing of globalization is just this pattern of interconnectivity captured by its homogenizing and differentiating trends.

Warfare in the contemporary sense entails a political description of the world diverging from an arena of sovereign states. For some decades, globalization has proved that this arena is no longer regulated or governed by the states themselves. Within the context of theoretical and institutional inquiry, the "phantom of sovereignty" burdens liberalism with categories unable to conceptualize the changing relation between politics (or, better, the political) and warfare, as John Crowley argues in the sixth chapter, "War, Politics, and Sovereign Violence." In a world where sovereignty has become a relative and even a contingent attribute, war does not constitute the denial of politics, but becomes one of its dimensions. Only if we acknowledge this, Crowley holds, can we coherently interpret the emerging global configuration of nationalist and postnationalist conflicts. Only in that way can we also experiment with resolution alternatives and undertake a *rational* defense of "sovereign violence" in cases of war, to the extent that violence and reason turn out to be interrelated concepts within the idea of justice.

Today, the crisis of the liberal conception of sovereignty involves above all the difficulties to designate its proper agent and, accordingly, to delimit its attributes. This is the concern of Pedro Francés-Gómez in "The Subject of Sovereignty." His chapter focuses on the formulation of a normative conception of sovereignty, universal or universalizable and serving as an alternative to both nationalist and statist interpretations, which see the nation as the true and single sovereign agent. The latter assumption, rarely questioned in academic debates, owes its authority mainly to the constitutionalism of the French Revolution. However, what is most significant in the interpretation of nation-states as *the* subjects of international law concerns the *recognition* of the nations' demands for sovereignty.

Against this view, Francés-Gómez proceeds to question the idea of assigning sovereignty to the nation. The attribution is mainly based upon the nations' will to achieve political self-constitution as independent states. The argumentative gap has been already discussed in previous chapters. Now it is revealing to note how this same will appears in demands for the recognition of sovereignty raised by political units other than states. If we glance at the growing variety of national and subnational entities created in liberal communities, then we get an idea of the complex picture of the sovereignty statute. In response, Francés-Gómez puts forward the normative conditions for a substitute idea of sovereignty: a procedural and deliberative conception that filters the major sovereignty aspirations made in the name of the nation. Conversely, the conception opens the way for a democratic reframing of the order of sovereign subjects.

Despite being "a horizontal space of states," built on the mutual recognition of its members, the order established by the Treaty of Westphalia is founded on an idealized model of state sovereignty—a model developed both by the realist and the neorealist approaches in international relations. Unsurprisingly, sovereignty is presented as an essential attribute of states, with the result that, for example, the problem of intervention not only upsets the balance of interdependence among states but also turns into an intractable issue within the parameters of the model. This is the argument of Kennan Ferguson in the following chapter, "Nationalism, Sovereignty, and Pluralism: The Case of William James." After he demonstrates its invalidity to address the crisis, Ferguson reformulates the liberal notion of sovereignty in pluralist terms. According to a pluralist conception (which Ferguson bases on the work of William James), sovereignty is an essential attribute neither of states nor of nations. It is, instead, a relational concept that denotes the aspiration to reach a fairer and more equitable balance among states than would otherwise be the case. Paradoxically, the problem of intervention becomes functional with this view. Hence, the intervention of a state can be justified in the name of the imposition of pluralism, which the intervention itself seems to invalidate. Such is the case especially in many instances of humanitarian intervention.

The ninth chapter, "Democratic Internationalism: A Defense of Deliberation as a Medium for Internationalism," pursues further this line of thought. Alan Gilbert argues that "global rivalry" among states prevents the fulfillment of the "promise" of national sovereignty, which pictures an ideal space for the community but in the end "rarely deliver[s] a common good to its own citizens or internationally." Only the civic action of social movements—a kind of action that Gilbert calls "democratic internationalism"—will keep that democratic promise alive. Their practices and institutions, the essay shows, would allow for the creation of a model of deliberative democracy "on a national and international scale."

Democratic internationalism can also be considered as a "sophisticated" version of pluralism, in line with the pluralist theory of James, that opposes the abandonment of foreign relations to hegemonic or oligarchic interests. To be sure, the politics of transnational civic movements does not constitute by itself a complete form of cosmopolitan governance. But the "global regimes" established to deal with issues like the banning of child labor or the creation of an international criminal court are examples of the potential reach of the international democratizing action by civic movements. And, for that very reason, they already provide the antecedents for a democratic, postnational world order.

In the tenth chapter, Eero Loone resumes the issue of intervention in the context of globalization. "Nationalism and Sovereignty Overrides: Permissibility of Interventions in Other Polities" recalls how intervention, which in principle is incompatible with the idea of sovereignty, has not always been fairly applied among states. Interventions reveal the precarious legitimacy of the idea of national sovereignty and demonstrate that the international order rests on a profound imbalance of power among states. On the other side, the demands in defense of human rights prove more and more their normative strength against the limits of state sovereignty. These demands, Loone points out, are examples of the virtual existence in our times of a "postsovereign world" whose theoretical features need to be worked out. Yet, he also notes, the search for a new consensus over the extent and legitimacy of intervention not only faces the resistance of traditional sovereignty (whose definition becomes ever more complex in a multicultural world) but also the risk of "the reemergence of colonialism under the guise of liberal values." The need for reform does not hide the difficulties involved in building a new normative reference to replace the nationalist reasons supporting nonintervention.

A new consensus might advance the creation of a world order where preference would be given to the rights of individuals over the rights of states; thus argues Teresa López de la Vieja in chapter 11. To a great extent, the normative path of the United Nations over the years has inaugurated a postnational, cosmopolitan order. However, as "Thinking Globalization, Rethinking Toleration" remarks, the task is not confined to states nor to the statute of international law. It demands the participation of individuals in a change that affects the very understanding of human rights. A democratization of the relations among states can only be envisaged through the reformist action of international civic movements (as Gilbert notes). But this same process entails a significant reconfiguration of the space of individual rights. For López de la Vieja, the opening up of frontiers becomes inefficient and even contradictory if it does not come with a new learning of toleration and a new acceptance of human rights. The cosmopolitan trend of the international community, hence, should rest on the global extension of the universalist experience of toleration.

Thus we arrive at the core of civil life. The third part of the book explores the changes of cosmopolitanism brought about by the intercultural and interethnic transformations of the public domain. The argument begins with a review of the cosmopolitan change of liberal citizenship. In "National Identities and Cosmopolitan Virtues: Citizenship in a Global Age," Bryan Turner examines the meaningful relation that exists between the model of citizenship, national identity, and the conception of masculinity. As he remarks, the political and cultural imagery of nationalism is based largely upon the narrative patterns of masculine heroism, clearly exhibited in the typical sequence of foreign oppression, military conflict, and national liberation. The continued viability of this triad becomes questionable with the introduction of postnational elements in the concept of citizenship and the transformation of the international order itself. Turner concludes by speculating about the possibility to develop cosmopolitan analogues of national-civic virtues, namely, "the virtues of a global city." Such an analogy becomes possible only if cosmopolitan virtue is practiced as "the necessary cultural envelope for the cultivation of transnational obligations of care and respect."

Closely related to cosmopolitanism is the issue of the multicultural extension of liberal citizenship. In chapter 13, Matteo Gianni examines the plausibility of a model of "differentiated citizenship" in response to the demands for political recognition raised by national minorities. "Multiculturalism, Differentiated Citizenship, and the Problem of Self-Determination" addresses the theoretical suitability of a differentiated citizenship to cope with the civic challenges of multiculturalism—an issue equally debated by liberals (Kymlicka), communitarians (Taylor), and postmoderns (Young). Gianni argues that a model of differentiated citizenship, if built on the principle of political equality, can contribute to strengthening the political resources of disadvantaged groups. The latter objective, and this is Gianni's specific view of self-determination, would aim at the fair, and differentiated, integration of groups in the political community. Against a purely anthropological or cultural interpretation, he favors a political treatment that faces the problem of "the effects of cultural membership on citizenship rights."

Multiculturalism is a multifaceted phenomenon combining ethnic, cultural, and civic-constitutional elements. In "Multiculturalism and Constitutional Patriotism in Eastern Europe," Judit Hell and Ferenc L. Lendvai reconstruct the evolution of nationalism in Eastern Europe. Its peculiar symbiosis of cultural and ethnic elements produced, as early as the second half of the nineteenth century, a kind of national identity hardly compatible with liberal constitutionalism. Hell and Lendvai review some of the perverse consequences of this configuration and focus the second part of their work on civil and institutional improvements that would lead to a patriotism not of the nation, but of the constitution. In contrast to the kind of identity nurtured by nationalism, "patriotism" based on the constitution inspires a kind of loyalty that reasonably combines some features of national identity with the identity formed by the constitution. This outlook, the authors suggest, may well turn into a preferred mode of dealing with the emerging nationalist and postnational order of Eastern Europe.

The next chapter addresses one of the most demanding issues in the debate on citizenship: the challenge to "accommodate" immigrants within liberal societies. In "Justice and Immigration: An Argument against Nationality as 'Cement' of Citizenship," Ricard Zapata-Barrero points out how the changing patterns in world immigration are raising novel demands in the political agenda. To the limited pluralism of liberal societies, immigration adds new forms of cultural and ethnic diversity that raise the need to redefine the access and membership conditions in the political community. The question, therefore, involves the normative foundations of the liberal model of citizenship and the related issue of the statute of nationality. In contrast with the liberal view that ties citizenship to nationality, Zapata-Barrero proposes to substitute residence for nationality as a fair criterion for political inclusion in the community. After all, recognition is not a concession, but a right acquired by many immigrants over years of residence—which means years of fiscal and civic contribution to the community. The "accommodation" of immigrants thus should be a step toward their recognition as subjects of rights, that is, as full citizens. Otherwise, the individuals and their cultural and ethnic communities will remain ghettoes inside the liberal community.

The final chapter is also a critique of the liberal orthodoxy concerning the recognition of rights. As José Rubio-Carracedo points out in "Globalization and Differentiality in Human Rights," the evolution of the conception of human rights involves the confluence of the universalist trend inaugurated by liberal constitutionalism with a differentialist trend advanced by the demands of multiculturalism and cosmopolitanism. However, in theoretical terms, the debate tends to polarize around universalist and differentialist claims. As the author reminds us, it has been precisely their joint action that has produced the widening of the recognition of human rights, from a first generation of civil and political rights, through a second generation of social and economic rights, to a third and a fourth generation of cultural rights, together with the rights to sustainable development, global peace, and rights of future generations.

Commenting on the World Conference on Human Rights convened by the United Nations in Vienna in 1993, Rubio-Carracedo contrasts the current level of recognition of human rights with the spirit, both universalist and differentialist, of the Vienna Declaration. As he shows, the Declaration is a persuasive document favoring a widening and deepening of the liberal recognition of new human rights, opening up a cosmopolitan horizon of community-building. This form of "moderate universalism" or cosmopolitanism, compatible with moderate versions of nationalism and multiculturalism, may in practice become a reasonable alternative to extreme nationalisms and differentialisms.

Glancing back, we can see the steps taken in this volume, which lead from theoretical revisions of nationalist theory to contrasting views on globalization and sovereignty to the concluding discussions of human rights. *Beyond Nationalism?* thus explores the civic and political challenges raised by a postnational, cosmopolitan reconfiguration both of the world order and of the spaces and civic networks of liberal societies.

Notes

1. The conflict has been elaborated by Benjamin R. Barber using the labels McWorld and Jihad. See his *Jihad vs. McWorld* (New York: Random House, 1995).

2. Compare in this context Anthony D. Smith, *Nations and Nationalism in a Global Era* (Cambridge, UK: Blackwell, 1995), *Theories of Nationalism* (New York: Holmes & Meier, 1983), and *National Identity* (Reno: University of Nevada Press, 1991); John Hutchinson and A. D. Smith, eds., *Nationalism* (Oxford: Oxford University Press, 1994); Omar Dahbour and Micheline R. Ishay, eds., *The Nationalism Reader* (Atlantic Highlands, N.J.: Humanities Press, 1995); Partha Chatterjee, *The Nation and Its Fragments*

(Princeton, NJ: Princeton University Press, 1993); Ronald Beiner, ed., *Theorizing Nationalism* (Albany: State University of New York Press, 1999) and Beiner, ed., *Theorizing Citizenship* (Albany: State University of New York Press, 1995); Joseph H. Carens, *Culture, Citizenship, and Community* (Oxford: Oxford University Press, 2000); José Rubio-Carracedo, José María Rosales, and Manuel Toscano Méndez, *Ciudadanía, nacionalismo y derechos humanos* (Madrid: Editorial Trotta, 2000); also Fred Dallmayr, "Nationalism in South Asia: Some Theoretical Points," in *Alternative Visions: Paths in the Global Village* (Lanham, Md.: Rowman & Littlefield, 1998) pp. 191-217.

3. A further analogy might be drawn between the status of susidiary nationalities and the status of economic undercastes or underclasses. In our globalizing world, the two statuses are frequently joined—in the sense that national and cultural minorities also tend to bear the major brunt of economic exploitation and deprivation.

Part I

Nationalism and Beyond

Chapter 1

Modalities of Consent, Compliance, and Non-Compliance: *Exit, Voice, and Loyalty* Reconsidered

Paul Thomas

English-speaking political philosophy was dominated for more than twenty years after the publication in 1970 of John Rawls's *A Theory of Justice* by a specific strand within liberalism (represented by Rawls, Dworkin, Ackerman, Nozick, and a host of lesser luminaries), whose goal was to state the principles of an ideal liberal constitutionalism, and whose end-product was a theory of rights and justice, a politically-constitutive project which specified the basic liberties which would be held by citizens in an ideal, liberal state.

John Gray has ventured the belief that late twentieth-century American liberalism's real province is not politics at all, but law, that it understands political philosophy as a branch of legal philosophy.[1] This view is a tempting one, not least because it enables or might enable us to locate such liberalism not just temporally but hemispherically. It struck many of us who attended the IPSA 1991 World Congress in Buenos Aires that political philosophy, to the extent that it is taught at all in Argentina (and by extension in other parts of Latin America too) is taught as a branch of legal philosophy. But be this as it may, there is also a specifically North American context for late twentieth century liberalism, just as we might expect.

There have been dissenting voices vis-à-vis the (by now waning) Rawlsian orthodoxy, to be sure, and I should be happy in what follows to be counted among them. William Connolly has indicated that self-confident assertion of democratic individuality must unavoidably be played out against a background of repressed cultural differences whose repression is not about to last forever.

Benjamin Barber has similarly indicated—on lines along which our Research Committee has been working in recent years—that multiculturalism can and must be defended against the accusation that identity-defining communities are inherently repressive. I agree with both of them that unabridged individualism inescapably involves serious losses of democratic equality—which is why that peculiarly American fetishization of individual autonomy, elevated over or beyond every other good as the precondition of all moral and political virtues, must not pass unchallenged. It has not passed unchallenged in the recent proceedings of our Research Committee; and it will not pass unchallenged in this collection of papers.

Political identity is above all a *relational* concept, involving membership. Citizenship, being a form of political identity, is a case in point. Yet member-ship—that which, if I am right, *makes* political identity relational—has remained remarkably unexamined across a wide spectrum of debates about citizenship, or about what is called "ethnic politics." Debate has been stymied because mem-bership per se has been seen in all too many recent discussions in rigidly binary terms that are less than appropriate to its complexity as a category. Membership, we are told—and we have been told, in one way or another, ever since the days of Max Weber—is fundamentally either "civic" or "ethnic." The former is generally held to be desirable because of its putative links with citizenship, seen in turn as a desideratum or even as a criterion of linch-pin. Civic membership commonly finds favor in liberal eyes, that is to say, because it is said to be freely and voluntarily chosen, because it is in principle revocable, changeable, contractual, and potentially universalizable. Civic identity so understood is thus in a sense both cause and consequence of something even more precious: it is based upon, and it leads into free association among uncoerced human beings considered as indi-vidual agents of their own destiny. Civic membership, association, and identity thus merge into a singular nostrum, a Good Thing that admits of being counterposed to or arrayed to that Bad Thing, namely "ethnic" membership, association, and identity.

This latter is commonly regarded in liberal circles as having something undesirable, or even disreputable about it, however inevitable or unavoidable it may be in practice. Ethnic membership, association, and identity have been variously characterized by those of a liberal persuasion as being unchosen, invariant, unchangeable, rigid, "natural," as "given," fixed, particularistic, and exclusionary.

I

In what follows I have no wish fatuously to deny that the "civic-ethnic" polarity exists in some fashion or another, or that it can count or have effects. But I do wish to claim that in certain respects it is overdrawn; that taken in and of itself, it cannot explain very much; and that it cannot do the work its liberal proponents wish to assign it. In particular, there are two implications of the supposed polarity between civic and ethnic membership I find quite unwarranted.

The first is that the civic and the ethnic are necessarily zero-sum categories, such that the more that obtains of the one, the less that obtains of the other—that the categories work, so to speak, at cross-purposes and at each other's expense. The second implication is, if anything, even more invidious. This is that civic identity and membership are in some sense more political or *more* properly political than ethnic identity and association. We might paraphrase this latter position as saying that the "civic," being by its very nature labile, open-ended, projective, and generative, points the way forward, while the "ethnic," being static, primordial, and backward-looking, cannot but be retrospective in character. Michael Ignatieff's *Blood and Belonging,* [2] for instance, distinguishes a good "civic nation" from a bad "ethnic nation." The former is composed of all those—regardless of race, color, creed, gender, language, or ethnicity—who "subscribe to the nation's political creed." The "ethnic nation," by contrast entails a polity whose members share (or think they share) a common original ancestry.

In contrasting the two, Ignatieff is in fact restating the preferred liberal scenario ever since Lord Acton's *Nationality* of 1862. Since Acton is more read about than read, it might be salutary to rehearse his main argument at this juncture. Acton envisages a depoliticization of ethnocultural membership to leave in place a purely civic-territorial conception of political membership. The state would generate whatever loyalty and solidarity it needed to execute its functions without calling upon or reinforcing the ethnocultural symbols of any one group within its borders.

> Our connection with the race is merely natural and physical, whilst our duties to the political nation are ethical. One is a community of affections and instincts . . . pertaining more to the animal than to the civilized man; the other is an authority governing by laws, imposing obligations, and giving a moral sanction and character to the natural relations of society . . . the nationality formed by the state, then, is the only one to which we owe political duties, and it is, therefore, the only one which has political rights. [3]

"Patriotism"—Acton means by this term attachment to good laws and institutions—will *alone* serve as the bond between citizens, even citizens lacking a common language, culture, and religion. Acton's distinction is repeated in a different register by Friedrich Meinecke's distinction between *Staatsnationen* (political nations) and *Kulturnationen* in his *Cosmopolitanism and the Nation State,* [4] which inscribes Meinecke within the large number of German nineteenth century writers who distinguished Germany from France in terms of the distinction between civic and ethnic nations—curiously in view of the fact[5] that one could not *be* a citizen of Germany (as opposed to Saxony, Bavaria, Prussia,

etc.) before 1912: just in time, one might be forgiven for thinking, for World War
One.

The problem here has to do with the fact that the civic/ethnic dichotomy has
in general not been as historically—and may thus not be as conceptually—distinct,
as those of a liberal persuasion might want us to believe. Ignatieff's contrast
between a "civic" and "ethnic" nation may not be absolute if we pause to consider
what "subscribing" to the nation's "political creed" has *meant* in historically
specific cases. The trouble with all too many arguments labelling something as
traditional is that of "the invention of tradition" in Hobsbawm and Ranger's
formulation: they select and even define what is to be counted as "traditional"
with some care. Arguments polarizing the civic to the ethnic are no exception to
this rule of thumb. To be sure, the kind of ethnic-based citizenship encountered
today in Israel, Germany, and elsewhere is scarcely without precedent; but the
precedents point in more than one direction.

The awkward fact of the matter is that, historically, examples of the
republican form of citizenship—Periclean Athens and the Roman Republic—were
highly exclusionary. Citizenship in classical Athens was at once highly
participatory, thus "civic," *and* highly restrictive, that is, heavily ethnic: citizenship
in the Periclean age was rigidly restricted to those born of Athenian parents. In
ancient Rome, there were (for a markedly long time) *gens*, vast groups united by
a professed belief in a common ancestry. But these did not define themselves as a
nation. *Natio* is Latin for birth, but quickly slides over into meaning a tribe, race,
people—especially if the people in question were deemed to be, and derogated as
being, uncivilized. Hence Sallust on *nationes ferae*, and Hieronymous on
innumeribiles et ferocissimae nationes; hence, also Varro, who used *natio* to refer
to a breed of cattle. More civilized people regarded themselves, and were supposed to refer to themselves, as a *gens*; only on the basis of such self-designation
could the Romans regard themselves not as a mere nation but as a *populus*. (Even
the fourteenth to the seventeenth century phase *gens anglorum* was designed to
distinguish the English from the Welsh, Scots, and Irish; we know too that the
news that the French Revolutionary army at Valmy in 1791 met Prussian cannon
fire crying "Vive la Nation!" provoked great distress among non-French European élites.) Nations may be defined by the beliefs, values, and sentiments of their
members; the Romans regarded themselves, not as a mere nation but as a *gens* or
populus, as believing in and valuing not themselves but the laws, institutions, and
territorial values they were positioned to worship.

But what of "ethnic" group attachments today? Clifford Geertz's well-
known explanation of these finds echoes in many, later "communitarian"
arguments:

> By primordial attachment is meant one that stems from the 'givens'—or, more
> precisely, as culture is inevitably involved in such matters, the assumed
> 'givens'—of social existence: immediate contiguity and kin connection mainly,

but beyond them the givenness that stems from being born into a particular religious community, speaking a particular language, or even a dialect of a language, and following particular social practices. These congruities of blood, speech, custom, and so on, are seen to have an ineffable, and at times overpowering coerciveness in and of themselves.[6]

The difference here from more recent communitarians like Michael Sandel (though not from precursors like Erich Fromm)[7] is that while Geertz's primordial ties issue in "coerciveness," Sandel's eventuate in "enduring attachments and commitments that, taken together, partly define the person I am."[8] The "sense of community" that to Geertz is "coercive" in to Sandel "constitutive"—more so, indeed, than "unencumbered" belief (whatever this is) might be. Which of the two is right cannot concern us here. What they share is the idea that ethnic self-understandings are rooted in some sort of deep primordial past and are inherited from generation to generation: people understand themselves as bound to each other by pre-rational, sentimental, primordial ties.

What this means is that we cannot assign political status simply to the "civic." The "ethnic," shorn of its primordial or primordialist baggage, works as a principle of explanation only to the extent that it, too, is understood politically. How then *are* we to understand the civic? By remembering that it, too, is a kind of association or membership, and that as such it has complexities all of its own. To put matters in a nutshell: ethnic membership turns out to be a much more complex category than its detractors would have us believe, while civic membership turns out to be a more complex category than even its *defenders* would have us believe.

To see this, we must stand back and take our bearings, reminding ourselves all the while that (as I indicated at the outset) that it is membership in general and not "civic" association in particular that has heretofore been undertheorized, and which will thus remain at the center of my concerns in this chapter.

II

In an important sense, the argument I am about to advance is not normative but descriptive. Its concern, in other words, is with what we mean *when* we talk about membership and identity, and not with what we ought to mean when we do so. If I may purloin the title of a justly famous book, my argument is that debates about membership and identity have thus far fixated themselves upon "voice" and "loyalty"—to the detriment of Albert O. Hirschman's third category, which is "exit."[9] It was not for nothing that Hirschman in *Exit, Voice, and Loyalty* chose to portray "exit" and "voice" as strategies that might, under certain circumstances, be tempered in various ways by "loyalty."

More specifically, "exit, voice, and loyalty" in Hirschman's celebrated formulation are "responses to decline"—to perceived decline or deterioration—in "firms, organizations and states." Whether or not states can be said to "produce" goods and services in the same sense that "firms" are commonly said to do is not my concern here, although it is clear that states can disappoint their members and frequently do so. My concern here is neither with firms per se nor with states per se (whatever these may be), but with organizations and categories of the kind that involve *membership* , and with membership itself as a portmanteau category that can in some senses admit to renewal or cancellation. Membership as such, that is to say, appears to involve a spectrum of possible actions, and of possible types of action, on the part of the member.

This in turn enables us to specify a spectrum of different kinds of membership, each of which is, I argue, characterized by a different exit verb. That the word "exit" can mean different things at different times in different contexts does nothing to undermine or dislodge Hirschman's approach. But it does complicate this approach in interesting ways. If exit and voice are options tempered at times by the existence or persistence of loyalty, as Hirschman believes, then it matters in what follows not only that "loyalty" admits of being read as "obligation" (as for instance in Josiah Royce's *The Philosophy of Loyalty*) but also that "exit" itself covers a variety of meanings (if not exactly a multitude of sins).

It is worth raising at this juncture a further complication having to do with membership of a state. My focus here is on modes of membership. Membership in or of a state is a subset of membership in general. But it is a particular *kind* of subset, any way you cut it. Voting in elections, which is the closest most members of most democratic polities get to participating in political (or state) affairs, is all too often dignified with the adjective "civic" and said to confer or represent legitimacy, rendering legitimate the political system that permits or requires periodic elections, as though every vote cast were also and at the same time a kind of vote of confidence in the political system at large. I am skeptical about such claims.

Whatever legitimacy the act of voting may confer is more immediately on the party or persons the balloteer thinks deserves his or her electoral support (*faute de mieux* , perhaps). Such support, as Hirschman is well aware, is in any case by its very nature provisional and can always be withdrawn the next time round if the party or person's performance in office is then deemed inadequate or not up to snuff. At another remove, that is to say, the vote of confidence (if this is what it is) is in the system that permits and requires periodic *re*-election of persons and ruling parties, and this system too is not to be equated with "the state." The case is obviously different in the instance of those who "live off" or "live for" politics, as in Max Weber's paradigm of politics not as a periodic recourse from below but as a "vocation" from above. Yet even here what gets legitimated by service, paid or unpaid, is not "the state" in any obvious sense but the *régime*, which is, after all, the actual source of livelihood.

At this rather rarefied and state-centered level of analysis, then, my decision to focus on exit verbs as signifiers of membership may seem unfortunate, or a rather unproductive tack to take. At this level, if things do not go well or turn out as expected, the available "responses to decline"—vote switching or (let's be dramatic) emogration in the case of the voter, resignation on principle or self-imposed exile in the instance of the office-holder—are not responses that appear to offer us very much in analytical terms. The point is, however, that these are "exit strategies"—and exit strategies about which Hirschman, let it be said once again, has some very interesting and characteristically paradoxical things to say—of a very particular kind. They are responses to a particular *kind* of failure, on the basis of which it would be unwise to generalize. To make sense of such decisions we must cast our net rather wider, and not remain within the confines of an untowardly "state-centered" orbit, for this orbit exists and can exist only within the compass of other decisions we are accustomed to making, and other memberships we are accustomed to enjoying (or suffering), in everyday life.

To follow Hirschman and think seriously about "exit" is to note something quite striking. This is that in everyday speech we commonly distinguish different modes of membership according to the verbs—I shall call them "exit verbs"—we use to govern termination of the kind of membership in question. We do so, moreover, unthinkingly to be sure, but in a remarkably consistent and systematic manner. There are memberships we *cancel*, memberships we *quit*, memberships we *leave*; there are others we can and may terminate if and only if we effect some *change*—not on the category to which we might belong but on ourselves as members or "belongers"; and yet others—I shall call them "No Exit" memberships—we cannot relinquish at all. (It is far from incidental to what follows that the above, fivefold distinction in no way corresponds to the simple-minded "civic"/"ethnic" distinction that was my starting point; that only the last two of my five categories bear any resemblance whatever to "ethnic" identity and membership, even as these are conventionally, and misleadingly, understood; and that even here, the relationship is tangential at best).

III

Cancel, quit, leave, change, no exit: let us take these, briefly, in order. Memberships I can *cancel*, or where the exit verb is "to cancel" are those where my status or identity as a member depends upon money: the payment of fees or dues. (One can cancel one's membership of the IPSA, though not of the gay community). By contrast, memberships voluntarily terminated by quitting, or where to *quit* is the exit verb, are those of groups or organizations (the soccer team, the debate squad, the PTA, but nor our family or our country) membership in which consists primarily in devoting time or rendering services to the group in question. (The key criterion this time is not monetary. Fees or dues may be required in addition to time and services, but so might payment for participation).

Third, memberships voluntarily terminated by leaving, or where "to *leave*" is the exit verb, are those whose membership depends upon the member's subjective identification with the group or organization in question, its aims and/or characteristics. Thus we are said to leave a church or religious denomination, or political party. (Members of such bodies may also pay fees or contributions but these again, are secondary, not primary, criteria for membership.) Fourth, there are memberships that can be voluntarily terminated if and only if we effect some prior *change* —upon ourselves, not the category. These are memberships that are not normally undertaken by choice and do not depend upon subjective identification. They are rather assigned by others according to objective criteria. (Subjective self-definition is the defining feature of "leave" groups, and of "leave" groups only). Examples would include our social class, our sexual orientation, the group that speaks the same language or dialect as we do, our nationality, or (in some instances) our religious faith.

Fifth and last, there are groups we might feel we would like to exit, but find we cannot. These are those I call "No Exit" memberships: of our families, our gender, our age set, of those who speak our *langue maternelle*. In these cases, we can't cancel or quit; we can't even really leave. (Of course, people are said to leave their families, when for instance they "fly the coop." But when we speak of someone's leaving the family, or of "leaving home," in that cold Beatles song of yore, we are referring to physical relocation, and not to the termination of membership. If for instance one leaves one's family for any number of reasons—to go to college, say, or because one despises one's relatives, or out of a fervent desire to go and live in Bolivia—one remains a member of one's family, one retains membership in it, like it or not—as the family's older denizens may well delight in pointing out).

A caveat imposes itself at this (taxonomic point). First, "Change" and "No Exit" memberships form what sociologists would call a subset within the five (to exit you have to change if you can: otherwise, you are stuck). In making this point we are distinguishing groups that are *organizations* from groups that are simply *categories*. Memberships that one voluntarily ends by cancelling, quitting, or leaving are memberships of *organizations*: change and "No Exit" memberships are memberships in *categories*, which are nonetheless sometimes, and perhaps misleadingly, given the name "communities." While categories are created by the *perceptions* of their members, or by those of others, organizations depend for their (continued) existence on the *actions* of their members—contracting, agreeing, covenanting, promising, establishing institutions, or actively (or on principle) identifying with the group's goals or aims.

Lest it be thought at this juncture that I am indulging in meaningless word-play, let me hasten to add that the five different modalities of membership, belonging, and identity I have outlined suggest five very different ways of configuring political membership and identity, each of which has a logic of its own that may not admit of reduction to that of (any of) the others. Each of them may reveal a different facet or aspect of political identity: any one of the above (linguistic) criteria, taken on its own, without reference to (any of) the others, can distort what is involved in membership or citizenship out of all recognition, or even to the point of absurdity.

It should already be clear that "civic" should on no account be taken to represent or stand in for political identity, or what is held to be good about political identity, at large. Even so, let us restrict ourselves for the purposes of argument to the civic side of the supposed polarity. And let us suppose—as it is only sensible to propose—that citizenship, the supposed leitmotiv of civic identity, is not normally to be regarded as the outcome of free choice but as something to which we are simply born.

There are then two alternatives. If citizenship is regarded as an inherited, inalienable characteristic, coterminous with nationality, it becomes an instance on "no exit" membership. If by contrast citizenship is to be regarded not as "natural" but as an outcome of what sociologists call "primary socialization," it comes under the modality of change. If citizenship is cultural, it is malleable and changeable by definition; if it is natural, it is not. If the "primary socialization" perspective is the staple of contemporary "communitarian" thinking it appears to be—and I see no reason to doubt this proposition—then the "liberal" theory that is its counterpart often takes it for granted that it is a set of shared beliefs, or a common commitment to a set of preferred political principles, that keep or should keep political formations together.

In this way, what I termed the "belief" modality of political membership and identity is often depicted as the only alternative to an illiberal, "ethnic" approach to political membership and identity. Citizenship on this seriously overdrawn view of it becomes nothing but a form of "change" membership: citizenship is supposed to be a, or *the* form of, membership involving the assertion of one's ethical autonomy, one's powers of judgment, and even one's very individuality. Historically—and unsurprisingly—this view has often depended on back projection, on to the idea of a fictitious or hypothetical "social contract," or on to the idea of "founding" as an act of consciously, intentionally establishing a constitution (the difference in a sense is one of personnel, not principle). Either way, consciousness, intentionality, authorization, and autonomy are understood to be the linch-pins of the argument, an argument that thus privileges not "primary" but "secondary" socialization. Membership, the only membership that dares to speak its name, is that which follows from conscious, moral attachment.

IV

Two separate but related points suggest themselves at this juncture. The first is raised by Hirschman: that commitment to revolutionary principles appears to fit the bill. Saint-Just, for example, spoke of "the public moment," in which the social contract is reviewed and reconstituted in action.[10] The second, which follows the logic of the first, and whose ironies are delicious to savor in any case, is that belief models of memberships and commitment, according to which we exit the category in question simply by changing our minds about its desirability or efficacy, *need not refer to actual states at all*.

Think for example of cosmopolitanism as this is defended by Martha Nussbaum and others: "We should give our allegiance to no mere form of government, no temporal power, but to the moral community made up by the humanity of all human beings."[11] Nussbaum does not shrink from invoking the authority of Diogenes the Cynic, and the Stoics at large in advancing such claims. This suggests that there has been, historically, a privileged relationship between the belief model of membership and morality; and that Nussbaum, in keeping with this, could have cast her net rather wider.

St. Augustine, too, attempted to characterize (if not exactly define) a new kind of membership, a new kind of morally rejuvenated "citizenship" in opposition to corruption—this time the corruption of the Roman Empire; and he did so by simply tracing out the ideas of eminent Roman thinkers to what Augustine considered their logical conclusion. He takes as his point of departure Cicero's celebrated representation of Scipio's definition of commonwealth, according to which "[t]he commonwealth . . . is the people's affair; and the people [*populus*] is not every group of men, associated in any manner [this would be a mere nation] but is the coming together of a considerable number of men who are united by a common agreement about law and rights and by the desire to participate in common advantages." (How similar to Rawls this sounds! But there is more to come.)

Seeking to use Scipio's definition to argue against the very existence of a Roman commonwealth, Augustine repeats Scipio's belief that rights presuppose justice and that, in consequence, "where there is no justice, there is no commonwealth." But no man who "takes himself away from the true God and hands himself over to dirty demons," Augustine deftly adds at just the right point, can have any justice in him. Nor indeed, by extension, can there be any justice "in an Assembly made up of such men."[12] Any citizenship worthy of the name must thus be undergirded by a shared, Christian belief. Augustine's argument is shrewd; it at once speaks against xenophobia *and* warns against the dangers of a false, purely formal type of membership—that of hypocrites, false friends, traitors, infiltrators, fifth columnists whose actions betray their multiple (and contradictory) allegiances. "Some there are who, covertly or overtly, join the enemy in abusing the God whom they have promised to serve. They are to be seen sometimes flocking to the theaters of the godless, and at other times to the churches with us." It may well be that the ultimate believers or Believers are those to subscribe to Utopias, for the City of God is nothing else than a Utopia in its fullest sense.

Citizenship, then, can be understood in principle as an expression or instance of "no exit," "change" or "leave" membership. But it can also be configured as an instance of "quit" membership, which, as you will recall, consists in and depends upon active participation in key enterprises, or performance of required, stipulated actions. Rights the citizen enjoys are understood as reciprocal, dependent upon the duties the citizen is enjoined to perform.

The gamut here stretches from Tom Paine's excoriation of his "sunshine patriots" to compulsory voting in El Salvador or Australia, and still further. There is nothing specifically modern about this gamut, the roots of which (in Europe) are feudal. The vassal, in exchange for a fief, and for the sake of protection of his person and his property, normally performed military or other services for his lord, services that were regarded as duties; the commutation of labor services into cash payments in the later Middle Ages is the origin (in the West) of the modern system of taxation. The duties of the citizen today are commonly seen to consist, I daresay, in the duty to obey the law; the duty to provide military service when called upon to do so; the duty (which is usually reconfigured as a right) to vote; and the duty (which no one regards as a right any longer) to pay taxes. Of these four, the last three have distinctly feudal origins: there is less that is new under the sun than many liberals commonly suppose.

V

This permits us to return to the supposed "civic-ethnic" polarity that was my starting point. Those who adopt this polarity more unquestioningly than I do, and who hang more weight on this hook than it can reasonably be expected to bear, make the "civic" the measure of the political, and this, I am suggesting, betrays a want of perspective. It effectively misreads the attainment of "civic" status as a yardstick by which—and in some cases, by which alone—moral progress and human autonomy may be said to have been furthered or even attained. Modern liberalism of the type that contents itself with making the "civic" foundational is to this extent untrue not only to the history of Western political theory at large, but also to its own nineteenth century liberal forebears like John Stuart Mill, though this cannot be my concern here.

To remain within the confines of the "civic" is to mistake an effect for a cause, or to treat autonomy as resulting from the attainment of what are purely formalistic rights, this being in many cases the most to which we can realistically aspire. The question this raises is of course whether we can or should set our sights rather higher than this, whether we can see beyond what Marx in his *Critique of the Gotha Program* called "the narrow horizon of bourgeois 'right'"—whether or not we take the next step and agree with Marx that his horizon needs to be crossed "in its entirety."

Merely to privilege the "civic" will do nothing to dislodge the various problems attendant upon the much more fundamental distinction between state and civil society as this was originally, and proleptically, outlined by Hegel. Much hangs here on who is to be our touchstone—Hegel or Tocqueville—whether civil society is to be regarded as an arena where people better themselves by associating with like-minded others, or whether it should rather be understood as a realm of material inequality, corporate power, and hierarchical order. If the latter is to prevail, and the brunt of my earlier work is to suggest that it *should* prevail, then we can specify that self-esteem is not going to be universal in civil society, that it will likely be sought elsewhere, and that (as Hegel in his manner was aware) the civically defined state is unlikely to provide a focus for it.

The glaring contemporary contradiction between economic inequality and a supposed political freedom for the individual, that is in reality the freedom of and for the market, is going to oblige the state to use its coercive power more often and more openly in the service of "stability," both international and domestic. This demands the eradication of vocal alternatives to capitalism. On the other hand, and at the same time, ineradicable differences among social groups and their respective cultural formations—which will surely be flexed and articulated at both the domestic and the international level—are going to intensify, and this very intensification (an ideological reflex of which is precisely the "civic"/"ethnic" axis of discussion) is everywhere going to challenge the *régime* of equivalence and what Marx termed "political emancipation."

In dealing with these problems—and we shall have to deal with them—we theorists are going to need all the help we can get. And this is far less likely to proceed from present-day Anglo-American liberalism than it is from serious reconsideration of Marxist state theories proffered by the late Nicos Poulantzas and others. For present purposes, let us remain content with considering the kind of cultural antagonisms that have increased so markedly in recent decades. It is of course to these antagonisms that New Social Movements speak. The activism of these NSMs, it is important to note, is not restricted to the topos of the political state, liberal or otherwise; it is not restricted to singular political and social issues but instead multiplies along the lines of intersection of various concerns, forces, and spaces. More is going on here than meets many a liberal eye. NSMs are not regulated by any singular concept of political subjectivity—and certainly not by a civic concept that could only stymie their understandings of themselves—and do not occupy the space of politics as this is conventionally understood. They tend rather to branch rapidly into contiguous issues, which is why they so often seem to more traditionally minded political theorists to be sporadic, disjointed, discontinuous—or even (depending on the eye of the beholder) as instances of a jagged postmodernity.

Such movements have been well-nigh ubiquitous in decolonizing struggles, as is well known, What is less obvious, perhaps, is their increasing purchase within major capitalist societies. The CND in Britain was a mass movement that mobilized opposition to state nuclear projects in the first instance, to be sure; but in short order in came to intersect with and branch out into contiguous environmental, antimilitarist, and communitarian activism through the 1960s and 1970s. Similarly with the May 1968 movement in France.

From a present-day perspective it may seem surprising that its focus should have concentrated as much as it did on relations between students and workers (and not between students and immigrants, or the unemployed, or women). But the relations upon which the French students chose to concentrate were the very sites of activism, contestation, and negotiation where nothing, not even the site itself, was taken for granted; to this extent our present-day perspectives, more broadly viewed, were formed by the May 68 events themselves.[13] Note also that the CND and May 68 movements were embedded in cultural forms of expression, which contributed over time to new formations of resistance to Thatcherism, Mitterandism, militarism and racism through the 1980s. In the United States the history of the Civil Rights movement and its legacy points to a related dynamic of intersection and ramification, embodied in the continuous emergence of new modes and sites of struggle: feminist activism, the movements of radicalized, racialized ethnic groups, and radical environmentalism are examples.[14]

Far from amounting to a destructive left-sectarianism, as is suggested by Todd Gitlin (in his recent *The Twilight of Common Dreams*)[15] and other avatars of the old New Left, NSMs gain their momentum from their transgression of normative divisions of state and civil society in ways that are very difficult for the state to contain. In this way "the distinction between human emancipation and the formal freedoms guaranteed by (conventional) politics is constantly underlined," while the latter are taken in and of themselves are undermined.[16]

It may well be the case that (in Habermasian terms) the "lifeworld" (or ensemble of background assumptions, shared understandings, and cultural traditions that form the horizon or presupposition of social action) is, as I write, being threatened by the functional needs of international capitalism and by those of the bureaucratic state, insofar as these are different. But we should not infer from this that the "lifeworld" is nothing but an inert recipient or victim of such initiatives (which are not uniform in any case, as Poulantzas was presciently aware). The "lifeworld" has had its own ways of bouncing back, and these have not proved uniform either. Nor are they likely to adopt the mantle of uniformity in an uncertain future.

What I can claim with some degree of certitude, and by way of conclusion, is that *to the extent* that NSMs challenge the pre-given distinctions between "the" political, "the" social, "the" cultural, "the" educational, "the" aesthetic, etc., they are not doing something altogether unprecedented. They are, rather, consciously or unconsciously following in the footsteps of those prototypical working-class radicals in and around the Chartist period in Britain who effectively challenged in advance such a division of society into separate spheres—spheres whose separation only subsequently came to be regarded as having been set in stone and as being, therefore, unalterable by political means. [17] That they *are* alterable by political means gives the lie to those who fail to question them—and particularly to those who base their claim on a "civic"/"ethnic" distinction that in turn takes this division for granted, as though it were a warmed-over variant of Lukács's capitalism as "second nature."

Where does this leave *Exit, Voice, and Loyalty*—and Hirschman's insistence that exit belongs to economics, voice to politics? [18] Since I cannot but concur with this liberal belief, it leaves the book in a privileged position, one it still deserves to occupy. Voice is indeed "political action par excellence," just as Hirschman says. [19] But how much *more* political voice would be if it were not reduced to the level of "a private, 'secret' vote in the anonymity" not of a supermarket but of a curtained voting booth! How much *more* political voice would be if it were not confined to "interest articulation"—to the articulation, that is, of interests that precede their political vocalization by emerging, fully formed and pre-given from the primordial economic realm!

Hirschman's no less admirable *The Passions and the Interests* ,[20] we might recall, had as its subtitle, "political arguments for capitalism before its triumph." It proffers and reconstructs these arguments with real panache, just as we might expect. And they work admirably—up to a point. Interests as such are indeed less "divers[e]" and capricious than passions, just as Hirschman argues, and passions did indeed need to be curbed and bridled accordingly. And they still do. But what of a state of affairs today where capitalism has long since triumphed, and at times crows triumphally? The "voice" that at first shores it up was that of the articulation and aggregation of interests, just as Hirschman says. But how quickly and astutely Hegel went beyond these in the light of Kant's *Third Critique*! How cleverly he noted that this same "voice" sounded not in the political arena or the state but in the economic arena of civil society's "system of needs"!

The categories shifted in remarkably short order, short enough to permit and encourage a new kind of category mistake. The "voice" that resounds from outside the economic realm has to do not so much with interest but with its (supposed) transcendence. It has to do with that capacity for disinterest(edness) that was encouraged to emerge in the nineteenth century by any number of British luminaries, and which today corresponds in some way with the concept of political "slack" Hirschman had already pinpointed in *Exit, Voice, and*

Loyalty—the ability to remain above the battle, outside the clash and clang of interests, and to judge according to the precepts of a "higher" sensibility it was the task of education, of enforceable state-sponsored pedagogy, to propound. This is the very disinterestedness that corresponds to a hypertrophied, formalized view of citizenship that is, as I write, under contestation from new social movements, from the dispossessed, from the marginalized, from the excluded, and (since 1968) from within the interstices of capitalist education institutions the mselves—not excluding the one I happen to teach at.

Notes

1. John Gray, "Autonomy Is Not the Only Good," *Times Literary Supplement,* 13 June 1997.
2. Michael Ignatieff, *Blood and Belonging: Journeys into the New Nationalism* (London: BBC Books and Chatto & Windus, 1993), 6-7.
3. John Acton, *Essays on Freedom and Power,* ed. Gertrude Himmelfarb (Boston: Beacon Press, 1984), 192-93.
4. Friedrich Meinecke, *Cosmopolitanism and the Nation State* (Princeton: Princeton University Press, 1970), 9-10.
5. Pointed out to me by Hans-Ulrich Wehler.
6. Clifford Geertz, *The Interpretation of Cultures* (New York: Basic Books, 1973), 259.
7. Erich Fromm, *Escape from Freedom* (New York: Avon, 1969), 40, 52.
8. Michael Sandel, "The Procedural Republic and the Unencumbered Self," *Political Theory* 12, no. 1 (1984): 90.
9. Albert O. Hirschman, *Exit, Voice, and Loyalty* (Cambridge, Mass.: Harvard University Press, 1970). In the section on membership and exit that follows, I should like to credit and acknowledge an unpublished, prize-winning essay by a former graduate student in my department, Elaine Thomas (no relation), which first gave me the idea about exit verbs.
10. Louis-Antoine de Saint-Just, *L'Esprit de la Révolution* (Paris: UGE, 1963), 20.
11. Martha Nussbaum, "Patriotism and Cosmopolitanism," in *For Love of Country: Debating the Limits of Patriotism*, ed. Joshua Cohen (Boston: Beacon Press, 1997), 7.
12. St. Augustine, *The City of God* , ed. V. J. Bourke (New York: Doubleday/Image, 1958), 469-71.
13. See A. Feenberg and J. Freedman, *When Poetry Ruled the Streets*, forthcoming.
14. See Paul Gilroy, *'There Ain't No Black in the Union Jack'*: *The Cultural Politics of Race and Nation* (Chicago: University of Chicago Press, 1988), ch 4; Raymond Williams, *Resources of Hope* (London: Verso, 1989), 187-244.
15. Todd Gitlin, *The Twilight of Common Dreams* (New York: Metropolitan Books, 1995).
16. Gilroy, *'There Ain't No Black*, 231, parenthesis mine; Gilroy's back-reference to Marx's distinction in "On 'The Jewish Question'" (1843) between real, "human emancipation" and purely "political emancipation" is here very conscious, and deliberate.
17. See Paul Thomas and David Lloyd, *Culture and the State* (New York: Routledge, 1997).
18. Hirschman, *Exit, Voice, and Loyalty*, 15.

Paul Thomas

19. Hirschman, *Exit, Voice, and Loyalty,* 16.
20. Hirschman, *The Passions and the Interests* (Princeton: Princeton University Press, 1977).

Chapter 2

Does a Homogeneous Conception of Nation Exist? A Typology of National Identities

Iván Vitányi

About the Homogeneity of the Nation

The nation has been the most important protagonist of history for the last five centuries. Millions of people fought and died for the sovereignty of their nation or to subjugate other nations. Wonderful thoughts and deeds and, at the same time, terrible crimes and faults were born in the name of the nation. The nation has been the most important subject of history in the last several centuries, though social classes and mankind were for some time its rivals. The term 'social class,' however, is no longer used as it was before (we call it layer or group). The lower social classes have lost their class identity. The upper classes have preserved it. They make use of it, but they do not speak about it.

A common global or planetary identity is not strong enough. Some of the identities placed between nation and mankind, for example the European, Atlantic, Arabian, Far Eastern, or Latin American identity, may gain more importance in the future. They are in the contradictory coexistence as Huntington describes our world.

Even the concept of the nation is contradictory. It has no universal and global definition; the given criteria can be used only under certain conditions. We speak about the German, Irish, Kurdish, Romanian, Swiss, Indian, Indonesian, American, Brazilian, Canadian nation though there are great differences between how, for example, the Germans, Swiss, Americans, or Kurds are nations.

Within the confines of some of these nations there are different ethnic groups, as in the case of the Americans. Nevertheless the influences of the original ethnic group can still be felt. Totally different kinds of nations include for example the Poles and the Swiss. The first one (the Poles) consists of a single ethnicity, the second (the Swiss nation) embraces three (or even four) national groups. There are nations speaking one single language, and nations where people have different mother tongues. There are languages spoken by several nations in several countries (like German, English, Spanish, Portuguese). Some ethnic groups speak the same language with small differences but are different nations, such as the Czechs and Slovaks or the Serbs, Croatians, and Bosnians. In these cases there are also cultural and religious differences. However, sometimes they are not more important ones than for instance within the American and Australian nations. Some of the nations have had their own state for centuries, while others have never succeeded in creating one. Thus they live within the confines of other states (like the Kurds or Basques). There are nations characterized by peasant traditions, others by industry, commerce, or shipping.

Thus, the concept of the nation can be defined only in an eclectic, pragmatic way. (As the young Stalin did, when during his emigration he studied this question in Western libraries. His famous definition is still valid today: "Nation is a historically developed, lasting community of the relations between language, territory, market and culture.") If we want to say more about it, we can try, but we have to know that we enter a very large and sometimes even dark forest. How can we see the woods through the trees?

May I mention here an example from the Hungarian past. The problem of the nation—its sovereignty, freedom, and unity—became extremely important before World War II, when Hungary found itself living between the empires of Hitler and Stalin. There was a group of young intellectuals who started a new movement for an independent Hungary. There were two wings within the same movement.

The first one—we may call it *nationalist*—raised the question: Who is Hungarian? And they had a radical answer: there are "deep" Hungarians and there are "thin" ones. (The nationalists used the same word, "thin," as Kohn and later Plamenatz did in their essays on the types of nationalism.)[1] They said that only the *deep* Hungarians were true, authentic members of the nation. But who belonged to the depths? Those whose parents, grandparents, and great grandparents were ethnically and culturally Hungarians. However, that was not enough. They had to follow the values, norms, and prescriptions of the deep Hungarians. They had, it was told, Hungarian hearts. But who had Hungarian hearts? It was decided by the *authentic depths*. (According to the notorious Nazi slogan: "das bestimmten Sie!")

I think this attitude is an archetype of nationalist behavior and discourse in thoroughly cultural terms. An archetypal behavior of some people within those nations who have the feeling that the national development was hindered or even stopped. If we want to understand the behavior of those nations we have to listen to this.

There was yet another wing within the same movement, which had a democratic answer to the problem. They said: to be a Hungarian (or Romanian, Serbian, Russian, German, etc.) is a choice. A Hungarian is someone who considers himself or herself to be a Hungarian. Franz Liszt must be regarded as a Hungarian, though his parents were not and he himself could not speak the language. But he manifested himself to be a Hungarian and nobody had the right to doubt it. On the other hand, Albrecht Dürer was a German, although his father was really a native Hungarian from the village of Ajtós. (*Ajtó* in Hungarian means door, *Tür*, Ajtós means Thürer, Dürer. So his name was a translation from Hungarian.) But the painter had never shown any empathy or nostalgia toward the homeland of his father.

Then we have to say that a homogeneous concept of the nation does not exist. Therefore—as usual in such cases—we have to analyze the system of dimensions where the investigated phenomenon comes into sight. I draw three dimensions that I think are the most important for further analysis. They are the following:

First, *the system of human communities*, especially of those that comprehend the entire society. There are two complementary types of human communities that comprise an entire given society: the *frame* and the *pole* organizations. They are and they were present even in the smallest and oldest human groups, in the form of tribes and genera. Everyone had to belong to one tribe and one of the genera within it. The whole life was built on that structure. The double character of poles and frames is one sine qua non of human society. The historical forms of *pole organizations* were (after genera) the casts, orders, classes, and (in Max Weber's sense) status groups; whereas the historical forms of *frame organizations* were tribe, ethnos, demos, polis, empire, and, later, nation.

Second, *the dimension of time*. As from the fifteenth century to nowadays—that is, the time range of modern society—the nations were the main frame, and the classes were the main pole, organizations. History became a battlefield of nations and classes. Howrever they were and they still are also conditioned by the times.

In a *first period* of its development, the nation was thoroughly based on, and connected to, ethnicity and religion. It was the time of primary accumulation of wealth and capital, and of the primary accumulation of power. It was the time of the new profane trinity of one state–one nation–one religion (*cuius regio eius religio et natio*). The accumulation of wealth and power was an aggressive, unjust, and even cruel process if we apply to it our measures. Nation and state were together in this process. From one point of view, it was a heroic fight for building up a new world; but from another, it was a merciless concentration of power using the nation-discourse.

In a *second phase*, new changes take place—if not everywhere but in the center of socioeconomic development, that is in the Euroatlantic region. Namely, the obligatory unity of the state and religion becomes looser in the process of secularization. Later the same thing happened, or began to happen, with the absolute unity of state and nation. The state is becoming an organization not of the privileged nation, but of all its citizens. The state has nothing to do with ethnicity, origin, color of skin, religion, conviction, *Weltanschauung*, or civic interest. The Afro-American black should be an emancipated member with equal rights in the same nation as an Anglo-Saxon, white, Protestant, a descendent of the Mayflower group. A double identity will be not only possible but usual. According to Robert Jay Lifton's expression: "Protean" personality develops, which means that the individual will be able to fulfill more than one single identity at the same time in a harmonious combination. [2]

But these phenomena are signs for the beginning of a new, *third phase* that I will discuss later. Now, we can summarize these processes in two main items. First, the political nation changes into a cultural nation. Second, the state loses the role of the most comprehensive frame-organization and becomes a pole-community, a center of culture (in the broadest sense) within the community of the nations. Many of us think that this role is not smaller and not worse than the old one. [3] There are, however, other opinions as well.

Third, the connections with the basic *models of socioeconomic development* (center, half-periphery, and periphery). If we want to distinguish, or even enumerate the different attitudes toward nation and national identity, this third dimension is extremely important. According to Wallerstein, the differences between the countries and peoples of the center, periphery and semi-periphery lay neither in the different genetic heritage of their people, nor in their different culture, nor only in the different level, but in the *different models* of economic and social development. [4] They are on different levels and the way they reached their levels has also been very different.

For example, in the center (Western Europe, North America, later Japan and other Far-Eastern countries) the development of market economy, nation-state and finally democracy was not only quicker, but also organic, autochthonous, home-made, and domestic. In the semi-periphery and periphery, East Europe, East-Central Europe, the Balkans, and formerly other regions, around the core, such as Scandinavia or Spain, they had the possibility to climb out of the pit, so in these countries the development was not only backward, but also nonorganic, artificial, and imported. The domestic conditions (for instance, the existence of a national bourgeoisie) were weak. The development had to be enforced by the state and by progressive groups around the state, but mainly through nondemocratic methods. Therefore, it was regarded by many people as something alien.

Draft for a Typology of National Identities and Behaviors

National consciousness, national identity, and national state configure three levels of analysis. They have different impacts when considered in the center of economical and social development (that is, in the countries of the center) than in the periphery and semi-periphery. Several alternatives have developed that create together the present typology of the modes of behavior connected to the nation. I will introduce them.

First Level: Extensive, Expansive, and even Aggressive (Illiberal and Preliberal) Types of National Identity and Behavior

During the time of the development of modern society and economy, as well as during the development of the nation-state, every West European nation belonged to this type. At that time, however, there were several ethnic groups trying to become a nation in the contemporary modern sense of the word. Other ethnic groups were losers, and they were not able to form an independent state. Some of them even disappeared as a nation, lost their language (as the Provençals or the Plattdeutsche), and today they do not fight for it any more. At the very most, they feel a nostalgia, learn the mother tongue as a third language, and try to preserve something from their cultural heritage and not only for touristic reasons. Others still fight, sometimes by cultural, sometimes by political means, and sometimes by bombs. They still consider that their fate should be changed.

The situation on the periphery and the semi-periphery is much more critical. National development started but had not ended, the possibilities became obvious but were not fulfilled. The nation-state developed very late, although inner national relations were not homogenized as in the center. Ethnic identities play in such cases a double role. On the one hand, it is of course understandable that every nation wants to live its own culture, have the own tradition and autonomy. On the other hand, *militant, aggressive nationalism* is developing. The nation becomes a value concept—one's own nation has a higher value,[5] while the other one is guilty. (That is the model of illiberal nationalism, exposed by Hans Kohn and John Plamenatz, and which was expressed in the notion of *deep* or *thick* Hungarianness analyzed above). This phenomenon is called "Jihad" by Benjamin Barber. This kind of nationalism goes together with everyday authoritarian behavior and political authoritarianism. The idea of the nation-state is the absolute power of one ethnic group (and very often of one religion). The power of the leading nation is used for discrimination, or assimilation, or both. The other ethnic groups have no autonomy and minority rights. In extreme cases this behavior leads to wars, such as the ones triggered in Karabah, Chechnya, Kurdistan, Bosnia, or Kosovo.

Second Level: Classical National Identity and Behavior

Both in the periphery and the center there is *a classical variation of national consciousness* (which should be called by many authors a liberal national identity.) It lays stress on the autonomy and flowering of national culture and on the nation-state, as well as on the relation between nation and state. At the end, it becomes tied to democracy. It does not want to discriminate and oppress other nations or ethnic groups.

The *consciousness of big nations* is again something different. In every national consciousness there is some pride, but especially in the case of the big nations. Both past and present reflect successes and victories. This is of course a national pride, which must be celebrated on every occasion. In the United States, the national anthem can be heard even on the occasion of a basketball game between universities—this is unimaginable in Hungary although there are as many nationalists (if not more) in Hungary as in the United States. The pride of big nations is more accepted than that of small ones. The great nation means power, which can be felt even today. It is not regarded as a historical accident, but as a virtue that gives them the right to judge. Maybe this attitude is also liberal, but a nonironic type of liberalism, which is (according to Richard Rorty) the first step to authoritarianism.[6]

Third Level: *Postmodern* Nations, or Behavior at the Time of Globalization

Now we have arrived at the crucial point in the sequence of problems. It is the *present* and here we find a *new phase* in the development of the nation question, which has new implications for our analysis.

To begin with, in the process of *globalization* the economic-political-cultural development gets beyond the phase of the nation-state. That is, the state and ethnicity are radically divided from each other. We find identities that go beyond the nation-state, such as the European identity. This kind of national feeling and consciousness is libertarian (in the ironic sense) and communitarian (in the democratic sense). National identity and national consciousness are now more concentrated around culture, but at the same time culture also loses its exclusivity and develops toward a multinational openness.

But, unsurprisingly, globalization has also a *dark side*. As mentioned above, Benjamin Barber has described these tendencies and shown how thoroughly connected they are to the process of globalization—namely, commercialization, uniformization, totalization. He draws the final conclusion that beyond, and instead of, nationalism a new type of totalitarianism threatens the world by means of a sort of infantilization of the individuals (who tend to relax their civic consciousness in "McWorld").[7] Fred Dallmayr added that this is a new form of nationalism itself.[8] Hence, McWorld becomes the twin brother (or sister) of jihad.

McWorld totalitarianism has really a mirror effect. Globalization can homogenize only the countries of the center and its own half-periphery. But neither its content (the behavior and culture of new democracies) nor its negative features have the same influence on other territories. Indeed, another kind of homogenization, uniformization, and totalitarianism threaten other regions. This situation and its negative consequences have been described by Samuel Huntington.[9] If it is so, the process called globalization does not create one but many homogenized new worlds. They are internally globalized-homogenized, while externally separated. In this new system, humanity will have the frame, whereas the different regions and cultures the pole, will have character.

A New Picture of the World

The problem is that all these modes of behavior and attitudes live together on the same globe at the same age. They live together, though the representatives of the different tendencies do not understand each other. Let's take the war in the Balkans. The Americans could not understand the anger of neither the Serbs nor the Albanians. Conversely, the people in the Balkans do not understand the Americans' pacifying interest. Neither Western nor Eastern politicians (together with Gorbachev) had foreseen that the possibilities offered by democracy would be used first by those who want more, and not absolutely democratic, power for their own nation or ethnic group.

The situation can best be characterized by a story. One evening during the 1980s I was the guest of the well-known psychologist Mihály Csíkszentmihályi. Csíkszentmihályi is of Hungarian origin, although he has never lived in Hungary. His wife is of Polish origin. At dinner her father and the couple's ten-year-old son were present. Hungarians and Poles lived for centuries in good relations. According to a proverb known in both countries, Hungarians and Poles are good friends. During dinner we spoke of course about our common past, common battles, common kings, revolutions, about our common fights (which all ended with defeat) against the Tartars, Germans, and Russians. After some time the son said:

> I am listening to you and I am happy that I'm neither a Hungarian nor a Pole, but an American. Because you have been talking for more than one hour about bitter defeats, unsuccessful revolutions, and oppressions. You have even been able to lose the same war twice: at the beginning and at the end. I am learning at the American school only about victories, there is no defeat at all in our curriculum.

Those who want to understand what's going on today in the countries that do not belong to the center of the world have to reflect upon this. What kind of a psychology can a person have who not only learns but also experiences continuous defeats. The essence of it is that the presented types of national identities and the modes of behavior and institutional structures belonging to them are not in a separate form present on the planet. We can not say that in certain places only one of the types is to be found, while elsewhere only the other types are present, as if in the center countries everyone moved beyond disintegrating nationalism, while in the periphery nobody did it.

The real differences lie in the proportions. Thus, the first level (expansive national behavior) is the most developed in the periphery area, has a lesser degree of representation in the half-periphery, and the least presence in the center countries. The second level (classical national behavior) has a moderate presence in all three areas and somehow forces a balance between the first and the third levels. If we now consider the third level (postmodern liberal national behavior), we can see how it is the most extended in the center area, but the least developed in the periphery countries (against the first level). In turn, it plays a growing role, though still not hegemonic, in the half-periphery area. The following table can illustrate the distribution of the different national ways of behavior:

3rd Level postmodern liberal national behavior			
2nd Level classical national behavior			
1st Level expansive national behavior			
	Center	**Half-periphery**	**Periphery**

Distribution of the different national ways of behavior in the countries of the center, half-periphery and periphery, areas (the intensity of the color shows the degree of development of each way of behavior.)

As a provisional conclusion, we can now infer that modes of national behavior, and, consequently, national identies do not form a loose mixture but rather a compound. We find this compound structure in each area of countries. So, national identities cannot be distilled in any chemically pure form, nor can they be historically and socially contextualized out of their compound-structure condition. Hence, to sum up, those who try to solve the contradictions must know that it is possible only through the transformation of the whole structure.

So, the question arises: Do we have an alternative? At the very beginning of the third millenium there are two main paths, two main alternatives or scenarios open up for our societies. The *first alternative* suggests that there will be less democracy and, accordingly, a minimal state in place of the welfare state, with bigger corporate authority. Individual freedoms will be safeguarded of course, but a weaker civil society will emerge from this corporate world. The scenario created goes together with national and ethnical neutrality on the one hand, and with a revival of expansive illiberal nationalisms and regionalisms on the other hand (that perfectly combines with the infotainment culture). A *second alternative* suggests that there will be more and stronger democracies,[10] more open societies.[11] Accordingly, the welfare state will be replaced by a welfare society, and corporate authority will not override political authority. There will be strong civil societies where individual freedoms will flourish, as will high culture. This scenario goes together with a liberal-communitarian-civic national consciousness—a developing planetary consciousness.

Is this second alternative possible at all? For the time being it is a Utopia. Naturally, to settle this question is not a duty of scientists. The future of civil society depends on the behavior of the members of civil society itself. Scientists and researchers can only analyze and discuss the trends and possibilities. There is no scientific proof for a positive or for a negative answer. But if human beings need positive Utopias, this is one.

Notes

1. See Hans Kohn, *The Idea of Nationalism: A Study in Its Origins and Background* (New York: Macmillan, 1944); and John Plamenatz, "Two Types of Nationalism," in *Nationalism: The Nature and Evolution of an Idea*, ed. Eugene Kamenka (New York: St. Martin's Press, 1967).

2. Robert J. Lifton, *The Protean Self* (New York: Basic Books, 1993).

3. I have developed this argument in Iván Vitányi, *A társadalom logikája* [The logic of society] (Budapest, 1994).

4. See Immanuel Wallerstein, *The Modern World System*, vols. I-II-III (New York-San Francisco-London: Academic Press, 1974, 1980, 1989).

5. See Benjamin R. Barber, *Jihad vs. McWorld* (New York: Times Books, 1995), 155-216.

6. See Richard Rorty, *Contingency, Irony and Solidarity* (Cambridge: Cambridge University Press, 1989).

7. Barber, *Jihad vs. McWorld*, 219-35.

8. Fred R. Dallmayr, "Nationalism East and West," paper presented to the international conference on *Beyond Nationalism? Sovereignty, Governance and Compliance*,

Málaga, June 1999.
    9. Samuel P. Huntington, *The Clash of Civilizations and the Remarking of World Order* (New York: Touchstone Books, 1998).
    10. Benjamin R. Barber, *Strong Democracy: Participatory Politics for a New Age* (Los Angeles: University of California Press, 1984).
    11. Karl R. Popper, *The Open Society and its Enemies* (London: Routledge and Kegan Paul, 1984).

Chapter 3

Nationalism and Typological Thinking

Manuel Toscano-Méndez

Translated by José M. Rosales

Beyond nationalism? The question raised by the editors is not easy to answer, among other things because it entails a series of interconnected questions: What do we mean when we speak of 'a postnationalist scenario'? Would that be possible, anyway? And if possible, would it be desirable? The main difficulty of these questions lies at the uncontrollable polisemy of the term 'nationalism,' to which it seems almost impossible to assign a precise meaning. Besides, it seems unreasonable, if not discouraging, to speculate about the future of a phenomenon so changing and diverse before establishing its meaning.

Thus, my argument will focus on a thesis concerning the social ontology of nationalism. Albeit tacitly, it performs an important role in the nationalist rhetoric. With the help of a conceptual distinction of evolutionary biology we can shed light on the nationalist tendency to represent the social reality of nations and the membership of individuals in the national community. This way of approaching nations and national identities usually distorts both the theoretical understanding and the normative characterization of the social scientist. However, it helps us differentiate a more scientifically balanced approach and gives us some clues to go beyond nationalism.

Nationalisms and Nationalist Demands:
A Necessary Remark

Undoubtedly, any prediction on the future of nationalism seems highly risky, if not senseless. For instance, at the beginning of the 1980s, who could have anticipated the demise of communism, the frantic course of events after 1989, and the reconfiguration of Europe's political map? Prudence is even more needed when we try to assess ethnocultural tensions and conflicts. They constitute "the most striking example of a general failure among the experts to anticipate social developments," as Jalali and Lipset have pointed out regarding the Cold War conviction, held by Marxist and non-Marxist social scientists alike, that many ethnocultural loyalties and identities would cede to modernization and transform or dissolve themselves into wider social entities. [1]

Furthermore, any exercise of futures anticipation entails of its own a remarkable dose of desiderata, as is happening currently in Spain on the debate on nationalism and the European political integration. On the one hand, Catalan or Basque nationalist demands, and particularly Basque secessionist demands, miss their point once we enter the space of the European Union—would it not be anachronistic to draw new frontiers at the time that current ones are disappearing? However, on the other hand, the nationalist vision of a "Europe of the peoples" underlines the growing loss of sovereignty by the states—and the emergence of new opportunities for small nations. The same happens with globalization, whose effects on nations and states can be instrumentalized in one sense or the other.

But the notorious difficulty of the debate lies in what Clifford Geertz called "the stultifying aura of conceptual ambiguity that surrounds the terms 'nation,' 'nationality,' and 'nationalism,'"[2] which the astonishing increase in the specialized literature for the past decades has not driven away. Nationalism has very different meanings, from the defense of cultural identity by a minority group to the aggressive expansionist politics by a state. Thus, it is common to distinguish the nationalism of ethnocultural minorities inside a wider state from the nationalism of the state's dominant group. But in each case we may find further differentiations, according to the typology drafted by Kupchan.[3] So, in the first case, the demands range from the recognition of the minority group's differentiated character to secession; while in the second, we find distinct levels of *state-claiming* or *state-building*, in which the identification with the state competes with alternative loyalties, or even turns into the main focus of mobilization and, lastly, of *state-expanding*, in which the state's nationalism fosters territorial demands or hegemonic aspirations in its international relations.

Yet can we find a common bond among the numerous politics we call nationalist? Traditionally nationalism has been taken as a political principle of legitimacy, built upon the relation of nation and state. That principle refers to the assumption that the political unit and the national unit *must* be the same. Otherwise, they become failures.[4] Indeed, properly considered, nationalism cannot be understood without the condition that it makes the nation the political community par excellence, the fundamental axis for the configuration of the political space and the organization of power.

But if we exclusively pay attention to this aspect, we get a partial, or even distorted, view of nationalist politics and demands. Then, for example, we would disregard the search for cultural roots and the promotion of national identity (language, folklore, history, etc.), or give them an instrumental use subordinated to political aims. These cultural motives are taken as proofs demonstrating the existence of a differentiated community. However, we should acknowledge the important role they play in educating the nationalist conscience.

In his research on the old nationalisms of Central and Eastern Europe, Miroslav Hroch has distinguished three stages in the formation of national movements.[5] First, the initial period, when small cells of activists, mainly intellectuals, consecrate themselves to researching and spreading a nation's distinctive features: language, history, customs, arts, popular traditions, etc. Yet this exploratory task does not imply the institution of a political project. That is precisely the endeavor of a second evolutionary stage, aimed to reduce the deficits of nation-building. Then new generations of activists launch patriotic upheavals to awaken the group's national conscience and receive a growing endorsement of their national political project. The process leads to a final stage, that not all the movements reach, when national identification has been widely spread throughout the different social classes and nurtures a mass movement, internally differentiated. This sequence reveals the fundamental role in the emergence of nationalist movements played by all sorts of literary activities, philological and historiographical research, interest in folklore or popular traditions, which, albeit politically meaningless at the beginning, provide the stuff upon which to build the group's national character and constitute the starting point of nation-building.

In his model of the evolution of national movements, Hroch combines three general groups of demands whose relative priority and timing vary in each case. Namely, the full deployment of a national culture, where a leading role is given to the local language through its use in public administration, the education, or the economy. Second, the rights and political institutions to support national self-government either of an independent state or within a state. And third, the creation of a full social structure in the nation. Of these three groups of demands, which correspond to the stages of the model, only the second addresses properly the issue of national self-government. Hence, if we were to focus mainly on it, we would miss the entire scenario of projects of the nationalist movements.

In particular, we may get a distorted vision of nationalist politics if, according to this principle of legitimacy, we take self-government, or the creation of a state, as the highest nationalist target. Accordingly, we might think that once this target is accomplished, for example, if a nationalist movement reaches independence and gets to create its own state, then it would no longer make sense to be nationalist. We might arrive at a postnationalist stage through the success of nationalism and the fulfillment of its aims. But history teaches us otherwise ever since the formation of new European states at the end of the First World War to the recent state reconfiguration in the Balkans. Thus we cannot expect the extinction of nationalism after nation-building and the division of the political space along national lines. On the contrary, it is reasonable to expect its continuation, or even its increase, through the boost of nationalizing policies by the new independent state. We may detect here a lack of vision rather frequent in studies on nationalism, as many tend to interpret it as the cause for the creation of new states and the drawing of new frontiers. Actually what happens is that nationalism comes afterward and is a consequence of such changes.

Rogers Brubaker has demonstrated that nationalism is not only the cause, among other factors, of the dissolution of old multinational state, but also the outcome of this process that, under novel forms, keeps going ideologically and politically in the new states.[6] It does not seem an irrelevant lesson that twice in the twentieth century the political map of Central and Eastern Europe has been massively redrawn along nationalist demands, without implying either the disappearance of nationalism or the solution to the national question in the zone.

If the studies of Brubaker represent a notorious advance toward the understanding of nationalism it is partly because of his analysis of the reconfiguration of national tensions after the nationalization of the political scene. Far from solving the national question, we are witnessing the emergence of the complex interaction of three antagonistic nationalisms: the *nationalizing* nationalism of the new independent states, a national minority that is left within the new state, and the nationalism across frontiers of what Brubaker calls "external national homeland"—a neighboring state politically interested in the fate of that ethnoculturally kindred minority. Conflicts in the Balkans or tensions in the states successors to the Soviet Union can be best studied through this triadic model.

If we accept Brubaker's persuasive analysis and combine it with the three groups of nationalist demands distinguished by Hroch, it is easy to see that national self-government, or the creation of a state, is not the final point of nationalism. Nationalism always comes under the form of a politics destined to remedy the deficits of national life and remove the obstacles impeding its realization. The nationalist discourse, therefore, can be interpreted as a series of variations around the fundamental theme of the expression of grievance against oppression and a call to defend the nation's interests.[7]

National self-government is accordingly understood as the way to amend such shortcomings of national life deemed to be caused by past injustices and to protect the nation against the supposed threats hanging over it. These motives are argued by nationalism in search of a state, but after a state comes into existence they still make sense. After independence it may be necessary to protect the national economy and foster the nation's own culture and language, thus achieving its hegemony in the different spheres of social life—or to complete the nation's social structure, thus avoiding the possibility that the relevant posts and positions are occupied by non-nationalists. Possible threats to national life may come from the existence of national minorities, immigration, foreign cultural influences, a weak record of local language, the investment of international capital, or the fact that a part of the territory or of the national population remains under the jurisdiction of another state—something that is viewed as constituting an amputation of the national body.

All these cases are deemed to represent a situation of weakness, injustice, or risk to the nation that should be amended or prevented. Accordingly, if all these variations of the nationalist theme share a common assumption, it is the belief in the value of a national life fully developed. This, in turn, explains the moral significance of the nation. Therefore, we should not focus the normative discussion of nationalism exclusively upon national self-government as a condition for political legitimacy, important as this may be. Nationalism, instead, should be regarded in more general terms as a response to the question, "What is the preferred setting, the most supportive environment, for the good life?" [8] If there is an assumption, more or less explicit, in the nationalist discourse, it is the idea that the national community constitutes the needed framework within which its members can lead a good life—and as a consequence, any threat to the community's integrity turns out to be harmful to its members. This assumption, that closely binds the identity to the well-being of the members, performs a crucial role in the nationalist rhetoric, whose persuasive resources greatly depend on its viability.

Thus, a proper study of nationalism must give account of these cultural and moral aspects of membership and identity both in theoretical analyses and in normative discussions. Michael Ignatieff does this in his *Blood and Belonging,* where nationalism is defined as a political ideal, according to which the peoples of the world are divided into nations and each nation has either a legitimate claim to self-government or a right to self-determination. But nationalism is regarded as a cultural ideal that likewise holds the claim that the nation provides the most fundamental membership and identification groundwork for men and women. [9] Also the justification for nationality by David Miller deals with it as the legitimate foundation for claims to self-government, but Miller adds two further conditions. The first is that national belonging is meaningful and relevant to the identity of individuals. And the second, that national communities draw frontiers that are morally significant, that is, they generate solidarity ties and normative expectations among their members. [10]

Therefore this moral or cultural dimension of nationalism, whose intellectual origins, according to Isaiah Berlin, can be traced back to Herder and the counter-

Enlightenment movement, are of great interest to our analysis. Berlin calls it "populism." [11] It stresses the idea of belonging, namely, what it entails to be a member of a national community and the way in which this condition confers meaning to the life of individuals, so that among the possible answers to the question of who we are, national identification stands out: I am French, Spanish, Irish, Flemish, Quebecois, or Catalan. In other words, the thesis gives special relevance to national identity among our ties and identifications and so takes the nation as the fundamental context for the life of people, their most achieved and significant social environment.

Its weight acknowledged, yet this thesis turns out quite vague regarding its meaning and normative consequences. Hence, it is possible to reconstruct this assumption of the nationalist discourse at least in two different ways—we'll call them the strong and the weak versions. To characterize the former, I will adapt the distinction between "typological thinking" and "population thinking" by the biologist Ernst Mayr, deemed to illustrate certain discussions around the evolution of the species that can be used productively in social philosophy. The weak version can be understood in terms of collective action and public goods, which offers a line of argumentation upon the protection of communitarian domains ("a context of choice," according to Kymlicka's rightful expression) [12] or shared cultural goods. For reasons of directedness, I will address below the former interpretation, toward which nationalist discourses tend generally to converge.

First, I would like to make a brief remark on the difficulties in identifying the reasons for nationalism. What is certain is that the reconstruction of certain assumptions in nationalist discourses entails a good dose of abstraction and simplification, which in turn move us away from the political contexts where such discourses take place. The problem is in that every nationalist discourse seems to argue its own reasons, depending on its particular historical situation as well as on specific social, political, and cultural circumstances. Given the variety of nationalist experiences, their local nature and the presumed singularity of their claims and circumstances, or their extraordinary eclectic nature that allow for the incorporation of arguments from the left and the right as well, we can legitimately doubt the existence of nationalist reasons in general. It is problematic to find an invariant core of nationalist discourses, that is, a set of arguments exclusively shared by all nationalists. One has the impression that a vague family resemblance barely exists, to use Wittgenstein's image, among them, and certainly nothing similar to a coherent doctrine.

In our case, we have difficulties with both interpretations. On the one hand, if we stick to the strong version, it hardly makes acceptable a rapproachment to liberalism. On the other hand, a weak version might be accepted even by non-nationalists. Herder himself, as quoted by Berlin, constitutes an eloquent example of this difficulty, as he is considered to be the intellectual parent both of nationalism and of cultural pluralism—a combination hard to sustain. Certainly he conceived of humanity as divided into cultural communities and took them as the vital contexts of individuals. But if we take into account the political ideal of congruence between nation and state, then at least in this sense Herder cannot be considered a nationalist. Anyway, our aim is to catch the meaning of the nationalist thesis that assigns individuals to national groups, each one of them having a unique identity. Now, if we may agree upon a general definition of nationalism, this refers to the affirmation and custody of the nation and of national identity.

The Strong Interpretation: Typological Thinking versus Population Thinking

What is the meaning of "typological thinking" and what usage may it have to clarify the "populist" or nationalist thesis we have been dealing with? The contrast between typological and population thinking was introduced by the famous evolutionary biologist Ernst Mayr to explain one of the greatest merits of Darwin's work. For Mayr, Darwin provided not only a huge set of empirical proofs in favor of evolution or an accurate mechanism to measure evolutionary change (natural selection), but he also decisively changed the view and the way of thinking of naturalists. Before Darwin, the traditional mode of interpreting the world had been to recognize, under the exuberant variability of nature, a limited number of types or fixed and immutable essentials.

Two aspects are especially worth pointing out, according to Mayr: first, that the typological thinking stresses the reality of types to the expense of the appearances of variability; and second, that there is no continuity among those types, for they are perfectly defined and neatly separated, so that there is no chance of gradual evolution among the species, as Darwin held. [13]

The genius conveyed by the author of the *Origin of Species* was to replace this traditional interpretation with what Mayr called "population thinking," which emphasizes the unique nature of every living organism. So, each one has singular features, which can be inherited by its successors, affecting its chances for survival and adjustment. Two innovative contributions can be pointed out here. First and foremost, the population thinking takes individual variations to be the main focus of attention. As a consequence, populations integrated by individual organisms can only be described collectively in statistical terms. But, furthermore, those populations are subject to continuous changes and variations, as their constituent members are, so that gradually they can generate new species. It is, thus, a complete reversal of the essentialist view: while it takes types or essentials to be real, and individuals only to the extent that they embody their groups' typical features, for the population view only the individuals are real, being the types' statistical averages, abstractions taken from populations in permanent change.

Mayr himself has pointed out the great advantages of this radical change of view, especially as it invalidated essentialism. The new methodology, insisting on the unique character of each individual belonging to a particular population, gave anthropologists a measurable tool of research that led very easily to empirical results.[14]

Now let us resume our argument. If we speak of nations instead of species, the contrast between typological and population thinking becomes apparent. Having in mind some formulations of the nationalist creed, we can recognize a close affinity to typological thinking. Thus, Kedourie condensed the core of the nationalist doctrine as stating that: 1) humankind is naturally divided into nations; 2) nations differ from each other as to certain features objectively verifiable; and 3) national self-government is the condition for political legitimacy.[15]

As we have said above, we are not interested in this last normative principle, but in the first two principles, which would come to reflect the social ontology of nationalism. Indeed, a number of objections can be put forward, as argued by authors who depict the modernity of nationalism: there is nothing natural in nations; the differences appealed to by nationalists turn out to be meaningful only in specific social contexts, when they are not deliberately distorted or invented; and the account of those differential features is open to an endless casuistry, inevitably partial, selective, and debatable.

But it is undeniable that nationalists firmly believe in the existence of nations and that men are grouped in national communities, which are deemed to have a special status among the various forms of human association. As argued above, the nationalist sees the nation as providing the social context best fitted to facilitate the members of that nation's life options, the framework including other forms of association. But now, the point is to remark how this social ontology of nationalism, as formulated by Kedourie, comprises a typological view, as it comes to represent the human world structured into separated, distinct nations (internally compact, self-contained within absolute borders.) Hence, each individual has a single nationality according to the features that define their membership in nations.

As Mayr explains, whoever thinks in typological terms as per race, assumes that each representative of a given race exhibits its characteristic features and differentiates herself or himself from individuals of other races according to their different conformity to their own types. Yet isn't this view too rough and unreal? Isn't it too unlikely, because of its extreme nature, in order for nationalists to recognize themselves in it? The fact that we have used terms of evolutionary biology, in referring to species, does not imply that we are focusing our analysis of ethnic nationalism in the strictest and most devalued sense. On the contrary, the most relevant issue raised by the distinction typological-population concerns the very ideas of nation and nationality.

For typological thinking appears basically in the substantialist or holistic conception of the nation, that confers entity and existence of its own to this kind of social aggregate. In general, nationalist discourses speak of the nation as something that transcends individuals, a real collective entity lasting over generations and time that eventually becomes the active subject of history, endowed with personality and interests of its own. For instance, it is enough to listen to how Basque nationalists speak of *Euskal Herria* (the Basque Fatherland) or the Basque People (with capital letters) as constituting something substantially different from the Basque citizens to corroborate that this conception of the nation is profoundly rooted and is something more than a question of words. This should not be surprising, given the continuous influence of nationalist historiography since the nineteenth century focused on the history of nations, or if we take into account, for example, that Durkheim, the distinguished sociologist, never had trouble arguing that France's identity and personality were one and the same from the Middle Ages to his own time. [16]

The problem is that this reified or typological conception of nationalism influences far beyond nationalist circles many studies on nationalism, that take for granted the existence of nations. Brubaker has vigorously pointed out this tacit assumption of nationalist social ontology in the debates on nationalism and the national question: "Most discussions of nationhood are discussions of *nations*. Nations are understood as real entities, as communities, as substantial, enduring collectivities. *That* they exist is taken for granted, although *how* they exist—and how they came to exist—is much disputed." [17]

Certainly, many of those debates have addressed the modernity of nationalism or its premodern roots, simply assuming the real existence of nations. So, when presuming that the world is divided into nations, a strong ontological compromise is taken that inevitably vitiates the whole discussion. As Brubaker suggests, special attention should be paid not to inadvertently introduce nationalist beliefs in the theories on nationalism, thus giving them theoretical endorsement. For "group realism," in Brubaker's terms, stains the discourse on the nation and so causes a confusion between "categories of practice" and "categories of analysis." The 'nation' is the category around which the discourse and the political action of nationalists is organized and, accordingly, it is necessary to analyze its usage by nationalists, without inferring acritically its existence.[18]

The population thinking, instead, reorients our understanding of the national question in terms of methodological individualism. It draws our attention toward the languages through which individuals interpret the social world, its interactive structures and institutions, but restrains us from giving a substantive existence to certain social aggregates or from taking them as the terms of our explanation. Furthermore, they present another advantage. To explain it, I would like to use the famous and revealing image by which Gellner described the transition from the agrarian to the modern world that produced the cultural homogenization of the political spaces: while the former looks like a picture by Kokoschka, multicolored and chaotic, the latter looks like a Modigliani, a surface distributed in different color stains internally homogeneous in neatly delimited figures. [19]

Putting aside Gellner's functionalist interpretation, I suspect that the vision *à la Modigliani* of compact sets and divisory lines unequivocally drawn, like the old maps, has an irresistible attraction for nationalists, precisely because of their leaning toward viewing the world from a typological standpoint. However, it is an optical illusion, as we hardly find that homogeneous color and division in real human societies. Again, from the population thinking point of view, reality looks more like a pointillist picture. When we see it close up, we discover thousands of small points of varying chromatic tones, instead of big stains or discontinuous leaps from one color to another.

Obviously, if the substitution of population thinking for typological thinking puts into doubt the way of representing national communities, it also changes the terms defining national membership and identity. Its advantage has to do with the skepticism toward the attempts to classify individuals along typological categories or to define them according to typical features. That way, if there is no archetype individuals must copy to become what they are, as their features are simply the result of statistical averages, then membership criteria tend to loosen. In other words, if we pay attention to the real identities of individuals, complex and varied as they are, we should then abandon any pretention of imposing on them a categorical identity along whith their membership.

The concept of "categorical identity," introduced by Craig Calhoun, is interesting to this respect because it allows us to catch the ambiguities of the modern representation of nationality and ethnicity, as well as their dependence on typological thinking. Calhoun establishes a strong contrast between the way of representing membership in premodern and modern societies: in the latter, social groups are understood as sets of equal persons, instead of complex interweavings of social positions or relations networks. That entails many important things: a sense of direct and symmetrical membership, in place of indirect and hierarchically mediated belonging. We associate it to the ideas of nation and nationality, where now participation does not come from the integration of local units into bigger ones, but from the individuals themselves.

At the same time, it has the effect of assigning a categorical identity, and not a relational one, to the individuals of the group, meaning a series of ethnocultural features shared by its members. This has been corroborated by anthropologists like Clifford Geertz when he explains the formation among African and Asian societies of "generalized ethnic blocs" nationwide: "A simple, coherent, broadly defined ethnic structure, such as is found in most industrial societies, is not an undissolved residue of traditionalism but an earmark of modernity." [20] An ethnic or national group then appears as a limited set of individuals, whose ties are defined more in terms of resemblance or common features than by certain types of relations. As Calhoun remarks, this opens the door to every kind of pressure toward the conformity and normalization of individuals, so that they become fixed in the national type.[21] In other words, the categorical character of national identity implies necessarily the idea that there exists a correct way of being a member of the nation. I do not think it is necessary to emphasize the risky consequences we all know may come from nurturing such expectations of correct identities.

Nationalism and Beyond

I cannot ensure that typological thinking acts as a necessary condition of every nationalism, although it is easy to see how the nationalist rhetoric shows a worrying proclivity to do so. The tendency may be more or less accentuated in each case, but it is present in nationalist discourses of all sorts, which assume the existence of the nation and assign a categorical identity to individuals according to their membership of the nation. Albeit I have tried to keep some distance, my experience as an informal observer for the past fifteen years of the political discussions on the national question in Spain leads me to think that a close affinity exists between typological thinking and the social ontology that constitutes the background to nationalist discourses and politics. This becomes apparent in many ways, but here I will focus on three aspects to illustrate the affinity.

To begin with, there is no doubt that behind the nationalist discourse, formerly the Spanish, now mainly the Catalan and the Basque, lies a substantialist conception of the nation, deemed as a collective entity lasting over time. The debates usually adopt a bias clearly ontological, as if the fundamental issue were which nations are state-nations: whether there is a Spanish nation, coexistent to the state, or different nations living inside the same state—a condition entailing their legitimate aspiration to national self-government or to independence. If in the past the Spanish nationalism denied the national reality of Catalonia or the Basque Country, today it is the nationalists of these communities who deny that Spain is a nation. So, given that their national projects are antagonistic, all share similar ontological assumptions concerning the existence of nations as historical entities. It seems as if, once the reality of a nation is established (which the nationalist takes as an irrefutable fact), the task that remains consists of deducing the political consequences of that fact. Because of the importance given by nationalists to the ontological affirmation of the nation, it can be fairly said that their discourse on national self-determination hides another on national pre-determination.

This becomes apparent in the declarations by nationalist parties that foster the recognition of the state's national plurality, as launched for example by the Barcelona Declaration of 1999. But they interpret this multinational nature as a picture by Modigliani, to resume Gellner's image, defined by the existence within a territorial state of two or more communities internally compact and well delimited. The contrast between the typological and the population views reminds us, rather, that there exists another way of describing diversity—one underlining the differences among individuals, instead of national communities. So we have citizens, and not nations, with varying sentiments of membership and identification. The difference lies in that the nationalist view recognizes and encourages pluralism within the framework of the state, but minimizes or suppresses it in the national community; whereas the second view makes no such distinctions and fosters the recognition of pluralism not only in Spain but also in Catalonia or the Basque Country, where the identifications of the citizens are plural, complex, nuanced, and changing.

This difference leads us to the other dimension of typological thinking, which closely binds the social ontology of nationalism to the assignment of a categorical identity to the members of the nation. This tendency is perceived with great clarity in the debates about languages: the fact that more than 75 percent of the Basques have Spanish as their mother tongue and speak it usually does not refrain Basque nationalists from declaring *euskera* as the genuine language of the country and impose the obligation to know it. It constitutes something akin to the Irish nationalists' attempts (as described by Joyce in his stories)[22] to revive Gaelic, designated to be the true language of Ireland, although the immense majority of the island's inhabitants, the nationalists included, speak English. As Conor Cruise O'Brien has pointed out, it is surprising, except for a nationalist, that the Irish Constitution of 1937 defines Irish as the first official language of the country, whereas English constitutes the language most used by the Irish in their everyday life.[23] These are examples of the categorical imposition of a fictitious identity that generates unreal expectations about what it means to be a good Basque or a good Irish, or about such essentialist claims that justify policies of linguistic or cultural normalization.

The third sign of the support and influence of typological thinking has to do with the claim that the sentiments of membership and identification of real people fit unambiguously within distinct categories. In the case of Basque nationalism, it is well known that one of its foundational dogmas, as formulated by Sabino Arana at the end of the nineteenth century, refers to the radical antagonism between being Basque and being Spanish. Despite the fact that, according to the polls, only a minority of the real Basques opt exclusively for one option or the other, while the great majority combine both identities in varying degrees, Basque nationalists hold the essentialist assumption of a fixed and excluding Basque identity. Also a Catalan nationalist leader some years ago expressed his grief for the "patriotic bigamy" of many of his fellow citizens, precisely because one can only belong to a nation and this requires an exclusive identification.[24] There is no better proof, coming from a moderate and democratic nationalism as the Catalan is, of the nationalist resistance to recognizing the real identities of the individuals, with their nuances and ambiguities, and of its claim to interpret them in terms of fixed, excluding categorical identities—a typological claim that mutilates the identities, plural and complex as they are.

We can now resume the initial question: Beyond nationalism? A condition to think of a postnationalist scenario consists of getting out of the typological view of the social world, so cherished by nationalists. That means changing our way of thinking about nationalism, nations, and national identities; and, particularly, about the relations we establish between nationalism and nationality. Gellner's suggestion of reversing the usual view in discussions of nationalism becomes especially relevant: so instead of adopting the view in terms of the nation or the national identity, we should adopt the reverse view. As nationalism declares itself to be at the service of the nation (a political action aimed to amend the shortcomings of national life), this reversal opens a quite different perspective.

It seems highly recommendable to abandon the imagined conception of the nation and its correlate, namely, the essentialist definition of national identity— an inescapable condition for a postnationalist scenario. But this suggestion should be applied to the theoretical understanding of nationalism and to the normative discussions on the national question. Briefly, the study of nationalism does not need to assume a nationalist social ontology. To use Brubaker's words, we should discuss nationalism in leaving for nationalists the belief in the nation and in categorical national identities. That would redound to the benefit of a more sophisticated analysis of nationalism: "We should think about nations," argues Brubaker, "not as substance but as institutionalized form, not as collectivity but as practical category, not as entity but as contingent event."[25]

Notes

1. R. Jalali and S. M. Lipset, "Racial and Ethnic Conflicts: A Global Perspective," *Political Science Quarterly* 107 (1992-93): 585.

2. C. Geertz, "The Integrative Revolution: Primordial Sentiments and Civil Politics in the New States," in *The Interpretation of Cultures* (New York: Basic Books, 1973), 257.

3. C. A. Kupchan, "Introduction: Nationalism Resurgent," in *Nationalism and Nationalities in the New Europe*, ed. C. Kupchan (Ithaca, N.Y.: Cornell University Press, 1995), 5-6.

4. E. Gellner, *Nations and Nationalism* (Oxford: Blackwell, 1983), 1.

5. M. Hroch, "From National Movement to the Fully-Formed Nation," *New Left Review* 198 (March/ April 1993): 6-7.

6. R. Brubaker, *Nationalism Reframed: Nationhood and the National Question in the New Europe* (Cambridge: Cambridge University Press, 1996).

7. Brubaker, *Nationalism Reframed*, 79.

8. M. Walzer, "The Civil Society Argument," in *Theorizing Citizenship*, ed. R. Beiner (Albany: State University of New York Press, 1995), 154.

9. M. Ignatieff, *Blood and Belonging : Journeys into the New Nationalism* (London: Vintage, 1994), 3.

10. D. Miller, *On Nationality* (Oxford: Oxford University Press, 1995), 10-11.

11. I. Berlin, "Herder and the Enlightenment," in *The Proper Study of Mankind*, ed. H. Hardy and R. Hausheer (London: Pimlico, 1998), 367.

12. W. Kymlicka, *Liberalism, Community and Culture* (Oxford: Oxford University Press, 1989).

13. E. Mayr, "Typological versus Population Thinking" (1959), in *Conceptual Issues in Evolutionary Biology*, ed. E. Sober (Cambridge, Mass.: The MIT Press, 1984), 14-17; *Una larga controversia: Darwin y el darwinismo* (Barcelona: Crítica, 1992). My attention to this distinction was drawn by the paper by J. A. Rivera "Contingencia y narratividad. 2. Mecanismos de autorrefuerzo," *Claves de Razón Práctica* 84 (1998): 37-45.

14. E. Mayr, *Así es la biología* (Madrid: Debate, 1998), 248.

15. E. Kedourie, *Nationalism* (New York: Praeger, 1960), 9.

16. E. Durkheim *L'éducation morale* (Paris: Presses Universitaires de France, 1992), 53: "Entre la France d'aujourd'hui et la France d'autrefois, il y a des différences, sans doute, mais ce sont, pour ainsi dire, des différences d'âge . . . Et, pourtant, entre la France actuelle et celle du Moyen Age, il y a une identité personnelle que nul ne peut songer à méconnaître."

17. Brubaker, *Nationalism Reframed*, 13.

18. Brubaker, *Nationalism Reframed*, 5.

19. Gellner, *Nations and Nationalism*, 139-40.

20. Geertz, *The Interpretation of Cultures*, 308.

21. C. Calhoun, "Nationalism and Ethnicity," *Annual Review of Sociology* 19 (1993): 230-31.

22. J. Joyce, "The Dead," in *Dubliners* (London: Penguin, 1992).

23. C. C. O'Brien, *Ancestral Voices: Religion and Nationalism in Ireland* (Chicago: University of Chicago Press, 1994), 85-87.

24. J. Triadú i Vila-Abadal, "Catalunya, nación plural," *El País*, 26 October 1996, 22.

25. Brubaker, *Nationalism Reframed*, 18.

Chapter 4

Nations within Nations—Nationalism and Identity Politics

Tuija Pulkkinen

From present political disputes it is readily concluded that discourse on nation is not merely confined to the context of nation-states. Much of the political action that today falls under the name of identity politics, that is politics in terms of gender, sexual orientation, or race in the name of minorities (or underprivileged majorities as in the case of women as identity) is literally phrased in term of "nations."[1] In this chapter I will argue that as a pattern of political thought identity-politics also bears a close relationship to what is historically understood as nationalism, and therefore can be judged as to its positive and negative effects with similar concerns that hold for the earlier political thought in terms of "nations."

However, I would like to underscore that in making this statement, close attention must be paid to varieties of nationalism in the past. The "nation" as a form of thought in connection with identity-politics has, I will argue, only a weak connection to the polity concept of nation that is most prevalent in the history of the western part of Europe and the United States, but rather is much more closely connected to the concept of nation that was defined in cultural terms and then developed into a political idea in which the ethnic and political ideas merged in Eastern Central Europe in the nineteenth century. In opposition to those who in the contemporary discussion seek to form a new polished concept of nationalism transcending the divergence of ethnic and civic thought,[2] I find the profound historical differences between the "Western European" and the "Central and Eastern European" type of conceptual development extremely significant and worth close analysis also for the purposes of the current discussion. In this chapter I propose to judge the contemporary identity politics on the basis of its having a structural connection to the pattern of thought, which I would refer to as the "nation-type" of political thought, and which is connected to the historical conflation of the ethnic and the polity versions of thought in terms of the concept of nation.

In the historical parts of this article I will use the Finnish history of thought in terms of nation as my prime example, in part due to my intimate knowledge of it which surpasses my knowledge of any other history. It is evident, though, that the pattern of conflating the ethnic and polity conceptions of nation that is apparent in Finnish political culture has by no means been an exception in Eastern Central Europe, and that the Hegelian influence that is eminent in Finland accentuates many elements that were present elsewhere in the domain of German thought in the nineteenth century.

I will begin my article with a compound history of the concept of "nation" in Europe, and then in my first systematic discussion I will analyze the different concepts of nation that I see as incorporated into this history. I then proceed to examine the case of Finnish nineteenth century thought from a historical perspective in order to highlight the connection between the Hegelian type of political philosophy and the Eastern Central European ethnic concept of the nation, which I analyze in my second systematic discussion connecting it to later Marxist thought and contemporary identity politics. In the final part I will consider and judge the merits and drawbacks of this nation-type of thought that is common to both the historical nationalism and identity-politics of today.

Conceptual History of "Nation"

Literature on the history of conceptual changes in European political thought and political vocabulary in European languages is fairly unanimous about the fact that a break in European conceptual history occurred around the year 1800. Many interpreters like to generalize this as the turn to "the modern" conceptual framework. Some writers do this by generalizing Reinhart Koselleck's term "Zattelzeit," from German conceptual history, and applying it universally to all of Europe as a general conceptual turn. Others, like Liah Greenfeld, seek to establish another general account of the conceptual development, in which the term "modernity" plays a central role.

However, as the writers of the *Geschichtliche Grundbegriffe* article "Volk, Nation, Masse" note, the conceptual development was not "one":[3] in Germany the Herderian turn around the year 1800 was unique in terms of its conflation of the concepts of *Volk* and Nation with ethnic, linguistic, and cultural overtones. The same conflation did not happen in the conceptual framework in France, England, or the United States where both terms prevailed without connection to ethnicity.

The earlier history of the concept of nation and the concept of people is also interesting in this respect. It is evident that for quite an extended period of time neither "people" nor "nation" were related to culture, language or ethnicity as we now understand them. According to those who have textually studied the terms deriving from the Greek *ethnos* or Latin *gens, populus,* and *natio* in European languages the history of the terms before the 1800 was already rich, and the relations between the terms had varied in different times and regions. According to the *Geschichtliche Grundbegriffe* article the Greek *ethnos* was used generally as an exclusionary term to designate those outside the *polis.*[4]

The Latin equivalent *gens* was used similarly, and *natio* was also used very closely in Roman times. In Rome, the word *populus* was used to distinguish the (inner) citizens of the Roman state from communities outside the center of the empire, who (or whose upper political stratum) were called *gentes* or *nationes*. Roman power was understood as power over "the peoples" it joined. In the usage of the ancient Romans and their successors, *natio* and *gens* referred to political units located outside the central area, including largely autonomous administrative areas, such as Bavaria and Bohemia in the Middle Ages. (The "German nation," on the other hand, was an unknown concept.)

For several centuries to follow, "the people" continued to primarily refer to either one of the poles of exclusion and inclusion in the central polity: either to the people of the state in a political sense (*populus*), or to "peoples" (*gentes, nationes*) as political and administrative areas in a given country, and the noblemen of such an area in particular.

Other meanings for each of these terms were also present. "People" in European languages could also refer to God's people in a theological sense or militarily or geographically to the population, or it could take on a sociological meaning by referring to a group's, crowd's, or society's lower orders. Another significant traditional usage of "nation" had to do with its etymological Latin meaning (*nascere* = to be born). *Natio* was used to describe a traveler's place of birth. Used in this sense, *natio* was a key concept, for example, in describing groups of university students, who organized themselves by provinces or "foreign nations," forming clubs (*nationes*) based on their areas of origin. The concept of a person's "birth nation" also appealed to the emotions and one's love of home. This notion of a person's "nationality" was, however, confined to the capacity of describing someone who was not at home, and thus it differed greatly from what we today refer to as a person's nationality. None of the conventional old usages of the terms referring to "people" or "nation" had any relation to culture, language, or ethnicity as we now understand them. Nor did they have the meaning of self-governing polity in the modern sense.

According to the *Geschichtliche Grundbegriffe* article, the fifteenth-century humanists first used the concept of "the people" as referring to a linguistic and cultural community as opposed to a political or administrative community. However, this usage remained marginal until the last third of the eighteenth century. At that point the work of the philosopher Johann Gottfried von Herder caused an essential change in the history of the concept of "people" in Germany. The concept of "people" radically took on linguistic, cultural, ethnic, and historical connotations and the German word *Volk* increasingly came to refer to a culturally defined community viewed as a single actor, with its own language and its own character.[5]

In the meantime, the concept of "nation" had undergone its own "modern" European change of meaning. Greenfeld places the "democratic" turn in the conceptual history of "nation" in sixteenth century England, where the notion of the sovereignty of the people thus constituting a nation was already discernible.[6] Without having to pinpoint the precise time and place of the conceptual change of the term nation, one can certainly say with a great deal of certainty that at the time of the French Revolution the new concept was already in use all over Europe. This new political usage entailed the ideas of popular sovereignty and general participation.

I would characterize the new political signification that emerged alongside the old established usages of the word "nation" in the following way: If the political space had previously been understood as being divided into rulers and subjects, the notion of "the nation" was now used to evoke a political space that was undivided. The nation is not composed of the rulers and the ruled. On the contrary, it is an entity that rules itself.

The idea of the nation as a self-ruling sovereign unit also entails a new concept: the citizen. It is precisely through the figure of the citizen that the ruler and the subject could coexist in the same person within the political community. The nation consists of citizens who are simultaneously both rulers and subjects. The notion of the citizen became increasingly bound up with the idea that everyone, and not just the elite, is a member of a self-ruling nation, and with the ideal of universal participation in the political process.

According to the *Geschichtliche Grundbegriffe* article, in France, up until the eve of the Revolution, the concept of the people was still used in the traditional sense, whereas the concept of the nation was already part of the new political practice. The concept of the nation became increasingly interwoven with representational politics, equality, and civil society in the context of the state. In revolutionary documents, the concept of the people was also gradually integrated into the new model of society. The Constitution of 1793 refers to the French people as a sovereign entity consisting of French citizens. In other words, in France, both *le peuple* and *la nation* were political concepts that were clearly bound up with the notion of sovereignty. Neither "people" nor "nation" were concepts used to express ethnic, linguistic, or cultural units.

In Germany, however, the concept of nation had an entirely different history. The humanists' idea of nation as based on language, culture, and history had resurfaced periodically throughout the centuries, alongside the established and more widespread usages of "nation." The old usages ("nation" as an independent administrative district and its upper classes, or a person's place of birth) were, however, dismissed when Herder remodeled the concept of "the people" at the turn of the nineteenth century. What happened in Germany was that the concept of the nation merged during the time of the French revolution with the new ethnic notion of the people. "The nation" not only no longer meant an area outside of the center of the country, or its political leaders, referring instead to a sovereign political community, but in Germany, it also referred to a sovereign political community based on an original identity of an ethnically, culturally or linguistically defined community. "The people" (*Volk*) no longer meant a subservient social group but referred to the ethnically founded nation itself. In other words, two concepts, "people" and "nation", merged with one another.

A "people" in the Herderian sense is an ethnic community joined by a common language, customs, and a common descent, which is understood to be concretely real. Herder's concept of the people also entails the view that a people's language and poetry are not external features but constitute elements of a "people" or "nation." Language and poetry render peoples and nations into what they are, meaning communities characterized by internal values. The nation also gains anthropomorphic features, including an attitude, a spirit, and a mind. Peoples lead their own lives. They do not necessarily require external embodiment in the form of the state. Herder envisaged a great garden of different peoples, in which no one was superior, and all had equal worth, and in which diversity was considered a richness.

Germany, unlike France or England, lacked a clear political center. This, some say, made it natural for the Germans to resort to linguistic and cultural definitions of nationhood, which subsequently underpinned the nationalistic ambitions of the German state. However, ethnic and political concepts of the people and the nation were also attractive to the smaller European nations, which had nonsovereign status as protectorates of various empires and countries. Among others in Eastern Central Europe, these nations included Finland. The new Finnish political vocabulary of the early nineteenth century drew heavily on German concepts and theories of the nation. German nationalism which was not centered around the state, but had an ethnic, linguistic and cultural emphasis, made it especially relevant to Finnish political conditions after the Napoleonic Wars.[7]

A Systematic Discussion

Nationalism, which in the past has for long been an area of study dominated by historians and historically oriented sociologists, has only recently attracted the wider interest of philosophers and political theorists. The previous task of the theorists was to present a plausible account of the phenomenon of nationalism, and theories were put forward to explain nationalism functionally and causally, as well as to discern and classify its various phases and types. Such well-known theorists of nationalism as Benedict Anderson, Ernest Gellner, Eric Hobsbawn, Hans Kohn, or Anthony Smith have certainly, in addition to explaining the phenomenon, each practiced a kind of political theory.[8] However, the new discussion in terms of political philosophy differs from the earlier theorizing in that it does not attempt to explain the phenomenon but rather directly questions whether thinking in terms of a nation is good or bad, and analyzes the content of this thought in relation to other types of political thought.[9]

In the philosophical discussion on nationalism terms such as "the nationalist," "the ethnic nationalist," and the "civic nationalist" have surfaced and begun to gain stability by occupying positions in an imaginary discussion between the advocates and opponents of views. The danger in this type of discussion is in the prospect that the abstract "-ists" and "isms" end up not finding much correspondence to positions that the political agents and writers of political texts actually have performed and perform by using the term "nation" in specific texts and contexts, and instead begin to take on a life of their own in relation to each other in a normative dispute between theoreticians. I would therefore emphasize the need to discuss in this area of political thought in close connection both to historical and contemporary contexts.

In a recent collection of articles entitled "Theorizing Nationalism" I think several writers are correct in pointing out that in the contemporary discussion, the contrast between "civic" and "ethnic" nationalism serves normative goals, usually in favor of liberal civic nationalism.[10] In my view, this may have the effect of incorrectly placing the ethnic and political concepts of nation, the difference between which I find to be of extreme historical significance and interest, on the same plane, as if they had been and were offering answers to the same set of questions. Actually the ethnic concept and the polity-concept of nation are not -isms that are created for the purposes of discussion, but are rather two different patterns of thought that have been formed in greatly differing circumstances and that both deserve analysis as patterns of thought by political theorists. One should recognize the genuine difficulty and futility of forming one position of a "nationalist" deriving from this conceptual diversity.

I am not, however, opposed to generalizing and theorizing the term nation. On the contrary, I am proposing a systematic connection between the nation-type of thought and contemporary identity politics. My suggestion is that the nation-type of political thought bears a much closer resemblance to the Eastern Central European type of political conceptualization than to a pure polity-notion of the French and the English usage of the word nation. The identity politics of gender, race, and sexuality are connected to the nation-type of thought with the parallel idea of a naturalized origin and continuity over time of the identity of the group concerned often connected with these political movements.

I find it useful to separate at least three different ideas connected with the concepts of nation and nationalism. First, there is the conventional understanding of nationalism according to which nationalism is closely related to the nation-state system. Hannah Arendt's discussion in *The Origins of Totalitarianism* is a good example of the clear and concise separation between "people" and "nations," in which the latter is understood strictly in terms of the system of nation-states. [11] In connection to the nation-state system, nationalism is an attitude invested in the glory of the state in opposition to other states, and loyalty toward one's state is the norm of nationalism. This may be the most common understanding of nation-alism, but it may also be the least interesting one, when considering the impact of nationalist ideas on political thought.

Second, there is the modern European political concept of nation, which is related to the notion of undivided polity. The main idea is the identity of the rulers and the ruled, and the concept of the citizen serves here as the sign of this identity. The nation is a self-governing sovereign polity. In the French political discourse and in the United States "nation" tends to be used in this meaning of a polity, often also in connection to the aforementioned meaning of nation within the system of nation-states, but very rarely in connection to ethnicity. As far as I can see, nationalism as an -ism has actually not been connected with the purely political concept of the nation until very recently. Only in the current philosophical discourse has "civic nationalism" been adopted as a term used to promote a conceptual move by which "nationalism" is reborn as the loyalty of a citizen to the political system of a self-governing sovereign democratic polity. Third, there is the concept of nation that is closely connected to the Herderian notion of a people as an originally identical cultural and linguistic ethnic unit. The Herderian idea is clearly separate from the two other conceptions of nation, and can either be connected or not connected to them. "Nation" when used as nearly synonymous to the term "people," does not necessarily need to be understood politically. The main idea is that peoples are originally and throughout time identical with themselves in a way similar to the way in which individuals are thought to be identical with themselves throughout time. For example, present day Bavarians are understood as being in a meaningful way "the same" as Bavarians in the middle ages, because of the self-identity of a Bavarian people or nation. In the history of Eastern Central European political thought in the 19th century, the idea of originally self-identical cultural ethnos and the polity-notion of nation seem to merge, forming the ethnic concept of nation.

Below I will engage in a closer and more detailed examination of the conflation of the political and the ethnic notions of nation as it occurred in Finland, where the nationalist thought in the middle of the nineteenth century was heavily influenced by Hegel's thought. The idea of one national mind and polity as a reflective self-command of that mind was the leading idea of this conflation. My suggestion is that the Hegelian political ontology in which a specific type of national thought is significant, cleared the path for several later developments, first and foremost, many of the central ideas in the subsequent Marxist thought, which was also prevalent throughout the same regions of Europe. I further suggest that this tradition of political thought is not irrelevant to present-day identity politics. However, I am not aiming to establish a historical connection here, although one might indeed be significant, rather I am merely pointing to certain systematic equivalences and their consequences.

Finland and Hegelianism

The myth of ethnic units as originally identical and of Finnish people as being one of these original units acquired extreme political significance in early nineteenth century Finland and has played a role in the political culture of the country ever since. The unique identity of Finns was founded linguistically, but it was also very effectively constructed in various other areas of knowledge, such as history, literature, and the arts during the course of the last century. According to the national narration, the Finns as an original unit from which all real Finns descend, have their origin and home at the great bend of the river Volga. They have "relatives," tribes figured often as "sibling peoples," in Eastern Europe, and they have their own history and their own literature, of which the folk poetry collected and recorded in great quantities during the active years of the nationalist movement of last century was the most original expression. Establishing the cultural identity of Finns and Finnish culture demanded great amounts of construction work from those engaged in the process of projecting it in the past as original.

The establishment of cultural identity was, however, not disconnected from the establishment of the polity. The issue was not so much that of Finland's position as a part of the Russian Empire and the ambition of achieving sovereign status within the nation-state system, but rather was more related to the establishment of a polity in terms of the modern notion of nation that deals with self-governing and participation. In this respect, a much bigger problem than Russian governance was the past "colonial" situation with respect to the Swedish empire and the continued position of the Swedish language as the language of the country's upper class, education, and law. Thus, the linguistic emphasis in the nationalist movement served as more than just the establishment of a mere cultural identifier; the language division along the lines of the rulers and the ruled of the old regime was an obstacle to the creation of a nation in the political meaning of the word. Cultural activity in the Finnish language was promoted in various ways by using its original nature as the real language of the real people as an argument, and it coincided with the issue of participation and the very form of the nation as a polity without the division into the categories of rulers and ruled. This occurred without any special emphasis on the nationalism of the type connected with the system of nation-states.

The total conflation of the ethnic and polity concepts of nation is amazingly clear on this linguistic level, in the Finnish language. The comprehension of a nation as an ethnic-linguistic original identity, equated with the polity idea of nation, in which citizenship as a position guarantees the identity of the rulers and the ruled is implanted in the political vocabulary that was coined by the "*fennomanian*" promoters of the use of Finnish in the public sphere. The words "people," "nation," and "citizen," which in other languages are not reminiscent of one another, are all based upon the Finnish term "people":

people = *kansa*
nation = *kansakunta* (people + community)
citizen = *kansalainen* (people + -er, as in Londoner)

Another important dimension in Finnish nationalism was, that when developing into a political force, the national movement was lead by thinkers who were deeply influenced by Hegel's system, the most significant of them being philosopher J. V. Snellman.[12] Despite the fact that neither the linguistically defined "Volk" nor "Nation" were central concepts for Hegel himself, his *Philosophy of Right* operates within the culturally defined German conception of political community of that time.[13] The most general of Hegel's terms in the area of social and political philosophy is *Sittlichkeit*, deriving from *Sitten* (habits or mores). When Hegel speaks about the *Geist* in respect to a given community, it may be interpreted more or less as the culture or something that these days we would call the "values and norms of a society or community in their constant process of change."

Significant to Hegel's conception of polity is the idea that the political unit (the state) is conceived of as a will, and that this will is supposed to ultimately be conscious of itself and be aware of what it wills. The self-reflective nature of a political community is its self-consciousness of the process of the change of the culture (habits and laws).

The themes of self-consciousness and self-reflectivity were extremely relevant in the Finnish national movement. It was all about the recognition of the specificity of Finnish culture, which had previously been acknowledged as nothing more than a lack of culture. With the posited originality of Finnish specificity which according to the national narrative had always existed, although it had thus far remained dormant, consciousness raising was now on the agenda.

Within the Hegelian framework the dominant political concept the state (*Swedish, Stat, Finnish, Valtio*) was conceived of primarily as a cultural community conscious of itself and in control of its own change by means of its functioning as a polity. [14] This was well suited to the situation of that time—there was, of course, no state of Finland within the European nation-state system; from 1809-1917 Finland remained a part of the Russian empire. Still, a distinct Finnish political publicity was emerging during the first decades of the nineteenth century, and the polity was conceived of in the nationalist minds as one, as the Finnish nation. J. V. Snellman for example would apply the term state to Finland in his texts, despite the fact that Finland was not an internationally recognized state. [15] Nor was his usage of the term intended to underscore the desire that Finland become a state, but rather it was determined by his concept of state, which was defined in terms of cultural self-recognition and action within a polity. His claim was that through this heightened self-recognition and self-governance, Finland had actually already transformed itself into a state. In his vision, it was a national *Geist*, the mind of the nation, comprised of the shared knowledge and shared held values in a community that reflectively governs itself, knows itself, and through the political action of its citizens plans a future for itself that is conscious of both its past and its present. The peculiar pattern of envisaging the nation, people, and culture as one mind and as a single agent became the most significant feature of the emerging political culture. [16]

The Second Systematic Discussion

The Hegelian twist in Finnish history points to three significant ideas that were woven into the fabric of national thought. First, there is the conception of the community as a single mind. Second, there is the idea of political processes as the self-reflectivity of the single mind. Third, there is the notion of the self-reflectivity of the single mind (the nation) that corresponds to the political process in a sovereign polity, which is all about the nation getting to know itself (self-consciousness) and consciously planning its future (self-governance). It is crucial to this pattern of thought that the resulting knowledge and will of the nation is considered to be radically one, and the polity is fundamentally thought to act as a single agent.

Later, Marxism continued the Hegelian pattern to a certain extent: the polity is one. It is, of course, not defined in terms of ethnicity, language, or state, but instead in terms of a future global community. The polity needs to be self-reflective and plan its future according to its past and present; it acts as a single agent and realizes a single mind. The Hegelian-Marxian tradition of political thought carries the themes of the original oneness and sameness of the political unit,[17] its self-knowledge and its self-governance being the goal. The problem in this is that this thought accompanies the assumption of a single mind, which can only result in an intense struggle regarding who should actually represent that mind. Heavy emphasis on the single will of the single agent (nation-form) quite understandably leads to fights over inclusion and exclusion, a low appreciation of difference in opinion, and a low tolerance of conflict. The result, in the worst case, is terror.

My suggestion is that it is possible to recognize the above-described pattern of nationalist thought in the identity politics of today. Identity groups, in other words, form "nations within nations" in which the first "nation" is understood as a conflation of the polity and the ethnic view of nationality (2+3) and the second "nation" is understood as referring to nations in the meaning that presupposes a system of nation-states (1). The aforementioned problems inherent to nation-type politics also arise in identity-political groups. In the last section I would like to briefly discuss the dangers, as well as the merits, of the nation-type of political understanding.

Identity-Politics and Its Limits

Feminism, at least during some of its phases, may easily be seen as an identity-political enterprise encompassing certain chief features of the above-sketched "nation-type" of political thought. The assumption of the original identity of the group "women" as distinct from the group "men" has been the most central assumption in feminist thought—at least until recently when it has been forcefully questioned.[18] The original identity has been founded either in nature or in culture, and either way, it has been the chief basis for politics.

Especially in the early second wave of feminism, one of the chief concepts in use was "consciousness raising." The movement sought to increase women's consciousness of being women, and to raise the claim for self-determination.[19] In the internal dynamics of feminism as an identity-political group the features of nation-type of politics became visible.[20] Because of the assumption of one culture, or one mind, of the community of women, the struggles of inclusion and exclusion grew. The question of whose experience was the "real" women's experience surfaced. Because the movement had historically mainly been in the hands of white, middle-class women, their experience had been interpreted as the women's experience. This began to be increasingly questioned as other women started to ask whether their different type of experiences were not women's experiences and they began to question the right of white middle-class women to monopolize the category "women."[21]

Another example of the nation-type of identity politics are gay, lesbian, bi-, and trans-gender issues. Within this politics, sexual orientation has tended to be treated as a quality belonging originally to a particular group of people that has originally always existed as a group even if individuals change, in a very similar manner in which an ethnic group is thought of as always having existed. This assumption has also recently given way for more constructionist views that pay attention to the historical coming into being of these categories of identification.

At the same time, the relevance of identity-politics has been put into question, which has occurred as a direct result of the frustration in dealing with the exclusion and inclusion in identity-categories and the necessity of forming one mind with regard to various questions in which a single common opinion is unavailable solely on the basis of shared sexual orientation.

Because of the dangers and difficulties of "nation-type" political thinking and practice, many would categorically dismiss it. In my view, the mere examination of the historical circumstances of each of the aforementioned examples of identity groupings suffices to convince me otherwise. At times there is definitely a need for identity politics, just as there are times in which it is appropriate to dismantle identity categories.

Identity-political groups are not based on natural identity, but rather are constructed. Nevertheless, the construction of identity-political groups does not occur randomly, but always in a specific context, and it is precisely this context that is the most interesting factor in these events. My suggestion is that identities are to be understood as moments in politics in the contexts of the presence of some specific wrong. These special political circumstances include "colonial" types of situations. But more inclusively they could be thought of as situations in which a claim for universality is presented, but a significant group among those who supposedly belong to that universality have no chance of meeting the standards of that universality. Charles Taylor has talked about "humiliating circumstances," but I think Jean Francois Lyotard's term *"différend"* best captures the essence of the phenomena. He has named *différend* a situation in which those who have been wronged cannot phrase the wrong done because the only language available for expression is the language of those who have wronged them, and there are no expressions in it available for the wrong done. Hegemony also is a concept that grasps some aspects of the peculiar contexts of identity politics. Usually those who are in hegemonic positions do not form a political identity group in the nation-type of way. It is those who are in a situation of a *différend* in a hegemonic situation that engage in an identity construction, often with naturalizing gestures of projecting the original identity in the past.

The Finnish speakers were culturally located in a *différend* type of situation in conjunction with the emerging notion of a modern polity and the hegemony of the Swedish speakers in the country. The same can undoubtedly be said of women in the situation of the cultural hegemony of men, as well of the naming and recognition of gay and lesbian specificity within the circumstances of heterosexual hegemony. Moments of identity politics as politics for naming and recognition are required and positive. The nation-type of politics in this sense is a necessary moment in politics.

From a normative position, therefore, more fruitful than an attempt to reinterpret the nation-type of political thinking into civic nationalism, I think, is to recognize its specificity as a type of political thought. On the basis of a proper analysis of the nation-type of political thought in the past, the drawbacks and dangers of this kind of thinking are evident. The critical attention based on the knowledge of the history of the nation-type of thought should be focused on the naturalizing gestures on identity on the one hand, and the demand of one mind on the other. The assumption of the original identity of any group should be questioned, as should the assumption of "one mind" or "one will" of an identity-positioned group. As a result, the identity of no group should be taken as a fact, but rather should be viewed as a transitory phase, which is significant in a specific moment of a political process.

Notes

1. "Lesbian nation" and "queer nation" are among "nations" frequently encountered in a search conducted on the term "nation" at any library catalogue.

2. See the discussion on different nationalisms in Ronald Beiner, ed., *Theorizing Nationalism* (Albany: State University of New York Press, 1999).

3. R. Koselleck et al., "Volk, Nation, Nationalismus, Masse," in *Geschichtliche Grundbegriffe. Historisches Lexikon zur politisch-sozialen Sprache in Deutschland*, ed. Otto Brunner, Werner Conze, and Reinhard Koselleck, Band 7 (Stuttgart: Klett-Cotta, 1992), 141-430.

4. *Ethnos* was used in contradistinction to the politically entitled citizens within it, collectively referred to as the *demos* or *politai*.

5. According to the *Geschichtliche Grundbegriffe* article, the notion "German nation" also long remained an unknown concept. It was thanks to the usages adopted by the German humanists around the year 1500 that the concept of nation began to take on linguistic, cultural, ethnic, and historical connotations and the humanists also forged "the German people" and "the German nation" into a single entity, furnishing it with a past by identifying ancient Germanic tribes mentioned in Classical texts with the Germans of the present day—an association that looks doubtful in the light of modern historiography. However, the humanist view was an exception that was ahead of its time. For several centuries, the concept of the nation continued to refer to a political and administrative area in a given country, and the noblemen of such an area in particular.

6. L. Greenfeld, *Nationalism: Five Roads to Modernity* (Cambridge, Mass.: Harvard University Press, 1992).

7. In connection with the Napoleonic Wars, Finland's status changed: after being a province in the Swedish realm, it became a Grand Duchy in the Russian empire with a fairly large field of cultural and institutional autonomy.

8. See B. Anderson, *Imagined Communities* (London: Verso, 1983); E. Gellner, *Nations and Nationalism* (Ithaca, N.Y.: Cornell University Press, 1983); E. J. Hobsbawn, *Nations and Nationalism since 1780* (New York: Cambridge University Press 1992); H.

Kohn, *The Age of Nationalism: The First Era of Global History* (New York: Harper & Brothers, 1962); A. D. Smith, *Theories of Nationalism* (London: Duckworth, 1971).
    9. A good example of this kind of discussion are the fifteen chapters in *Theorizing Nationalism*, ed. Ronald Beiner.
    10. Ronald Beiner, I think, is right in pointing out in his introduction that the political-philosophical project shared by Yael Tamir, Charles Taylor, Michael Walzer, Will Kymlicka, and others in his volume aims simultaneously at liberalizing nationalism and sometimes the necessary accommodation with nationalism ("Introduction" to his *Theorizing Nationalism*, 7). The distinction civic/ethnic in the service of this project is problematized in Bernard Yack, " The Myth of the Civic Nation" (in *Theorizing Nationalism*, 103-18), and Kai Nielsen "Cultural Nationalism, Neither Ethnic nor Civic" (in *Theorizing Nationalism*, 119-30), but not specifically in historical terms.
    11. H. Arendt, *The Origins of Totalitarianism* (San Diego: Harcourt Brace & Company, 1967).
    12. T. Pulkkinen, "Kommentar" (Commentaries of J. V. Snellman's University lectures on *Sedelära* [*Sittlichkeit*]), in J. V. Snellman, *Samlade arbete*, Vol VII-XII (Helsinki:Statsrådets kansli, 1996-98).
    13. G. W. F. Hegel, *Philosophy of Right*, tr. T. M. Knox (Oxford: Oxford University Press, 1967); orig. *Grundlinien der Philosophie des Rechts oder Naturrecht und Staatswissenschaft im Grundrisse* [1821].
    14. More precisely in my *The Postmodern and Political Agency* (Jyväskylä: SoPhi, 2000).
    15. J. V. Snellman, *Samlade arbete*, I-II (Helsingfors: Statsrådets kansli, 1991-99). See for further analyses, O. Jussila, *Maakunnasta valtioksi. Suomen valtion synty* [From a province to a state. The birth of the Finnish state] (Helsinki: WSOY, 1987).
    16. In Snellman's case the unity of the single mind was clearly founded in language. For him thought cannot be thought but in a language, and people sharing a language necessarily also share much in terms of thought. Thus linguistically differentiated communities may be treated as different "minds," their truths and their good/bad, right/wrong conceptions differ significantly. Later Finnish nationalists accentuated (and simplified) the thought—the slogan: "one language, one mind" was present in Finnish political culture throughout the century. See also T. Pulkkinen, "One Language—One Mind," in *Europe's Northern Frontier. Perspectives on Finland's Western Identity*, ed. Tuomas M. S. Lehtonen (Jyväskylä: PS-Kustannus, 1999), 118-37.
    17. I have in *The Postmodern and Political Agency* analyzed more precisely the differences of what I call Hegelian-Marxian political ontology and liberal political ontology.
    18. I am referring to the problematization of the given nature of identities "man" and "woman" by Judith Butler and others in the last few years. More precisely in the chapter "Identity-Lesbian" in my *The Postmodern and Political Agency*.
    19. More precisely in the chapter "Women, Nations, Citizens" in my *The Postmodern and Political Agency*.
    20. The connection between feminism and Hegelian-Marxian tradition of political thought is also not historically surprising as much of the early second wave feminism grew out of Marxist student movements.
    21. Sojourner Truth's "Ain't I a woman" from an 1851 Women's Convention has been a much cited phrase disclosing the new realization of falsely constructed identity of women in feminist literature.

Chapter 5

Self-Determination without Nationalism

Omar Dahbour

Disaggregating Nationalism and Self-Determination

In discussions of the norms that ought to govern international relations, the principle of self-determination has often been invoked as an important, even foundational, value underlying the legitimacy of states. It has also been the case that self-determination is applied to nations, when they are regarded as distinct from states. In fact, it has sometimes been assumed that nations are necessarily the primary, even the only, international actors to qualify as properly self-determining. This linkage between self-determination and nations is made by most scholars of nationalism, both those who adopt a favorable stance toward it and those who are critical of it—and it is this linkage that I want to challenge. One urgent task in global ethics today, it seems to me, is to reconceive the concept of self-determination in such a way as to disconnect it from complicity with nationalism and the legitimation of nation-states.

This was, of course, the view of Alfred Cobban, in an important (if now neglected) work on nationalism at the end of the Second World War.[1] The human rights abuses that nationalists have perpetrated, the social inequalities that they have institutionalized, and the wars they have started, have been amply documented and need no recapitulation here. A whole new vocabulary of political atrocities has had to be invented to describe these things. But the point that Cobban emphasized was that, despite all this, there is a real issue that has been raised by nationalist movements—the issue of what constitutes genuine political self-determination. Attempting to minimize or dismiss the very problem that is the occasion for so much political conflict in the twentieth century—a temptation of so many critics of nationalism (including myself)—is not a constructive solution. So we need instead, I would argue with Cobban, to disaggregate the idea of self-determination from that of national identity—and therefore to make room for a nonnationalistic treatment of what constitutes the legitimate boundaries of a political community.

Parenthetically, the practical benefit of doing this is to enable us to make distinctions between the huge variety of contemporary political movements making claims to self-determination. The inability to distinguish a concept of self-determination from the nationalist concept of it means that these movements come to seem essentially alike—and we are forced into either wholesale condemnations of self-determination movements as a result of the abuses and crimes of some of them, or into wholesale acceptance of these movements, all the while attempting to ignore the very real conflicts and atrocities that some of them perpetrate. Later in this chapter I will formulate a principle that I hope will enable us to distinguish between legitimate and illegitimate claims to self-determination (as well as mention how certain cases do or do not fit this principle); but for now, I want simply to make the general case for disaggregating self-determination from nationalism.

Now, let's examine, for a moment, two examples of this consensus about an essential connection between nationalism and self-determination—those found in the works of Elie Kedourie and Michael Walzer. Kedourie defined nationalism as basically equivalent to the doctrine of national self-determination.[2] Self-determination, for him, was the idea that our values and actions ought to be self-chosen, that is, that they ought to be products of the exercise of our will (an idea he traced to Fichte and Kant).[3] Autonomy therefore becomes the primary political value—and the belief in the necessity of the autonomy of nations is an inevitable consequence of this.[4] Of course, Kedourie regarded this belief as having disastrous consequences; but, from his point of view, there was nonetheless nothing contradictory about the idea of national self-determination. It was an inevitable result of the modern belief in political autonomy as the supreme social good. As he put it, the belief that self-government is better than good government underlies the aspiration to self-determination, whether nationalist, democratic, populist, socialist, or otherwise; and this belief is quite mistaken.

Walzer, while differing with Kedourie's negative assessment of nationalist movements, accepts the same close linkage of nationalism to self-determination: he defines nations in part as communities that seek self-determination.[5] The ways that Walzer characterizes the idea of self-determination suggest that there is nothing particularly problematic about nations pursuing it. On the one hand, such a goal is simply the result of the brute fact that the state is the only means in modern politics of insuring that communities can carry out decisions about common goals.[6] Nations desire states because states enable them to achieve their goals, whatever they are. On the other hand, from a global perspective, national self-determination is simply the application of democratic principles to international relations. It is the very meaning of political liberty for communities, as well as for individuals.[7]

Both defenders of nationalism such as Walzer and critics of it such as Kedourie assume that self-determination is a principle that can be readily applied to nations, whether with beneficial or deleterious results, depending on one's viewpoint. But I want to argue that advocacy of a principle of national self-determination yields no positive consequences, not because, as Kedourie maintained, the very idea of self-determination is undesirable, but because the ends to be served by this principle do not necessitate its application to nations. I therefore wish to agree with Walzer that self-determination is the democratic principle of international relations—though only as long as it is *not* deemed applicable to national groups. But I also want to agree with Kedourie that, if self-determination is defined in an unrestricted sense that does not allow limitations to be placed upon it by other principles or goals, it cannot be the paramount political good, since it would exclude or override other important needs and considerations.

National self-determination can be most simply defined as the idea that nations ought to be able to live within a state of their own choosing. Parenthetically, I will, throughout, distinguish nations—as defined in terms of ethnic criteria—from peoples, as the populations of already existing states. Advocates commonly claim that this principle is close to self-evident, given some prior general commitment to democratic and/or liberal principles. But upon closer examination, it is anything but obvious that nations are the entities that should determine state boundaries and citizenship criteria. I will not here go into the conceptual problems with arguing that nations ought to have this role. Rather, I will contend that acceptance of a principle of national self-determination, properly understood, does not yield the goods commonly attributed to it, and that an alternative interpretation of the general idea of self-determination is necessary in order for these goods to be obtained.

What I wish to do here, in other words, is to ask whether the ends that a principle of national self-determination are designed to serve are in fact served by it. This is different from offering justifications for such a principle, justifications which I have criticized elsewhere. Rather, I want to take the purported claims made for the principle at face value, asking whether we need such a principle to achieve the ends for which it is designed. What ends? There are four—namely, the goals of national liberation, cultural rights, democratic self-government, and regional autonomy. It is instructive to note that these are goals that the principle of self-determination of peoples recognized in international law does not directly address, since it is designed to serve the interests of already existing states in relation to one another, rather than those of substate peoples or groups.

Four Goals of Self-Determination

1. National Liberation

The principle of national self-determination is often regarded as important in that it constitutes a theorization of the normative content of so-called national liberation movements. A critique of colonialism is therefore seen to be one important benefit of affirming such a principle. But this view rests on a confusion about the meaning of the term, "nation." For national self-determination to have any specificity as a principle, it must rest on a distinction between already existing states and nations that may or may not have states of their own. Otherwise, national rights would become indistinguishable from a general principle of political self-rule.

Of course, in common parlance, including in the anticolonial movements of the mid-twentieth century, "nation" often referred to the people inhabiting a state or colony. Yet, this distinction sometimes came out even in canonical anticolonial writings; for instance, Frantz Fanon makes a distinction between the "nationalist" party, on the one hand, and the peasant movement, on the other, in describing resistance to the French in Algeria in his book *The Wretched of the Earth*. Nevertheless, it is fair to say, I think, that there is confusion about this term, when used in the context of "national liberation."

What is national liberation? It is simply self-rule for the colonies—the assertion of the principle of political sovereignty, in accordance with existing international law, for territorially distinct political entities. Of course, this principle was not generally recognized prior to the various anticolonial resolutions and documents issued by the United Nations and other organizations in the 1940s, 1950s, and 1960s. But the important point here is that the idea of national liberation or anticolonialism is not equivalent to the notion that separate nations, ethnicities, tribes, or cultures have the right to states. In fact, it is apparent in Fanon and others' writings that such a concept—sometimes designated as "tribalism" in the colonial context—was a grave threat to the project of national liberation as they conceived of it, since it threatened to undermine the stability of newly emerging states within the former colonial territories.

Understood in this way, then, national liberation does not involve a determination of legitimate boundaries in accordance with national homelands—a key goal of invoking a principle of national self-determination—but merely the extension of the right to self-rule to political territories in which it currently does not exist. It must, of course, also be noted that this goal is now a largely historical one. But certain parties in contemporary international relations persist in attempting to apply the rhetoric of national liberation to current situations, however inappropriately.[8] Such attempts employ the language of national liberation, but not the core idea, which is that of a consistency principle: namely, if some peoples have self-rule, all other peoples are entitled to this right. The particular boundaries and membership of the political units within which they are entitled to exercise this right, however, are not at issue, so long as people can express their political will *somewhere*.

2. Democratic Self-Rule

One way to extend the original notion of national liberation to incorporate nationalist claims to self-determination is to take the idea of democratic self-rule as the essential normative claim embodied in self-determination, and this is the second goal often claimed for this principle. But while international law recognizes political sovereignty, or internal self-rule, as a right of the peoples of existing states, and this right was eventually extended to colonized peoples, there might still be other groups existing neither in independent states nor in colonial territories who deserve to be self-ruling. Obviously, when Walzer refers to national self-determination as the democratic principle applied to international relations, he has this in mind. So applying self-rule to so-called "captive nations," or to, as Walzer puts it, "nations that ought to have been independent," is what is supposedly at stake in asserting a claim of self-determination for nations.[9] It is, in this view, simply an extension of democratic self-rule to a category (similar to colonies) previously unserved by this principle.

But things are not so simple. On the one hand, what criteria are used to determine if a nation is "captive" or ought to have been independent? As Lea Brilmayer, for one, has recently pointed out, reference to historical grievances or injustices leads to a quagmire of conflicting claims in which every nation can see itself as deserving, unfairly treated, captive, and so on.[10] This is especially the case if we consider that claims to self-determination by nations are not only assertions about independent statehood as such, but also about the correct boundaries for states.

On the other hand, the problem with conceiving of national self-determination as a principle of democratic self-rule is that if it is a democratic principle, it is one in a very different sense from that which is presently recognized in international law. National self-determination is a democratic principle only in the sense that it is a principle of consent to membership, not of political participation as such. Yet, nationalists want to argue that nations have a right to determine their membership in states as a corollary to the right of persons to political participation. Of course, since a truly unconstrained self-determination of membership would result quite quickly in anarchy (as there would be no way to adjudicate conflicting claims), a criterion is needed, and this is, unsurprisingly, membership in specific national groups.

But once this is admitted, consent to membership is no longer democratic, since absent membership in a national group, people have no right to participate politically at all, on this account. Furthermore, membership in a nationality cannot itself be determined democratically. So, if certain persons are found not to be members of a particular nation, they have no right to membership in a state within which they may always have lived (and of course, do not necessarily have a claim to membership in any other existing state either). This consequence is not the result of atavistic prejudices in one or another nationalist movement, but of the fact that there are inevitably limits on any process of democratic consent—some point at which the process *cannot* be consensual—and this point has traditionally been, for good reason, at the determination of membership. If nationalists now assert their right to self-determination on democratic grounds, it means that nations will have a right to determine themselves which states they recognize as sovereign over them. But of course that will also mean that other nations, individuals, and groups will, in particular cases, not be able to exercise this right.

3. Cultural Rights

Denying nations the right to determine within which state they will live seems harsh, if that is to mean that their cultures and livelihoods may be under threat from a hostile majority of another nationality. So a third understanding of national self-determination has been as an assertion of the rights of nations to cultural expression. The idea is that nations possess distinctive cultures that require independent states for their protection. Otherwise, national cultures may be suppressed by other nationalities that are dominant within the same states. If this does not happen, the state may still become neutral in relation to national cultures, in which case an important dimension of cultural identity will be lost.

Despite the claim that national cultures are subject to suppression or irrelevance without nation-states, the case that a principle of national self-determination is necessary to counteract these possibilities cannot be made successfully. Such a case is based on three assertions, none of which warrant the general right of self-determination that nationalists seek. First, there is the assertion that cultures are necessarily national cultures—or, to put it differently, that people necessarily care whether national cultures as such are preserved or not. To begin with, the idea that national cultures are things (or facts) is generally erroneous: cultures tend to be syncretic, even those that are presently thought to be stereotypically "national." Furthermore, it is not clear that people group their own cultural practices in the neat bundles of national cultures of which nationalists are so fond.

The second assertion is that (nation-)states are necessary for (national) cultures to flourish (that is, not simply to survive). But this is itself dependent on the idea that what is significant about human culture are the kinds of practices that states make possible—for instance, official languages, holidays, flags, sports teams, and the like. From a nonnationalist perspective, this looks like a trivialization of culture, rather than its apotheosis. Finally, the third assertion is that national cultures risk suppression by states committed to other cultural practices. Surely, this is the best reason for a right of self-determination on cultural grounds, since obviously this sometimes happens. But it is only an argument for a remedial, not a general, right; that is, in cases of the suppression of a national culture, that nationality would have a right to self-determination—but only as a last resort. It would be a last resort because a right of cultural expression is not equivalent to the right to a state, though it might be that a state would be the only remedy in cases of systematic cultural suppression or discrimination. In any event, such a remedial right does not generate a general principle of national self-determination; it is more appropriately formulated as a right of individuals to cultural expression, a right already extant in international human rights law.[11]

4. Regional Autonomy

Nationalists, however, would object to an individualist interpretation of culture, maintaining that national cultures exist within a territorial context in specific regions. So the fourth interpretation of national self-determination amounts to an argument for regional autonomy, since the regions within which nations have their homelands need a right to independence in order to protect the local basis of their national communities. My view is that the need for regional autonomy is the impetus for many claims to self-determination and I want to argue below for a regionalist or, more precisely, an ecoregionalist version of this idea. But first it must be determined whether a need for regional autonomy is served by claims to a specifically nationalist concept of self-determination.

This concept is often invoked today in contexts where there seems to be some desire for a greater decentralization of political authority to regions or localities. Rationales for this include greater political accountability, fairer allocation of resources, and freer expression for local cultures. Does national self-determination serve these at least potentially legitimate needs? To answer this question, one must first ask whether political independence for nations is a necessary condition for greater regional autonomy.

Claims to national self-determination are claims that nations have a right to establish states of their own. In doing this, nations seek recognition for themselves as sovereign actors internationally. Yet, this also requires that new nation-states seek to have the stability and internal cohesion of already existing states. A decentralized state—one which recognizes greater regional autonomy—would tend to undermine this quest for international respectability. Nationalists, in other words, seek to mimic, rather than challenge the dominant, centralized form of the state. In acquiring statehood, nations tend to seek means of unifying the new state—and autonomy for regions within the state would work against this. So (more often than not) as nations gain statehood, substate regions lose their autonomy.

Furthermore, statehood cannot guarantee that these new states—or the regions that comprise them—will gain fairer access to resources. For one thing, redistributions across state borders are harder to achieve—even to argue for—than intrastate rectifications of prior inequities. For another, as mentioned above, new nation-states tend to centralize resources, rather than allowing regions greater scope in their allocation.

Finally, establishing nation-states may disrupt existing patterns of cooperation between groups within regions, since the primary criterion for state membership would not be locality, but nationality. "Laws of return," as well as so-called ethnic cleansing, will tend to destroy longstanding forms of regional life shared by different nationalities in the process of creating new nation-states.

Some Cases to Examine

Is there anything left of the idea of self-determination after excluding the four above-mentioned reasons for invoking the principle? I argue below that there is, as long as self-determination is construed in such a way that the nationalist uses of the principle are precluded. Before considering how to do this, however, a word might here be said about a few cases of self-determination claims that I would consider illegitimate on the basis of the arguments just given. Then, after reformulating the principle, I will mention some instances to which it might legitimately be applied.

Consider first, the case of the Puerto Rican independence movement; second, the case of the Baltic republics such as Lithuania that seceded from the Soviet Union around 1990; third, the French Quebec secessionist movement in Canada; and fourth, the independence movements of regions such as Scotland within the United Kingdom. In each of these cases, I would argue, a case for self-determination has not been adequately established, since they rely on some of the problematic claims just discussed. While a thorough treatment of these cases would involve detailed examination of a number of considerations, a few comments will have to suffice for now.

First, in the case of Puerto Rico, the issue is whether Puerto Ricans can claim to have a right to political independence based on the idea that they are in a colonial situation. The problem with this claim is that, although Puerto Rico does exist in a kind of limbo between full incorporation into the United States and separate statehood, this condition is not necessarily one that the Puerto Rican people have rejected or would (or will) reject—since there have been referenda in which all three political options were under consideration. This is not to say that there may not be a case to be made for independence; but it is to say that Puerto Rico does not require national liberation in the sense of being able to invoke a right to statehood.

Second, take the case of Lithuania: did the Lithuanians have a right to secede from the Soviet Union on the basis of lack of consent to the regime? In order for Lithuanian nationalists to establish their case for self-determination, they would have to argue that Lithuania was in some way distinguishable in terms of political rights from the rest of the Soviet Union, so that the proper venue for determining consent would be the population of that republic—and not that of the USSR as a whole. But there is no evidence that Lithuanians had significantly fewer political rights than Russians or other peoples under the Soviet system, since the state denied substantive political rights to citizens of all nationalities. Without demonstrating a disenfranchisement that is distinct from that of the population of the country as a whole, the idea that Lithuanians could unilaterally withdraw from the union for the reason that they did not consent to it any longer makes no sense.

Third, in the case of Quebec, claims that the survival of French culture in the province mandate political independence have been made. But, if survival is indeed at stake, it is not the result of Canadian government policies (which have been as rigorously multicultural as those of any government in the world)—and would not therefore necessarily be ensured by changing governments. Furthermore, there is some question as to whether most Quebecers actually desire or need the cultural accoutrements of statehood, which would be the only certain result of independence.

Finally, in the British Isles, Scottish and other independence movements have made self-determination claims on the basis of a supposed need for autonomy from the English. But, while there may be a legitimate case to be made for greater regional autonomy within the UK, statehood is not required for this to be achieved. Statehood would only be warranted if there were significant evidence (which there is not as far as I know) that the British government were discriminating in systematic fashion against these regions. Absent this evidence, only a claim to national identity—not one to regional autonomy—would provide a reason to seek statehood. But, as I have argued, national identity cannot, in the event, be a basis for claiming self-determination.

A Non-Nationalist Account of Self-Determination

So, while peoples do have legitimate needs for political sovereignty, democratic self-rule, cultural rights, and regional autonomy, many cases—such as those mentioned above—where national self-determination is specifically at issue are not instances where these needs are unmet. And, if there are significant problems in these areas, the principle of national self-determination will fail to address them adequately.

First of all, the sovereignty of non-self-governing peoples is a legitimate concern, in the few places where it may still be at issue; but it is met by existing international law, which has increasingly recognized self-government as a basic entitlement. Second, democratic self-rule cannot be applied to the question of membership without contradiction. As long as peoples are provided with the opportunity for participation in some political system, membership should not be an issue, since it is irresolvable by democratic means. Third, while the cultural rights of peoples are an important consideration, they do not require a national principle in addition to currently accepted human rights law, which recognizes culture as an individual right. Finally, regional autonomy, while a need unmet in current international law, is also unserved by a principle of national self-determination, since such a principle threatens to re-create the problem in new ways.

Self-determination therefore seems to be a principle that would best serve to provide for greater regional autonomy within existing states—or for justifying secession from these states when no regional autonomy seems possible. To redefine the principle in this way, while avoiding the problems of the nationalist definition, requires a reconsideration of the basic ethical concept. Three elements in the basic definition of self-determination are worth consideration for this purpose: a particular meaning given to the concept of autonomy, a definition of an agent or self who seeks self-determination, and a principle that provides a limitation on when a claim to self-determination would be warranted.

Let's begin with the last element, a principle that provides an ethical constraint on the application of a norm of self-determination. In this case, the principle would be the existing body of international law that mandates particular rights of existing states in relation to one another. The nationalist principle seems to justify violating international norms when nations invoke their rights to a state. Any redefined principle of self-determination must therefore be generally compatible with existing international law, not because, as some nationalists might claim, there is a bias in favor of already existing states, but because the maintenance of international peace requires respect for the autonomy of states except in cases of grave violations of human rights.

The second element is the specification of the proper agent or self who could claim self-determination. In traditional international law, existing states are generally the only legitimate agents. But in the newer law of human rights, the agents who can legitimately claim rights include individual persons. Nationalists seek to add nations to this list; but this seems unwarranted for the reasons given above. As previously noted, regions, defined not in terms of ethnic identities, but in terms of geographical or ecological characteristics, would be legitimate agents who could claim a right of self-determination under certain conditions. This is because it is the goal of regional autonomy that is most clearly unserved by existing legal doctrines that privilege states and individuals. It is not these entities, but rather substate regions, that may lack the autonomy appropriate to particular ways of life.

A non-nationalistic principle of self-determination should therefore be designed to highlight the problem of what has been called "regional exploitation" or "internal colonialism"—the differential status and power of regions within existing states. It is important to note two things about how such a principle would differ from the nationalist one. First, it would be a remedial, not an unconditional, principle, since a legitimate claim to self-determination would be designed as a remedy for specific injustices or inequities and absent such specifics, no claim could be made. Second, unlike a nationalistic principle of self-determination, a revised principle should not be primarily aimed at achieving state power for a substate group, but at a more equitable rearrangement of relations within existing states. This is because nothing is necessarily gained and much could be lost by turning regions into separate states: achieving state power leads to new structures of domination in order to preserve state sovereignty, while regional autonomy leads to limiting the power of states in relation to substate regions. [12]

Self-determination should therefore be understood as a principle applicable to regions in terms of distinctive ways of life, or ecologies, specific to those regions. So, I would argue, we need an ecoregional principle of self-determination in the sense that it would be designed to protect the autonomy of regions that embody particular ecologies—that is, relations to the natural environment and the distinctive political and economic arrangements resulting from those relations.

Finally, the third aspect of self-determination—a particular concept of autonomy—can be defined in terms of the absence of constraints on regional development and sustainability in accordance with local cultures and ways of life. Here, I want to refer to Allen Buchanan's definition of the necessary condition for claiming self-determination. The condition is that of a particular kind of autonomy that constitutes what he calls the elimination of "discriminatory redistribution." [13] By the latter term he means the forcible reallocation of resources and productive capacities from one group to another within a state or the forcible imposition of an inappropriate mode of development upon a group by a central government.

Eliminating discriminatory redistribution will facilitate the maintenance of regional cultures and ways of life and the ability of regions to sustain these cultures. But it will do so without justifying nationalistic prejudices or state power, since regions are to be understood in terms of ways of life rather than the identities of persons or groups. Problems of injustice affecting individuals or groups can usually be dealt with according to existing principles of civil or human rights, properly understood. It is only the issue of the domination or exploitation of regions by centralized authorities (and by other regions acting through centralized authorities) that currently remains unaddressed.

An Ecoregional Principle of Self-Determination

There is, however, an important difference between Buchanan's formulation of a principle of discriminatory redistribution and my own. While he refers to redistribution of resources between groups of any kind, I would restrict the principle to counteracting discriminatory redistribution only between regions. This, then, is the point at which I want to differentiate my own position from Buchanan's.

It ought to be noted that discriminatory redistribution is actually the last of three justifying grounds for secession, in Buchanan's view (note that he refers to secession, not self-determination as such, which he regards as too vague a notion for use in international law). The first two grounds are: systematic violations of human rights, on the one hand, and unjust seizures of territory, on the other. About these, I would concur with the first ground, but argue that existing human rights law already addresses this condition adequately. As for the second ground of unjust territorial seizures, I would disagree that it can be an adequate ground for self-determination for the reason that—as with democratic consent—there is no baseline or beginning point from which to judge what is just or unjust. Such seizures (usually from war or invasion) must be judged on the merits of the results—their effects on the peoples involved—and not on the basis of some prior existing condition.

So we come to the third ground for secession or self-determination (and I, unlike Buchanan, have no inherent objection to using the broader term, as long as it is clearly understood to be a remedial right used to address specific injustices); this is the idea of eliminating discriminatory redistribution. I would argue that Buchanan's use of this idea as applying to all groups is too broadly defined, since groups defined racially, ethnically, religiously, or in terms of other ascriptive characteristics have recourse to existing rights doctrines in order to describe and criticize discriminatory state policies. It is the regional and ecological dimensions of injustice that require a different principle, since they do not refer to group identities that might be the basis of discrimination, but to the exploitation of natural resources and the imposition of social institutions that mandate or prevent particular forms of life for local communities.

Does this concept of self-determination account for the legitimacy of self-determination movements that are not necessarily based on the types of claims criticized earlier? Several examples might indicate how this could be the case. Consider, first, the claims of American Indians, not only in the United States, but also in Canada—and for that matter, in some Latin American countries (including, perhaps, the Zapatista movement in Mexico). The central contention of American Indian demands for territorial autonomy has been that only under this condition can they sustain their distinctive ways of life. Reference is therefore made to the idea that regions with large Indian populations need autonomy in order to maintain a particular relationship with the land and resources of those regions. So a principle of self-determination that emphasizes regional autonomy will naturally provide grounds for asserting a right of self-determination in these cases.

Second, consider Tibetan demands for autonomy within China. In this case, the crucial fact is the actual denial of the cultural rights of the Tibetan population by the Chinese state; this—and not an abstract definition of cultural rights as necessarily requiring a state—is what gives a warrant for the claim to autonomy. Whether or not full independence is mandated becomes a judgment about the extent to which Tibetan autonomy will ever be possible within China.

Third, there is the case of the former Yugoslavian republic of Bosnia attempting to establish an independent state. This example suggests that democratic consent becomes a legitimate consideration only under conditions of an existing or imminent abrogation of a people's political rights. As Yugoslavia was transformed increasingly into a Serbian state, Muslims were put into an extremely precarious situation—with mounting evidence of human rights violations, discriminatory redistribution of land and other property, and even-tually, genocidal attacks. In such a case, the people that could legitimately consent or dissent from membership in a state had already been defined by these discriminatory policies—so Bosnian independence was warranted as a last resort in the face of this discrimination.

Fourth, the Palestinian independence movement in the territories occupied by Israel indicates that, where there are today legitimate calls for national liberation, they should be understood as based on the lack of political rights and/or the result of policies of discriminatory redistribution. It is this political disenfranchisement of the Arab population—coupled with the probable continuance of discriminatory redistribution even if Palestinians in the occupied territories were incorporated within Israel as full citizens—that gives the demand for a Palestinian state its legitimacy.

These examples—especially when paired with the ones discussed above—will, I hope, indicate that it is possible to make ethical distinctions between legitimate claims to self-determination based on the idea of eliminating discriminatory redistribution between regions (or upon the real denial of political or cultural rights) and illegitimate claims based on various justificatory uses of assertions of national identity.

Finally, I want to take note of a potential problem with using the idea of discriminatory redistribution to define self-determination. As Buchanan notes, using the concept of discriminatory redistribution as a means of distinguishing legitimate from illegitimate claims to self-determination seems to require prior agreement about what constitutes a just distribution of resources. Without this, no consensus, philosophical, legal, or political, could be expected about when discriminatory redistribution is occurring.

But, as Buchanan maintains, it may not be necessary to reach agreement about a philosophical concept of justice before agreement could obtain concerning cases. What is required is a mid-range, or substantive, conception that would indicate when discriminatory redistribution is occurring. As he notes, there is an historical example of this—namely, colonialism—that did provide a basis for both philosophical and legal agreement about the necessity of redress (and this occurred without agreement on how to characterize the conception of justice or rights underlying condemnations of colonialism). Yet, Buchanan is somewhat at a loss as to what such a mid-range concept of justice might be in the postcolonial world.

I would argue that this is where reformulating self-determination—and discriminatory redistribution—in ecoregional terms lends itself to providing just such a mid-range concept of distributive justice. In discussions of the environmental impact of economic development policies over the last twenty years, a new international consensus has emerged that rejects the old concepts of growth and modernization that were used to measure development. Instead, a new concept of sustainability has come into play as a means of gauging when development policies are appropriate for regions and ecosystems and when they are not. If development policies are unsustainable in terms of a region's natural resources and social structures, then it can be deemed unjust. So discriminatory redistribution, when applied to ecological regions (rather than social groups of all kinds), occurs when unsustainable development policies, including schemes of land tenure and resource allocation, are imposed.

Of course, the concept of sustainability has been the subject of much debate (as was that of colonialism) in terms of what it actually means, how to measure it, and whether or not it is compatible with development policies of various kinds. Views of these matters range from those that advocate "sustainable growth" to those that argue for the fundamental incompatibility of sustainability with development of any kind.[14] But such a debate also occurred about how to define colonialism—which did not prevent the international community and most political philosophers from characterizing it as unjust.

In the end, the aim of formulating a principle of ecoregional self-determination based on the elimination of discriminatory redistribution is to create enough autonomy for different ways of life to allow them to coexist within the same polity. Furthermore, it is important that these ways of life be defined not in terms of perceived kinship ties, as with the nationalist definition of culture, but in terms of distinctive forms of interaction with the natural world and of the different social institutions that result from those interactions.

In other words, self-determination must become a political goal that, rather than serving to justify the acquisition of state power and the romanticization of national, ethnic, and tribal commonalities, instead legitimates limits on centralized states and the protection of diverse, but equally sustainable, ways of life. This reformulation may appear to some as remote in light of the domination of international relations by conflicts between great powers and transnational corporations on the one hand, and by atavistic nationalist or fundamentalist reactions to these forces on the other. But it is some consolation to realize that—as in some of the examples discussed above—there are an increasing number of movements of regional autonomy and ecological resistance in contemporary global society that cannot be subsumed under (or consumed by) these seemingly intractable dichotomies. Since philosophical awareness of the true import of such political movements inevitably lags behind, it is as a contribution to theorizing them that the approach to self-determination outlined above has been offered.

Notes

1. Alfred Cobban, *The Nation State and National Self-Determination* (London: Oxofrd University Press, 1947).

2. Elie Kedourie, *Nationalism* (London: Hutchinson, 1960), 31.

3. Kedourie, *Nationalism*, 76.

4. Kedourie, *Nationalism*, 22.

5. Michael Walzer, "Nation and Universe," in *The Tanner Lectures on Human Values*, vol. 11, ed. G. B. Peterson (Salt Lake City: University of Utah Press, 1990), 554.

6. Michael Walzer, *Spheres of Justice: A Defense of Pluralism and Equality* (New York: Basic Books, 1983), 44.

7. Michael Walzer, "The New Tribalism: Notes on a Difficult Problem," *Dissent* (Spring 1992), 165.

8. Rupert Emerson, "Self-Determination," *American Journal of International Law* 65 (1971): 459-75.

9. Walzer, "New Tribalism," 166.

10. Lea Brilmayer, "Groups, Histories, and International Law," *Cornell International Law Journal* 25, no. 3 (1992), 559.

11. James Nickel, *Making Sense of Human Rights: Philosophical Reflections on the "Universal Declaration of Human Rights"* (Berkeley: University of California Press, 1987).

12. Lewis Mumford, *The Culture of Cities* (New York: Harcourt Brace Jovanovich, 1938).

13. Allen Buchanan, *Secession: The Morality of Political Divorce from Fort Sumter to Lithuania and Quebec* (Boulder, Colo.: Westview Press, 1991).

14. See, for some discussion of these debates, M. Redclift, *Sustainable Development: Exploring the Contradictions* (London: Methuen, 1987), and Vandana Shiva, "Recovering the Meaning of Sustainability," in *The Environment in Question*, ed. P. J. Cooper and Palmer (London: Routledge, 1998),

Part II

Globalization and Sovereignty

Chapter 6

War, Politics, and Sovereign Violence

John Crowley

What is a "political solution" to a conflict? Like many theoretical questions, this has circumstantial origins. It so happens that the first draft of this chapter was written in the spring of 1999 during the NATO bombing campaign against Yugoslavia. A feature of public debate about the rights and wrongs of the war was general agreement that it was not "political." Both opponents and supporters of military action called for a "political solution" to the problems of Kosovo. The only difference between them was that supporters of the NATO perspective regarded such action as a *pre-condition* for a political solution. The failure of the Paris and Rambouillet negotiations in early 1999 to produce a generally acceptable agreement was precisely what was judged to justify the war. On the contrary, critics of the NATO campaign claimed that a political solution was what should have been pursued *instead of* military action. To that extent, nearly everyone would agree that the Yugoslav government's acceptance of a de facto UN protectorate in Kosovo in exchange for a NATO cease-fire represents the reestablishment of the previously suspended political process.

Yet, in spite of this consensus, something seemed wrong. What, after all, could be more "political" than a war conducted under the aegis of constituted authorities, aimed at effecting a change in the distribution of power within Kosovo in particular and Yugoslavia in general, and furthermore saturated by analysis of its effects on the legitimacy and stability of the Yugoslav government? What could be more "political" than a public debate on the significance of universal human rights, on the circumstances in which force might be used to promote them, and on the relation between the moral basis and the institutional legitimacy of the use of force? Surely, in this case at least, war was—for better or for worse—a *mode*, rather than the "opposite," of politics.

Thus, a circumstantial running commentary on current affairs leads into the heart of political theory. For profound conceptual reasons, but also for practical prudential reasons that the war of 1999 clearly illustrates, theories of politics are generally—perhaps necessarily—theories of war. Clausewitz states that war is the prosecution of political objectives by certain specific techniques. Foucault provocatively flips that famous dictum, and suggests that politics be analyzed as the continuation of war by other means.[1] Weber offers a sociological bridge between the two perspectives by defining the state in terms of the specific means at its disposal: the use of force.[2] But to base the state's existence as a state on its capacity to monopolize the legitimate use of force is to make the *possibility* of war—albeit, internally, in the peculiar form of its successful avoidance—central to politics. War between states therefore appears as a natural expression of the state's characteristic features at the point where the claim to monopoly no longer operates. Carl Schmitt arguably pushed to its logical conclusion the Weberian idea of force as the "joint"—what is called in both ordinary and theoretical French "*articulation*," but often lazily translated into English as "articulation"—between internal and external sovereignty. Conversely, liberal theory—of which Rawls and Habermas are exemplary—strongly rejects this "warlike" view of politics. But it does so in a way that tends implicitly to validate it, by defining politics normatively as a realm of reason, absolutely distinct from war, and therefore dependent on the empirical absence of war. In this sense, a liberal theory of politics that did not offer a theory of war would be analytically vacuous.

My contention here will be that standard liberal theory in fact fails to offer an adequate conceptualization of the relation between "politics" and "war," and is therefore, if not vacuous, at least less normatively compelling than it aspires to be. In order to substantiate this claim, I propose to focus first on the practical politics of war, with particular emphasis on the theoretically crucial gray areas characteristic of the internal conflicts absurdly called "civil." These empirical observations usefully clarify the more general theoretical issue of the relation between "reason" and "violence"—often misleadingly equated with that between politics and war. Since the criticisms in the first two sections focus largely on contemporary common sense, as expressed particularly in media debate, more theoretical argument might seem little affected by them. In fact, as I propose to illustrate by internal critique of Rawls and Habermas, this is not true.

Furthermore, a coherent theory of the distinction between politics and war is not simply something that Rawls, Habermas, and others contingently fail to provide. It is, even in principle, not available. And this problem goes deeper than the structure of liberal theory, and affects any attempt to bring within a single framework the political issues of *foundation* and *justification*. Any political authority subject to challenge needs to establish itself, or it by assumption simply fails to exist. Its ability to justify itself in the eyes of its challengers is, of course, one possible mode of establishment. But what if such justification fails? The answer is crude and simple: if it is to exist at all, it must necessarily establish itself by other means—means that ignoie the challengers for the purposes of justification (although other logics of justification may be at work)—means that, in at least a minimal sense, are violent. We reach here the point where politics and war merge in the body of what is classically known as the "sovereign."[3]

War as a Mode of Politics

What the 1999 conflict in the Balkans illustrates is that war is very widely regarded as something strictly separated from politics and in some sense opposed to it. The idea is of course plausible, and it is easy enough to understand how it has come to be generally accepted. Nonetheless, when it is pushed a little harder, a number of interesting and important unresolved difficulties emerge.

The best way of getting to grips with the problem is simply to look empirically at what is going on in conflicts such as those of the former Yugoslavia, Algeria, or Northern Ireland—to take just three quite different examples. I make no attempt here to describe them, still less to analyze them, in detail. It is possible, however, to offer a characterization based on certain generic features. A "political" solution is usually defined as one in which the use of violence is suspended; cease-fires and truces therefore play a crucial role in the political process by opening spaces for negotiation. Furthermore, a *durable* political solution requires not merely the suspension of violence but some kind of guarantee against its reemergence. There is usually strong emphasis on disarming paramilitary groups and somehow taking their weapons out of circulation. A complementary objective is "reconciliation"—a ambiguous notion that covers a wide range of processes involving various kinds of forgiveness and fo rgetfulness.[4] Whatever precisely it may entail, reconciliation is intended to remove the *basis* for the reemergence of violence, just as disarmament reduces the capacity to exert it.

It is striking that such processes stand in an ambiguous relation to the idea of sovereignty. At one level, the suspension of violence in such cases restores the state in the conventional Weberian sense, since the characteristic feature of the violence suspended was to be amenable neither to suppression nor to legitimation. Yet the *way* in which it does so seems to derogate from the idea of statehood. The suspension of violence is not an instance of one party's claim to the monopoly of the legitimate use of force, nor the consequence of the success of such a claim—in many cases it is indeed quite the opposite, namely, the recognition that armed confrontation has produced stalemate, and is likely to continue to do so. Pacification thus involves the renunciation, within a specific sphere judged to be political, of *all* claims to the legitimate use of violence, including those of the juridically sovereign authority—hence the central issue of amnesty. The juridical sovereign does not, however, thereby cease to exist. Indeed, its status may even be reinforced in the nonpolitical sphere by its newfound modesty in the political sphere: "peace processes" usually involve, among other things, heightened repression of the kind of petty crime that tends to flourish in the interstices of political violence. But the limits and legitimacy of the use of force by, for example, the British government in Northern Ireland or the Israeli government in the occupied territories are in practice (and are, at least tacitly, recognized in principle to be) within the scope of negotiation. Such negotiated processes are thus predicated upon the suspension of sovereignty, in both the strictly legal and sociohistorical senses. They aim of course at the ultimate disappearance of political violence, and to that extent at the reestablishment of sovereignty, since what characterizes distinctively political violence is precisely its claim to legitimacy. However, the means they use to obtain the temporary suspension of violence necessarily recognize the existence of fundamental political conflict. Conversely, what characterizes a strictly sovereign perspective on political violence is the refusal to recognize it as political or its perpetrators as people one can "do business with," and therefore the denial that its suppression differs from that of ordinary criminal activity. What outsiders regard as civil war, sovereign governments call "policing" or "law enforcement," or at most—through clenched teeth—"pacification."

Less theoretically, we may say simply that the condition for the kinds of peace processes illustrated in various ways in Northern Ireland, South Africa, Lebanon, Mozambique, and many other places, is a partial suspension of questions about *legitimacy*. Conversely, when, as in Algeria for instance, such a condition cannot be met, not just reconciliation but even minimally civil peace prove elusive. Whether this suspension involves the explicit recognition of the equal legitimacy of all positions—which means, in practice, legitimizing the past use of violence—or the explicit or tacit denial of legitimacy to any use of violence, makes little difference. The key point is simply that such a framework admits no privileged position: at least for the limited purposes of the ongoing process, non-state actors are regarded as having, de facto, the status of a kind of quasi state—with, indeed, a higher degree of criminal immunity than international law now grants to the officeholders of legally sovereign governments.

Clearly, the suspension of sovereignty in this sense opens a political space for negotiation, aimed ideally both at practical compromises on issues of special urgency and at the development of new principles of legitimacy more broadly acceptable than those against which, or in the name of which, past political violence was used. What is far less clear is how to draw the line between this process and the prior condition of armed confrontation. Yet, unless such a line can be drawn, the claim that there is something uniquely, or even distinctively, "political" about the negotiation process is difficult to sustain.

In practical terms, the line exists as a matter of fact. It is precisely one of the key things that parties to a peace process agree on. But its function is primarily symbolic and illocutory. It announces publicly the possibility of a solution, and the legitimacy of the process, and thereby possibly contributes to making such a solution possible. It also, for the same reason, has a tactical purpose that is by no means insignificant: to lock the parties in to the process by prior commitments that raise the costs of failure. What this generally means in practice is making erstwhile "terrorists"—now accepted, however reluctantly, as people to "do business" with—(e.g. the IRA) accountable for the process to their outside sponsors (e.g. the U.S. government) and thereby acquiring some degree of leverage over them. These are risky tactics, of course, since they create issues of "face" that secret contacts do not, and in addition the stability of negotiators' commitments cannot be guaranteed when even limited democratic criteria of representativeness and accountability are in operation. The principle, nonetheless, has been adopted, often effectively, in a wide variety of cases.

However, if this is to be regarded as the line dividing politics from nonpolitics, it is crucial to note that it is permeable in both directions. On the one hand, secret contacts between governments and insurgents with whom, ostensibly, it would be unacceptable to "do business" are an almost invariable feature of civil strife in the broad sense. The British government has conducted secret discussions with representatives of the Provisional IRA on a number of occasions since 1972, in parallel with often brutal counterinsurgency operations. The National Party government in South Africa had been talking to the ANC since the mid-1980s, even as it deployed its particularly vicious undercover forces against the very same opponents. Similarly, there was no obvious change in Israeli strategy or tactics to reflect the secret discussions that led to the Washington agreement. On the other hand, violence is an integral part of the political processes of discussion and negotiation—not in any deep conceptual sense, but simply because both the tactical use of force or the threat to use force, and the inability of participants in talks fully to control splinter groups, are a central issue.

Let us take just one example: the Northern Irish "peace process" as it has developed since the agreement signed in April 1998 by most of the relevant political actors, including Sinn Féin, with the strong backing of the UK, Irish, and U.S. governments, and ratified by parallel referendums in Northern Ireland and the Republic of Ireland the following month. The quotation marks around "peace process" underline both that this is what everyone calls it, and that there is sharp disagreement about what the words mean. Even such an apparently straightforward notion as "IRA cease-fire" has been the subject of persistent semantic wrangling since, empirically, it clearly cannot be equated with the literal suspension of violence. In a sense, of course, such ambiguities are the whole point of processes of this kind: only if all parties can make some plausible claim to have "won," and if no one looks too closely at the inevitable fabrications and misunderstandings, can any stable solution be achieved. But what this means is simply that violence is at the heart of the political process, just as politics was always at the heart of the war. Thus, the carefully maintained ambivalence about the relations between Sinn Féin and the IRA and the resulting brinkmanship over weapons "decommissioning"—which eventually led to the suspension of the institutions established by the 1998 agreement—are not failures of the process, but characteristic features of it. We may, on normative grounds, prefer impartial deliberation to bargaining based on a balance of power; and we may, further, reasonably argue that deliberation and violence have no theoretical or empirical connection. However, where bargaining aimed at a modus vivendi is the limit of the practical best, things get more complex. No doubt there are excellent normative reasons to prefer the ballot box to the Armalite—to adapt the standard Northern Irish phrase—but it is implausible to regard them as belonging to radically separate worlds.

Reason, Violence, and the "Political"

The theoretical implications of these empirical observations are far from straightforward. Even if the attempt to equate politics exclusively with reason, and violence exclusively with war, were abandoned, it might still be possible to draw a more subtle line between a higher form of politics, grounded solely in reason, and a debased form inseparable from violence. As we shall see, this is what Rawls and Habermas do by their dismissive critique of the notion of a modus vivendi. In order to deal with this argument, it is not enough to point to the *empirical* prevalence of interest-driven bargaining in supposedly deliberative contexts, which no one really denies. What has to be challenged is the *normative* significance of the ideal deliberative perspective. The issue, in other words, is the relation between reason and violence as it impacts on the notion of the political.

I do not wish to argue here that one should reject the conceptual distinction between reason and violence, still less that violence might be somehow superior to reason if looked at from the appropriate angle. Such views are in fact surprisingly common, especially perhaps in the French intellectual tradition. In Derrida, for instance, violence becomes a kind of quasi-metaphysical category based on a confluence of Bataille, Lacan, and Levinas.[5] The essay *Force de loi*[6] is most explicit in this respect, particularly in its reading of Benjamin, but the fascination with the moment of foundation or origin, associated in terms of the fixing of meaning with the critique of structuralism, is a leitmotiv of Derrida's work in general. One possible consequence is that "reason" and "violence" may become simply interchangeable, as different ways of describing the asymptotic point of origin: the point irreducible to interpretation or explanation. By this time, however, violence in any ordinary, concrete sense, as something people may do to other people, has entirely dropped out of the equation.

Another, rather different, denial of the superiority of reason to violence is at work in the celebration of emancipatory violence. The *locus classicus* of this reversal is Sartre's famous, or infamous, preface to Fanon's *Les damnés de la terre*.[7] Here, at least, the concrete reality of violence is not elided: as Sartre puts it, when the native shoots the settler, both the oppressor and the oppressed disappear, leaving a dead man and a free man. The political point is that such violence does not increase the amount of violence in a social system, but merely displaces and rearranges it. Domination is, in the terms of Bourdieu's sociology, *symbolic violence*; real violence, so long as it is politically informed, is not "worse," but "better." But sociology, of course, offers no basis for such normative judgment, especially when it has resolved violence as a relation between people into violence as a relation between social positions. At least in Bourdieu, what serves to justify such normative statements, which are increasingly common in his work, is a largely unargued criterion of "transparency"—one that is ultimately quite close to metaphysical concern with the "origin."

More generally, what is at stake is the tendency of violence to become an object of *fascination* rather than of analysis. Such fascination can work in two apparently opposite ways. On the one hand, violence may be regarded as that about which nothing, ultimately, can be said.[8]

On the other, it can become a purely erotic-aesthetic obsession. The status of Sade in French intellectual life, and the way in which Kubrick's *Clockwork Orange* has been received in France—much to the chagrin of Anthony Burgess, the author of the book on which the film was based—are indicative of this climate. It is fairly clear, however, that fascination, whether positive or negative, is here an obstacle to understanding.

The question, therefore, is whether it is possible to find ways of talking about violence that are both analytically useful and morally defensible—that keep in touch, in other words, with both the fundamental *moral* fact that violence involves suffering, and the epistemological commonplace that the victim's position is not *sociologically* privileged. At its most general level, I shall simply avoid this question. My aim here is more modest: to suggest a framework capable of bringing some aspects of violence at least within the domain of political theory in order to support the negative theorem that normative support for reason against violence—which I fully share—cannot be based on assigning them to radically separate worlds. For this purpose, some kind of definition or criterion is useful. What I shall regard here as irreducibly violent is *the application of force, with the potential to inflict pain, to a victim capable of giving consent, without that victim's consent*. I do not mean that everything one might appropriately regard as violent fits this criterion; rather that anything that fits it would meet almost any standard for violence. Furthermore, the definition raises some serious difficulties, particularly with regard to the perpetrator's intentionality and to the victim's "capacity

to give consent." However, even if we restrict ourselves to the most straightforward cases, where both the use of force and the denial of consent are entirely
deliberate, it is still capable of proving fruitful.

The most interesting consequence of this approach is the light it throws on
the conception of reason as communicative, of which Habermas is currently the
most influential proponent. Is violence "irrational" in the sense that its use is
something that could never be regarded as legitimate in a context of free
discussion? The answer is a complicated one, since it depends not only on the
ideal conditions relevant to the justification of principles, but also on the presumed
characteristics of the situations to which they are designed to apply. If these are
imperfect, violence may in practice have a role to play. Many people regard as
legitimate in principle both a punitive criminal law and the use of violence, in
certain circumstances and subject to certain restrictions, to combat profound
injustice. They may be wrong, but the argument that some people's consent may
count for less—because they are criminals or exploiters—is certainly not
obviously irrational. While it may conflict with a Kantian view of equal moral
worth, it is even universalizable in the straightforward sense that it is both
intelligible and empirically observable to defend one's use of violence by
recognizing one's victim's equal entitlement to it. However morally unpleasant,
this is not obviously incoherent or self-contradictory. To make sense of violence
in terms of "monological" reason, on the other hand, is far more difficult.

This point is reinforced by consideration of the empirical forms that violence
takes, at least in its political manifestations—regarding as "political" for these
purposes contexts where the infliction of pain is associated with a claim about its
legitimacy that exceeds the personal relation between perpetrator and victim. A
wealth of evidence suggests that such violence is in a very real sense a mode of
communication. Recognition of the victim's capacity to give consent is essential
to the process, and indifference to consent is not usually an expression of callous-
ness or lack of moral imagination, but a deliberate form of symbolic violence
superimposed on the infliction of physical pain. Indeed, it is precisely in its most
horrible forms (torture, mutilation, sacrilege, etc.), which tend to be symbolically
charged, ritualized and usually stereotyped, that violence has the most clearly
defined discursive dimension.[9] Furthermore, communication in such cases
exceeds by design the bilateral relation between perpetrator and victim. Extreme
violence is usually staged for the "benefit" of a group of spectators.[10]

Nor is this discursive dimension of violence peculiar to such extreme cases.
A terrorist bomb is always, among other things but quite consciously, a demons-
tration of the capacity to cause murderous explosions and therefore a threat,
express or implied, to do it again. Whether or not it takes place in an ongoing
context of negotiations, it is thus usually, in a very tangible sense, a discursive
move.[11] This is precisely why cease-fires (as in Northern Ireland) do not really
take violence out of politics. Furthermore, this relation is at least partially

reversible. Just as violence is, among other things, a form of discourse, so discourse habitually involves a dimension of violence. As post-structuralist theory has stressed, the language of politics often affirms or denies identities, affiliations, memories, dignity, or pride, and it has a capacity to inflict emotional pain quite comparable to certain forms of mental torture. In more practical terms, and in some ways more importantly, the language of deliberation, especially when public, has real effects, both deliberate and unintended, often indistinguishable from the straightforward use of violence. Mental torture and symbolic humiliation are fairly natural preludes to physical extermination.[12] Genocide in Rwanda started, in a very tangible sense, on the radio; and legal codes in many countries define, for very good reasons, criminal offences of "incitement to (racial, religious, etc.) hatred."

This does not mean, of course, that all forms of human communication are violent or that differences between modes of violence in terms of kind or of degree are morally indifferent. A consequence is, however, that normative arguments about violence cannot simply rely on reason as defining an inherently nonviolent mode of interaction. Even in an *ideal* deliberative situation, from which violence is *ex hypothesi* excluded as a valid mode of interaction, it is at stake with regard to the *nonideal* conditions of ordinary social interaction. The *justification of violence* is not some kind of absurd scandal, but one of the most routine of political issues. Furthermore, the relation of violence to reason has to do with tensions within the idea of reason itself. Violence is perhaps *unreasonable* rather than *irrational* ; and, as we shall see with reference to Rawls, reasonableness and rationality are very different faculties.

These observations have distasteful implications and raise a series of awkward philosophical problems, which is perhaps why even those who do succumb to the fascination of violence generally prefer to avoid them. In addition, the classic response to the challenge is deeply unsatisfactory. Thus Carl Schmitt grounds the "concept of the political" in what he calls "anthropological pessimism."[13] This, in his view, is one answer to two supposedly identical questions: whether "man" is good or evil[14]; and "whether man is a dangerous being or not, a risky or a harmless creature."[15] "Pessimism" states, of course, that man is evil and dangerous. Furthermore, Schmitt regards the only other possible answer as "optimism"—the claim that man is inherently good—and this as absurd. "[A]ll genuine political theories presuppose man to be evil, i.e., by no means an unproblematic but a dangerous and dynamic being."[16] It is no doubt true that no political theory would subscribe to Schmitt's "optimism," but that does not entail "pessimism" because the questions themselves are loaded. As the use of the word "evil" (in a nonmoral, nonethical sense) implies, what Schmitt calls "anthropology" is really theology. In the absence of his theological presupposition, what changes is not the answer but the question. The truly political question is whether human intercourse is a risky business. This has superficial similarities to Schmitt's formulation, but in dropping not just the category of "evil" but also that of "man"—as implying a supposedly uniform "human nature"—it is in fact quite different. However, dislike of Schmitt's answers has tended to preclude criticism of his questions, [17] with the result that something like his "optimism" tends to be tacitly adopted by his intellectual opponents. This makes it impossible even to formulate the problem of violence as an object for political theory.

It is impossible here to take this line of thought any further. What I wish to do is simply to draw from the understanding of contemporary political conflicts, and of the conceptual relation between reason and violence, that I have sketched so far two postulates that, if valid, would point to a series of unacknowledged gaps in political theory. *First*, politics and war are not sharply distinct forms or spheres of activity; reason and violence are not strictly separate modes of interaction; and still less can the two binary oppositions be neatly superimposed and correlated. *Second*, whatever ethical or moral judgment one may wish to make about violence, it relies on extrinsic considerations. The *use* of violence may, in practice, be self-limiting in many contexts; but the claim that violence is in principle a legitimate resource does not seem to be self-contradictory or self-undermining. Perhaps the most concise way of bringing together the two postulates is to state, in line with my opening remarks, that the idea of a "just war" (whether *in bello* or *ad bellum*) is inherently and profoundly political, and necessarily based on an appeal to reason.

All this may seem blindingly obvious. In fact, whether or not people would accept the postulates as stated above, they are habitually denied or ignored. An anecdote may clarify the nature of this denial. In 1998, I was asked to contribute a short piece on the "peace process" in Northern Ireland to the journal *Critique internationale*.[18] The main purpose in the editor's mind was to assist understanding of the reasons for, and the meaning of, the unexpectedly comprehensive "Good Friday" agreement finalized on April 10th 1998 and endorsed by referenda in both the North and the Republic the following month. Defining myself by contrast with Gerard Delanty's analysis of the peace process as reflecting the emergence of a post-ethnic and post-nationalist form of political consciousness opening a space for Habermasian deliberation,[19] I had sought to stress the shifting balance of power, social cleavages, and political aspirations that had facilitated a messy compromise by which most parties agreed to fudge the key underlying issues and which, far from excluding violence, was intimately involved with it. Wishing to stress that such compromises were as much the stuff of politics as higher-minded deliberation, I suggested the title *"L'espace du politique* [the space of the political] *en Irlande du Nord."* The editor and managing editor disliked the title, which they took to miss the key feature of the peace process, namely the *reemergence* of politics as a result of the suspension of violence. They therefore suggested titles on the lines of *"Le retour du politique"* [the return of the political]. I came to fight quite hard to get my point across, precisely because it cuts against the grain of what now seems to be accepted thinking about the nature of politics. Eventually, we agreed on *"La pacification du politique,"* a better and more explicit title than the original: the idea of "peaceful politics" clearly points to the conceptual coherence and empirical possibility of "warlike politics."

Rawls and Habermas on Moral Pluralism and Political Conflict

If such implicit preconceptions about the nature of politics and its relation to reason, violence, and war were simply a reflection of lack of thought or of the influence of journalistic clichés, they would not require extended discussion. I wish to suggest, however, that this is not the case. The presumption that politics "reemerges" in places like Northern Ireland as the guns fall silent is central to contemporary political theory, and, precisely because it is not usually examined at all closely, is a significant source of weakness.

The problem is at its most striking in the work of John Rawls, particularly in his attempts to revise his theory to respond to criticism of *A Theory of Justice*. The focus for the issues raised here is what Rawls regards in his later work as the "fact of pluralism." By this he means the empirical fact of deep conflicts around fundamental values in contemporary societies, and the absence of any reasonable or rational standard according to which such conflicts might be adjudicated. Pluralism, understood as the irreducible diversity of "comprehensive conceptions of the good" thus has a *moral*, and not simply *factual*, status: it is both the cause of conflict, and a constraint on the institutions designed to cope with conflict. As we shall see, what is ultimately at stake is the significance for democratic theory of the sociology of conflict, which is implicit in the notion of "stability" to which the second version of Rawls's theory gives great prominence. In a word, contemporary liberalism and its communitarian critics *need* a theory of conflict, but are prevented from acquiring one because of their commitment to a peculiar idea of pluralism. They are thus forced to write conflict out of the scope of theory just as they claim to be theorizing it. For the moment, however, I shall concentrate on Rawlsian exegesis.

Any discussion of Rawls must take into account the significant differences between the two book-length versions of his thinking on social justice.[20] For my purposes here, the key point is the changing role of the notion of "stability," which points to a subtle, unacknowledged shift at the most fundamental level, namely the *point* of the whole exercise, the *purpose* the theory is intended to serve. The most basic premise of any theory of justice is a set of assumptions about the kind of people who make up a society, and the various ways in which they interact. Simplifying very crudely, TJ reasoned from the structural necessities of cooperation, whereas PL gives priority to a newly salient fact of (reasonable) moral pluralism. The kind of people whose interactions produce pluralism in this sense are essentially the bearers of comprehensive doctrines. It is plausible enough to consider that any free society is highly likely to include significant groups of citizens strongly committed to incompatible but reasonable comprehensive doctrines. However, Rawls provides inadequate evidence for the primacy attributed by him to this problem, and, quite apart from his argument, adequate evidence is not in fact available.

The starting point is again the complex relation between TJ and PL. Rawls's own statement is at once accurate and subtly misleading: "the account of stability in part III of *Theory* [sc. TJ] is not consistent with the view as a whole. I believe all differences are consequences of removing that inconsistency. Otherwise these lectures take the structure and content of Theory to remain substantially the same" (PL, xv-xvi). In fact the differences caused by the new account of stability are far-reaching (although, tautologically, TJ is *otherwise* unaffected) because they affect not simply the substantive content of stability but its very theoretical status. To put the contrast very crudely, TJ is a theory of justice sensitive to the social context of its reproduction, whereas PL is a theory of social order and of the role of justice in promoting it. However, this conceptual reversal is never stated or defended.[21] Rather it arises from features peculiar to PL that are justified primarily in formal rather than substantive terms, namely, the fact of pluralism and the related distinction between comprehensive and political liberalism. The distinctive contribution of PL, compared to TJ, is the implied claim that stable justice is necessary for the *collective survival* of a society primarily threatened by *political conflict* arising from the clash of reasonable comprehensive doctrines. The underlying theme, in other words, is a simple dichotomy: "mortal conflict moderated only by circumstance and exhaustion, or equal liberty of conscience and freedom of thought" (PL, xxxi). This implies two distinct assumptions: (1) that the clash of doctrines necessarily produces severe political conflict, and (2) that nothing else produces conflicts of comparable severity. Neither is satisfactorily established.

With respect to the first assumption, even granted the existence of fundamental doctrinal opposition between at least some groups in any given society, it does not follow that civil war is just around the corner. Despite the massive historical significance of the post-Reformation European wars of religion, they are just an illustration from societies of a very different kind,[22] and they do not constitute proof. Rawls himself appears ambivalent on this point, and seems to hesitate in PL between a robust view of politics and a strongly antipolitical reference point of a society entirely without conflict, expressed by his constant concern to insulate justice from politics ("in the wrong sense"), and to distinguish sharply justice as fairness from a "mere" modus vivendi. In the absence of theory of belief and motivation, the conflictual implications of comprehensive doctrines are simply indeterminate.

The case is if anything stronger with respect to the second assumption. One way of looking at the issue is to consider the idea of "circumstances of justice," a phrase used in TJ (and carried over into PL) to refer precisely to the basic problem the theory of justice is designed to solve: "although society is a cooperative venture for mutual advantage, it is typically marked by a conflict as well as by an identity of interests. There is an identity of interests since social cooperation makes possible a better life for all than any would have if each were to live solely by his own efforts. There is a conflict of interests since persons are not indifferent as to how the greater benefits produced by their collaboration are distributed, for in order to pursue their ends they each prefer a smaller to a larger share" (TJ, 4). The conflict of interests referred to is a political problem requiring a political solution. Rawls provides a series of convincing reasons for believing that the political management of social cooperation would be more effective, and more widely acceptable, if it was based on principles incorporating an ideal position of impartiality outside politics. It is important, however (and entirely consistent with Rawls's theory), to stress that the issues are not thereby removed from politics, nor are the underlying reasons for conflict somehow dissipated. The precise extent to which, in various circumstances, class conflict, say, may be a threat to social order is an important question of political sociology. Rawls's failure to address it makes his emphasis on the primacy of doctrinal conflict seem merely dogmatic.

A complementary angle is provided by Rawls's insistence on circumscribing the domain of justice by rationality (the moral power to define conceptions of the good) and reasonableness (the willingness to accept fair terms of social cooperation). From the perspective of a theory of justice this limitation is perfectly understandable. If all established positions and all forms of belief and behavior deserve equal respect, any current injustice is simply entrenched. [23]

The view of social and political conflict that it produces is, however, so thin-blooded that it is hardly relevant at all. Accepting, as a constraint on justice as it relates to social order, the status quo with respect to the actual distribution of comprehensive doctrines within society, including the weird, the wacky, and the downright nasty, is a recipe for vacuousness, but so is failure to take account of the circumstances that create the problem one is trying to solve. The distinction is a matter of judgment, to which Rawls gives insufficient attention. "prejudice and bias, self- and group interest, blindness and willfulness, play their all too familiar part in political life. But these sources of unreasonable disagreement stand in marked contrast to those compatible with everyone's being fully reasonable. . . . It is unrealistic—or worse, it arouses mutual suspicion and hostility—to suppose that all our differences are rooted solely in ignorance and perversity, or else in the rivalries for power, status, or economic gain" (PL, 58). In other words, even if people were in fact reasonable and rational, political conflict would still occur. No doubt this is true, but unless it can be shown that in a more just society people would be less prejudiced, biased, and blind—and Rawls drops in PL his previous attempt to argue for this (TJ, 453-512)—it is not very interesting. Removing grounds for reasonable conflict simply leaves *unreasonable* conflict as the only threat. Perhaps this is not really a problem of justice. From the point of view of social order, however, it is very much *the* problem. It is hardly controversial to suggest that civil peace may be threatened by unreasonable people with guns, and that no shared principles of justice are likely to be available to justify restricting their activities. Indeed, unreasonable people *without* guns are just as much of a problem: less dangerous, perhaps, but more difficult to deal with in an approximately just society.

What is at issue here is ultimately whether the concept of "reason ableness"—and therefore the underlying idea of "reason"—can do the work Rawls intends it to. Certainly his own ambivalence hardly helps his case. How does the idea of a "comprehensive doctrine" express "rationality"—the moral power to define conceptions of the good? In Isaiah Berlin's well-known version of moral pluralism, moral knowledge is inherently limited by *value* pluralism, which is neither individually nor collectively subjective, but objective, so that the idea of a "comprehensive doctrine" is incoherent. Rawls is aware of this, and indeed pays lip service to it (PL, 197). As he says, "Only ideologues and visionaries fail to experience deep conflicts of political values and conflicts between these and nonpolitical values" (PL, 44). But he is uncomfortable with the idea, and elides its implications. Ultimately Rawls's pluralism is quasi-monistic, in the sense that it postulates a plurality of value monisms, and he apparently speaks for himself when he says "that there are . . . many reasonable comprehensive doctrines affirmed by reasonable people may seem surprising, as we like to see reason leading to the truth and to think of the truth as one" (PL, 64). Skepticism about one's beliefs is in this respect an important issue, and Rawls is ambivalent between the (plausible) view that no form of political liberalism can legitimately *demand* skepticism and the (unsubstantiated) view that beliefs held skeptically cannot really be moral beliefs at all. There is no room in Rawls for "extreme views weakly held,"[24] although many people would I think find them familiar—and perhaps congenial. While Rawls is not consistent here, one aspect of what he is saying is that only ideologues and visionaries subscribe to comprehensive doctrines. If so, if rationality is ultimately incompatible with reasonableness, much of what is distinctive about the later Rawls simply evaporates.

Such inconsistencies are hardly trivial, but it is possible to interpret them more charitably. Let us therefore redefine the problem—much more narrowly than Rawls himself—as the threat to a just social order posed by doctrinal differences between reasonable people. The characteristic postulates that other threats are less significant and that nonmoral social orders are inherently unstable are not essential to this formulation. The familiar solution offered by Rawls is the idea of an "overlapping consensus." However, Rawls fails to prove the effectiveness of an overlapping consensus in promoting social and political order; and furthermore the political efficacy of liberalism in this respect, including the kind of consensus it involves, derives precisely from those features that Rawls feels most uneasy about defending.

The idea of an overlapping consensus arises in PL at the conjunction of two requirements: that principles of justice should be stable, [25] in other words that their implementation should promote a sense of justice, and should therefore not be self-defeating; and that they should actually be acceptable to all reasonable citizens. However, these rather uncontroversial requirements are also, in a further twist, subject to the logic of a "well-ordered" society, i.e., one "effectively regulated by a public conception of justice" (TJ, 5). The reason for the twist is Rawls's sharp distinction between a (nonmoral) modus vivendi and an overlapping consensus "moral in both its object and its content" (PL, 126).

Rawls defines a modus vivendi as any set of institutions supported by the conjunction of private advantage rather than by public argument. He advances two distinct reasons for his vehement rejection of such an idea. On the one hand, he expresses skepticism about its effectiveness in principle: "social unity is only apparent, as its stability is contingent on circumstances remaining such as not to upset the fortunate convergence of interests." (PL, 147). On the other hand, by definition, no modus vivendi can be the focus for a well-ordered society. Presumably they are intended to reinforce each other, but the first is in fact vacuous: no one would seriously suggest that any society could be maintained *solely* by its members' individual material satisfaction with their share of the fruits of social cooperation. The objection to viewing justice in terms of a modus vivendi therefore depends entirely on the theoretical persuasiveness of the idea of a well-ordered society. It was initially derived from the "Aristotelian principle," but this is valid only within comprehensive liberalism. Within the terms of PL, therefore, and for the purposes of this discussion, the idea of a well-ordered society must be judged by its practical implications. There are three difficulties in this respect.

First, Rawls's emphasis on publicity (PL, 66-67) ultimately commits him to the transparency of the political sphere as a criterion of a good society. Yet, on his own terms (PL, 133-172), the same political principles may be supported by different reasons from the perspective of the various available conceptions of the good—although the requirement that such reasons be articulated publicly limits the extent of difference. Furthermore, transparency is not simply unnecessary, but potentially *self-destructive*. So long as it is assumed that people entertain serious disagreements (and otherwise Rawls's whole exercise would be pointless), prudence would seem to advise against bringing it all out into the open. The limited but genuine success of current political transitions in South Africa and Northern Ireland suggests that there is more to be said for opaque and immoral political fudges than Rawls is prepared to envisage.[26]

Second, the effectiveness of an overlapping consensus in reducing political division is not satisfactorily established by Rawls. The general idea—which is plausible enough—is that people with divergent comprehensive views should be able equally to accommodate a common political perspective. Rawls's distinctive contribution, however, is to make the content of the consensus *moral* and to restrict its scope to those comprehensive views eligible on grounds of reasonableness. Yet the capacity of such a consensus to be politically effective is impossible to evaluate in the absence of an analytical theory of the causes of social conflict, which Rawls completely fails to provide.

Finally, a characteristic feature of PL is Rawls's suggestion that the idea of an overlapping consensus is simply a more systematic and sophisticated formulation of something that is already available within the practical political tradition of the West, namely, the principle of tolerance. His attempts to prove this are unconvincing. Thus, in the pre-liberal era, he suggests, "Intolerance was accepted as a condition of social order and stability. The weakening of that belief helps to clear the way for liberal institutions. Perhaps the doctrine of free faith developed because it is difficult, if not impossible, to believe in the damnation of those with whom we have, with trust and confidence, long and fruitfully cooperated in maintaining a just society" (PL, xxv). This suggests that free faith involves no change in the nature of faith itself. Yet the historical development of liberalism is inconceivable without the decline in religious faith characteristic of the skeptical and deistic eighteenth century. "Belief" in intolerance did not simply decay in a vacuum. By contrast it is striking that early understandings of (legal) toleration were—in Britain at least—not the opposite of but *premised upon* doctrinal intolerance. [27]

Conversely it is arguable, as a matter of historical interpretation, that legal toleration was a condition for the development of doctrinal tolerance rather than a consequence of it. Again, the link between social cooperation and belief in damnation seems merely facetious. After all, some religious doctrines prescribe belief in the damnation of the majority of one's *coreligionists*, and to the extent that such a belief is socially self-contradictory, it tends as much to the erosion of faith as to "free faith." Finally, toleration was born in societies that, by no standard relevant to Rawls's discussion, could be regarded as just.

A different but perfectly plausible interpretation of the historical development of liberalism, along the lines sketched in the previous paragraph, would in fact be incompatible with the whole thrust of Rawls's theory. In PL, Rawls considers various possible objections to the idea of an overlapping consensus. One that he clearly believes would, if valid, be damaging is that it necessarily implies skepticism about the truth of comprehensive doctrines, and is thus incompatible with the holding of any such doctrine. His statement, and rebuttal, of this objection involves, however, the fallacy, explicitly endorsed in PL, that "belief" is a purely cognitive notion. [28]

In fact, convictions have degrees of commitment attached to them, not simply degrees of intellectual certainty, and the practical effect of skepticism is usually diffidence with regard to implementation rather than intellectual doubt. Indeed, if toleration *is*, plausibly enough, the "only workable alternative to endless and destructive civil strife" (PL, 159), what makes it work is ultimately the feeling that things may be true in some sense without being worth killing for, whereas in previous centuries commitment and belief were inseparable. The possibility that rationality might ultimately be unreasonable (using both words in the Rawlsian sense) is within the logic of PL, but Rawls refuses to admit it. He does of course recognize that liberalism has effects on society, to the point, ultimately, of turning many or most people into liberals of some kind. What he is not prepared to accept is that these effects, because non-liberals clearly have no reason to endorse them, might provide a *justification* for liberalism. However, contrary to what he suggests, the historical evidence of the development of liberalism does not support the view that a derivation of liberalism acceptable to non-liberals is available.

A similar tendency to set the limits of theory by reference primarily or exclusively to justice is apparent in Habermas. Although Habermas presents his debates with Rawls as a "family quarrel," their theories actually differ quite sharply. In particular, although Habermas does start from value plurality as a social fact, the ethic of discussion is not really pluralistic, and certainly does not postulate the incommensurability of values. (Arguably, of course, if my earlier suggestion is correct that Rawls, despite his Berlinian references, is some kind of closet monist, the difference may not be so sharp. This is a central theme in their recent debate, Habermas regarding their positions as closer than Rawls is prepared to accept.) Furthermore, he explicitly disclaims a close theoretical link between justice and social order, or stability in the modified Rawlsian sense of PL. In so doing, he obviously denies that justice based on reasonable agreement is a sufficient condition of order, although it is fairly clear that he does envisage some kind of necessary relation. However, the way in which he does so is revealing. The extent to which justice may contribute to social order is, he says, an empirical question—about which theory has little to say (*Débat sur la justice politique*, 41). Social order is thus ultimately not "thinkable" but rather the condition prior and radically external to rational thought that makes politics and political theory possible. (Habermas does not say this, but the combination of his silences and what he does say implies it.) In times of civil war, therefore—or simply of severe social conflict involving, through bad faith or other mechanisms, the utter failure to communicate—theory can only be silent.

Habermas is understandably unhappy with Rawls's unsatisfactory conflation of justice and social order via the notion of stability. But in denying that order is an appropriate subject for theory at all, he remains within the same format. "Reason" and "violence," as he presents them in passing at the beginning of *Faktizität und Geltung*—without justification or expansion—are polar opposites.

There is no space here for violence as a mode of discourse, or for the overlap of politics and war, that characterize most pressing political problems. The bounds of reason are set by "serious" participation in discussion, thereby tacitly assuming, in the formal structure of the theory, the motivations, the "sense of justice" in the Rawlsian sense, that are supposed to be internally grounded. The best indicator of this difficulty is the undue emphasis Habermas is forced to put on the developmental psychology he borrows from Piaget, and later from Kohlberg. The link between the transcendental conditions of public discourse and the empirical, sociopsychological disposition to engage in it is ultimately a spectacular leap of faith. Habermas is thus vulnerable to the same charge as Rawls: to put it very crudely, that he offers a theoretical approach to justice that only works against the kind of institutional background—itself a contingent and fragile historical achievement—that makes such an approach, if not strictly unnecessary, at least optional. Justice in approximately just societies, so long as they are approximately insulated from a deeply unjust world, is an important moral issue, but not, by definition, a burning practical one.

Foundation, Justification, and Compliance

These internal difficulties in Rawls and Habermas, which could be equally illustrated from a wide variety of other thinkers, show how the journalistic clichés about "politics" and "war" have a close parallel in contemporary theory. To put things in more abstract theoretical terms, what is ultimately at stake is the ambivalence at the heart of the notion of "compliance," which seeks to conjoin two ideas: the *fact* of acceptance (of authority generally or of specific instructions), and the *reasons* for it. The presumption, implicit in Rawls, Habermas, and many others, is that there is a close internal connection between the two: that ungrounded acceptance (say de facto "social peace") is different *in practice* ("less stable"), and not simply morally, from acceptance based on recognized legitimacy. Conversely, the moral character of social institutions contributes to their practical stability. There is nothing wrong with this as a normative aspiration. As a sociological analysis, however, it is less plausible than it appears at first sight.

The participants in any activity may have a wide variety of reasons for following its rules. Does such diversity make a difference, or is the fact of compliance of independent significance? It is easy enough to agree that identification of a rule as a rule requires evidence of compliance over time in a range of circumstances, and some grounds for postulating future compliance. In other words, reasons for compliance are constitutive of rules, and not simply incidental to them. In particular, the ability *in general* to punish noncompliance depends on the existence and plausibility of such reasons.

From the point of view of political theory, laws are a highly significant category of rules (taking law in a broad sense, regardless of, say, the detailed hierarchy of legal norms). Let us therefore consider the question: how do the reasons for compliance with law—the basis of civil, or political, obligation, as they are often termed—relate to actual compliance? It is immediately apparent that this question is in principle indeterminate unless the nature of the activity presumptively regulated by law is further specified. This may not seem to be of great practical relevance. Yet a glance at contemporary theory reveals a tension between two distinct, but conceptually related, answers. On the one hand, the central activity to which law pertains is considered to be the realization of social justice, following Rawls's dictum that "justice is the first virtue of social institutions, as truth is of systems of thought." The issues are, therefore, the nature of justice, the reasons for behaving justly, their capacity to produce just behavior, and the implications of their failure to do so. On the other hand, law is theorized in terms of social order, the key issues being mutatis mutandis identical.

What makes this tension interesting is precisely that the two sets of problems are not strictly distinct. A theorist of order could perhaps, in principle, disregard justice, although even here the possibility that unjust arrangements might be inherently unstable needs explicit discussion and cannot be dismissed out of hand. A theorist of justice, however, is inescapably confronted with the problem of order. Justice is, indeed, a kind of ordering, in something like the mathematical sense. Specifically, a set of just arrangements is characterized, among other things, by patterns of motivation and behavior that are, at the very least, widespread; and by institutions that effectively permit the correction of injustice. Human rights, for instance, require application—often involving force—and not simply enunciation. How rules might become socially embedded and effective is thus the key problem in any theory of justice. In practice, theories can broadly be divided into those for which order is some kind of background condition (of a "cultural" nature, for instance), and those that regard order as deriving from the operation of the rules that it underwrites (what scientists might call a "bootstrap" structure).

The bootstrap version, which is clearly the more theoretically ambitious, is characteristic of the most interesting contemporary theories. Justice and order thus emerge simultaneously, and the principles of *foundation* and *justification* must in some sense converge. In other words, whatever might in principle be regarded as justifying some social arrangement must also be assumed to sustain it in practice.

The ambivalence about the nature and status of law naturally extends to compliance, and thus brings us back to our starting point. It would be tempting, but wrong, to distinguish neatly between the perspective of social order, from which only the *capacity* to enforce compliance matters, and the perspective of justice, from which the ability to *justify* such enforcement is vital. In fact the two issues blur, because the distinction depends on the theoretically indeterminate question of the *reasons* for noncompliance. We may agree with the currently standard liberal paradigm that actual or latent conflict in which all parties are "reasonable" can be fully resolved by reference to justice. But what makes people reasonable, and what are the consequences of their not being reasonable?

A fairly standard answer, which Habermas and Rawls in particular both reflect without being entirely comfortable with it, is that reasonableness only makes sense within a set of established and generally accepted institutional constraints, which in turn make just coercion possible. But what this means is that justice flourishes, if at all, in the shadow of violence. Foundation in principle may be consistent with justification, but actual historical origin is generally unjustifiable. This is the core of Foucault's critique of the social-contract tradition.[29] Considering the relation between politics and war, Foucault seeks to show how a theorist who is often assumed to have addressed the issue explicitly (Hobbes) in fact evades it. Although war—in the peculiar Hobbesian conception of the "state of war," where actual fighting is almost immaterial—is conceptually linked to the origins of political order, all trace of actual conflict is removed within the Commonwealth. Foucault generalizes this observation to the social-contract tradition generally, which he views as handicapped by its legalistic conception of power, equated with sovereignty and in turn with the enunciation of law. On the contrary, the political-historical writers that Foucault analyzes, and that he relates to the conceptual origins of racism, regard law as a decorative structure behind or beneath which the traces of past war, and its present-day continuation, are clearly visible if one chooses to look. While he does not exactly endorse this view, he does regard it as more consistent with his own perspective on power than the legalistic tradition which remains the mainstream within political theory. The social contract, as Foucault puts it, is signed, if at all, in blood.

And even this understates the problem, since a just order must, in principle, be founded anew each time it addresses non-compliance, which cannot be presumed to be reasonable. Thus, the justification of violence is not an incidental or occasional feature of political authority, but something very close to the inherent nature of justice itself. No system of law operates by reason alone—otherwise it would not be necessary at all. Violence and reason, which Habermas and Rawls distinguish strictly, therefore have, at the very least, an inherent instrumental relationship within, and not simply as a derogation from, the idea of justice. War is an aspect of politics, and not its negation. Thus, contemporary liberalism is haunted by the ghost of sovereignty—in the strong Schmittian sense that Agamben appropriates for rather different purposes—and yet is entirely unequipped to exorcise it. The sword of justice is an inherent attribute of the sovereign because it is quite simply what justice means in an unjust world. Yet the swish of that sword is precisely the point at which war and politics merge, and justification and foundation part company.

Notes

1. Michel Foucault, *Il faut défendre la société. Cours au Collège de France. 1976*, (Paris: Gallimard / Seuil, 1997).

2. Weber's term is *die Gewalt*, which has in German more complex connotations than "force" in English. It can, in particular, mean both "administration" and "violence."

3. On this, see further Giorgio Agamben, *Homo sacer. 1, Il potere sovrano e la nuda vita* (Turin: Einaudi, 1995).

4. On the political dimensions and problems of reconciliation, see the papers collected in *Cultures & Conflits*, forthcoming; in particular John Crowley, "La pacification du politique: quelques réflexions sur les transitions immorales."

5. "Violence and metaphysics" is the title of the essay on Levinas in the early collection *L'écriture et la différence* (Paris: Seuil, 1967). The theme of violence and origin, however, runs through the *whole* book, and is ultimately what gives it its unity.

6. Jacques Derrida, *Force de loi. Le "Fondement mystique de l'autorité"* (Paris: Galilée, 1994).

7. Frantz Fanon, *Les damnés de la terre* (Paris: Maspéro, 1961).

8. References on this point are extremely numerous. A good recent statement is Jean Leca, "Violence et ordre," in Jean Hannoyer (ed.), *Guerres civiles. Économies de la violence, dimensions de la civilité* (Paris: Karthala-CERMOC, 1999): 315-26.

9. I refer here in particular to the studies collected in Françoise Héritier (ed.), *De la violence* (Paris: Éd. Odile Jacob; volume 1, 1996; volume 2, 1999); and Hannoyer, *Guerres civiles*. See also John Keane, *Reflections on Violence* (London: Verso, 1996).

10. It should be stressed that some important cases seem to detract from this characterization, most strikingly the Nazi genocide. Such exceptions obviously cast doubt on the ability of the indications given here to offer any basis for a *general* "theory" of violence, whether in philosophical or sociological terms. A useful philosophical discussion of this point is Myriam Revault d'Allonnes, *Ce que l'homme fait à l'homme. Essai sur le mal politique* (Paris: Seuil, 1995).

11. A useful statement of the instrumental analysis of political violence, with particular reference to terrorism, is Yves Michaud, *La violence*, 3rd edition (Paris: PUF, 1996).

12. A helpful summary of these multifaceted interactions between discourse and violence is Vivienne Jabri, *Discourses on Violence. Conflict Analysis Reconsidered* (Manchester: Manchester University Press, 1996).

13. Carl Schmitt, *Der Begriff des Politischen* (second edition, 1932). English translation: *The Concept of the Political* (Chicago: University of Chicago Press, 1996).

14. "The distinction is to be taken here in a rather summary fashion and not in any specifically moral or ethical sense." (*Concept of the Political* : 58)—whatever that might mean.

15. Schmitt, *The Concept of the Political*, esp. §7. An unusually interesting recent variant on the "anthropological" perspective is Wolfgang Sofsky, *Traktat über die Gewalt* (Frankfurt: S. Fischer Verlag, 1996). Sofsky attempts explicitly to include within the analysis of violence the understanding of the fascination it often seems to exercise.

16. Schmitt, *The Concept of the Political*, 61.

17. This tendency is broad, but by no means universal. Schmitt's thought continues, for instance, to exert significant influence among left-wing critics of liberalism. See, for example, Chantal Mouffe, ed., *The Challenge of Carl Schmitt* (London: Verso, 1999).

18. John Crowley, "La pacification du politique en Irlande du Nord," *Critique Internationale* 1 (1998): 35-42.

19. Gerard Delanty, "Negotiating the Peace in Northern Ireland," *Journal of Peace Research* 32 (1995): 57-64; "Habermas and Postnational Identity: Theoretical Perspectives

on the Conflict in Northern Ireland," *Irish Political Studies* 11 (1996): 20-32; "Social Exclusion and the New Nationalism: European Trends and Their Implications for Ireland," *Innovation: The European Journal of Social Sciences* 10, no. 2 (1997): 127-44.

20. *A Theory of Justice* (Cambridge, Mass.: Harvard University Press, 1971) [hereafter quoted as TJ]; *Political Liberalism* (New York: Columbia University Press, 1993) [hereafter quoted as PL]. Rawls's subsequent debate with Habermas [*Journal of Philosophy* 92, no. 3 (1995)] introduces some additional complications that will be referred to where necessary but not discussed in detail. References are to the French edition [Jürgen Habermas and John Rawls, *Débat sur la justice politique* (Paris: Éd. du Cerf, 1997)], which contains Habermas's *Politischer Liberalismus*, Rawls's *Reply to Habermas* (49-142; quoted here as RH), and Habermas's *Einbeziehung des Anderen*.

21. Indeed, it is explicitly denied on at least one occasion: "I have not supposed that an overlapping consensus is necessary for certain kinds of social unity and stability." (PL, 149). The context is the (correct) emphasis on the fact that an overlapping consensus is not a political compromise. But the denial remains, in view of Rawls' discussion as a whole, essentially unconvincing. In his own words, "social unity . . . as deriving from an overlapping consensus on a political conception of justice suitable for a constitutional regime. . . . is the most desirable conception of unity available to us; it is the limit of the practical best." (PL, 201-2). Rawls is in fact consistently ambivalent about the status of a "modus vivendi": is it a kind of "social unity and stability," albeit a morally inferior one; or is it too thin and too dependent on a contingent balance of power to qualify as "stable" at all? I think it is easy to show that in PL Rawls clearly prefers the second answer. The ambivalence is on the other hand more marked in RH, where Rawls retreats slightly from some of the less plausible positions criticized here.

22. Whether they even illustrate Rawls's point is in fact arguable. The theological differences between, say, Anglicans and Catholics in late seventeenth-century England were minimal, and their political outlooks in nearly all respects were quite compatible. There was certainly far less difference than between either and the Puritans. The real issue was geopolitical. Catholics were regarded as *traitors* because of (supposed) subservience to the interests of France or Spain, even more than as *heretics*. Conversely tolerance had as much to do with a diminished sense of external threat (especially after 1745) as with internal politics. Mutatis mutandis, the difficulties faced by European Muslims may be analyzed in a similar way.

23. This is the point of Joshua Cohen's article "Moral Pluralism and Political Consensus" [in David Copp et al. (ed.), *The Idea of Democracy* (Cambridge: Cambridge University Press, 1993)], which was a critique of Rawls's "The Domain of the Political and Overlapping Consensus" (*New York University Law Review* 64, no. 2 (1989): 233-55; also reprinted in Copp et al., *The Idea of Democracy*, 245-69), in which the distinction between reasonable pluralism and pluralism *tout court* was not made. It was directly responsible for Rawls's adoption of the idea of reasonable pluralism in PL. A similar critique of the principles of justice in TJ was made by Brian Barry [*The Liberal Theory of Justice* (Oxford: Clarendon Press, 1973)], on the grounds that the "difference principle" takes greed, which is unjust, for granted and implicitly validates it. This, however, is not a criticism that Rawls has incorporated.

24. A self-description reportedly given by the English historian A. J. P. Taylor [Alan Watkins, *Brief Lives* (London: Hamish Hamilton, 1982), 178].

25. As we have seen, "stability" may also characterize the society regulated by principles of justice. The extent to which this elastic usage is deliberate and legitimate is unclear. On the resulting difficulties, see further David Copp, "Pluralism and Stability in Liberal Theory," *Journal of Political Philosophy* 4, no. 3 (1996): 191-206.

26. For a broader theoretical perspective, see John Crowley, "La transparence du politique et ses limites: négociations d'intérêts et pluralisme 'moral,'" *Politique et Sociétés* 17, no. 3 (1998): 37-58.

27. Iain Hampsher-Monk, "Is There an English Form of Toleration?" *New Community* 21, no. 2 (1995): 227-40.

28. As he puts it: "it is vital to the idea of political liberalism that we may with perfect consistency hold that it would be unreasonable to use political power to enforce our own comprehensive view, which we must, *of course*, affirm as either reasonable or true" (PL, 138; my italics). The same point crops up in much of the current literature on moral pluralism, and seems to have axiomatic status. Yet, it is hardly self-evident. Of course, "I believe that x" is trivially equivalent to "I believe that x is true." But this is not what is relevant here. Sentences of the form "I believe in x" cannot generally be rephrased as "I believe that y is true" without loss of content.

29. Foucault, *Il faut défendre la société*.

Chapter 7

The Subject of Sovereignty

Pedro Francés-Gómez[1]

> Der Staat selbst ruht auf allgemeinen Vernunftbegriffen; ist allenthalben
> der gleiche oder ähnliche. Was ist nun das eigentliche Nationale?
> Ich denke: gegenseitiges Verstehen zwischen Repräsentirten und Repräsentanten,
> und darauf gegründetes Wechselvertrauen.—Nun giebts etwas, worüber ganz gewiss
> Einverständniss herauszubringen ist: die bürgerliche Freiheit. [2]

J. G. Fichte

Introduction

The concept of sovereignty is in crisis. Most, if not all, current literature on the topic focuses on the inadequacy of the classical concept of sovereignty. The concept established by Bodin and the early international law theorists, and developed, after the American and French revolutions, into the normative idea of the nation-state as subject of international law, is no longer tenable. Surprisingly enough, a common way to expound the problems of the classical understanding of sovereignty is to refer to (very classic) sovereignty claims. In particular, to the various sovereignty claims posed by nations without a state, and, perhaps less frequently, to quasi-sovereignty claims posed by economic or political inter-national organizations. Both national communities and multistate organizations are demanding at least part of the allegiance that citizens were supposed to pay only to their countries, and the international recognition that only states used to enjoy.

Under certain political conditions, both national communities and multistate organizations exercise de facto powers traditionally reserved for the sovereign. These instances do not seem to show a concept in crisis, but rather the dispute about the same old scarce, valuable, and useful resource (the supreme social power). It is undeniable that the occasional virulence of this dispute is forcing theorists to reconsider old ideas about the allocation of sovereignty, but so far it is hard to point to a real change in the received concept.

The distinction between "concept" and "conception" introduced by Rawls in regard to justice might be useful to explain this seeming contradiction. It is possible to distinguish between the concept of sovereignty and conceptions of sovereignty. What seems to be in crisis is, of course, the particular conception of sovereignty that emerged from Westphalia and developed along the Enlightenment and Romantic ideals of patriotism. According to this conception, sovereignty is the legitimate absolute power uniquely exerted by the nation-state (through its legal representatives) and recognized both by the people (authority in the internal sphere) and by other states (autonomy in the international sphere). Despite the crisis of this conception of sovereignty, the concept itself seems to be intact.

Sovereignty claims could not be explained otherwise: national minorities would not claim sovereignty if it were thought of as a meaningless or historically superseded idea. The same goes for multistate economic and political organizations. They demand allegiance from the citizens and claim legitimacy for the power they exert. And these claims are based on the supposition that post-modern citizens are able to sincerely commit themselves to collective projects, and to rationally justify and accept the legitimacy of the (sovereign) power exerted on them. That is, these claims have the same basis as the traditional sovereignty claim of the nation-state.

I will suggest that the talk about the crisis of (the conception of) sovereignty expresses our difficulties in defining a precise subject for the concept: a proper sovereign. The modern conception of (absolute, indivisible, non-delegatable) sovereignty had a precise subject: the Monarch, the Nation, the State. Today, the received theories of exclusive sovereignty sound simplistic and unconvincing; but no satisfactory alternative has been developed. Therefore we lack a sound definition for one of the essential parts of any conception of sovereignty. We lack any normative (that is universal) idea about how to define the "who" who is sovereign. Other components of the concept (faculties, limits, scope, ways of exertion, etc.) are of no use if we cannot define a subject for them. An approximate empirical description of whom is actually claiming sovereignty, exerting sovereign powers, or recognized by others as such, is always possible. But empirical descriptions would be of little help to solve normative questions such as: Is there a right of intervention in other polities? What is a legitimate constitution? To what extent are states obliged to hand part of their sovereignty over to international organizations? And so on. These questions require a plausible normative theory of sovereignty. And the absence of a sound normative definition of the subject of sovereignty hinders in an important way the possibility of developing such a theory.

My contribution will be an attempt to construct a normative notion of the subject of sovereignty. Normative constructions are rather peculiar pieces of theory: they are essentially debatable. By this I mean that there is just no other way to establish normative notions and practices except by discussing and criticizing them (either around a table or through our acts in the world). Hence, the suggestions I will be presenting are wide open to discussion. They could never claim to be true, but only adequate or valid; and this only as the result of your taking them as such.

As a methodological preamble, I would like to mention what I consider the main sources of my proposal: since the task I have taken on is that of normatively constructing a subject, I will use as inspiration the ideas of Hegel in the *Phenomenology of Spirit*. I do not aim to be faithful to the Hegelian text (whatever that would mean); I will take it as a model because it can plausibly be interpreted as a philosophical—indeed phenomenological—narrative about the constitution of the self. According to Pinkard's reading, on which I will rely heavily, Hegel's story about the social constitution of the self is neither a metaphysical postulation nor an empirical history; and I believe this is exactly the kind of approach one should use in order to construct the subject of sovereignty. Of course the subject we are interested in—not a subject of knowledge, but the abstract (probably collective) subject of sovereignty—does not explicitly appear in the *Phenomenology*, but in other writings. I will attend particularly to Hegel's *Philosophy of Law*, and some of Fichte's writings, where the political subjectivity of the state is more clearly set. And of course, the treatment of concrete constitutional matters requires a contemporary approach; German idealists were influenced by political and philosophical contexts too removed from ours. I consider that Habermas's procedural understanding of democracy will be more helpful at this point.

I must insist that I will use these authorities merely as a guide (I do not embrace the method or the comprehensive views of any of them). In fact, my reflection will be stated in the more familiar language of analytical moral philosophy, abounding in economic and game-theoretical idioms, and this will additionally veil the ideas I take from Hegel, Fichte, or Habermas.

First, I will review the ongoing dispute between "nationalists" and "statists" to show how both parties share a common premise about who is the subject of sovereignty—both seem to be convinced that the nation is essentially the source of all sovereignty. I will hold that there is no rational basis for this conviction. The normative reconstruction of the *Bildung* or formation of a subject capable of saying "I am sovereign" in a politically meaningful way will help me to suggest an alternative for that undisputed premise. The construction of such an alternative and a reference to its consequences will occupy the rest of my chapter.

The Undisputed Premise:
The Nation as the Subject of Sovereignty

Contemporary theorists concede that the nation-state as the only depository of sovereignty is giving way to a variety of local communities and multinational organizations that are bound to share the title of sovereign. The nation-state is based on the conviction that every nation is entitled to constitute an independent state. A "nation" in the politically relevant sense can be defined as a "territorially based community of human beings sharing a ditinct variant of modern culture, bound together by a strong sentiment of unity and solidarity, marked by a clear historically-rooted consciousness of national identity, and possessing, or striving to possess, a genuine political self-government."[3]

However, there are few examples of states in which a nation thus defined coincided from its beginnings with the kind of polity that became what in post-Westphalian language was called a sovereign state. Most westerners (and almost all non-westerners) live in multinational states. Nationalist ideology reminds us of this fact every day. Nationalism adopts several forms and degrees: from the struggle for mere recognition to the open claim to secession. Whatever the allegations, they are based on the premise that nations are sovereign, so that they have the right to exercise supreme power over their nationals on a determinate territory; and the right to international recognition as independent and self-governing political communities. This is what I call a normative premise about who is the subject of sovereignty. The normativity of this premise was expressed, for example, in the third article of the Declaration of the Sacred Rights of Men and of Citizens (Paris, 1789): "The nation is essentially the source of all sovereignty; nor can any individual, or any body of men, be entitled to any authority which is not expressly derived from it."

Nationalists claim that the nation is the proper subject of sovereignty, while the state (as the king before) would exercise sovereignty only by way of delegation. The position of the defendants of state (or popular) sovereignty (as opposed to "national" sovereignty) is not theoretically different[4]: they tend to allege that their state comprises a single nation. The quarrel between nationalists and "statists" is often about the existence of some nation or other. When the existence of a separate nation within a state is taken for granted, the advocates of state sovereignty move to pragmatic arguments in defense of the status quo, with the simple aim of avoiding political change or secession. These pragmatic arguments are convincing only as long as nationalists see secession as a threat. They are bound to fail when practical problems eventually disappear or are reasonably solved, because they do not challenge the premise that the subject of sovereignty is an entity called "the nation." The fact is that both parties have the same underlying political theory: sovereignty lies in the nation and, at least contemporarily, is exercised through the means of a complex apparatus called the state. (This is why nationalists struggle to have a differentiated state, while non-nationalists have to insist that there is just one nation within the existing state). However, this premise has no rational or historical foundation—in fact, it comes from the ambiguity in the use of the term "nation." [5]

International law theorists have pointed out the ambiguity I am referring to, and the consequent necessity of a clarification. To cite just one example, Hannum writes:

> Most discussions of "self-determination" begin with an attempt to break the concept into its component parts: what constitutes the relevant "self," and in what manner should its fate be determined? The former includes subjective and objective components, in that it is necessary for members of the group concerned to think of themselves as a distinctive group, as well as for the group to have certain objectively determinable common characteristics . . . . Of course, everyone belongs to many different groups at the same time, and the difficulty arises in determining which are the relevant groups for purposes of respecting the principle of self-determination . . . A glance to contemporary conflicts is all that is needed to expose these difficulties, many of which appear during attempts to define the relevant borders. Within the two islands of Ireland and the United Kingdom, for example, the relevant "self" might be both islands taken together, despite their ethnic mix of English, Scots, Welsh, and Irish; each island separately, despite the mix of the first three in Great Britain and of Irish and Scots in Ireland; the two existing states; or each ethnic/geographic group, which would include at least the four separate entities of England, Scotland, Wales and Ireland, with from zero to two additional groups (Irish Catholics and "British" Protestants) in Northern Ireland. Citing a multitude of equally irreducible situations will not advance our thinking very far.[6]

As a first step to clarify how to define this elusive self, I propose to look closer to the "who"—the subject—that is claiming to be a nation, and therefore to be "the source of all sovereignty," in our times.

Who is "The Nation"?

Sovereignty claims come from various kinds of groups. Without trying to be exhaustive, we can cite ethnic groups, cultural groups, peoples historically attached to some territory or just conventionally united. The so-called ethnic nations may not occupy a definite or geographically united territory and may not share the same religion or worldviews; sometimes they do not share a single language. The trait they choose to identify themselves is a common descent; but then, several descents may be found in what is called an ethnic group, and there are always people of mixed descent who are included. [7] And, of course, people of the same ethnic background may populate different independent and sovereign states. Groups of the second kind are formed by people who came to consider themselves as a unity because they have historically developed a distinguishable culture over a certain territory—although this territory may not have precise boundaries. In cases of this sort, when descent is not the means to defining the group, and there are no clear territorial boundaries, common language and culture may play the key unifying role. Third, those groups that do not share either a clear common descent or a single language and culture have to resort to myths of their origin. Groups that allege that they constitute a unity of faith, because they share a common religion, could be considered a subclass of this kind. As a fourth set of cases I cited conventionally united peoples. I refer to those claims for sovereignty simply based on a collective decision supported by private associations and other states, and open to actual political implementation—the sovereign state of Liberia would be an example of this.

One could suspect that this variety is due to the fact that the groups currently demanding sovereignty are marginalized peoples, whose cultural traits have been truncated and disfigured, and whose original territories have been stolen by more powerful nations, organized as (aggressive) states. According to this suspicion, the historically successful nation-states should show all the characteristics that defined national sovereignty (those that are missing in communities currently claiming sovereignty). They should be the historical "natural" development of a group of culturally and territorially linked people into a self-governing organization capable of eliciting both allegiance from members and recognition from similar autonomous groups. However, this account would hardly describe the actual history of the formation of recognized sovereign states. Among sovereign states one can observe as much variety as in less-recognized communities.

By way of example, one can cite Switzerland, a confederation with several languages, cultural backgrounds, and religious faiths; Germany, now a federal state that originally reunited several religious factions historically opposed, and had contested and movable boundaries; Russia, a country of which Hegel remarked that the ruler could not even say how many languages were spoken under his territory (the same could be said of China, India, Brazil, etc.); the United States, whose unity is based in original myths about individual freedom, republicanism, and democracy that are very differently assimilated and understood by the heterogeneous ethnic and cultural groups of immigrants; Canada, a really singular country that contains two major western traditions together with a rich variety of indigenous nations plus highly differentiated groups of immigrants; and so on. In sum, the normative case of a single nation in a single territory constituting a single state has almost never existed.

It is clear that there is little or nothing "natural" in the development of nation-states. They are constructions. They were constructed in different epochs according to different beliefs and degrees of moral development, and perhaps this establishes certain differences among them. But the fact that they succeeded in keeping themselves as independent self-governing societies, and the right they acquired to do so through recognition in the international sphere, does not prove anything about the alleged relationship between nation, sovereignty, and state.

Thus, most political discourses and scientific literature on sovereignty accept a premise that, beyond grand declarations, is not founded on historical data. If we want to elucidate who is the proper subject of sovereignty, we had better leave this misleading premise aside and start anew with a normative theory, that is, a rational reconstruction of the notion of subjectivity that matches the concept of sovereignty. I propose to start such a reconstruction with a brief reflection on what is actually implied (but seldom explicit) in the formation processes of would-be subjects of sovereignty.

Subjects of Sovereignty:
The Initial Will and the First Proponents

Only one thing is common to all recognized nation-states and all groups claiming nationhood and sovereignty: their very will to be or become sovereign. This will implies establishing aims such as the subsistence (creation) of political unity, or the international recognition of a right to self-government. Our search for the subject of sovereignty should start, then, by analyzing how it is possible for groups of persons to exhibit such a will. From an empirical point of view, the search would focus on facts about collective beliefs and actions (as marks showing the will of a collectivity). From a normative point of view the challenge is to reconstruct the conditions under which a (shared) will for sovereignty can be born, grow, and develop into an articulate form of nationalist (or "statist") ideology. Of course, this reconstruction will disregard the fact that in real societies sovereignty rights are usually already assigned and effectively exercised. Being normative, my argument does not try to describe the actual historical processes through which state and/or national sovereignty are claimed, struggled for, and achieved. These processes never start from scratch, particularly in complex modern societies. My argument is intended to show the requirements for rationally explaining what is going on when a claim for sovereignty comes to be public.

Let us begin this reconstruction by assuming, as it may very plausibly be done, that the conviction about a group's right to self-government does not arise unless there is a reason for it to arise. A reason must be understood as a belief such that, when combined with the appropriate individual desires or interests, may play an efficient cause for a rational agent to act. Surely, the reason I am referring to will not be a simple one. It will certainly be a compound of private interests, metaphysical judgments, political circumstances, and so on. Whatever the factual reasons, once the conviction about people's rights has emerged, it involves deep changes according to a logic of their own. When a right is soundly defended as rational, it entails a change in worldview: it is considered to have always been there, so that many past actions will be reconceptualized as violations of such a right. Deep changes in worldviews are neither immediate nor easy. The first claimants must undoubtedly be ambitious persons (like the old European royal dynasties, or the Romantic historian and writer), political élites in the hope of grabbing power, outstanding economic agents in search of influence and profit, or enlightened minorities leading the way to political enfranchisement. In sum, some person or small group of persons may come to see her/their position as an unjustly deprived one; but improvable through a change in the location of the legal supreme social power.

Now, it is clear that a change in the location of the supreme social power is a goal well beyond the capacities of a single person or small group. The goal is necessarily a collective one. The first proponents of the right to sovereignty must procure the assent and cooperation of a sufficiently numerous set of people.

Cooperation and the Constitution of the Subject of Sovereignty

At this point the mechanisms of rational cooperation are set in motion. Its first stage is to constitute the set of individuals who are willing to cooperate. Among rational individuals, cooperation will occur only if it is mutually beneficial. Therefore, the first proponents must be able to convince (not merely to persuade) others not only of the legitimacy of their claim, but also of the beneficial effect that adherence would have for those who choose to adhere. To convince requires more than words, it requires commitment.[8] The first proponents must be committed to grant other persons approximately the same return they expect—for an unfair distribution of the cooperative benefit would not elicit cooperation. But profits in terms of free self-government are difficult to guarantee, so that the establishment of cooperation will depend on a return that can be produced more or less at will: recognition.

The first proponents came to see themselves as full members of a group that is entitled to certain rights of freedom and self-government. They are committed to recognize membership and similar rights to those who in turn recognize their authority as members of such a real, preexisting group.[9] Thus the community of cooperation is constituted through the dialectic of mutual recognition: only those recognized as members by the qualified representatives of the community can enter the community; but the community in turn needs the recognition conferred by the candidates who want to be considered members.

This dialectic is facilitated, of course, when the first proponents are the members of a ruling dynasty or an established political bureaucracy. In this particular case, recognition is a two-person deal: proponents offer equal treatment as citizens to their subjects; the citizenry, in turn, validates the claim to legitimate power put forward by the ruling group. The facticity of the effective monopoly of force does not eliminate, however, the necessity of a mutual recognition of this sort in order to establish the community as a sovereign one. [10]

The community succeeds (establishes itself as a source of normative authority) when a critical number of people commit themselves to its definition (thus contributing to the collective effort of forming the community). The individual succeeds (achieves her wanted social identity) when she is actually granted admission as a full member, and thus recognized by other members as entitled to equal participation.

What I have called "dialectic of mutual recognition" is dependent on the will of the parties, but this does not mean that it is an arbitrary process. The recognition (admission) granted by the members constitutes themselves as well as others, so once they define who they want to be as a group, they cannot grant membership to whomever they please, on pain of self-contradiction. If they grant membership, say, to someone who is not strongly committed to self-government as the main aim of the group, they would be recognizing that they are not very committed either. So once the standards of belonging and cooperation (the basic normative agreement) are set, admission is, in one sense, objectively limited. The immediate consequence is that the willingness to enter a well-defined group is not enough for someone to be granted admission; and exclusion may be justified on "objective grounds."

The community being constituted by the dialectic of mutual recognition—in other words, the cooperative group—tends to choose some external trait that facilitates the objectivity of the inclusion/exclusion transaction and that helps guarantee conditions of universal participation, or mutual understanding. [11] Common history, connected and closed territory, and shared language may be some of these external traits and conditions. But they are by no means decisive. They are subordinated to the objective of creating a collective self capable of achieving what a single individual or small group cannot. True, historical and cultural factors may help to establish the channels of communication in early stages of the community's formation process. Afterward they may serve as useful resources to keep the unity and morale of the group. But they are always fuzzy concepts and contingent facts. The backbone of the community is the cooperative will of the members, which can be explained in terms of individual self-interest.

In sum, the community and the identity of each member are simultaneously defined through normative commitments and through the process of exclusion/inclusion in which mutual recognition consists. First, the community is constituted by autonomous acts of personal commitment; then, the community becomes a source of normativity for each member. If this process ends up in the development of mutual identification and solidarity, and in the genesis of mutual obligations and rights, then the first proponents have achieved their initial objective: the constitution of a self-conscious cooperative group.

The Activity of the Sovereign Self

Once the community is constituted internally, it tends to confront other communities and singular agents in a competitive way. We can call this confrontation the struggle for external recognition—for the rights and status of the members of the group vis-á-vis the group itself are already recognized. At this stage, the rights of the community are proclaimed and the actions of other agents may be socially conceptualized as violations of these rights. Since the shared ambition (now declared as right) of the community may be hindered by these violations, the group will strategically act against violators, as the only way to achieve self-government in practice. Once communal rights are taken for granted, claims for sovereignty, independence, or secession may be made public, and war (or aggressive self-assertion) may be declared against violators of sovereignty—a just war, from the internal point of view of the community. I have to point out that the "internal point of view" of a group involves more than just a biased perspective. It must involve a concept and practice of "rationality" according to which the true and the good are defined. This is the only way to establish the community's rights as universally true, and the kind of aims of the group as normative reasons for action. The concept of "rationality internal to a tradition," described by A. McIntyre, would be a good approach to what is meant here by "internal point of view." [12]

The success of this process, the actual self-government of the group, will depend on many different internal and external factors, whose analysis does not belong to philosophy. I want to stress the only factor that seems to me essential from a normative point of view: the truthfulness and reasonableness of the first proponents' motivation and plans, as well as their readiness to renegotiate the terms of their proposal if reasonably requested by other members or membership-candidates. The reasonableness of these motivations, plans, and requests would be measured, in principle, against the "rationality internal to a tradition" both accepted and transformed through the dialectic of mutual recognition.

A strong commitment to the relativity of reason would lead us to affirm that the heuristic process I am describing could happen between any kind of cooperative beings, as long as they share (or come to share) in a conception of rationality. This in turn would leave us with no critical stance from which to judge the legitimacy, say, of a "sovereign" group of Islamic fundamentalists, Nazi white men, or whatever. If groups of this kind manage to obtain external recognition, their legitimate sovereignty has to be accepted. If they do not, still they would be right to claim, from their internal point of view, that they do constitute a sovereign community and that the irrationality, error, or wickedness of other peoples is depriving them of recognition.

A less strong commitment to the relativity of reason would give us resources to criticize certain kinds of motivations, plans, and requirements. This is the path I try to indicate below.

Truthfulness and reasonableness (here tokens for discursive commitments) are requirements of successful communication. And without a successful communication the constitution of the community would never be achieved, because it could never gather the individuals' consent. For the individual, the struggle for external recognition appears as a competition among allegiances: ideally, she can pay her allegiance to one of several communities. When one of the competing communities tries to impose itself through force and coercion, while another successfully uses its communicative powers—particularly if this use implies setting up a formalized system of rights of access to public discussion and collective decision making [13]—the latter can be predicted to get more support from rational individuals.

It must be observed that the allegiance of the individual and the success of the community thus described are at a normative level, and may not coincide with the political status quo. That is, the individual may be forced to accept a sovereign to whom she would not pay uncoerced allegiance. That subject would never be seen as the "true" or proper sovereign. As for the community, it can succeed in constituting itself as authoritative for its members without getting formal political recognition because of the obstacles interposed by a competing (hostile) community. My point is that, at a normative level, this struggle is won by the community disposed to set up the system of rights and institutions necessary to channel individual aims into the collective will through true communication (or even through uncoerced bargaining). Coercion (as well as persuasion or sham) may succeed temporarily, but eventually, only a community built on the premises necessary for the cooperative construction of norms will be authoritative for its members, and could convincingly claim autonomy (that is, sovereignty) against others.

When a community based on free participation and cooperation (let's call it legitimate for its members) competes with another, which tries to impose itself coercively, it is no wonder that the first becomes strong and capable of posing rational claims which, in turn, give it an advantageous position in the political and conceptual negotiations for sovereignty. Such a community would erect itself as the proper subject of sovereignty for its members and for impartial external agents, and the effective exercise of its right is only a matter of time, opportunity, or political expediency.

The Failure of the Sovereign Self

On the contrary, when the first proponents fail to establish free channels of communication and negotiation inside the forming community, they will not get the allegiance of a critical mass of candidates for membership. In this case, there are two open paths. The first one is to go on negotiating the definition of the community. Through subtle modifications of the aims and description of the group it may be possible to give access to persons to whom it was previously denied. This requires, of course, the existence of candidates disposed to enter the group under new (perhaps more democratic) conditions. Depending on the success of this attempt, the group may either reach a critical number and go on to establish a legitimate community, or it may not. In the second case, it has to transform the aim of self-government into the ideology of a political party that plays in the democratic field of an already existing sovereign polity (along with other parties). The nationalist party is, thus, a monument either to the inadequacies of the first proponents' plan and attitude or to the efficiency of the existing state in providing solid grounds for individual allegiance.

The second open path is the constitution of a closed community. In this case, the integration through participation is abandoned in favor of integration based on what I will call pre-modern personal loyalties. Groups of this kind are bound to be always minorities in liberal societies. Claims to full sovereignty may be out of the question because their very survival is always in peril. In view of this, they may pose claims for partial sovereignty; or they may accept the degree of autonomy they may enjoy within a tolerant state, while endlessly longing for a broader self-government. In any event, they could not be regarded as legitimate subjects of sovereignty by enfranchised individuals, but only by "believers" who share in the strict convictions that support pre-modern forms of social integration; therefore, they will never achieve full external recognition.

Think for example of Jehovah's Witnesses. Under a democratic constitution, they would certainly constitute a sovereign community in regard to the religious beliefs and ethical rules of the members (the religious leaders would be the ultimate authority in this regard for the members). However, they are not taken as authoritative regarding their own children's care in cases when their religious beliefs would lead them to impede necessary blood transfusions. The same could be said of the gypsy community in regard to its traditional ways of imparting justice.

Conclusion

This sketch tries to establish the normative character of the subject of sovereignty without the prejudice of nationhood as the only candidate. My argument is directed to an enfranchised individual who, in order not to be subjected to another's will, aspires to be a full citizen in a democratic community. Such an individual represents minimum conditions of rationality. In other words, that person represents the underlying assumptions of the dominant and more universal understanding of rationality. These assumptions establish the conditions for the general acceptability of a normative argument. If such an enfranchised individual accepted my construction, I would take it to be rational, and so a good candidate for a correct definition of the proper subject of sovereignty.

The tentative conclusion of this reflection is that the only rationally acceptable subject of sovereignty is the product of a free social normative construction involving both the political rules of the collective opinion formation and decision making and the personal allegiances and self-images of the individual members. This process and its outcome are rational for the individual because it was freely initiated and no single participant was obliged to adhere. Each participant can normatively reconstruct the reasons for her to accept the commitments implied by an honest process of mutual recognition. Specifically, rights of free political participation and access to public discussion, as well as basic equal rights protecting life and well-being, will be the minimum required conditions to consider it rational to take part in the constitution of a self-conscious political community. In this sense, Habermas is right when he suggests that popular sovereignty has withdrawn into democratic procedures and the demanding communicative presuppositions of their implementation. [14]

Enfranchised individuals will not accept as legitimate the decrees of an illegitimate sovereign, no matter what fiction is used to rhetorically justify its actions. Nobody will accept torture, political persecution, or limitations of her rights just because they are decisions of the sovereign. There are no sovereigns over our lives, bodies, and thoughts except us. Millions of people just leave their homelands and move to freer or safer countries. With this act they do not show a lack of commitment to their political community; they do show that they are committed to their only legitimate political community: that in which the conditions for freedom and participation are preserved. Or, as Fichte put it, "a true State of Right, as never has been seen in the world . . ., for the freedom grounded in the equality of all those who have a human face." [15]

Sovereignty is essentially linked to legitimacy; and legitimacy can only be defined as rational acceptability. And only universal rights and democratic procedures can secure individual rational support. This is why the proper subject of sovereignty must be a community freely built by the interactive normative decisions of its members and recognized in a free dialogue with other agents.

Once a proper subject of sovereignty reaches its maturity, you can call it "nation" (as well as other names). The point is that nationhood should be understood, in this case, as the product of the negotiations that give rise to a proper sovereign, not as the necessary natural condition for sovereignty.

All this does not mean that only individualistic (or capitalistic) democracies can be subjects of sovereignty. On the one hand, the negotiations that normatively constitute a polity do not occur in a vacuum. They take place in the midst of traditions and concrete political cultures, which provide not only the stage but also the constructive elements of those transactions. Certain traditions and political cultures may not coincide with the liberal-democratic western tradition; however, they can be seen as legitimate and hence proper subjects of sovereignty as long as basic political rights and fair procedures (no matter how they might have been secured) are safeguarded. On the other hand, the range of normative expectations created among the members of the community depends on the aims of the first proponents; and those aims may not be comprehensive but limited to some area of common interests (cultural self-organization, commercial regulation, judicial guarantee, etc.). When aims are not comprehensive, the legitimate communities brought about do not certainly need to be states, but they still may be sovereign subjects for the normative range they cover.

At the end I have to come back to the first statement: sovereignty is in crisis. Of course it is. It is not only that the dominant conception of sovereignty has changed. Rather, the very concept of sovereignty, the frontier concept that Giorgio Agamben perspicaciously explained as being under the law and above any law, does not exist any more. [16] The sovereign is always under the law; not the positive law, but the necessary commitments entailed by open communication and expressed in democratic procedures and basic rights. We cannot meaningfully apply the classic concept of sovereignty to the conditional exercise of relative, limited, and partial powers that most local, regional, national, and international communities exert. If Habermas is right and sovereignty has withdrawn to democratic procedures, then sovereignty has simply ceased to have its classic meaning.

It is tempting to say that there can be no subject for a concept that does not exist as it used to. However, I prefer the more positive conclusion that through a proper system of rights and democratic procedures (the backbone of a thinkable universal state), a unique legitimate social normativity will emerge. And those affected will, at least in principle, sanction such social normativity, as the will to which they are committed to subject themselves. In this I coincide with Blatz, when he writes:

> To the extent that members of these communities construct these norms competently, the norms are thus legitimate and socially real norms. In this way, instances of these sorts of communities [bound together by accountability recognition] enjoy normative sovereignty within the range of normative

expectations covered by their constructions . . . . There is nothing that states have in this regard that non-state associations cannot have.[17]

Notes

1. Part of this work was realized during a stay as visiting scholar at the Department of Philosophy, Northwestern University, funded by a grant of the Spanish *Ministerio de Educación y Cultura*. I gratefully acknowledge the support of these institutions. For the edition of the text, I would like to thank John Welch.
2. "The State itself is based on general rational concepts; the same or similar everywhere. What is, then, actually national? I think: the mutual understanding between represented and representatives, and a mutual trust grounded on it.—Now, the agreement can be certainly reached about something: civil freedom," J. G. Fichte, "Aus dem Entwurfe zu einer politischen Schrift im Fruhlinge 1813," in *Saemtliche Werke*. Siebenter Band: *Zur Politik, Moral und Philosophie der Geschichte,* ed. J. H. Fichte (Berlin: Verlag von Veit und Comp., 1846), 549.
3. K. Symons-Symonolewiz, "The Concept of Nationhood: Toward a Theoretical Clarification," *Canadian Review of Studies in Nationalism* 12 (1971): 221.
4. For an illuminating account of the historical origin both of the differences between "nationalists" and "statists," and of the sameness of their underlying convictions, see J. Habermas, *The Inclusion of the Other: Studies in Political Theory*, ed. by C. Cronin and P. De Greiff (Cambridge, Mass.: The MIT Press, 1998), 105.
5. Habermas reminds us of the historical changes of the meaning of "nation" and its political implications (*The Inclusion of the Other: Studies in Political Theory*, 110-11). He also analyzes the contingent social necessities that led to the general acceptance of the nation as the subject of political self-determination. He stresses that "one cannot explain in purely normative terms how the universe of those who come together to regulate their common life by means of positive law should be composed" (115). This is why "Democracy must take the form of a national democracy because the "self" of the self-determination of the people is conceived as a macrosubject capable of action and because the ethnic nation seems to be an appropriate entity to fill this conceptual gap—it is viewed as the quasi-natural substrate of the state organization. This collectivist interpretation of the Rousseauean model of self-legislation prejudices all further considerations" (135).
6. H. Hannum, *Autonomy, Sovereignty and Self-Determination: The Acommodation of Conflicting Rights* (Philadelphia: University of Pennsylvania Press, 1990), 31.
7. G. F. A. Werther, *Self-Determination in Western Democracies. Aboriginal Politics in a Comparative Perspective* (London: Greenwood Press, 1992) and S. H. Hashmi, ed., *State Sovereignty. Change and Persistence in International Relations* (University Park: Penn State University Press, 1997) provide vivid and updated examples of ethnic groups currently demanding and negotiating sovereignty within nation-states.
8. The meaning of this assertion will be only partly explained in what follows. I derive it from the "Normative Pragmatics" developed by Robert Brandom in his *Making It Explicit* (Cambridge, Mass.: Harvard University Press, 1994), 243-66.
9. The kind of recognition I am referring to here has something in common with what Blatz calls "accountability recognition" as the form of recognition that "establishes only joint or multilateral and shared authority to determine the content, interpretation and applicability of norms. Instead of accepting the other as authoritative and normatively self-determining with respect to some range of conduct or decision making, and thereby

accepting limits upon our own norm determining behavior, we only acknowledge the other's right to explore with us the justifiability of acting or being in matters of common interests. . . . Accountability recognition can serve to establish norm-determining relationships and thus is apt to *found* normatively sovereign communities." In C. V. Blatz, "Community, Recognition and Normative Sovereignty: Reaching beyond the Boundaries of States," in *Perspectives on Third-World Sovereignty. The Postmodern Paradox*, ed. M. E. Denham and M. O. Lombardi (London: Macmillan, 1996), 64-65.

10. Not surprisingly, the metaphor used by Hegel in order to explain his abstract account of mutual recognition as constitutive of the self is the struggle between master and slave. In Hegel, *Phänomenologie des Geistes* [1807], ed. by J. Hoffmeister (Hamburg: Felix Meiner, 1952); *Phenomenology of Spirit*, trans. by A. V. Miller (Oxford: Oxford University Press, 1977), § 178-96. I cannot be faithful to the concrete Hegelian ideas at this point for I am not distinguishing all the stages involved. In my opinion, the constitution of the community (that is, the social institution of the set of "objective" norms which determine the borders of the community and the rules that the members have to observe) and the constitution of each member's self are simultaneous and "internal," so to speak, to the community. In a second stage, the subjectivity (the self) of the community is constituted through a similar process of mutual recognition among individual communities; this is the "external" recognition. However, from the methodologically individualistic point of view I am adopting, these two stages are not just two versions of the same process. They overlap; they influence each other: the process of external recognition may influence the internal constitution of the community, therefore shaping the identity of its members, who possess the active will in both processes. Unfortunately, I cannot pursue this idea here.

11. The paramount importance of the exclusion-inclusion process is acknowledged by Fichte in the clearest possible way: *"Also in dem Umfassen und im Ausschliesen in und von einem geschichtlichen Selbst besteht die Volkseinheit"* ["the People's unity consists in the accepting and excluding in and of a historical self"], J. G. Fichte, "Aus dem Entwurfe zu einer politischen Schrift im Fruhlinge 1813," 566.

12. A. McIntyre, *Whose Justice, Which Rationality* (Notre Dame, Ind.: University of Notre Dame Press, 1988), 4-10.

13. Here I am following the ideas put forward by J. Habermas in "Citizenship and National Identity." In J. Habermas, *Between Facts and Norms: Contributions to a Discourse Theory of Law and Democracy*, trans. by W. Rehg (Cambridge, Mass.: The MIT Press, 1996). 491-515; esp. 495-97. Habermas pursues the thesis that the current form of sovereignty is expressed in the acceptance of a common procedure of opinion- and collective will-formation among free and equal citizens, rather than in the agreement about authority or in the allegiance to the nation. Thus he writes: "The nation of citizens finds its identity not in ethnic and cultural commonalties, but in the practice of citizens who actively exercise their right to participation and communication" (495).

14. Habermas, *Between Facts and Norms*, 486.

15. Fichte, "Aus dem Entwurfe zu einer politischen Schrift," 573.

16. G. Agamben, *Homo Sacer. Il potere sovrano e la nuda vita* (Torino: Einaudi, 1995).

17. Blatz, "Community, Recognition and Normative Sovereignty," 76.

Chapter 8

Nationalism, Sovereignty, and Pluralism: The Case of William James

Kennan Ferguson

The problem of sovereignty is central to the question of nationhood. Long seen as essential to the identity of states and thus the highest aspiration of nationhood, sovereignty is to states what liberty is to individuals: theoretically, the right to determine one's own actions without interference. Like the politically constituted subject, the ideal state is conceived as autonomous.

Sovereignty is thus understood as the ultimate aspiration of a nation, its fundamental completion. Yet sovereignty has never fulfilled this promise; the history of state sovereignty is also a history of coercion, war, and intervention. The first half of this chapter builds on contemporary examinations of sovereignty that identify its exclusions and limitations, arguing that the underlying theoretical construction of sovereignty also fatally undermines its ideals.

On the other hand, the deployment of the philosophy of sovereignty has had many variations in its complex history, both salutary and pernicious. In the second half of the chapter I explicate an alternative conception of sovereignty, one that celebrates the heterogeneity of nations and states as central to comprehending the significance of a state's self-identity. At the beginning of the twentieth century, as is well known, the United States was engaged in its most wide-ranging imperialist expansion ever, increasing its control over such distant countries as Hawaii and the Philippines. In this historical period an explicit connection was created between anti-imperialism and the celebration of autonomy, and it was in the thought of William James that these connections are most overtly made formal. Through these connections an alternative, pluralist conception of sovereignty emerged, one with the potential to inform contemporary understandings of international relations.

Intersections of Sovereignties

Sovereignty as a conceptual basis for national autonomy has emerged over the last four centuries as the dominant theoretical basis for understanding relationships between states. The idea that states have the moral and political right to ultimate self-governance, as developed by Jean Bodin and Thomas Hobbes, is largely taken for granted in the formulation of international policy and state relations. And yet the problem of sovereignty, the theoretical justifications for the unconditional dominance of state-centered absolutism, are increasingly contested, within both academic thought and everyday practices.

The end of the Cold War, the dominance of transnational capital, and the explosion of information and communication technologies are customarily given as the reasons for this contestation. But the inconsistencies of sovereignty far predate these contemporary events. From its intellectual founding, sovereignty has needed to neglect or repress alternative conceptions of authority; the problems of founding a state and the problems of founding an intellectual justification for that state have been intertwined from the beginning. [1]

In attempting to replace the complex arrangements of theological authority and economic feudalism with a specifically political nationalism, the architects of sovereignty constructed a world where authorization for political action was limited to the state and where political identities were reduced to citizenship. Yet in this construction—and in the necessary overthrow of these previous authorities—these theories reconstituted human identity in ways that subverted the goals of sovereignty; in creating political identities that resisted previous powers, they created political identities that could resist the new governance as well.

Hobbes, for example, famously grounded the authority of the sovereign in the protection of the individual: it is the Leviathan who protects each person from the "war of all against all" that naturally arises from the essential equality of men. In doing so, of course, he necessarily privileges the autonomy of the individual as not only the purpose of the state but also its cause. His fictional "state of nature" narrative serves to position the state as the necessary counterbalance to the inherent sovereignty of man. Without the contractual unification of autonomous humans, their autonomy sabotages itself. To create the sovereignty of the state, Hobbes must produce the sovereign individual. He recognizes that this causes sovereignty to be based on intrinsically unstable support; thus the limitation that one is free from one's political obligations when the sovereign threatens one's life.

The sovereignty of the state, therefore, is based on its exact opposite. If individuals are truly sovereign, as Hobbes insists more strongly than anyone before him, then state power is vestigial and parasitic. In this conception, it is the power of the Leviathan that must be strengthened in order to simultaneously protect and obliterate this individual sovereignty. But it is also the individual who must acquiesce in this obliteration. It is the individual who is the implicit reader of Hobbes's text, a reader who will subsequently reason that the power the state has is justified.[2]

Positioning this conflict as central to the sovereignty project explains many of the peculiarities that arise in the history of sovereignty. Both Hobbes and Bodin, for example, insist on the impossibility of sovereign alienation: they both insist that the rights of monarchs cannot be relinquished, circumscribed, or estranged. Yet their very insistence points to their apprehension about its possibility. One may ask: why bother to insist that the impossible cannot happen? Similarly, as David Campbell has pointed out in his work on Bosnia, the entire premise of Hobbesian order necessarily bases itself on the (putatively) inescapable reality of disorder. The work of subject formation, that of the individual and of the nation, therefore serves to justify the exclusion, even the violent exclusion, of those who are unable to be integrated into the sovereignty that is presupposed as necessary.[3]

In other words, Bodin and Hobbes construct a system in which the autonomy of the subject and the authority of the state are interdependent. And yet autonomy by its very nature is supposed to be, well, autonomous: absolute, independent, and unconstrained. There is an unacknowledged complexity to the existence of interdependent autonomies. Additionally, these mutually iterated sovereignties, that of the subject and that of the state, cannot possibly coexist: as Daniel Warner has noted, the claims of the state upon the individual are limited by no power external to the state.[4] Even when the Hobbesian relation between state and populace is reversed, as in Rousseau's insistence that the people instead of the government are sovereign or Hegel's aspiration that the state is merely the concrete manifestation of the will of the people, the sovereignty of the individual cannot coexist with the will of the nation. The hierarchy of freedom and authority that each constructs, for all the differences between the two thinkers, results in the dissolution of subjectivity into citizen.[5]

Thus the project of politics becomes the negotiation of these incommensurable yet mutually foundational ideas. "The new modern world of spatially separated sovereigns and subjects having been constituted," as Rob Walker puts it, the theoretical project becomes "that of working out how it could be put back together again—how individual and collective, public and private, state sovereignty and public sovereignty, and so on, could be reconciled."[6] Those questions and paradoxes, in short, have underlain the question of sovereignty—and thus of individual subjects, nation-states, and politics generally—throughout modernity.

Other alleged sources of sovereignty are similarly troubled by the bases of its very creation. The Treaty of Westphalia, often identified as the emergence of interstate sovereignty by international relations scholars, is a turning point in the establishment of a horizontal space of states as Europe's primary actors. The Westphalian logic that underlies the mutuality of state recognition is generally understood as that which gives nation-states the authority to speak for the populations which reside within: each government, however constituted, recognizes (or does not recognize) another government as its sovereign equal.

It was not the Peace of Westphalia that created this system wholesale, of course.[7] But the system that emerged in fits and starts during the course of the seventeenth century reached a particularly idealized form in the treaty, an idealized form still with us. The need of those who controlled the mechanisms of state to formalize and mediate relations of power with others served to 1) create an interstate system, and 2) reify the legitimation of those individuals as the sole and authentic leaders of "their" territories and peoples, a legitimation that was constituted from without as well as from within.

There are two noteworthy aspects to this process. The first, as historical accounts cannot help but note, is that the sovereignty of states did not immediately become widely accepted upon the signing of the treaty, even in Europe: the Holy Roman Empire continued until the beginning of the nineteenth century, and many cities and fiefdoms in areas such as present-day Italy fiercely resisted statist consolidation.[8] State sovereignty, in other words, was not instantly triumphalist; the battles between it and other forms of political power both pre- and ante-date Westphalia.

Most accounts of the history of interstate acceptance of sovereignty explain these battles as a delay in intellectual development. F. H. Hinsley, for example, explains that Westphalian conceptions did not immediately become ubiquitous due to people's inability to epistemologically comprehend that the world was "composed of separate political communities."[9] This analysis may seem correct in hindsight, but only if the development of the contemporary interstate system was in fact teleologically inescapable, if the contemporary arrangements of the state-system are the absolute and correct answer to the problems of the distribution of political power. For those for whom authority ought not be reducible to the state—on the other hand, for those whose identities exceed, undercut, or are more complex than that of "citizen"—the conception of the spatially limited but absolute power of the state was seen as disabling, pernicious, or even sacrilegious. Indeed, for many it continues to be so.

The second noteworthy aspect is that the ideal of Westphalian sovereignty is profoundly dependent on that which it denies, in ways profoundly akin to the dependencies of Hobbesian sovereignty. International sovereignty, the exclusive and total authority within the borders of the state, can be neither truly exclusive nor total; if the international system is that which endows this authority, then that authority is always based at least in part on the recognition of those from without the state. The very existence and being of a "sovereign entity," then, "presupposes an institutional framework in which it is recognized by others." [10] The goal and design of sovereignty, to be free from dependence on alternative sources of power, is therefore subverted by the recognition that is constantly needed to constitute it.

That such recognition is at least partially dependent on extrasovereign sources has long been emphasized by those who want to displace the "realist" approach to international relations and replace it with approaches that emphasize norms and institutions. [11] But even the vast majority of these theories do not fundamentally critique the dilemmas of a putative sovereignty that relies on institutional frameworks; their authors accept the idea of sovereignty unproblematically as the precondition of their theories and then attempt to show how norms and organizations mitigate the anarchic effects of that sovereignty. States, that is, are seen as existing as sovereign entities around which networks of control and recognition are to be built; those networks are not properly seen as constitutive of the very existences and definitions of the sovereign states.

The constituted nature of sovereignty is made more tangible first through accounts that show the evolution of the idea of sovereignty as itself a normalizing development: one that is historically located, partial, and in constant need of reinscription. [12] Second, the fact that claims to sovereignty are necessarily oriented to external constituency (e.g., China decrying the involvement of human rights organizations and the United States in its "internal affairs") undermines the very claim on which they are based, both in audience (to whom is China speaking?) and in intent (Why does China feel the need to speak at all?); that fact of exteriority belies the understanding of sovereignty as intrinsically autonomous. [13] Third, this difficulty is made manifest in the practices of sovereignty, for example the oft-noted incongruity that countries who most insist on the actuality of sovereignty (e.g., the United States) are also in the habit of repeatedly finding vindications for interstate intervention.

These difficulties, intrinsic to the very concept of sovereignty, have resulted in many voices in international relations over the course of the twentieth century calling for the abolition of the concept in politics and political science. Well-respected international relations scholars—Charles Merriman at the turn of the century, Harold Laski and Léon Duguit in the First World War period, and R. M. MacIver and Jacques Maritain at mid-century—argued that the concept of sovereignty lacked legal foundation, historical precedent, philosophical usefulness, or empirical authenticity. [14] Sovereignty, they asserted repeatedly, is a bankrupt concept, used by states as a cover for intervention, as a justification of blindness to human suffering, as an excuse to inflict ruthless cruelties, and it should thus be banished from the lexicon of international concerns.

And yet the language of sovereignty continues unabated: it is perhaps the most used and reused trope in the international vocabulary. A government wishes to turn aside criticism of its treatment of a minority culture? Sovereignty. What is bolstered by the Law of the Sea? Sovereignty. What does the World Trade Organization protect? Sovereignty. What American resource is threatened by creeping one-worldism? Sovereignty.

In other words, to hope to reject the terminology of sovereignty entirely is undoubtedly implausible, though there are still those who would have us move "beyond sovereignty." [15] For one, it is deeply enough ingrained at this point that its use would be relatively impossible to terminate. But not only does it underlie the linguistic structures and normative assumptions of interstate relations, the term also continues to have useful purposes: serving as a theoretical and utilitarian bulwark, for example, against the excesses of international capital and global homogenization. An idealized national independence also has intense rhetorical and emotional force in the case of those peoples forced to undergo hundreds of years of colonialism under the brutality of Western imperialism. [16] Sovereignty clearly has its uses. And yet the intrinsic contradictions within the very concept make it impossible to use unproblematically.

These recognitions of the difficulties of sovereignty have led in recent years to an explosion of scholarship that addresses the sovereignty problematic in a new way: as a historical process that replaces one set of political predicaments with new ones. The modern difficulties are negotiated through a variety of means, each well explicated by contemporary theoreticians of international relations: for example, through the displacement of ontological insecurity into constructing a threat of the "foreign" (Richard Ashley, David Campbell), by focusing on the role of non-state actors with negligible access to state decisionmaking (Rob Walker, Cynthia Enloe), or by examining the underlying symbolic construction of state legitimacy (James Der Derian, Michael Shapiro). [17] Still others, such as Cynthia Weber, confront the concept of sovereignty directly, arguing that one can understand it only as an historical "simulation," wherein the false oppositions of "intervention" and "sovereignty" are seemingly adversarial but in fact continuously justify one another, where sovereignty and threats to sovereignty replace and reinforce each other. [18]

What these approaches all have in common is the recognition that sovereignty is not an essential or natural characteristic of states. Instead, they look at the ways in which states construct themselves in relation to philosophical, linguistic, and historical practices. It is these practices that give rise to sovereignty: sovereignty as a crucially multifarious artifact, a part of the international world that always works fragmentarily. Sovereignty, they show, promises a closure that will never come.

The Pluralistic Outlook

Instead of further reiterating the ultimate indecipherability of sovereignty, however, I want to use the remainder of this chapter to investigate a particular historical conception of it, a way in which it was popularized as an appropriate vehicle for national identity. Before the absolute conflation of sovereignty with ideology that was a hallmark of the Cold War, before the Germanic conception of a fascist sovereignty as the culmination of a people's solidarity, before the Wilsonian iteration of sovereignty as the automatically liberal/capitalist goal for peoples not yet competent to achieve that goal, before all these was an understanding of sovereignty that both helped form contemporary conceptions of sovereignty and provided a convincing alternative to them.

For the American philosopher William James, the right of a people to determine their own destiny was morally crucial. Akin to many of these other versions, his was a "strong" conception of sovereignty. It was seen as central to the rights of states, the substance of international relations, and the ethical practice of governance; James emphatically did not have the latter-day suspicion of the goals of the nation-state. National independence stood as the highest good to which a people could aspire, and its achievement was to be celebrated.

But intrinsic to Jamesian sovereignty was a radically pluralistic streak, one that went missing even two decades later in the Wilsonian ideology of self-determination that ostensibly resembled James's. For James, the ability to create one's own destiny was sacrosanct, but it remained an ability that was informed by and dependent on others. States, like individuals, could never truly exist on their own, he argued; it is only through difference and contestation that either can truly reach their full ability and achieve the richness of a well-lived life. This pluralistic epistemology set James's philosophy and international politics apart, both from his contemporaries and from those who came after him.

It is of primary importance to distinguish Jamesian pluralism from the later philosophic trajectory of the concept of "political pluralism." The better-known pluralism that emerges during the course of the twentieth century (e.g., that of Robert Dahl), in which the state functions as a formal but normatively empty structure through which various interest groups contest one another, bears virtually no resemblance to James's celebration of pluralist difference. [19] Nor does one of its offshoots, namely, the occasional use of the term "pluralism" within the field of international relations instead of "liberalism" or "idealism" comes from a further segregation of the term from James's original meaning. For James, pluralism and difference is an aspiration; without the opposition of other ways of making sense of the world, he argues, life can have no significance. For latter-day pluralists, on the other hand, pluralism is an inconvenient fact of modern-day life, requiring states and systems to negotiate those unpleasant dissimilarities of political coalitions and interest groups. Such a conception relies on a severe impoverishment of plurality, positioning difference as exclusively organizational, that is, as consisting of "autonomous organizations within the domain of a state."[20]

The central tension in James's philosophy was the same as the central tension in his politics: the conflict between, on the one hand, the creation and valuation of difference and, on the other, the existence of (and people's preference for) systems that demand unity. According to James, philosophy and politics both required the attempt to take proper account of the shared senses of lived experiences as well as the unalterably separate nature of these experiences.[21] That other people could live in ways that are unusual to us, even alien to our standards, is what gives meaning to our own ways of life, according to James.

James told a personal parable in a public lecture to drive the point home. He informed his audience that, from a train traversing the North Carolinian wilderness, he looked out the window and saw a scarified land: a clearing where trees had been blasted from the ground, a cabin rough-hewn and out of plumb, a serpentine fence going nowhere and a protection from nothing. Squalor in the midst of a sylvan idyll, this clearing was an affront to James's sensibilities, at least at first: it showed the very baseness of man's development and his generalized disregard for the beauty of nature. But upon further reflection, and upon discussing the ethos of progress that informed the denizens of nearby comparable homes, James realized something far different was at work.

It was not that the residents did not see this house as an affront to nature. Like James's, their understanding was that such a clearing was antithetical to the natural order. But unlike him, they saw such an affront as a victory: the working-man's ability to transform the disordered wilderness into civilization. The clearing, James pointed out to his audience, "which was to me a mere ugly picture on the retina, was to them a symbol redolent with moral memories and sang a very paean of duty, struggle, and success."[22] James recognized that his own limitations blinded him to the "significance" of such constructions; his cultural and social position discouraged an ability to understand the legitimacy of others' worlds.

This is not merely the tolerating liberalism of the late twentieth century, in which one is meant to endure the dissimilarities of others. James did not simply allow others to destroy "their" woods while leaving his in peace (or, worse, attempt to convince these others that their figurative struggle against nature was wrong, or misguided, or contraposed to historical reality). Instead, his is a constitutive, active, embrace of the *need* for difference: James considers himself transformed, elevated, and educated by this incidental encounter with a way of life dissimilar to his own. Without this realization, James recounts, he would have continued his life intellectually impoverished, blind to the legitimacy of the rural land-workers' views.

Sovereignty, Dependence, and Difference

So what, exactly, is the relationship between a Jamesian radical pluralism and the aforementioned sovereignty problematic? One noteworthy aspect of the relationship is historical: James became well-known to the American people not only for his construction of pragmatism but also for his public pronouncements—letters, essays, speeches—against American imperialism. A second is the degree to which internationalization and globalization were central questions in his time; when James begins to be interested in international affairs, the international economy was more integrated than it is presently.[23] A third aspect is that these two interests emerged in tandem: it was essentially during the last decade of his life when he emerged both as a publicly renowned pacifist/anti-imperialist and as a pluralist. As James was becoming increasingly interested in pluralism, he was also positioning himself against his former student Theodore Roosevelt in a series of letters published in national newspapers. In these letters James defended the right to dissent publicly, the right to self-governance, and ultimately, the right for other nations to exist on terms the United States might never understand.

Though this aspect of his thought is overlooked in most philosophical biographies, it was well known at the time and contributed to the popular reception given to both his philosophy of pragmatism and pluralism. Publicly, James was most closely identified with his criticism of McKinleyite imperialism. The capriciousness of the Spanish-American War, the annexation of the Philippines, and the United States's involvement in the overthrow of the Hawaiian monarchy all drove James to speak out against the imposition of American power on other countries.[24]

His public stance was slow in appearing. Privately, James was critical of the "madness" of the American Congress as early as the sinking of the *Maine;* he already saw in such "perfectly honest humanitarianism" the seeds of the imperialism to come.[25] As the crisis with Spain escalated, James became fascinated with the ways in which the psychology of crowds was stimulated and exercised by an administration interested in expansion, and he began to suspect the ideological underpinnings of the creation of excitement and heroism that enabled the U.S. government to act in violent and warlike ways.

But it was not until the turn of the century that James was publicly (and vociferously) criticizing the McKinley administration's peremptory colonization of the Philippines. In a series of letters to influential newspapers, James began to decry the American involvements abroad, identifying as "hegelian" the misguided idea that all countries should have the same goals and aims, and that the United States was thus in a position to show the way to other states. The fundamental multiplicity of humanity, he argued, makes the domination of others fundamentally immoral; the United States, therefore, did not and could not have the right to control the destinies of other countries. James's public pronouncements until his death continued likewise: he persisted in his outrage at imperialism in all its forms, and he continued to openly criticize it despite his failing health.

James's arguments were in clear contrast to the Mugwumpery for which other prominent anti-imperialists of the time were known. Even beyond the actual Mugwumps, for whom imperialism's worst effects were the corruption of the ideals of America and the coarsening of the nation, other predominant anti-imperialists gave dubious reasons for their opposition to imperialism. E. L. Godkin, editor of the *Nation* and the *New York Evening Post*, was famous for his antipathy to the American imperialism of the time, but he based his opposition on what colonialism did to the U.S. Constitution, and what close contact with "alien, inferior, and mongrel races" would do to Americans.[26] Edward Atkinson's famed opposition to American involvement in the Philippines came in large part from his conviction that American boys would return from abroad infected with "venereal disease."[27] Andrew Carnegie, with more money behind him than the rest of the anti-imperialists, fulminated publicly about the cost of imperialism, the damage to American "moral fiber," and the loss of international respect.[28] All three of these public figures shared, in their opposition to the expansionist foreign policy of the McKinley and Roosevelt administrations, a concern not for the non-Americans being invaded and killed but for the damaging effects of colonialism and imperialism on the citizens of the United States.

James, on the other hand, argued against expansionism on the grounds that the American presumptions that underlay imperialism were neither necessary nor even beneficial to the colonized. The United States, he argued, could not understand other cultures and thus had no right attempting to shape or control them. The sovereignty of other nations, for James, was not exactly the same as the individual pluralism he professed, but it was the same mistrust of absolutism and unity undergirding both. The internal truth of different individuals and the internal truth of different cultures, he believed, are linked; one cannot believe in the empirical authenticity of the first without also recognizing the latter. The recognition of these truths, for James, necessitated respect for these others, be they peoples or countries. It is injurious for a country to impose its system of government on another—not merely for the country imposed upon but for the ethical constitution of the empire-minded country. The latter needs to discover how to learn from alterity rather than merely conquering it.

The reason for the United States not to annex the Philippines, for example, had more to do with the liberties and rights of the Filipinos than with the effects of that annexation on Americans. In this James was resisting both the imperialist's language of the necessity to improve the Filipino character (in fact, he pointed out, the United States was killing Filipinos) and the anti-imperialists' nativist focus.[29] In one series of arguments against American intervention in the Philippines James inveighed against the emotional and intellectual distance that the Americans perpetuated between themselves and the Filipinos. The United States, he said, tries to organize the world according to its own principles and conceptions, and it thus ignores the possibility that those who are objects of American intrigues "could have any feeling or insides of their own . . . that might possibly need to be considered in our arrangements"(*W*, 160). He argued that it was impossible for U.S. politicians to regulate the "souls" of the Filipinos, since these politicians could not even understand other Americans' souls.[30]

Years later, in 1904, James continued to argue that American interventionism in the Philippines was primarily an inability to let other countries constitute their own national identities. "No people," he argued, "learns to live except by trying" (*W*, 179). And American concerns, though concealed in a cloak of morality, could not adequately justify the oppression of others, even if those others do not correspond to particularly American conceptions of the moral: "if they fail to be good exactly according to our notions, is not the world full even now of other people of whom the same can be said . . .?" (*W*, 179) James overtly draws the parallels between the autonomy of individuals, which he positions as universally accepted by his audience, and that of nations, which deserve the same liberties, even if they fail to live up to what Americans perceive as their responsibilities.

Philosophically, James made possible a hermeneutics of cultures; politically, he demanded acknowledgment of the right of other peoples to determine the terms for their own existence. His conception of sovereignty is clearly tied closely to nationalism (there is no hint in his writings, for example, that the Philippines are not naturally unitary), but the underlying language of legitimacy of nationhood is changed. No longer should it be the United States, or even the West, that defines which countries are worthy of sovereignty and which need to be pushed to that point of readiness; it should be those countries themselves. Such "international comparisons," James argues, "are a great waste of time—at any rate, international judgments and the passing of sentences are. Every nation has ideals and difficulties and sentiments which are an impenetrable secret to one not of the blood. Let them alone."[31]

Sovereignty, in this conception, is self-legitimating, accruing naturally to a people. The distance between nations makes it consistently unjust for the people of one country to claim to know what is better for a people than the people themselves. That the United States imposed its own version of control over the Filipinos constitutes a fundamental affront to this version of sovereignty.

The same affront reemerges half a century later, when the United States "relinquishes sovereignty" over the Philippines in 1946. As Roxanne Lynn Doty points out, the term "sovereignty" continues at this time to operate at a purely symbolic level. What, for example, is one to make of the fact that the United States continues to determine policy for the Philippines in the areas of trade (occasionally in direct violation of the Philippine Constitution) and in the regulation of arms purchases? What, Doty asks, is the meaning of the term "sovereignty" when all its "empirical referents" appear to be "missing?"[32] The version of sovereignty prevalent in the United States at the time (and presently) encourages such actions; a Jamesian interpretation would overtly proscribe them.

James's combination of respect and pluralism extended beyond his interest in international state affairs, of course. For James, the political tendencies toward monism were as strong within the United States as without. Indeed, he saw the two as inextricably linked: as the modern world was constantly being systematized in increasingly unitary ways, individuals within that world were subject to increasingly strict mandates for homogeneity. And homogeneity, for James, was the "hegelian" demand that all people behave, talk, and think in one allegedly correct way; the same concern, in fact, that underlies much contemporary opposition to market globalism.[33] As opposed to this, James wanted to celebrate those people who were overtly not like him, for it was they who could teach and change him: people who loved war, people who hated nature, people who believed in the afterlife, Cubans, Hawaiians, Filipinos.

In these cases James found it not only possible but necessary to look beyond his own beliefs, his own most treasured aspirations for humanity, in order to understand where they conflicted with others' ideals. He wanted to see ideas with which he disagreed fully realized; he did not merely want people to understand views that conflicted with their own, but to actually hope to see those other views actualized. He wanted those who agreed with him to see their own shortsightedness. This kind of pluralism arises from not only a true commitment to the possibility of forms of difference but also a recognition of the legitimacy of those forms.

James's international pluralism is not Wilson's later liberalism; where Wilson endeavored to give other countries sovereignty, it was a sovereignty along the lines he envisioned, a specifically pro-American, free-market, ersatz-Caucasian sovereignty.[34] Those countries that failed to meet Wilson's standards of authenticity, such as Mexico or the Soviet Union, found themselves on the other end of interventions. James's radical pluralism, conversely, encouraged the autonomy of those peoples who specifically differed from American values: those were the countries who most deserved to make their own way in the world. Not only was it the height of arrogance to want to mold those countries into pale replicas of the United States, James believed that without their continued practical experimentation the entire world would be impoverished.

These aspects of Jamesian pluralism can also continue to inform other aspects of politics, even in a post-imperialist world. For example, the narrow focus on democratically representative elections currently evinced by U. S. foreign policy often supports this particular form of governmental legitimation at the expense of human rights, minority rights, and civil liberty. What is fundamentally improved by a popularly elected tyrant immediately suppressing dissent and quashing opposing viewpoints? James shows that instruments of dissent, such as a free press and private associations, have as much civil import as majoritarian rule, if not more. James reminds us that forms of opposition are important in their own right, that the ultimate goal of societies and governments should be not stability but rather the opportunity to express disagreement.

But even further, James reminds us that it is from opposition that we discover those things that are most important to us. In doing so, he creates a different way to think about sovereignty: not as an interstate system of recognition but as the countenance of alterity that makes identity meaningful. To endorse the sovereignty of others—be they states or individuals—can be as much about challenging ourselves as about demanding recognition. It can be the realization that we are always involved with others, even in asking to be let alone. It can be an engagement with the world based on terms we do not ourselves control.

Notes

1. For many years, in fact for much of the history of political philosophy, the problem of founding has continued as a conundrum for philosophers reaching from Hobbes to Rousseau to Arendt to Rawls to Derrida. See Bonnie Honig, *Political Theory and the Displacement of Politics* (Ithaca, N. Y.: Cornell University Press, 1993).

2. Richard Ashley emphasizes the degree to which it is the rationality of the individual that sets him up as "the modern *sovereign*." See his "Border Lines: Man, Post-structuralism, and War" in *International/Intertextual Relations*, ed. James Der Derian and Michael Shapiro (New York: Lexington Books, 1989), 265.

3. David Campbell, *National Deconstruction: Violence, Identity, and Justice in Bosnia* (Minneapolis: University of Minnesota Press, 1998).

4. Daniel Warner, "Searching for Responsibility/Community in International Relations," in *Moral Spaces: Rethinking Ethics and World Politics*, ed. David Campbell and Michael Shapiro (Minneapolis: University of Minnesota Press, 1999), 9.

5. See Steven Johnston, *Encountering Tragedy: Rousseau and the Project of Democratic Order* (Ithaca, N. Y.: Cornell University Press, 1999), esp. 75-89.

6. R. B. J. Walker, "Forward," in *Sovereignty and Subjectivity*, ed. Jenny Edkins, Nalani Persram, and Véronique Pin-Fat (Boulder, Colo.: Lynne Rienner, 1999), x.

7. Nor, as Jens Bartleson reminds us, is the concept of the "international" reducible to the advent of the modern state. On the other hand, the two are logically linked, both made possible through shared historical and political developments. See *A Genealogy of Sovereignty* (Cambridge: Cambridge University Press, 1995), 209.

8. Alexander B. Murphy provides a nuanced historical reading of these periods in his essay "The Sovereign State System as Political-Territorial Ideal: Historical and Contemporary Considerations" in *State Sovereignty and Social Construct*, ed. Thomas J. Biersteker and Cynthia Weber (Cambridge: Cambridge University Press), 81-120.

9. F. H. Hinsley, *Sovereignty*, 2nd ed. (Cambridge: Cambridge University Press, 1986), 159.

10. Alexander Wendt and Daniel Friedheim, "Hierarchy under Anarchy: Informal Empire and the East German State," in *State Sovereignty as Social Construct*, 240-77, 247.

11. See, for a few samples of this approach, James N. Rosenau, *The Study of Global*

Interdependence: Essays on the Transnationalism of World Affairs (New York: Nichols, 1980); John A. Vasquez, *The Power of Power Politics: A Critique* (New Brunswick: Rutgers University Press, 1983); Robert O. Keohane, *After Hegemony: Cooperation and Discord in the World Political Economy* (Princeton: Princeton University Press, 1984) and, co-edited with Joseph Nye, *Transnational Relations and World Politics* (Cambridge: Harvard University Press, 1972); or, more recently, Ernst B. Hass, *Nationalism, Liberalism, and Progress* (Ithaca, N. Y.: Cornell University Press).

12. Cynthia Weber, for example, engages in an extensive and invaluable historiography of ways that "practices of sovereignty" are used to undergird the legitimacy of the state, in *Simulating Sovereignty: Intervention, the State, and Symbolic Exchange* (Cambridge: Cambridge University Press, 1995).

13. For further reflections on this paradox, see Richard K. Ashley and R. B. J. Walker, "Reading Dissidence/Writing the Discipline: Crisis and the Question of Sovereignty in International Studies," *International Studies Quarterly* 34, no. 3, 367-416.

14. Charles E. Merriman, *Studies in the Problem of Sovereignty since Rousseau* (New York: Columbia University Press, 1990); Harold J. Laski, *The Foundations of Sovereignty and Other Essays* (New York: Harcourt, Brace, 1921) and *Studies in the Problem of Sovereignty* (New York: Howard Fertig, 1968); Léon Duguit, *Law in The Modern State* (New York: Viking Press, 1919) Robert MacIver, *The Web of Government* (New York: MacMillan Company, 1947); Jacques Maritain, *Man and the State* (Chicago: University of Chicago Press, 1957).

15. Maryann K. Cusimano, *Beyond Sovereignty: Issues for a Global Agenda* (New York: Bedford, 2000).

16. Many of these issues are raised in the excellent essays collected by Mark Denham and Mark Owen Lombardi in *Perspectives on Third-World Sovereignty: The Postmodern Paradox* (London: MacMillan, 1996).

17. Richard Ashley, "Untying the Sovereign State: A Double Reading of the Anarchy Problematique," *Millennium* 17 (1988), 227-63; David Campbell, *Writing Security: United States Foreign Policy and the Politics of Identity* (Minneapolis: University of Minnesota Press, 1992); R. B. J. Walker, *One World, Many Worlds: Struggles for a Just World Peace* (Boulder, Colo.: Lynne Reiner, 1988); Cynthia Enloe, *Bananas, Beaches and Bases: Making Feminist Sense of World Politics* (Berkeley: University of California Press); James Der Derian, *On Diplomacy: A Genealogy of Western Estrangement* (New York: Basil Blackwell, 1987); Michael J. Shapiro, *Violent Cartographies: Mapping Cultures of War* (Minneapolis: University of Minnesota Press, 1997).

18. Weber, *Simulating Sovereignty*.

19. Robert Dahl, *Pluralistic Democracy in the United States* (Chicago: Rand McNally & Co, 1967) and *Dilemmas of Pluralist Democracy: Autonomy vs. Control* (New Haven, Conn.: Yale University Press, 1982).

20. Dahl, *Dilemmas of Pluralist Democracy*, 5.

21. William James, *Writings, 1902-1910* (New York: Viking Press, 1987), 1159-82. Hereafter *W*.

22. "On a Certain Blindness in Human Beings," *Talks to Teachers on Psychology and to Students on Some of Life's Ideals* (New York: Norton, 1958), 133-34. Two noteworthy commentators have taken this story of James's very seriously and argued that it plays a central role in James's political thought; I am indebted to both George Cotkin's *William James, Public Philosopher* (Urbana: University of Illinois Press, 1989) and Joshua L. Miller's *Democratic Temperament: The Legacy of William James* (Lawrence: University Press of Kansas, 1997).

23. Robert Wade, "Globalization and its Limits: Reports of the Death of the International Economy are Grossly Exaggerated," in *National Diversity and Global Capitalism*, ed. Suzanne Berger and Ronald Dore (Ithaca, N. Y.: Cornell University Press, 1996), 73-74.

24. Two recent authors of note who have helped to rectify this situation are Cotkin, a historian (see 123-51) and the literary critic Frank Lentricchia. See his essay "The Return of William James." *Cultural Critique* 4 (Fall 1986): 5-31.

25. Letter to Théodore Flournoy, June 17, 1898. *The Letters of William James and Théodore Flournoy*, ed. Robert C. LeClair (Madison: University of Wisconsin Press, 1966), 72.

26. In *The Nation,* January 13, 1898, 23, quoted in Robert Beisner, *Twelve against Empire: The Anti-Imperialists 1898-1900* (New York: McGraw-Hill, 1968), 76.

27. Edward Atkinson to William McKinley, January 26, 1899. Cited in *Twelve against Empire,* 97-98.

28. *Twelve against Empire*, 174.

29. However, James had played a considerable part in building the rhetoric of "American manliness" that was used as a pretext in both the Spanish-American War and the Philippines. See Kim Townsend's *Manhood at Harvard: William James and Others* (New York: W. W. Norton, 1996) and Roxanne Lynn Doty, *Imperial Encounters* (Minneapolis: University of Minnesota Press, 1996), 30-42.

30. *W*, 161; see also Cotkin, 138-39.

31. William James to Mrs. Henry Whitman, October 5, 1999, *Letters of William James*, ed. Henry James (Boston: Atlantic Monthly Press, 1920.) Quoted in Joshua Miller, *The Democratic Temperament*, 58.

32. Doty, *Imperial Encounters*, 94.

33. See, for example, Benjamin R. Barber's *Jihad vs. McWorld* (New York: Times Books, 1995).

34. Though many have commented on Wilson's "diplomacy of idealism," the book that best captures this central ambiguity in Wilson's international affairs is William Appleman Williams's *The Tragedy of American Diplomacy* (New York: Dell, 1962), esp. 52-83.

Chapter 9

Democratic Internationalism: A Defense of Deliberation as a Medium for Internationalism

Alan Gilbert

Introduction: Globalism, Sovereignty, and Seattle

In my book *Must Global Politics Constrain Democracy?* I explored the thesis that great power rivalry has important anti-democratic effects on citizens at home (what I called the *anti-democratic feedback hypothesis*).[1] For instance, in American history, the charge of "foreign enemies" from the Alien and Sedition Acts of 1798 to the Truman-McCarthy era has chilled domestic, common good-oriented movements. Citizens at home thus often have common interests with ordinary people in other countries against the interests of their own state(s). I suggested that because of global rivalry, national sovereignty promised but rarely delivered a common good to its own citizens or internationally. Only a robust, citizen-based, deliberative democracy—a regime only embryonically embodied in protest movements and, more rarely, opposition movements in parliamentary democracies (which are better seen as capitalist oligarchies with parliamentary forms)—could do that. Emphasizing movements from below across national boundaries, the view I defend is called *democratic internationalism*. This chapter will sketch practices and institutions consistent with deliberative democracy on a national and international scale.

Capitalism—a system that "knocks down all Chinese walls" in the words of the *Communist Manifesto*—has, nonetheless, reached a new stage in the era of "free trade" and "globalization." The December 1999 protest in Seattle against the World Trade Organization, focusing on the issue of outlawing child labor and requiring decent standards for workers as well as restricting capitalist poisoning of the natural environment, highlighted the crimes of "globalization." Rising "wealth" and trade benefit some, but dispossess many, especially in the less developed countries. Free trade often sharply increases the gap between the rich locally and internationally, and the majority, especially the very poor (as this chapter will suggest, a similar phenomenon has occurred in the wealthy countries, particularly the United States). Whether, as Amartya Sen has suggested, development in the most dire circumstances can be focused on the capabilities of each person and relieve the special oppression of women is also a question that must be met by *democratic* sovereignty. In this regard, the protests in Seattle—one useful model for movements in other country and internationally—have shown a way.

Illustrating the impact of global politics on a domestic presidential system, President Clinton abandoned "free" trade and also held out for decent standards concerning labor and the environment.[2] He sought to help his protégé Al Gore, who needed votes from workers and environmentalists—a striking example of *the democratic feedback* of globalism on presidential politics—in the context of fierce protest from below. But Mayor Paul Allen struck out viciously at the demonstrators, declaring martial law in downtown Seattle and arresting mainly nonviolent protestors for exercising freedom of speech. A photograph of a cop firing a tear gas canister at a Red Cross worker, standing out in the crowd, graced European newspapers, and such publicity suddenly metamorphosed Seattle's municipal government into a global, Mayor Daley-like symbol of repression.[3] Fukuyama as well as advocates of the democratic peace hypothesis speak casually about democracy. In the era of globalization, real democracy places citizens willing to fight for it against the odds.

This chapter deepens democratic internationalism's conception of a common good by exploring a theory of deliberative democracy. It then considers the promise of novel, nonviolent movements, a panoply of possible reforms to make contemporary oligarchy more democratic, and new international regimes, prefigured in the Ottawa Convention Banning Land Mines, restrictions on greenhouse gases, and other initiatives of the post-Cold War era.

The first section contrasts internationalism with pluralism. The second shows how a conception of deliberative democracy permits principled resolutions of otherwise intractable ethical disputes. The third assesses nonviolent movements for social change. The fourth section criticizes abstract visions of cosmopolitan governance, and it includes suggestions, instead, about the importance of global regimes on particular issues, such as outlawing land mines, curtailing the emission of greenhouse gases, barring the use of children as soldiers, and founding an international criminal court. Though not previously applied to the international arena, pluralism explains American diplomatic isolation on each of these issues as a consequence of unchecked particular interests. In contrast, internationalism maintains that only movements from below—perhaps multilateral in setting—can realize these and other common good-sustaining regimes.

The fifth section focuses on Downs and Rocke's principal/agent account of presidential escalation of a losing war or intervention abroad to resurrect a candidacy. That view suggests the likely corruption—to some extent—of any democratic regime. But internationalism stresses the energy of citizens rather than—solely—political reforms. The sixth section considers a sophisticated realist objection to this argument as a whole. That criticism might contend that anti-democratic feedback harms most citizens rather than instigates political cooperation, thus supporting realism not internationalism. The last section notes the impermanence of reform and the distance, as well as promise, of deliberative democracy.

Internationalism versus Pluralism

Internationalism is a theory and policy appropriate to any nonaggressive democratic regime or movement.[4] Since Aristotle, Plato, and Thucydides, political theorists and historians have considered it. Yet the absence of internationalism in contemporary political science, until now, reveals an oligarchic skew.

In the post-Cold War era, however, broad interest has also emerged in the thesis that democracies do not go to war with one another. As neo-realism (Krasner, Gilpin, Keohane, Waltz) and internationalism stress, some versions of this view conceal a pattern of American aggression against democracies in the less-developed countries. Nonetheless, the very existence of the interdemocratic-peace argument underlines a novel, post-Cold War hope that the section on globalization and cosmopolis examines below: that the realization of democratic regimes in many countries may limit belligerence.

Internationalism reinforces this trend. For it raises a question *internal* to neorealism about what effect Great Power rivalry has on a domestic common good—antidemocratic feedback—and demonstrates that any well-formulated realist view, supposedly concerned only with power, *must* include harms to citizens at home. It thus shows that the dominant paradigm in the American Cold War "science" of international relations cannot sustain its argument against democracy.

Through striking historical examples, internationalism warns citizens against the likelihood that presidents will intervene against democracy abroad to circumscribe political alternatives and "resurrect" themselves.[5] It identifies a hierarchically controlled press, academia, and mainstream politics—Morgenthau's "academic political[-media] complex"—as obstacles to nonaggressive democratic practices. It emphasizes the fierce ideologies of antiradicalism, racism, and sexism that stigmatize others as "enemies" (in refusing to commute a sentence of death on Ethel and Julius Rosenberg for "stealing nuclear secrets," President Eisenhower, for instance, focused hostility on her).[6] Thus, internationalism sanctions insurgencies from below like the anti-Vietnam War movement to make an oligarchy with parliamentary forms more democratic. In addition, it suggests that further steps toward democracy could reduce the possibility, and domestic harms, of aggression.

A pluralist view of American democracy purports that organization by the disadvantaged, that is, the union movement, the civil rights movements among blacks, Chicanos, and Native Americans, feminism, the gay and lesbian movements, and the like can balance the power of the rich and secure a common good. A disconcerting international consequence of that view, however, has long gone unnoticed.[7] For what group in America, one might ask, defends the autoworkers for U. S. companies in Santiago or Johannesburg and offsets the political power of GM and Ford?[8] On a pluralist theory, no one does. The section on globalization and cosmopolis probes this unacknowledged consequence of pluralism that accounts for the isolation of the U. S. government, in thrall to particular interests, on treaties concerning land mines, exploitation of children as soldiers, and the like.

Contrary to pluralism, internationalism underlines the damage done by global rivalry to democracy at home and the interest of most citizens in opposing (neocolonial) aggression as well as the harms accompanying "free" trade and "globalization." It creates some hope that domestic protest can accompany international resistance to U. S.-sponsored domineering and restores the moral attractiveness of pluralism (we might thus see democratic internationalism as a *sophisticated* pluralism). Further, only activity from below would realize innovative regimes, possibly including, as we will see, the outlawing of major war.

Democratic Deliberation and Moral Controversy

In a democratic regime, citizens sometimes engage in fierce moral disputes, which, if untempered by mutual regard across conscientious differences, can lead to violence. Influenced by metaethical relativism, however, many scholars believe that such clashes derive from incommensurable, *underlying* ethical premises. Holders of different positions live, as it were, in disparate moral worlds.

That account, however, denies the possibility of the central, democratic virtue of civility or what Thompson and Gutmann call *civic magnanimity*. Such magnanimity recognizes "the moral point of view of others even though we disagree with it"[9] and derives from liberalism's core moral standard: mutual regard among persons of differing comprehensive views.[10] In addition, we can often discern a common ethical basis in complex moral disputes that pivot mainly on social theoretical and factual clashes. Such empirical conflicts frequently make political as well as theoretical disagreements intractable.

For instance, at a high level of abstraction, plausible social and political theories start from the core *moral* insight that securing a common interest among citizens is a decisive political good (level 1). Then they add factual and social theoretical claims (level 2) that, if challenged—as democratic internationalism questions the silence of pluralism on global affairs—lead to clashing, complex ethical and political judgments (level 3).[11]

A deliberative democratic critique of realism, applicable to pluralism, also clarifies the structure of the public controversies that are the subject matter of Thompson and Gutmann's *Democracy and Disagreement*.[12] Starting from Morgenthau and Niebuhr, my argument shares Thompson and Gutmann's aim of defining a reasonable deliberative process that can mitigate *often intractable* clashes (clashes to which there is, at least currently, no objective solution). Such deliberations, however, as I have emphasized, arise from core *recognition of persons*: a mutual insight into equal basic liberties and sufficiently cooperative economic arrangements—the difference principle—to uphold democracy (Rawls) or into the substantive, fundamental rights of each person—liberty, basic opportunity, and fair opportunity—and relevant, derivative conditions—reciprocity, publicity, accountability.[13] Although Thompson and Gutmann see *reciprocity* as a "condition" for deliberation, my way of putting it—that reciprocity derives from a core insight into the dignity of each person—underlines its *substantive*, political content. Their other conditions—accountability that involves a growing recognition of members of other cultures and those not yet born; publicity to each individual of the laws and policies that affect her—have similar, substantive content.

Thompson and Gutmann rightly suggest that a history of deliberations often shifts and strengthens—by a bootstrapping process—its conditions: "This capacity of deliberative democracy to encourage changes in its own meaning over time illustrates one of its most important qualities. Deliberative democracy expresses a bootstrap conception of the political process: the conditions of reciprocity, publicity, and accountability that define the process pull themselves up by means of the process itself."[14] Over time, they hope that such a democracy can "meliorate" core injustices: "[T]he level of opportunity [for example] does not represent some immutable standard, objectively determined outside the political process . . . Just as citizens and public officials in the 1930s came to see social security for financial protection in old age as part of a social minimum, so in the 1990s the vast majority are coming to regard guaranteed health care as a basic opportunity."[15]

Thompson and Gutmann contrast their vision with a "proceduralism" that encourgages citizens to adhere to certain common rules and, as it were, to keep their differences out of the public sphere. But such an approach hardly erases those disputes, especially concerning basic questions of justice, such as the oppresion of workers, women, and minority groups, that eventually surface in extraparliamentary conflict. Thompson and Gutmann also reject a "constitutionalism" that downplays elections and looks for public reasons solely to a Supreme Court. For such a regime removes the people—and political deliberation—from democracy.

On behalf ot that view, however, one might note that protection of the core liberties of each citizen underlies any decent process of deliberation. Ideally, a court can defend or expand these liberties against transient, popular pressures. Some such judicial institution must play a central role in an equal-rights-based theory of democracy. Thus, Dworkin's vision of a Constitution of abstract principle, registered especially in the Bill of Rights, models a Rawlsian or Rousseauian conception. That view contrasts with a notion of judicial decisions as an ad hoc historical process so that, for example, the Supreme Court might grant "due process" to blacks but not to gays. [16] But even the best court cannot, by and large, substitute its reasons for democratic deliberations, and, as we will see, protest movements among citizens.

Through public reasons—reasoning that appeals, however inadequately, to the interests of all—deliberative democracy provides some chance to mitigate basic injustices:

> We do not presume that these background circumstances [for deliberative democracy] are easily created or maintained. But citizens and officials should not use the injustice of inequalities in liberty and opportunity as an excuse for neglecting to deliberate or failing to develop a more deliberative form of democracy. On the contrary, because deliberative democracy relies on reciprocity, publicity and accountability, it stands a better chance of identifying and meliorating social and economic injustices than a politics that relies only on power, which is more likely to reproduce or exacerbate existing inequalities. [17]

Despite its virtues, however, Thompson and Gutmann's argument has two fundamental flaws. First, they fail to discuss relevant questions in social theory, in particular, why deliberation has worked so slowly to overcome glaring injustices or how deliberation can remake growing oligarchic influence over government policy. [18] By contrast, this argument stresses the existence of oligarchy and *antidemocratic feedback* that undermine such deliberations.

Further, a social theoretical emphasis would strengthen Thompson and Gutmann's restrictively moral account of internationalism. For instance, they praise the shift to a wider *accountability* to American citizens and others involved in the Clinton administration's endorsement of the International Biodiversity Treaty. If such diversity is protected, "the human world will be better off," and it will have "more intrinsic value." [19] The antidemocratic-feedback argument, however, underlines the nonmoral as well as moral interests of citizens in a panoply of such proposals.

Second, Thompson and Gutmann fail to see struggle from below as a *driving force* in democratic deliberations. For instance, social security became an issue in American politics through the radical-led formation of unemployment councils and union drives; sit-down strikes created industrial unions. As in the case of the Vietnam War, deliberation often occurs *only* as a result of such conflict. In this context, the Montgomery bus boycott and sit-ins at southern lunch counters suggest a democratic promise in civil disobedience to which I will return.

Experiments in Nonviolence

Internationalism encourages us to imagine favorable conditions for democratic deliberation, ones arising either from the reform, due to mass rebellion, of existing regimes, or from nonviolent or violent revolution. A refined pluralism or deliberative view, however, can see civil disobedience, or more radical protest, as an instrument to offset the elite's power and promote public reflection.[20] In addition, although in a nuclear era violent revolution has been possible, as in China, Vietnam, Cuba, Algeria, Guinea-Bissau, Mozambique, Nicaragua, and elsewhere, radicals have lacked the vision to sustain novel, more democratic regimes. In this context, we might envision, as an alternative, militant, nonviolent movements, respectful of the humanity and dignity of others, which, nonetheless, relentlessly challenge unjust authority.[21] For in protesting the waste of human life by current governments, nonviolence emphasizes the value of life. Through self-sacrifice, it offers hope for a transformative regime, one less responsive to aggression with additional bloodshed and more tolerant of political differences.

From Henry David Thoreau[22] to Martin Luther King Jr. and Barbara Deming,[23] Americans have contributed to the theory and practice of civil disobedience. They have celebrated the capacity of each individual to say no to great injustice.[24] They have thus participated in a still embryonic, international movement, joining their voices to those of Tolstoy, Gandhi, Dom Helder Camara,[25] Denise Levertov,[26] and many others. Their efforts have led so far to a few, striking, twentieth-century successes—the struggles for independence in India and Ghana, the American civil rights movement, and the South African Truth Commission.

Some critics of nonviolence mistakenly argue, however, that proponents, like older utopians, seek merely to petition an elite. They take the fact that a ruling class will not peacefully abjure even horrifying injustices to rule out, by itself, succesful nonviolent campaigns. But as Deming notes, nothing about a mass, militant, nonviolent movement requires "begging." For instance, noncooperation overturned the Kapp putsch in Germany (1920) and the French general's revolt in

Algeria (1961). The collapse of Soviet-style dictatorships in Eastern Europe occurred without violence. [27] A self-conscious nonviolent movement would only have deepened these changes.

Put differently, some suppose that a Gandhian movement could work against the "nice" British but not against the Nazis. But this objection disregards the brutality of English colonialism. It also ignores the need for a revolutionary situation, as in Eastern Europe in the late 1980s, that will allow a mov ement—whether nonviolent or violent—to succeed.

Deming concurs with Stokely Carmichael's critique of utopianism: "Look, you guys are supposed to be nice guys and we are only going to do what we are supposed to do . . . We demonstrated from a position of weakness. We can not be expected any longer to march and have our heads broken in order to say to whites: come on, you're nice guys. For you are not nice guys. We have found you out." [28] Conjuring Lorenz's biology of aggression [29]—she might better have invoked Niebuhr's realism—Deming insists that almost no one is politically "nice" in the required sense, and emphasizes the power of revolt.

Further, in the experience of nonviolent movements, the leader's visions came to encompass "a beloved community." Thus, Gandhi renamed the "untouchables" *harijans* (the children of God) and fought for Hindu-Muslim unity. Martin Luther King Jr. opposed the Vietnam War, supported the Memphis sanitation worker's strike, and initiated the poor people's movement. [30] Each foresaw a revolution in social as well as political equality. In a last speech to the Southern Christian Leadership Conference, King mused:

> There are forty million poor people here, and one day we must ask the question, why are there forty million poor people in America? When you begin to ask that question, you are raising questions about the economic system, about a broader distribution of wealth. When you ask that question, you begin to question the capitalistic economy. I am simply saying that more and more we've got to begin to ask questions about the whole society. We are called upon to help the discouraged beggars in life's market place, but one day we must come to see that an edifice which produces beggars need restructuring. It means that questions must be raised. You see, my friends, when you deal with this you begin to ask the question: who owns the oil? You begin to ask the question: who owns the iron ore? You begin to ask the question, why is it that people have to pay water bills in a world that is two-thirds water? These are the questions that must be asked. [31]

King had "been to the mountain top" in a vision; he did not expect to join others there:

> Like anybody I would like to live a long life. Longevity has its place. But I'm not concerned about that now . . . I may not get there with you but I want you to know tonight that we as a people will get to the promised land. [32]

If the means can work, nonviolent movements can undertake radical democratic projects. Thus, despite historic differences, a nonviolent revolution might simply *be* a communist or radical democratic movement. Further, not just novelty or elite attack, but psychological insecurity and status differences within the movement have long inhibited fair conversation on "Quaker-vegetarian parttle" (Trosky); "*I* am a good person; I would never consider violence." In contrast, Gandhi saw violent resistence as better than acquiescence to oppression.[33] Millions of people have participated in twentieth-century battles, nonviolent as well as violent, against injustice. We need respectful, mutual conversation not only in the current dissarray but also as a characteristic of democratic resurgence.

Globalization and Cosmopolis

Internationalism favors the realization of a common good within each country and strengthens democratic arrangements domestically; it also stresses, across borders, mutual support from below. Nonetheless, a critic might suggest, it does not adequately address the threat to such goods represented by globalization. For instance, contemporary regimes such as the International Monetary Fund that make loans contingent on "anti-inflationary" cutbacks in social programs already enforce economic antidemocratic feedback.[34] The globalization of capital, this critic might maintain, further undercuts the possibility of local democratic transformations.

Moreover, the augmenting inequality in the United States mirrors, though less shockingly, a worldwide pattern. Recalling Honderich, Thomas Schelling notes:

> If we were to think about a "new world order" that might embark on the gradual development of some constitutional framework within which the peoples of the globe would eventually share collective responsibility and reciprocal obligations . . . what actual nation, existing now or in the past, might such an incipient world state resemble? . . .
>
> I find my own answer stunning and embarrasing: [apartheid] South Africa.
>
> . . . We live in a world that is one-fifth rich and four-fifths poor; the rich are segregated into the rich countries and the poor into the poor countries; the rich are predominantly lighter skinned and the poor darker skinned; most of the poor live in homelands that are physically remote, often separated by oceans and great distances from the rich.[35]

The term *apartheid,* which Falk also stresses, underlines the *excessive,* racist evil of contemporary international distribution and indicts "geogovernance." Yet this name conceals the harms done to many whites, and the way racism is used, as a form of divide and rule, to legitimize such practices.

In amplifying existing inequalities, global and domestic capitalism follow a course long ago theorized by Marx. Oppression highlights the optimism, utopian temper, and, ironically, vagueness—despite an underlying critical impulse—of David Held's cosmopolitan countervision:

> The achievement of taking steps towards the realization of democratic autonomy within a nation-state or region—important as it unquestionably is—would be but a milestone on the road to the establishment of a cosmopolitan democracy with global reach. While, initially, those communities which enable policy and law to be shaped by their citizenry are likely to pursue such a future, the possibility is held out [the passive grammar betrays the questions: by whom? through what measures?] that the conflict between a person's obligation *qua* citizen to obey the regulations of a particular community, and his or her obligation to obey internationally recognized rules, might eventually be overcome, as more and more states and agencies affiliated to the new democratic order. The principles of individual democratic states and societies could come to coincide with those of cosmopolitan democratic law . . . democratic citizenship could take on, in principle, a truly universal status. [36]

Held contends that some form of federated democracy—one might imagine Marx's communism or radical democracy—is desirable, but suggests few measures to achieve it. [37] Further, despite securing arms for humanitarian interventions, that regime would have to be mainly federal, noncoercive, and restricted. As Held acknowledges, following Kant, any *armed* global *state*—for instance, one generated by repeated humanitarian interventions—would pose a significant danger of despotism. [38] As we will see, the starvation occasioned by the UN boycott of Iraq adumbrates this possibility. Surprisingly, however, Held also advocates substituting an "efficient, accountable, international military force" for those of particular states.

His coeditor, Daniele Archibugi, envisions reforming the United Nations. She recommends creation of a "people's assembly" alongside the state representatives in the General Assembly to give voice to citizens and minorities, abolition of the Great Power veto in the Security Council, and the like. Though improvements, such reforms would only make a federation of diverse powers a little less unequal. To trumpet modest reforms as "democratic" world governance is misleading. [39]

Similarly, on Kaldor's account, the European Community, for instance through launching multilateral, humanitarian intervention in the former Yugoslavia, has eroded state sovereignty. Projecting the Helsinki Citizen's Assembly's attempt to inject serious debate into the wasteland of contemporary politics—Kaldor invokes Havel's concept of "Living in Truth"—she envisions a more participatory regime.[40] Though morally compelling, however, like Falk's image of humane governance, her account is frail.

In addition, capitalism has long been internationalistic. Visions of globalization as an instigator of oppression—or a generator of democratic cosmopolis—are both, probably, overstated.[41]

Nonetheless, an objection to democratic internationalism based on globalization has an important grain of truth. No arrangements in a particular country or group of countries—even those resembling the radical democracy I have sketched—will halt the fluidity of international capital; unchecked from below, capitalism exacerbates inequalities. Yet in particular cases, furthering deliberations and a common good, such political arrangements would be a striking improvement. Moreover, radical example might inspire democratic feedback. Thus, international movements of workers and other oppressed people as well as peace—notably in Eastern Europe—and green movements that go beyond national borders illustrate such possibilities.

Further, for particular international goods, such as outlawing land mines, diminishing greenhouse gases, forbidding the use of children as soldiers, establishing an international criminal court, and barring major wars, nongovernment—including non-United Nations—groups can play a decisive role. These examples illustrate Keohane's notion of cooperative regimes.[42] Yet in the post-Cold War era, they also highlight surprisingly backward features of American diplomacy, underlining the difference between pluralism, which abandons foreign policy to uncountered oligarchic interests, and internationalism, which remedies this foreign-policy defect of pluralism through democratic resistance.

First, the unusual award of a 1997 Nobel Prize to Jody Williams and the Committee to Ban Land Mines—composed of one thousand organizations from sixty nations that led an impromptu, successful campaign—provoked Russia's President Yeltsin to reverse his stand and support an antimines treaty. Only the United States holds out. Though the Clinton administration insists that South Korea needs mines, the South produces twenty times the wealth of the North, and, with a massive American presence,[43] is able to defend itself. What is the "security" value of continuing to seed mines between these regimes for the next ten years compared to that of cutting back on the annual killing of twenty-six thousand civilians and the maiming of others? In the poor countries, wars have already "planted" 100 million such weapons, claiming dozens of new victims daily. Yet, led by Defense Secretary Cohen, the Pentagon plans to use mines widely in any future war and strives to undo even a separate, yearlong ban on this weapon.[44]

Ironically, Americans initiated this campaign. Bobby Muller, a paraplegic veteran, formed Vietnam Veterans of America, which galvanized the International Committee to Ban Land Mines. As he underlines: "$3 antipersonnel land mines have killed more people than all the Cold War weapons of mass destruction combined."[45] In 1992, Senator Patrick Leahy of Vermont fought for a U. S. ban on exporting land mines as well as for a rehabilitation fund for victims. The Canadian regime broke with the Cold War model of "consensus" and supported the treaty. Yet President Clinton told Muller flatly that he could not risk a breach with the Pentagon.[46] Once again, in Morgenthau's words, the American government squanders the *substance* of democratic power to chase its illusory shadow. In November 1997, diplomats from 120 countries approved the antimines treaty. As Muller reflects, "It is . . . sad that this country, which played so important a part in getting this campaign off the ground, is, at the end of the day, a no-show."[47]

Second, to stem greenhouse gas emissions, Europe has cut back on coal. Britain and the Netherlands, for instance, base electricity on natural gas. In the late 1980s, East Germany burned 300 million tons of lignite; in 1995, reunified Germany consumed only 130 million tons. In contrast, coal burning generated 56 percent of American electricity in 1996 compared to 50 percent in 1980.[48] As German foreign minister Klaus Kinkel remarked: "How can the Americans, with around 5 per cent of the world's population, go on accounting for a quarter of its greenhouse gases?"[49]

Though still an issue of controversy, the role of human activity in causing dire, long-run shifts in the earth's climate is recognized by most scientists. Carbon dioxide, methane, and nitrogen oxide, transparent to sunlight and generated by fuel combustion, trap heat emitted by the Earth. Further, according to a 1995 UN report, carbon dioxide stands at a 30 percent higher level in the atmosphere than in preindustrial times. Scientists predict that emissions could push up the Earth's temperature two to six degrees by the year 2100—current temperatures exceed by only five to nine degrees those of the last ice age—and elevate sea levels six to thirty-seven inches. Heat would expand ocean volume and melt glaciers, inundating islands and shorelines. Contributing to Western arrogance, these changes would especially affect such less-developed countries as poor, populous, and low-lying Bangladesh.[50] These alternations would shift climate zones, worsen floods and droughts, make heat waves more lethal, and extinguish some ecosystems.[51]

At the December 1997 Earth Summit in Kyoto, the European Community proposed cutting three gases that contribute to the greenhouse effect 7.5 percent below 1990 levels by the year 2005 and 15 percent by 2010. The Clinton administration initially held out for a 1990 standard, but it finally agreed to a level 7 percent below that of 1990, to be achieved by 2012.[52] Withdrawing its original offer, Europe then agreed to cut back only 8 percent from 1990 by 2012, Japan 6 percent. In addition, against European resistance, the conference adopted a U. S. suggestion to curtail three other gases—hydroflourocarbons, perflourocarbons, and sulfur hexachloride.[53]

America had previously resisted such measures. At the 1992 Earth Summit in Rio, because of U. S. opposition, other nations made reduction to a 1990 standard by the year 2000 a "voluntary" goal.[54] Through gas burning, automobiles contribute centrally to global warming.[55] Yet American manufacturers have shifted production from cars to light trucks, which emit 20 percent to 100 percent more carbon dioxide.[56] In 1990, after Iraq invaded Kuwait, Senator Richard Bryan of Nevada introduced legislation to increase the fuel economy of all vehicles 40 percent by 2001. To lobby against this bill, the auto companies hired FMR Group and John R. Bonner. Despite support from fifty-seven senators, a filibuster defeated it.

In 1992, backed by environmentalists, Clinton won the Democratic nomination. Speaking in Detroit on 21 August, however, the candidate alleged that fuel efficiency might not be technically feasible, a justification for subsidizing industry "research" instead of enacting higher efficiency. When the Sierra Club editorialized against the wastefulness of sport utility vehicles, the Big Three pulled their ads from *Sierra* magazine.[57] But the Sierra Club is not the president.

Thus, with the exception of the Biodiversity Treaty, the U. S. government has not only refused to lead for an international common good, but rather, catering to *particular* interests, it has lagged behind. As I emphasized, pluralism explains, though it does not counter, this ignoble pattern. Yet according to a *New York Times* poll, 65 percent of Americans support swift, even unilateral, action to restrict greenhouse emissions.[58] As internationalism stresses, however, without mass protest, democratic opinion cannot check oligarchy. In a global context, internationalism, once again, appears to be a sophisticated pluralism. Yet for the present, Americans are, comparatively, unorganized. In Europe, green movements—and, consequently, more effective public awareness of ecology—stimulate better policies.

Still, having just rejected the land mines treaty and cognizant of the dangers of global warming, the Clinton administration agreed to a decent accord. By the year 2000, scientists project that, unchecked, the United States would emit 13 percent more greenhouse gases than in 1990, 30 percent by 2010. Thus, if upheld by the Senate, the treaty would significantly curtail U. S. emissions.

In addition, the Clinton administration will offer five billion dollars of research incentives for companies to adopt fuel-efficient technologies. For instance, boards of education might commission new schools with geothermal heat pumps, mirroring the Choptank Elementary School in Cambridge, Maryland, which will cut greenhouse gases 40 percent compared to conventional technology and save, over the next twenty years, four hundred thousand dollars in energy and maintenance cost; according to Terry Peterson, manager of green-power marketing at the Electric Power Research Institute, financed by the energy industry, in many parts of the United States, wind power will soon underprice fossil fuel; for an Energy Department study, Ford predicted that it could manufacture an electric van, using fuel cell technology, that would get 32 to 34 miles per gallon, more than double today's Econoline; with research subsidies, the Solar Energy Association estimates that its growth might accelerate from 27 percent to 40 percent per year, and reduce the cost of clean—sun based—electricity by 25 percent.[59] After the Kyoto conference, the auto companies announced the possibility of cutting out 99 percent of carbon dioxide emissions. Underlining the comparative ease of transition, this startling alternative highlights the corruption of presidential policy since Reagan as well as that of the auto manufacturers.[60]

At Kyoto, the United States proposed setting overall goals to curtail greenhouse gases in each country and issuing allowable emissions certificates to specific corporations. These firms could then engage in "emissions trading," namely, trying to undercut their targets and sell the remaining certificates, at a profit, to less fortunate companies domestically or internationally. The treaty would also establish a multilateral organization to encourage firms in the rich nations to invest in cleaner emissions in the poor ones.

Stressing that industrialized nations have caused the problem yet seek to fob off the cost of curtailing global warming on poor countries, the latter, led by China, have demanded serious cuts. Neither the U. S. Senate nor the Clinton administration, however, will sign the treaty unless the industrializing countries join. In addition, even though the treaty creates a novel international framework to deal with global warming, scientists warn of its inadequacy, distinguishing between serious climatic disruptions, which are now regarded as probable, and catastrophic ones—for instance flooding in Bangladesh or New York—which further action may avert.[61]

In addition, 191 governments have now ratified the International Convention on the Rights of the Child, which bans the use of soldiers younger than eighteen. Yet the United States is one of only two countries that have not signed. Catering to conservative ideologues who fear "government intervention" in the family—as if war were not a government activity affecting families—the United States resists a ban on a malevolent practice of which it is not even a part.

The *Human Rights World Report for 1998* contends that selective American commitment based on economic convenience or strategic interest, poses a growing threat to efforts to defend the rights of, for instance, Chinese or Central Africans. Invoking a realist insight, it concludes: "U. S. arrogance suggests that in Washington's view, human rights standards should be embraced only if they codify what the U. S. government already does, not what the United States ought to achieve."[62] In Keohane's idiom, in an increasingly established human-rights regime, such conduct exacts costs in contempt—as well as lack of cooperation—from others.

But lone U. S. opposition to global treaties on behalf of particular interests did not emerge in the Clinton administration. For thirty years, from Truman until Ford, the United States refused to ratify the United Nations' Convention on

Genocide, for fear it would be applied to American persecution of blacks. [63] This tyrannical interest is more that of a ruling class than of the specific companies, suggested by pluralism. But what in the Cold War appeared narrow, vicious, self-interest now appears as arrogant, isolated, and inexplicable. [64]

Finally, to deal with genocide and other war crimes by individuals, many governments support a permanent international criminal court. The Security Council has, so far, mandated ad hoc tribunals for the former Yugoslavia and Rwanda. But beyond the 22 million civilians already forcibly uprooted, the UN High Commissioner for Refugees estimates that thirty-five civil wars may force another twenty-five million to abandon their homes. Provoked by rape and other forms of sexual abuse in the Balkans and Central Africa, women's organizations and human-rights groups have successfully campaigned for the inclusion of crimes against women—a major moral advance—among crimes of war. [65]

Across diverse state systems of common law, military justice, and civil law, the ad hoc tribunals have worked out common standards. Testifying to a United Nations committee of legal experts, American Justice Gabriel Kirk McDonald noted: "We at the Yugoslavia tribunal brought together 11 judges, all from different systems in different countries, and we were able to draft rules of procedure and evidence that we believe met the needs of all systems." [66] Further, as chief prosecutor in Bosnia, Louise Arbour of Canada, warned: "[T]here is more to fear from an impotent than from an overreaching prosecutor."

Yet the United States holds out for a Security Council veto over cases to be brought before this tribunal. The Pentagon fears that American soldiers might be charged with war crimes. As Arbour responds: "an organization should not be constructed on the assumption that it will be run by incompetent people, acting in bad faith, for improper purposes." [67] But the worry probably reflects a deeper sense about American policy. To protect particular interests, for instance, past criminality in Vietnam, continuing CIA involvement in torture and murder in places such as Haiti, and possible future misconduct, the United States seeks to place itself above an international law that applies to others (except those nations that also have a veto on the Security Council). [68]

As Connie Ngondo, executive director of the Kenyan branch of the International Commission of Jurists, suggests: "the . . . criminal court could be used to harass the nations of the south." Thus, parochial American policy encourages defection from an impartial, common-good-oriented court, undermining the rule of law. The British Labour government, however, has broken with the United States. Instead of allowing a veto by any permanent member over each case by refusing to send it to the court, Britain proposes joint state action—if the Security Council is already discussing a conflict—to postpone proceedings for a *limited* period.

Will Leadership in a Democratic Movement
Eventually Become Problematic?

Using a principal/agent model, Downs and Rocke contend that compared to prime
ministers, presidents have electoral incentives to prolong losing wars or intervene
against other representative regimes. The agent has knowledge that the principal—the voters—lack, and can use this information selectively to lend illusory
promise to such ventures.[69] If a war's costs are too high, the principal has only
belated electoral rejection as a way to punish the agent (as Downs and Rocke note,
this mechanism could dismiss a president who made reasonable decisions that
turned out badly).[70]

Any belligerency, however, may trascend a public threshold for loss of life,
after which de-escalation or withdrawal cannot prevent electoral defeat. Through
escalation and calls for patriotism, however, a leader may still hope to survive an
election.[71] Comparatively, parliamentary systems more easily translate citizen
discontent into shortening the prime minister's term and diminish "gambling for
resurrection." Though fought against a dictatorship, Thatcher's war with Argentina over the Falklands Malvinas is, however, a counterexample. To a lesser
extent, even parliamentary leaders engage in temporary popularity-instigating
foreign adventures.

Downs and Rocke's theory contrasts with George Ball's assumption that,
with escalation, chauvinism sweeps the whole citizenry: "Once we suffer large
casualties, we will have started a well-nigh irreversible process. Our involvement
will be so great that we cannot—without national humiliation—stop short of
achieving our complete objetive." [72] But such arguments deny the possibility—in
the case of Vietnam, the reality—of movements from below. They disregard
institutional alternatives.

Given the privileges and psychology of leadership[73]—a tendency to
domineer—and the principal/agent separation, distortion is likely in any system
(even a radical democratic one). Though more concerned with the common good-
sustaining potentials of protest movements than most realisms, Downs and
Rocke's view also suggsts the likely deficiencies of any democratic politics.

But internationalism accepts these cautions. A radical democratic regime
need not be Clintonesque—or Reaganesque—in its corruption. Yet short of
vibrant movements from below, it would, very likely, become somewhat corrupt.

Downs and Rocke's argument underlines the distance between reasonable
practices and presidential "gambling." Critical of U. S. interventions against parliamentary regimes, it allows for a vigorous—nonapologetic—version of the
democratic-peace hypothesis; except where the elite can drape "the enemy" in
racist, antiradical garb, the principal's knowledge about the good of other free
regimes curbs the agent's belligerence. This theory also reinforces a democratic
internationalism *from below*, one cognizant of the importance of institutional

reforms, but focused on citizen action rather than the beneficence of (ordinary) leaders.

A Democratic Realist Criticism
and an Internationalist Rejoinder

Considering this internationalist critique as a whole, a sophisticated realist might respond: doesn't the emphasis on antidemocratic feedback underscore the harms to most citizens arising from Great Power rivalry? Realists, however, expect such abridgments of the common good; democratic internationalists do not. Thus, your argument shows that some version of realism must be right.[74]

But this criticism makes three errors. First, it overlooks causally important variations in domestic institutions. Though antidemocratic feedback affects every regime, if Downs and Rocke are right, when compared to presidencies, parliaments mitigate "gambling for resurrection." Thus, the fundamental realist move—an abstraction of powers competing in international affairs from generalized regime types as well as particular configurations of institutions—fails. Further, even a democratic realism, such as Morgenthau's concerning Vietnam, cannot account for such institutional variations without abandoning this core realist starting point. In contrast, democratic internationalism highlights the interplay of global conflict *and* particular domestic settings.

Second, international politics results in *democratic,* not just antidemocratic, feedback. Such feedback can involve solidarity from below, for example, in the case of the Spanish republic or between the Jacobins and the Haitian Revolution,[75] as well as from above, for example, to compete effectively with rivals, today's adoption of parliamentary forms—and perhaps some civil liberties for citizens[76]—by fomerly dictatorial regimes.

Robert Putnam stresses two-level games in which international settings stimulate particular domestic policies, and contradict the unitary state model employed by neorealism, otherwise minority domestic groups invoke global pressures to push for preferred measures[77] ("from above" here refers to groups within the elite in contrast to a "unitary state"). Putnam uses the example of negotiations over energy prices at the Berlin Summit of 1978 and domestic conflicts. But interactive pressures for adopting parliamentary institutions, preventing major wars, or barring the use of nuclear weapons might also be considerable.[78]

A sophisticated realism might, however, take such democratic effects into account. Since democratic feedback contributes to a common good, it undercuts *this* objection. Further, as ordinarily formulated, realism is a statist view. In contrast, internationalism stresses robust citizen democracy and transnational solidarity.

Third, democratic internationalism does not say that citizens *must* achieve a common good domestically, but rather, that they *can*. It suggests reforms from below to make a realization of such goods more likely. Contrary to the self-misinterpretation of official realism, sophisticated realism also envisions a common good and, through internal critique, merges with an internationalist view. But the first response—that, in explanations, domestic institutions matter, and that interplay of spheres, not one-sided emphasis on powers in the global realm, is vital—differentiates democratic internationalism from even a sophisticated realism.

The Erosion of Reform and Democratic Movements

Even in a radical democratic conception, pluralism depends on the truth of the claim that disadvantaged people can organize themselves to offset prevailing interests and policies. In an oligarchy with parliamentary forms, however, such organization yields, at best, temporary results. Though reform movements have sometimes won particular demands, they then tend to decline. Mainstream political and media hostility speeds their erosion. For instance, in contrast to the vibrant civil rights movement of the 1950s[79] and 1960s, most black teenagers today face unemployment, gangs, or the army. Despite the emergence of an integrated elite, American cities are divided into two worlds. Further, income inequality, harming most whites as well as minorities, is growing.

Antidemocratic feedback exarcerbates these trends. In the Reagan-Bush era, for example, warnings of an "Evil Empire," a rapidly increasing military budget, a soaring deficit ("supply-side economics"), and borrowing from Japan fused with the Iran-Contra and Cocaine-Contra affairs and cutbacks in domestic social programs.

In contrast, the power of democratic example is unusual—consider the impact of Gandhi on King[80]—and often occurs through internationally influenced, slow-to-emerge movements. Where elite power is covert, concentrated, near to office, and costless to individuals,[81] democratic power falls outside prevailing circles of influence, is surveilled[82] and thus dangerous to participants, and often stems from mass revolt from below.

Now democratic theory mandates for each citizen not just a right to vote or even to participate in deliberations but also an equal voice in setting the public agenda. If we imagine ourselves in a Rawlsian ideal sovereign assembly, we would need to be able to say that the basic institutional structure and policies of our society uphold equal freedom. But mainstream arrangements stem or reverse democratic movements and undercut such freedom. *Anti-democratic feedback* has been a decisive, though long unrecognized, obstacle to a deliberative regime.[83] Furthermore, shadowing, a narrowing oligarchy, even once-dominant pluralism is a declining theory in American universities. [84] The policies, institutional reforms, and international agreements noted above would go a long way toward allowing citizens a genuine say on important issues. Some of these measures could, even now, be realized. Within American and other parliamentary regimes, however, the emergence of even this degree of democracy would probably require nonviolent social revolution.

Must global politics constrain democracy? No. Does such politics constrain democracy in the United States and elsewhere? Markedly. In the gulf between these two responses lies the need for renewed debate and democratic movements.

Notes

1. Alan Gilbert, *Must Global Politics Constrain Democracy? Great-Power Realism, Democratic Peace, and Democratic Internationalism* (Princeton: Princeton University Press, 1999). This chapter is a revised and shortened version of chapter 5, "Deliberation as a Medium for Internationalism."

2. The U. S. government also let the talks collapse for nefarious reasons. Agribusiness has tried to force genetically modified foods on Europe, producing massive protest, especially in England. Ironically, Clinton and Labour prime minister Tony Blair sided with Monsanto, which, with blind imperialist avidity, had mixed genetically modified material in all the soy it tried to market to vegetarians in the United Kingdom. Due especially to the protest in Seattle, the U. S. was unable to strong arm Europe into supporting "free" trade for such products.

3. See *El País* and the *International Herald Tribune*, 2 December 1999.

4. Rawls, "The Law of Peoples."

5. George Downs and David M. Rocke, "Conflict, Agency, and Gambling for Ressurrection: The Principal-Agent Problem Goes to War," in *Optimal Imperfection? Domestic Uncertainty and Institutions in International Relations* (Princeton: Princeton University Press, 1995), ch. 1. As Clinton's 1996 bombing of Iraq illustrates, a president may also—though insecurely—be leading in the polls. Nonetheless, the circumscription of this effort—"not one American life was lost"—betrays democratic influence.

6. See Adrienne Rich, "For Ethel Rosenberg," in *A Wild Patience Has Taken Me This Far* (New York: Norton, 1981).

7. Alan Gilbert, *Democratic Individuality* (Cambridge: Cambridge University Press, 1990), 318, n. 20.

8. As obvious illustrations, Charles Wilson and Robert McNamara, CEOs respectively of GM and Ford, became secretaries of defense under presidents Eisenhower and Kennedy.

9. Dennis Thompson and Amy Gutmann, *Democracy and Disagreement* (Cambridge, Mass.: Harvard University Press, 1996), 84-91.

10. John Rawls, *A Theory of Justice* (Cambridge, Mass.: Harvard University Press, 1971), ch. 1; Thompson and Gutmann, *Democracy and Disagreement*, 79-91, invoke "mutual respect."

11. Gilbert, *Democratic Individuality*, chs. 5, 13.

12. Thompson and Gutmann's *Democracy and Disagreement* identifies features of deliberative democracy that encourage provisional resolutions to specific moral disputes. It thus represents a step forward compared to Habermas's and Benhabib's conception, which

stresses a noncoercive, "ideal speech situation," and Cass R. Sunstein's exploration of freedom of speech in *Democracy and the Problem of Free Speech* (New York: Free Press, 1993). Such deliberative conceptions make Dewey's notion of a "democratic public" more specific.

13. Rawls's conception applies Rousseau's notion of a *general will* as a will to equality—a will to uphold the basic freedom and independence of each citizen—to a modern, plural regime. Thus, respect for the rights of each is a *precondition* for democratic deliberation. For the rule of mere democratic procedure could result, through successive majorities—"will of all"—in favor of disenfranchising different groups, in a steadily shrinking electorate.

14. Thompson and Gutmann, *Democracy and Disagreement*, 352.

15. Thompson and Gutmann, *Democracy and Disagreement*, 218.

16. Ronald Dworkin, *Life's Dominion* (New York: Knopf, 1993), ch. 5, especially 119-20. The latter conception is Justice Antonin Scalia's.

17. Thompson and Gutmann, *Democracy and Disagreement,* 349, 347.

18. Many current deliberative conceptions share this flaw. For example, Sunstein, *Democracy and Free Speech* , overemphasizes Madison's commitment to deliberation at the expense of his primary fealty to commerce (Gilbert, *Emancipation and Independence: The American Revolution, Haiti, and Latin American Liberation*, forthcoming, ch. 5).

19. Thompson and Gutmann, *Democracy and Disagreement*, 161-62.

20. For example, after the Second World War, Togliatti—the Italian Communist leader—proposed such a view.

21. Barbara Deming, *Revolution and Equilibrium* (New York: Grossman, 1971).

22. Thoreau rightly admired John Brown and had no paradigm of mass, nonviolent resistance.

23. Adrienne Rich's "The Hermit's Scream," in *What Is Found There: Notebooks on Poetry and Politics* (New York: Norton, 1993), 57-61, explores Deming's thoughtful, passionate activism, her eventual linking of the struggle for peace to combating violence against women.

24. George Kateb, "Nuclear Weapons and Individual Rights," *Dissent* 33, no. 2 (1986): 161-72.

25. As Bishop Helder Camara put it, "When I gave charity to the poor, people called me a saint. But when I asked *why* men and women are poor, people called me a communist" (quoted by Vincent Harding, *Martin Luther King: The Inconvenient Hero* (Maryknoll, Mass.: Orbis, 1996), 126.

26. Levertov, "With the Seabrook Natural Guard in Washington," in *Light Up the Cave* (New York: New Directions, 1981).

27. Gene Sharp, *Making Europe Unconquerable: The Potential of Civilian-Based Deterrence and Defense* (Cambridge, Mass.: Ballinger, 1986), ch. 2.

28. Deming, *Revolution and Equilibrium*, 10-13.

29. Before he emigrated to the United States, Lorenz was a Nazi. His (socio)biology has reactionary undertones.

30. Yet Gandhi warned against strikes and tended to control too tightly the movement he led. Under pressure from LBJ, King tried to talk the Mississippi Freedom Democratic Party out of demanding full recognition—replacing the racist Mississippi delegation—at the Democratic Convention of 1964; he also, reluctantly, supported use of the National Guard against the Watts rebellion. Both traveled a complex, ambiguous course toward important clarities.

31. Cited in Harding, *Martin Luther King*, 125.

32. Cited in Harding, *Martin Luther King*, 127.

33. Mahatma Gandhi, *Essential Writings of Mahatma Gandhi,* ed. Raghavan Iyer (Oxford: Oxford University Press, 1994), 253.

34. Cheryl Payer, *The Debt Trap* (New York: Monthly Review Press, 1974). The

IMF could require cutbacks of, say, military budgets. The elite in the borrowing state would, however, resist; hence, the Fund's preference for harming the poor and ravaging a common good.

35. T. C. Schelling, "The Global Dimension," in *Rethinking America's Security*, ed. Graham Allison and Gregory F. Treverton (New York: Norton, 1992), 200; Richard Falk, *On Humane Governance: Toward a New Global Politics* (University Park: Pennsylvania State University Press, 1995), 51-52.

36. David Held, *Democracy and the Global Order: From the Modern State to Cosmopolitan Governance* (Stanford, Calif.: Stanford University Press, 1995), 232-33.

37. Held, *Democracy and the Global Order*, 278-80. In "Democracy and the New World Order," in *Cosmopolitan Democracy: An Agenda for a New World Order*, ed. David Held and Daniele Archibugi (Cambridge: Polity Press, 1995), 88, 114-15, he notes, in passing, "the deficiencies" of the United Nations—its domination and financing by the Great Powers, particularly the United States—which he traces to the state system "with its deep structural embeddedness in the capitalist economy." Likewise, Norberto Bobbio, "Democracy and the International System," in Held and Archibugi, *Cosmopolitan Democracy*, 32, gestures at contemporary obstacles.

38. Held, *Democracy and the Global Order*, 229-30.

39. Daniele Archibugi, "From the United Nations to Cosmopolitan Democracy," in Held and Archibugi, *Cosmopolitan Democracy*, 140-42, 152-58.

40. Mary Kaldor, "European Institutions, Nation-States, and Nationalism," in Held and Archibugi, *Cosmopolitan Democracy*, 90-93.

41. Stressing positive features of the contemporary global environment, David Held, "Democracy: From City-States to a Cosmopolitan Order?" *Political Studies* 40 (1992): 26, unlike Marx, downplays its harms: "What is new about the modern global system is the spread of globalization in and through new dimensions of activity—technological, organizational, administrative and legal, among others—and the chronic intensification of patterns of interconnectedness mediated by such phenomena as the modern communications industry and new information technology."

42. Overlapping with Kenneth N. Waltz's emphasis in *Theory of International Politics* (New York: McGraw-Hill, 1979) on restricting the four *ps*—poverty, pollution, population, and proliferation—they realize international public goods.

43. The U. S. stations 38,000 troops in South Korea.

44. *New York Times*, 3 May 1998.

45. Francis X. Clines, "Militant Veteran Wages War against Land Mines," *New York Times*, 3 December 1997.

46. Clines, "Militant Veteran Wages War." Even General H. Norman Schwartzkopf signed a letter to the president, supporting the ban.

47. Clines, "Militant Veteran Wages War."

48. James Gerstenzang, "Germany Powering Way to Efficiency," *Denver Post,* 17 November 1996, A12.

49. William Drozdiak, "World Increasingly Disdainful of Powerful US," *Denver Post,* 13 November 1997, A27.

50. William K. Stevens, "Kyoto Agreement Only a Beginning in Fight against Global Warming," *New York Times,* 12 December 1997.

51. William K. Stevens, "Talks on Global Warming Open in Kyoto," *New York Times,* 12 December 1997.

52. Future presidential candidate Gore's appearance at the conference presaged this change. Retreating from, though not quite abandoning, his one time stand on global warming, Gore moved cautiously between environmentalists and the oil companies. James Bennet, "Senate Fight to Be Tough," *New York Times*, 11 December 1997. Within the administration, Tim Wirth, undersecretary of state for environmental affairs, fought for major reductions, lost, and resigned (John H. Cushman Jr. and David F. Sanger, "No

Simple Fight: The Forces That Shaped the Clinton Plan," *New York Times*, 28 November 1997).

53. William K. Stevens, "Global Emissions Accord Gets Nod: But US Hedges on Volatile Issue," *New York Times*, 11 December 1997.

54. Charles J. Hanley, "Warming Hot Topic for 150 Nations," *Denver Post*, 30 November 1997, A30.

55. So does the burning of rain forests, which diminishes absorption of carbon dioxide by trees.

56. Keith Bardeuer, "License to Pollute: Trucks, Darlings of Drivers, Are Favored by the Law, Too," *New York Times*, 30 November 1997, A24. The figure varies from city to city with the severity of auto inspection.

57. Bardauer, "License to Pollute." This withdrawal cost the journal 7 percent of its advertising revenue and forced the editors to shorten it.

58. John H. Cushman Jr., "How Climate Change Treaty Could Affect US," *New York Times*, 12 December 1997.

59. John H. Cushman Jr., "How Climate Change Treaty Could Affect US," *New York Times*, 12 December 1997.

60. Warren Brown and Martha M. Hamilton, "New Cars Would Cut Emissions by 99%," *Washington Post*, 18 December 1997.

61. W. K. Stevens, "Kyoto Agreement Only Beginning," and "The Coming Battle over Kyoto," editorial, *New York Times*, 12 December 1997.

62. Robin Wright, "Rights Group Argues US Poses a 'Growing Threat,'" *Denver Post*, 5 December 1997, A3.

63. United States Civil Rights Congress, *We Charge Genocide*, ed. William L. Patterson (New York: International Publishing, 1949). After the civil rights movement, President Carter signed the agreement. Yet during his tenure, the larger pattern of U. S. human-rights policy remained abysmal. See Noam Chomsky and Edward Hermann, *The Political Economy of Human Rights*, vol. 1: *The Washington Connection and Third World Fascism* (Boston: South End Press, 1977). Since leaving office, however, Carter has provided striking leadership for a common good.

64. Like Carter, Clinton and Gore are aware of the relevant moral and intellectual issues. That these two men—who have sought "leadership" relentlessly since they were teenagers—cave in to particular interests is sad.

65. Secretary of State Madeleine Albright has spoken out on this issue. Barbara Crossette, "Legal Experts Agree on an Outline for a World Criminal Court," *New York Times*, 14 December 1997.

66. Barbara Crossette, "World Criminal Court Having Painful Birth," *New York Times*, 13 August 1997.

67. War crimes are uncommon. With the highest stakes, however, as for those concerning an armed world state, an analogous response would not be persuasive.

68. Barbara Crossette, "Prosecutor Proposes Permanent International Criminal Court," *New York Times*, 9 December 1997.

69. This knowledge is often problematic. Two friends of mine, both Vietnam veterans, relate the routine in their companies. They would go as far away from battle as possible, get high, return after five to seven days, and report a "bloated body count."

70. Downs and Rocke, "Conflict, Agency, and Gambling for Resurrection," 67.

71. Downs and Rocke, "Conflict, Agency, and Gambling for Resurrection," 59-67, 72-75, offer a striking mathematical interpretation of their theory.

72. Cited in Downs and Rocke, "Conflict, Agency, and Gambling for Resurrection," 69.

73. Plato's "city in speech" deprives guardians of spouses, children, and personal property. Marx's proposal that worker-officials, modeled on those of the Paris Commune, should receive wages no higher than those of a skilled worker also attempts to counter this

danger (Gilbert, *Democratic Individuality*, ch. 8).

74. I owe this objection to George Downs.

75. Robin Blackburn in *The Overthrow of Colonial Slavery, 1776-1848* (London: Verso, 1988), 222-26, 258-59, stresses this high point of Jacobinism.

76. The failure to consider individual rights in the democratic-peace literature is startling.

77. Robert D. Putnam, "Diplomacy and Domestic Politics: The Logic of Two-Level Games," *International Organization* 42, no. 3 (1988): 428-29, 434-35.

78. Glenn H. Snyder and Paul Diesing, *Conflicting Nations: Bargaining, Decision-Making, and System Structure* (Princeton: Princeton University Press, 1977), 510-25. William Clark of Georgia Tech and Kenneth Schultz of Princeton are currently working on the role of such interactions in the expansion of democracy.

79. The Montgomery bus boycott.

80. Sudarshan Kapur, *Raising Up a Prophet: The African-American Encounter with Gandhi* (Boston: Beacon Press, 1992).

81. Perhaps I should say costless in terms of official persecution or sentencing. The wretchedness and servility, characteristic just below the surface, of elite politics is—at least for some—a detriment.

82. Michel Foucault, *Surveillir et punir. Naissance de la prison* (Paris: Gallimard, 1975); David Caute, *The Great Fear: The Anti-Communist Purge under Truman and Eisenhower* (New York: Simon and Schuster, 1978); Ellen Schrecker, *No Ivory Tower* (New York: Oxford University Press, 1986); Griffen Fariello, *Red Scare* (New York: Norton, 1995).

83. Among democratic theorists, Cohen and Rogers, *Inequity and Intervention* (Boston: South End Press, 1986) discuss the domestic impact of the U. S. war on Nicaragua. See also Rawls, "The Law of Peoples."

84. The original proponents of pluralism—Dahl and Lindblom—now believe that the "power of large corporations" is inconsistent with democracy. Charles Lindblom, *Politics and Markets* (New York: Basic Books, 1977); Robert A. Dahl, *A Preface to Economic Democracy* (Berkeley and Los Angeles: University of California Press, 1985). Only radicals like Walzer and Joseph M. Schwartz, *The Permanence of the Political* (Princeton: Princeton University Press, 1995), hold to it, as a postrevolutionary conception (Gilbert, *Democratic Individuality*, 350-51).

Chapter 10

Nationalism and Sovereignty Overrides: Permissibility of Interventions in Other Polities

Eero Loone

Introduction

The actual human world is multicultural, whether we do or do not like the fact. Descriptively, multiculturalism involves something more than just idiosyncrasies. Cultures (and their political subcultures) can be incommensurable. They can be opposing. Nazism and democracy provide standard examples of opposing political cultures. [1] Liberalism has not been universally accepted as an actual operational ideology. Cultures may even just include lists of values that have only common entries, but the ranking orders of entries (priorities) are different. Political cultures of the USA and Canada differ significantly on how they assign weights to certain values and rights. [2] Cultures have core values and distant borderlands.

Western media and public opinion have been increasingly vocal during the last decade in presenting demands for action anywhere on the globe to impose certain Western standards of behavior. These demands presume that everybody has a duty to settle injustices everywhere. A British politician, Douglas Hurd, said that this presumes the West has an imperial role, but the latter view has been rejected by public opinion. [3] Incompatibility of value presumptions creates tensions and weakens policy-making capabilities. There are unsettled questions about the legitimacy of actions that do not involve national defense and about capabilities to act (for example, capabilities to suppress a civil war, or to prevent an execution, or to stop the production of dangerous drugs).

Globalization certainly involves increases of capacities for some actions by individuals, non-state collective actors, and states outside their primary locations. Possibilities for overt and covert interventions have grown both for the largest and for middle-ranking states (possibilities for covert interventions have grown for all states).[4] Interventions within other states are obviously incompatible with traditional ideas about sovereignty, although in the nineteenth century some states were considered more sovereign than others; intervention in Turkey was thinkable, intervention in Russia was non-thinkable. The Rushdie case has demonstrated that interventions by developing countries within the Western world are at present conceivable.

Earth is exhaustively divided into multiple polities or states. Antarctica is a sole gray area; permanent human settlement in Antarctica requires support by states. Some of these states have an identifiable majority and/or dominant culture (or culture-kind). Some have also identified themselves with a particular culture or a culture-kind. These states claim sovereignty over defined territories and persons. Actions by a state inside another state without the permission of that particular other state override the sovereignty of that particular other state. Sovereignty overrides lessen the status of a polity from that of a legally independent actor to that of a legally dependent actor. Protectorates and colonies are not legally independent actors and they are not self-determining polities. Permissibility of sovereignty overrides seems to create a two-tier system of polities similar to the system of colonialism.

Interventions are illegal under international law. Rules about legality may be changed. Claims about the legitimacy of sovereignty overrides on human rights issues suggest that we are entering a post-sovereignty world, where voters in a country *A* (for example, Iran) may properly decide, what it is politically correct behavior in a country *B* (for example, the United States). Therefore, we should inquire whether it would be advisable to change the present laws. Obviously, if voters in the United States are to be allowed to decide on proper length of skirts in Iran, but voters in Iran will not be allowed to decide what is blasphemy in the United States, then we would have a system of colonialism. There is a problem of meaningful consensus on action warrants in a multicultural world. If God's rights are higher than human rights, then God's rights may justify intervention over "Western" human rights (for example, on the issue of blasphemy). If severing a hand is not an unusual or necessarily a cruel punishment, then it is not a human rights violation.[5]

The object of these examples is to indicate sources of some problems about producing generally acceptable reasonable and reasoned solutions in a multicultural world. Acceptability is not just a matter of words. UN document writers had become quite adept at producing texts that were discoursively[6] acceptable for thin liberal democracies, Islamic societies, and Soviet-type communist states. The statements in these documents are not always vacuous, although explicit textual consensus does not equate with behavioral consensus. Some governments still torture or just restrict liberties of their subjects. If there is no meaningful consensus on specific action justifiers, could there be other universal rational grounds that would justify sovereignty overrides or, vice versa, uphold non-interventionism?

This chapter will investigate possible permissibility and even obligatoriness of interventions within other states and the charge of the reemergence of colonialism under the guise of liberal values. My primary interests within the present chapter are those of normative analysis. I will confine myself to nationalism, although relevance to democracy (and sometimes liberalism) will be indicated. Nationalism might oppose a sovereignty override permitted by liberals. Nationalism might support a sovereignty override permitted by democrats. My own viewpoint will be (I hope) generally democratic and also a version of pragmatic pluralism. This allows me to support liberty without a previous commitment to some particular U. S. or U. K. liberal theory.

A strong premise of this chapter is that war is a crime. In general, Walzerian treatment of just wars will be assumed to provide the standards.[7] This is not a premise that has been universally shared within humankind from the time of its emergence up to our present. During various intervals of its existence, humankind or its parts have sometimes glorified war. I am not just referring to Nazis. Rulers and groups in the past have thought it proper to extend the areas they rule by means of war. While particular instances of these actions may have been condemned, the kind of activity was not necessarily impermissible. There is a difference between condemning execution for heresy and condemning execution of a Catholic (or a Lutheran), for the reason that he or she was judged guilty for belonging to the right religion.

Obviously, any war involves at least two sides. I do not think self-defense should be totally condemned. My premise is that killing is sometimes justified (although never a pleasure or a positive value). This is a standard Lockean position, which has also had some more recent supporters. A war of aggression is a crime; resistance to a criminal act is not a crime. Genocide equals war. Genocide is crime. Resistance to genocide is not a crime. For an absolute pacifist, what follows is mostly superfluous (although some of the arguments might be modified for nonviolent relations of domination).

Clarifications of the Conceptual Network

Sovereignty

Sovereignty, as used within the present chapter, is first and foremost a legal concept that applies to states. A unit is sovereign if it is the highest decision-making authority within its borders and if there are no higher authorities that may change its laws, alter its governmental decisions, and overturn rulings of its courts. The existence of international law based on consent of states presents no difficulties for this concept. H. L. A. Hart has discussed cases such as the obligatoriness of existing international law on new states. He found that these seeming exceptions do not invalidate the concept of sovereignty as it is ordinarily applied to states within international affairs.[8] There is, of course, a domestic sense of "sovereignty," which refers to issues of supreme authority within a state (for example, sovereignty of a monarch or of people). This presents no major relevance for solutions of the problems of the present chapter, although issues of domestic sovereignty have been predominant in some political conflicts.

There is a difference between legal and sociopolitical sovereignty. H. L. A. Hart mentioned the case of puppet governments in states that were sovereign on paper. Ukraine and Czechoslovakia were UN members in 1975 but neither was sovereign in a sociopolitical sense. The General Secretary of the CPSU and Politburo of the CPSU had power to give orders to Ukraine and Czechoslovakia. The administrations of the latter units could be (and sometimes were) dismissed by the CPSU authorities. Krasner asserts that the Westphalian system has always been a behavioral regularity, and that the Westphalian model has never been an accurate description of reality. He justifies his case within the confines of the descriptive sociopolitical notion of sovereignty.[9]

Prudence constitutes something different from having to accept orders. It may be prudent for a small and weak country to formulate its laws and policies in a way that avoids opposing the expressed wishes of the governments of the USA or, for example, Iraq. It may be prudent even for the USA to avoid some confrontations with Japan. Sovereign governments are not always prudent. They can be misguided. They can be irrational. The exercise of prudence by a state does not mean it has lost its sovereignty in either a legal or a sociopolitical sense. A prudent individual is still an individual actor and not necessarily a dependent being. Discussion of prudence, misguidedness, and (ir)rationality of an actor differs from discussion of sovereignty of an actor.

The growing interdependence of economies has added another dimension to the area of international prudence at the same time that it does not equal post-sovereignty. Moreover, no actor ever has full or real control over the world market, although some have obviously more control than others. In the nineteenth century, the United Kingdom or France or the USA had no control over world business cycles or inflation rates, yet we do not doubt they were sovereign countries. I am not sure whether there exists a method to measure increases or decreases of the size of the set of rational options open for government decisions on domestic and international economic matters between, for example, 1899 and 1999. Whatever the changes, the governments would still be sovereign in both legal and sociopolitical terms.

The European Union has grown from an intergovernmental organization to a quasi state. Law, courts, common citizenship, and, at present times, money are matters for government, and the EU has staked claims to make authoritative decisions in all these areas. Nevertheless, EU legislation is still subject to state veto and may be seen as international law, although it deals with matters internal to states. If the EU will develop into a federation, then there would just be a new sovereign (federal) state to replace more than a dozen old ones. This will not be a case of post-sovereignty.

Traditional realist models of international relations assume that humanity is divided into sovereign states. These states are assigned the status of the highest-level component units of the international order and they are claimed to be the sole constituents of this decomposition level. Contemporary critics allege that there are other actors on this highest level or that the system has more dimensions than just one. For example, Ansell and Weber have argued that the international system is best understood as an open system, in contrast to standard realist closed system models. Nevertheless, they also point out that sovereignty still exists and has to be taken into account in IR theories.[10] Obviously, IMF, World Bank, and (possibly) WTO are influential actors within the international system and do not belong in the same category with multinational corporations or with states. The IMF, World Bank, and WTO do not have armed forces or police units and cannot engage in wars on law enforcement. A multinational corporation might (in theory) employ armed persons and order them to act against some governments. This would be quasi war, for they would not be entitled to claim the right of self-defense.

The USA is a sovereign state in the traditional sense of the word. In internal U. S. politics, there are no politically influential groups that advance the demand to subordinate the U. S. Congress, president, and Supreme Court to decision-making by other bodies or persons. China and Iraq are also sovereign in the traditional sense of the word. Thus, there are some important cases in which sovereignty still exists.

Interventions

An *intervention* of a state A within a state B is a set of actions by state A without the permission of the state B. If the action is carried out with permission by the state B, it has to be freely given by state B for it not to qualify as an intervention. Interventions are made to produce specific changes in other polities, such as placing under arrest a drug-running president and delivering him to courts of the intervening country or dismissing an independent-minded Euro-communist Communist Party secretary and replacing him with a Stalinist servant of the Soviet Union. The goals of intervention are compatible with the preservation of the polity as a unit or a separate entity (although they may reduce the independence status of a polity from separate actor status to client status and its sovereignty to a pure legal fiction). Interventions in this sense are supported by force, although in some cases there might be no need for actual violence. If Ruritania sends its policemen to Blobotania to apprehend a Ruritarian citizen there, and it has no permission from Blobotania, then this is obviously a case of a use of force.

Wars in a strict sense involve attempts to destroy or change other entities as entities and resistance to these attempts.[11] There are kinds of actions in other polities, which are located in the border zone between interventions and wars in a strict sense. If a state *B* is transformed into a colony of the state *A*, then the state *B* is preserved as a kind of virtual entity, although its political regime and international status will have been changed. Imposition of a constitution on a state *B* by a state *A* provides us with another example of the gray area. A blockade of Blobotania by Ruritania is usually seen as a case of war, because states are presumed free to enter into relations with other states, and this permission applies to citizens of relevant states (subject to both sets of relevant laws). Participation in a civil war in Ruritania by other states will be classified as war and not intervention for the purpose of the present chapter, if the outsides do not want to change the borders of Ruritania against the wishes of Ruritanians. Wars and grounds for participation in civil wars will not be investigated in this chapter.

Refusal to accept a state into membership of an organization of states is not, in itself, an intervention, even if setting up democracy or abolishing capital punishment are made sole prerequisites of admission. There may still be gray areas. For example, let Blobotania have borders only and only with the Commonwealth of the Independent Ruritarian States and the Common Market Union of Western Seaside Continent. Let both the Commonwealth and the Common Market operate prohibitive import and transit tariffs. These actions may, in practice, be equal to economic blockades and the resulting situation will fall into the gray area.

Any action of a state *A* within a state *B* without permission of the state *B* is deemed to create a *Lockean state of war*. Interventions, in the strict sense, constitute therefore a specific kind of Lockean state of war. Starting a war is, under standard Lockean presumptions, an unjust act and the resulting war will be unjust for the state *A* . There may be exceptions or overrides.[12] These have to be strong and include safeguards against arbitrariness.

Actions by permission are not interventions. A treaty may provide for the legality of such actions and, if it is a legitimate treaty, the actions will be legitimate. UN membership imposes a condition to refrain from aggression and to use force only in self-defense. If Ruritania breaks its treaty obligations, then actions of other states against Ruritania (in some cases, inside Ruritania) will not be interventions. They will also probably be just, even if they involve violence.

Interstate coercion is different from interventions. We have interstate coercion of state B by state A, if the state A induces the state B to act according to commands (desires) of state A. For example, let Ruritania wish Blobotanian laws to be written in Ruritanian (although parallel texts in Blobotanian would be admissible). Let Blobotania be dependent on exports to Ruritania and on Ruritanian transit. Now, let Ruritania introduce an 800 percent tariff surcharge on all goods crossing their mutual borders and let it state that the surcharge will be abolished at once when Blobotania stops discriminating against the use of the Ruritanian language in Blobotania. This will be a case of interstate coercion as distinct from an intervention. A threat of war against a state B would also be a case of interstate coercion, even if the state A does not intend to incorporate the state B or make it a colony. [13] Interstate coercion may produce both target-specific governance and external override spaces in other polities. In the nineteenth century, Western powers used both methods in dealings with Turkey and China. [14] These results decreased sovereignty of the target states and created a two-tiered system of sovereignty. Some countries were more sovereign than other ones. Obviously, this situation was supportive for the growth of nationalism in target countries.

Outside *coercion* of a state can be exercised by non-state actors. The World Bank supplies an obvious example. Multinational corporations and private international financial actors are sometimes said to have been involved in outside coercion of states by exercise of their economic power.

This chapter will deal with interventions in the strict sense. The wider issues of outside coercion will not be investigated here. I am not assuming by default that outside intervention (and coercion) is always good or bad, desirable or undesirable. I am seeking to find some rational and reasonable criteria for decision making about interventions in democratic polities. The extendibility of these criteria to other kinds of coercion needs separate investigation.

Nationalism

The word 'nationalism' is an overfuzzy and often descriptively near-vacuous expression for negative evaluation of others in English. [15] Its use persuasively defines the user as non-nationalist. [16] There are no sacred nationalist source-texts like those by Marx on Mao. Of course, liberals have no Marx of their own, but *On Liberty* by J. S. Mill could certainly be regarded as a member of the foundational set of liberal texts. Nationalists have no shared sacred texts. Some nationalisms involve claims that make it impossible for other nationalisms to share foundational texts with these nationalisms.

'Nationalism' is actually a family of concepts. Roger Scruton pointed out that 'nationalism' has at least two basic meanings. It may refer to a sentiment or an ideology of attachment to a nation and it may refer to a demand or theory that state should be founded on a nation.[17] Ernest Gellner used the word 'nationalism' only in the latter sense. He allowed 'nationalism' to refer to sentiment and ideology, if these accompanied the claims about the setup of states (and delimitation of their borders).[18] Standard Soviet theory was closer to the former sense of the word (as defined by Scruton). It treated nationalism as a wrong or evil theory about interests of a nation being higher than interests of the working class (this entailed that attachment to a nation was less important than attachment to working class).

I shall use the term *ethnopolitical nationalism* to refer to a political program (and ideology and sentiment) that provides legitimation criteria (or rights claims) for setup of states. Setup involves "installation" and "uninstallation" and something that may be called "operating system" or "environment." Ethno-political nationalism provides answers to questions about who may legitimately make decisions about founding a new state unit, preserving or not preserving an existing one, and delimiting its borders. It also provides criteria for decisions about some properties of political regimes that are legitimate.[19]

A *strong ethnopolitical nationalism* claims that (i) most humans belong to (ethnic) nations, (ii) only nations are justified in making decisions about the setup of states, and (iii) political regime of a state has to be congruent to the culture of the nation(s) that had installed this particular state. A *very strong ethnopolitical nationalism* claims that (i) all humans belong to (ethnic) nations, (ii) only nations are justified in making decisions about the setup of states, (iii) each nation is entitled and obliged to set up its own state, and (iv) political regime of a state has to be based on the culture of the nation that had installed this particular state. Obviously, an ethnopolitical nationalism may include a rationality constraint, which means it will allocate similar rights to all ethnic groups. A very strong ethnopolitical nationalism is still compatible with mutual political consent of two ethnic nation-states about their mutual borders and even about the rights of members of another ethnic group to settle and operate inside a state of another ethnic group. What it will have to insist on is that the foundational decisions are to be made by the ethnic groups and their states.[20] In practice, strong ethnopolitical nationalisms could live with interstate agreements on some minority rights, but they might not be compatible with minorities having a right to share decision making on issues of sovereignty.

Nazi nationalism differs from a very strong ethnopolitical nationalism in that it introduces additional criteria (a) in case of controversies and conflicts, the rights of the German nation override the rights of all other nations, and (b) some nations have no entitlement to set up their own state. Nazi nationalism also alters assertion (iv) of the strong ethnopolitical nationalism, that it, the political regime of a state has to enforce the culture of its nation (and the culture of the objectively most valuable nation, namely, the German nation). Any nationalism that supports an absolute priority order of values of nations is a Nazi-type nationalism.

Weak ethnopolitical nationalism asserts that (a) some humans are members of ethnic nations, (b) ethnic nations are the highest decision units for setup of states, and (c) states have an obligation to support the survival within their borders of ethnic nations that legitimately participate or have participated in the setup decisions. A law that regulates the language of subtitles of imported films or of TV programs would be perfectly justified for weak nationalism.[21]

Ethnocultural nationalism asserts that ethnic identity is a valuable human trait and ethnic groups have a right to their culture. The term "culture" is used here in an anthropological on sociological sense and not solely to designate results of artistic activity. Obviously, culture in this sense is a constituent property of a group (a set of humans). Some myths may belong to a culture, but shared actual behavioral patterns are not mythical. *Strong* ethnocultural nationalisms will insist on the objective existence of a unique intrinsic priority order of cultures (with the highest rank awarded to the culture whose members do the insisting business). *Weak* ethnocultural nationalisms will insist on indexical priority orders (the culture *A* is assigned the highest rank for the members of the culture *A*, the culture *B* is assigned the highest rank for the members of the culture *B*, etc.)

Statist nationalism is a normative doctrine about sovereignty. It is an ideology that claims that there are no legitimate actors above states and that no state is justified in restricting the liberty of another state in its internal affairs. Actions against other states to prevent harm to oneself are, of course, justified. Obviously, some statist nationalisms might claim privileges for their own state to act against or within other states, while denying these privileges to other states. Strong ethnopolitical nationalisms are also statist nationalisms, but the opposite does not hold. A multiethnic state can pursue statist nationalism. A statist nationalism may be variously combined with ethnocultural nationalisms. Most U. S. Americans seem to hold a hidden default position that is analogous to strong ethnocultural nationalism, with "America" (=USA) being substituted for the ethnic entity. Of course, "Americans" differ on what they accept as the hidden default settings of the U. S. culture.

Concepts of nationalism are not singularly entailed by assertions about whether ethnicity is a myth or something real. The force of nationalist arguments would be seriously undermined, if nations were to turn out to be fictitious entities (or fictitious collections of humans). Ethnicity is certainly a difficult concept to analyze, but it makes sense to presume it refers to something nonfictitious. Talk about Poles or Ukrainians in Canada presumes that they are identifiable by some other socially relevant property that is independent of Canadian citizenship. Moreover, this other property is one they have in common with many inhabitants of Poland and Ukraine. I shall be using the word *ethnie* to designate these sets of humans.

Overrides

Noam J. Zohar used the concept of overrides to discuss the political morality of interventions in Western and Talmudic traditions. In any practical issue, justificatory arguments involve more than one warrant providing principles. A principle may override another one. Kant's categorical imperative is an example of an override principle. It provides for an absolute override on all other principles within his system.[22] Locke argued that self-defense provided an override to the principle that killing other humans is wrong (both for individuals and governments).

Override principles may be arranged in a strong unique order. Nazism, Russian communism,[23] Islam, Christianity, and liberalism support monistic systems of unique orders for override principles. Pragmatism and pluralism would oppose these absolute orders, although this does not necessarily entail absolute arbitrariness (even under the guise of extreme cultural relativism).

Ethnopolitical nationalisms are first and foremost doctrines about a kind of actor whose interests or demands override interests or demands of other kinds of actors in matters of setting up and operating states. Statist nationalisms and ethnopolitical ones may share support for popular sovereignty, but they differ about the constitution of *populus*. Therefore, their views about specific sovereignty overrides may differ.

The actual humanity is multiethnic and multicultural. A single culture and a single ethnicity can, at present, be imposed only by forcible destruction of all other cultures and many of their members. Variety may also be valuable and humans are certainly right to hold a particular culture precious for them.[24]

Individual *ethnies* or parts of *ethnies* may have been incorporated into a state by conquest and held within it against their will. In this case, the sovereignty of their particular state will be contentious for them and the problem about sovereignty overrides becomes a political issue. They may also have been participants of an initial social contract that they continue tacitly to accept as valid. They may have entered a state to become members of a state nation (immigrant countries), and possibly even to switch their ethnic identity. They may have entered a country as refugees, to become members of the state operationally, but not by positive identification. In the latter cases, sovereignty of the specific state will not be contentious for the cultural group. Before the First World War, nearly all state borders in Eastern Europe were contingent results of conquests. Might does not create right.

It is a truism that there is no identity between ethnic and state boundaries. What follows is that ethnicity may be involved in discussions about override warrants for actions in other states. If the legitimacy of the variety of culture-kinds is granted, then these discussions are rationally and reasonably legitimate. It does not follow that the proposed override criteria will always be rationally and reasonably warranted.

A Note about Democracy

This chapter is premised on the idea that democracy is desirable, if it is feasible.[25] Democracy is feasible in industrial (and supposedly postindustrial) societies. It might not have been feasible in pre-industrial societies (there are still some of these extant around the globe). Of course, this generalized support does not entail specific support for a particular form of democracy. Politics is a matter of actions, agreements, and disagreements. It cannot be premised on arbitrary justificatory principles, but one should not think political solutions wrong if philosophers cannot derive these solutions from universal principles.[26]

Democracy cannot supply a unique, universal, and sufficient override principle for all particular situations. For example, Dahl has pointed out that a theory of democracy cannot include decision criteria for the choice of the "people," that is for delineating the membership of the set of humans empowered to make the decision about the choice about the setup of a political entity.[27] It is also true (or highly probable) that a democratic world (=Earth) government is at present still not feasible. These examples do not mean that inimicability to democracy cannot count as an argument to justify opposition to some policies for many particular situations. They just point to some overrides even to the most likable principles.

Intervention against Genocide

Let us start with an example. Vietnamese invasion of Cambodia replaced a well-organized system of mass murder, mass slavery, and mass villeinage by a Hobbesian-justifiable absolute monarchy. This particular monarchy was set up as a client state of the invader state.[28] This was a solution to problems of preventing or halting mass murders, which prioritized preserving life over all other values, rights, and issues. The solution was compatible to one of the basic tenets of the Hobbes-Locke tradition about justifiable ends of government. According to this tradition, government is a legitimate corporation or body to use force (violence) to protect the lives of members of a specific individual compact or commonwealth. Lives cannot be always protected with talk or fines, if no recourse to force (violence) is available as a last resort. It is true that there was no compact about asking the Vietnamese in. There is no possibility to set up a compact under a genocidal regime against that regime. In cases like Rwanda, Burundi, and Nazi Germany, there were no interventions. Actually, UN forces in Rwanda had orders not to use force for both the protection of victims of genocide and themselves.

Given the actual plurality of value sets in a world with pluralism of cultures, there are extremely few consensus candidates for highest values, irrespective of cultures. I am upholding the following claim, although it cannot be supported by full argument here:

> (1) Preservation of humanity takes rational and reasonable precedence over all other values.

Within rational and reasonable politics, we are entitled to accept that we do not yet know the real, ultimate, absolute ordered list of value priorities, particularly in a multicultural world. Therefore, if the very strong statement (1) is not acceptable, then there is a weaker form that will not make any practical difference:

> (2) Preservation of humanity takes rational and reasonable precedence politically over all other values.

Both (1) and (2) will support an override to democracy. What they claim is that if we have to save the existence of human species at a cost of substituting autocracy for democracy, then it would be a right action for us (of course, given there are no other options).

A relevant weaker candidate for justificatory reasons to support a sovereignty override would be:

> (3) Preservation of individual human life takes rational and reasonable precedence politically over all other values, except in case (2).[29]

We cannot place (3) above (1) or (2) because this would mean we should sacrifice humanity to preserve a life of one human only. The choice will be terrible, but if somebody will have to be sacrificed to capture mad terrorists with their fingers on the trigger to launch an overall nuclear war, then the present arrangement of priorities entails that it would be right to kill the terrorists and to suffer human losses in the process of destroying them.

Genocide is mass murder on a particularly large scale, destruction of the humanity or of its large part. There will be no rationality and reason without humans.[30] Intervention against genocide will be warranted if we accept (1) or (2). If we do not want to equate genocide with the preservation of humanity itself, then a weaker version of (2) should be entered into the above list of priorities (3). This version should refer to a subset of humanity.

There are many additional problems, for example, about intermediaries between (2) and (3). We can ask whether preventing mass murder takes precedence over preventing a single murder, or whether defending my country (that is, my polity) can be equated with (3). They are all about location of a particular value in a particular priority order.

If honor is more valuable than life, then the assertions (2) and (3) are wrong. In this case, it would be permissible to carry out mass murder or even destruction of humanity to preserve or vindicate honor. If rights are more valuable than humanity, then the assertions (1) and (2) are wrong and (3) is inadequate. This does not make sense. Rights are claims. No humans, no claims. Therefore, there are override limitations to discourse carried out solely in the language of rights.[31]

A government that carries out mass murders of its subjects is not legitimate in rational and reasonable terms. Sovereignty override to prevent or stop genocide is permissible.

Permissibility of a kind does not depend on particular feasibility. Full justification of an action has to take the latter factor into account. Physical and logistic resources for intervention to stop genocide have to be available before the occasion happens. Fire brigades have to be trained and available before a fire starts. Moreover, permissibility and feasibility do not entail particular political obligations. Vietnam was not politically obliged to intervene in Cambodia. Zohar has also pointed out that there might be moral overrides to orders for citizens of state *A* to be sent to state *B* to kill and be possibly killed for reasons other than self-defense.[32]

Feasibility involves an issue of long-term presence. Given a culture that equates power with a license to use physical force, prevention of genocide might mean setting up a permanent colonial-type regime. This will mean a return to the nineteenth-century world and will certainly not be compatible with democracy in the target polity.

Nazi-type nationalisms are compatible with support for genocide. They have to oppose genocide only and only if the object is the *ethnie*, which has been allocated the highest place in its priority list of values of *ethnies*. They are perfectly compatible in theory with obligatory genocide against lower-valued *ethnies* (and have actually carried out this policy). Statist nationalism (of a state *A*) does not necessarily have to support genocides, even if genocide happens outside of the state *A*. Statist nationalism may be compatible with the admission that there are some overriding universal human values, but this admission might not be sufficient to allow intervention against genocide in other policies and will certainly (in practical terms) be incompatible with the admission that other states may intervene against genocide in state *A*. The result might be a freeze of action capabilities.

Of course, the government of state *A* that is incapable of dealing with genocide within its territory by a part of its population against another part might turn to other governments for assistance. The actions of other governments in this case will not be interventions in the sense of the present chapter because they will be acting not against the will of the government of state *A*, but rather will be assuming the capacities of agents for the state *A*.

There is no necessary connection between support for genocide and other types of ethnopolitical nationalisms. If an ethnopolitical nationalism claims that ethnicity is the highest value for (live) humans, then it has to oppose genocide. The opposition would be warranted by general considerations about there being no *ethnies* without humans, and by less general reasons like the destruction of an *ethnie* being a loss to humanity. Protection of an *ethnie* against destruction used by other agents will override any other values.

Other Humanitarian Interventions

To eat and drink are requirements or needs. A human cannot stay alive without food. This is also a case of a multicultural consensus, although some cultures would not consider it to be the moral duty or a political obligation of a government to feed their people. For example, they might think this is best left to private enterprise within free markets, and that poverty is, in any case, a just punishment for being lazy, immoral, or not properly obeying God(s). Of course, other cultures might hold that government is there for feeding the people (or, at least, the citizens). Statistically, the latter view has been more widespread during the existence of full-time governments among humankind.

It is not feasible to distribute food in another country if the government of this country opposes our government's carrying out the distributions (intervention was defined above as use of force inside another policy without its permission). Globalization increases the membership in the set of practically available charity recipients, but charity differs from force-feeding.

Statist nationalism of a state *A* is incompatible with acceptance of the right of other states to carry out humanitarian intervention within the state *A*. In general, if a state *A* adheres to statist nationalism, then it will have to oppose humanitarian interventions (as distinct from humanitarian aid). If it accepts a colonialist kind of world where states of the second tier are not full-fledged sovereign entities, then, of course, interventions in the second tier states will be permissible, but statist nationalism of the state *A* will be opposed to classification of itself as a second tier state.

Nazi-type nationalisms exclude humanitarian consideration of *ethnies* (and individual members of these *ethnies*) that are placed lower on the priority list of *ethnies*. Nazi-type nationalisms would probably exclude any kind of humanitarian considerations altogether, and this has been their actual practice. I am not prepared to state at present whether this is logically entailed by their starting point. Given the general properties of these nationalisms, logical considerations would not greatly matter.

Other types of ethnopolitical nationalism may accept humanitarian consideration and some of them (the mild variety) could be essentially compatible with these considerations. They would still oppose intervention (in the sense argued above), but they could support giving and accepting humanitarian aid. The actual decisions on these matters would, of course, be a matter of particular politics and resources.

There are some difficulties with multiculturally acceptable entries to the list of humanitarian actions deemed to provide warrant for interventions. Female political leaders have been known to support what we call female genital mutilation (and which is deeply abhorrent to me). Sending in male marines to stop female circumcision seems to be a deep wrong. The override warrants have to transcend particular cultures and civilizations to avoid the charges of colonialism and of hypocrisy.

Protection of Property

Government involves setting up rules about property. Any claim by Ruritania that its legal rules and social customs about property have to take precedence inside Blobotania over Blobotanian rules and customs means that Ruritania claims sovereignty over Blobotania. This amounts to an attempt to erode sovereignty of a particular state but may not be supported by references to globalization. If Ruritania sends its forces into Blobotania to prevent Blobotanian government taking over a piece of land owned by a Ruritanian to build a new road (although compensation at market value was paid), then it has committed an act of aggression. Rules about property are to be made by polities themselves. We may hate these rules in some other state, but it is their affair. Nationalization of the Suez Canal by Nasser was not a crime and did not warrant an intervention.

Statist nationalism of a state *A* is on the whole incompatible with acceptance of the right of other states to intervene in the state *A* on issues of property. Strong varieties of statist nationalism would allow the state *A* to intervene in other states for this reason, but without granting reciprocity. Ethnopolitical nationalisms would not differ from statist nationalism in this area. In any case, once we accept interventions in "defense" of property, we cannot give full support to democracy. Therefore, the issue and its solutions are not nationalism specific.

There is a specific kind of illegitimate property. This is slavery, full ownership of a human being by another human being. Let us assume that it is feasible to send an expeditionary force into Ruritania to free all slaves and to enact a law making slavery illegal (this must also mean that Ruritanians will not reintroduce slavery after the intervention force will be withdrawn).[33] If Ruritania is a sovereign state, this would be illegal under international law, given that Ruritania has not assumed an obligation to outlaw slavery. Violent suppression of the slave trade on the high seas is not an intervention for the reason that the high seas lie outside polities.

There are, at present, large numbers of Russian prostitutes in Western Europe who are actually held as slaves of their "employers."[34] They are illegal immigrants, their passports are held by brothel-keepers, and they are subject to murder threats if they should complain to the police. If intervention against slavery is right, then it would be right for Russia to send in police to Germany to check up on contracts of Russian prostitutes without the permission of the German government.

There is a difference between humans and inanimate objects.[35] The issue of slavery is not properly an issue about property. It is an issue about who is to be counted human and thus involves the priority levels assigned to mass murders. In moral priority lists of evils, slavery is located just under mass murders. Slavery is utterly reprehensible, but assertion (1) still holds. Of course, the feasibility requirement may also override our decision to use force both to free individual slaves and abolish slavery in other polities without their consent.

Nazi-type nationalisms allow that the political interests of the superior *ethnie* would ground the decisions about interventions against slavery in other polities. Other very strong and strong nationalisms do not entail support for slavery. Whether they would allow intervention or even starting a war to liberate slaves in other countries would depend on particular policies of particular nationalisms. Of course, interventions against slavery may be overruled on grounds of preserving the international order. These grounds are not nationalism specific and will be discussed in the last sections of this chapter.

Protection of Religion

Protection of religion might mean protection of a particular religion within a state that has many religions. It could also mean installation of a religious state by outside intervention or intervention to protect a religious state. Violent crusades or jihads have been considered legitimate by large sections of humanity during many centuries. Everybody is not a Western liberal. A religious party in Estonia put up candidates at the 1999 general elections. It advocated the use of state (and state-run education) to install Lutheran Christian values into Estonian minds as the means of producing a decent and non-corrupt state. They do not, of course, advocate intervention in other polities for this purpose, but they are definitely not liberals, and they are ethnopolitical nationalists. Their electoral support is actually very low and they did not succeed in getting anybody elected to the Estonian Parliament. There are also non-Christian cultures that insist on setting up and maintaining a religious state for their own particular religion.

Both liberalism and democracy are incompatible with a religious state (a Scandinavian type of state religion will not matter). Supporters of a religious state will in practice be supporters of a particular religion. Statist nationalism and ethnopolitical nationalisms are compatible with both the setup and the operation of a religious state. This does not mean they automatically accept a crusade or jihad or that they will automatically produce a religious state. A Nazi-type ethnopolitical nationalism involves a crusade. Moreover, it really accepts that only one crusade is the true crusade, although a polity that is governed in accordance with a Nazi-type nationalism might politically tolerate for the time being crusades by lesser allies (there can be no equals for a Nazi-type nationalism).

There is no necessary connection between a religion and a nationalism. There could be a factual connection between a religion and an *ethnie* (all or most of its members could share the same religion). Nevertheless, nationalisms can accept that religion or a particular religion is not an integral part or property of a nation.

If a religion is unique to an *ethnie*, then there will be no reason for the ethnopolitical nationalism to support the spread of this religion outside the *ethnie*. There will be demands for interstate coercion and intervention if members of the *ethnie* will be prevented from exercising their religion in another polity. There is still no necessary warrant for intervention in other polities in this case because ethnopolitical nationalism accepts sovereignty as an override.

A non-religious state or a state with a wrong religion may be evil for a religion R. Given a system of sovereign states, coexistence of states with various religions (inclusive of some secular states) will be possible. To set up a world government in a present multicultural world will mean to make a decision (among other decisions) about relations of the future world government with a multitude of actual religions. There is no good reason for sincere Muslims in Muslim countries to support abandoning sovereignty of their countries for a global Christian, or even secular, government. Survival of sovereignty is a means to deal with actual (descriptive) multiculturalism and provide some tools for legitimate conflict management. Obviously, the fact of existence of a multitude of *ethnies* provides another warrant for not treating world government as a realistic option at present.

Intervention to protect religion (e.g., against atheism) or a religion (e.g., against another religion) is incompatible with the sovereignty principle. Within the "European" tradition of the last three centuries and also under UN law these interventions are not permissible and the target state enters into a just war mode, if it uses force to oppose an instance of this kind of intervention.[36] Statist nationalism adheres to the tradition and is, of course, theoretically compatible with it. Nazi-type ethnopolitical nationalisms will allow cases of intervention within this goal type to be legitimate, if they are carried out against *ethnies* of lower value. Other ethnopolitical nationalisms will also not admit that intervention to protect religion or a religion is legitimate. A reciprocity principle or Kantian universality rule about protection of religion being inadmissible as a warrant for intervention will be compatible with non-Nazi-type ethnopolitical nationalisms.

Installation and Operation of Democracy

Statist nationalism is compatible with democracy. There is no logical or social necessity for setting up a democracy under statist nationalism, but it will be certainly incompatible with a limitation of the right of a state to install and operate a political regime (with possible exceptions involving the issue of genocide, as argued above). Therefore, if a state wants to install and run democracy, it is permitted to do this under state nationalism. Of course, installation and running of a democracy[37] will not be feasible if the population does not understand and support this particular kind of political regime. Compatibility does not mean entailment. State nationalism will allow any state to install and maintain the regime this particular state likes. Interventions on regime setup and operations are prohibited. This is a practical solution in a world that is actually multicultural (and not even quite industrial everywhere). Realist theories of international relations assume state nationalism.

Sovereignty can be used as a warrant in an argument that opposes intervention by Blobotania for the purpose of introducing democracy in Ruritania. This does not mean the victorious powers were morally wrong to set up democracies in (Western) Germany and Japan after 1945. There was no German state any more and Germany had to be restarted as a polity. Japan was certainly a polity, but the totality of defeat had changed its status from sovereign to nonsovereign polity.

Obviously, an attempt to install democracy by intervention (against an unwilling government) will mean war and war is a crime. Moreover, it will always be an attempt to install a particular instance of democracy, and, thus, it will also be in conflict with social contract or consent justification of a state. It will be another case of a crusade.

Ethnopolitical nationalisms are also not necessarily be incompatible with democracy. The reasoning is analogous to that of state nationalism. They would likewise oppose interventions to impose democracy in other polities.

What has been under discussion in this section is not the desirability of democracy, but rather the desirability and permissibility of using armed force to set up democracy in other states against the will of their governments (and even populations). Ruritanians are not politically obligated to set up and operate political regimes in Blobotania. Egyptians are not politically obligated to set up and operate political regimes in Iraq, Israel, Spain, Germany, Panama, and the United States of America, even were it feasible for them to do this. It would also be wrong for them for reasons of sovereignty and nationalism. Of course, the argument also establishes that it would be wrong to impose authoritarianism or a feudal monarchy on another polity for these same reasons. People have to work out their salvation themselves. The concepts of nationalism and sovereignty do not justify imposing nasty regimes on outsiders.

Jack Snyder and Karen Ballantyne have produced persuasive evidence about the contribution of human rights' NGOs to Rwandan massacres. Insistence on freedom of broadcasting in an agricultural state with long-standing internal conflicts between categories of population and non-Western views on power enabled legalized hate propaganda.[38] Notwithstanding globalization elsewhere, Rwandan or Burundian populations can do without close ties with the corporatist industrial world. Introducing democracy and liberty by force into mainly preindustrial societies can lead to disasters.[39] Democracy has to grow. Interventions might ensure that multicandidate elections will take place without much violence but they will not change deep-rooted political structures, judicial and penal systems, and culture as a whole.[40] Thomas Pogge has pointed out that although it is not reasonable to advocate slavery, colonialism, or authoritarianism, there are many areas outside common values that may be presumed in a pluralist international system. His examples included the number of parties, ownership of means of production, and whether basic civil liberties or basic social and economic needs come first.[41]

Interstate Governance

We allow government to interfere with our liberty for the protection of liberty of everybody. Designated persons may enter our homes without our permission, they may take away our property or arrest ourselves. These actions may not be carried out at will. Arbitrary use of force is not equivalent to rule-governed force. Some forms of rule-governed use of violence are considered legitimate by large majorities (although anarchists would not concur). Rules and institutions allow for protections of individuals and groups against arbitrary and nonlegitimate use of force. This is why governments and law exist. In case of dispute, there are courts of law, and they may find against government.

There is no world government. There is no court to appeal over illegitimate or unjust intervention and no institution of enforcement for the rulings of this court. Thus, false claims cannot be institutionally separated from true ones. There is a Liberal Democratic political party in Russia (led by Mr. Zhirinovsky) that is neither liberal nor democratic in the ordinary Western sense. Philosophical disputes over the concept of meaning would not help us, if a Russian liberal democratic government would intervene in Poland and Germany to set up a Liberal Democracy in Mr. Zhirinovsky's meaning.[42] In the cases of Germany, and Poland, there is NATO. In a hypothetical case of, say, Latvia, there will be no NATO.

States rationalize their policies under the guise of humanitarian motivation. This supplies an additional argument about the need for proper institutional authorities to legitimize or restrain interventions.[43] Miles Copeland, a former U.S. government operative, has definitely supported the normative view that interventions to oppose democracy are proper and desirable, if an authoritarian government will support U. S. policies, but a democratic one will oppose them.[44] Philip Darby has shown that in the late 1940s, the United States supported nationalism if it was anti-communist, and opposed nationalism if it was communist.[45]

External intervention is also profoundly unsettling in regard to the international system.[46] It de-legitimizes the concept of a separate state without setting up a new legitimate institutional order.[47] Moreover, the right to intervene has to be reciprocal and universal, if humanitarian interventionism is not to become a cover-up for a colonialist system. If the USA is to be allowed to intervene in Iran or Iraq or Yugoslavia on grounds deemed acceptable in liberal political thought, then Iran, Iraq or Yugoslavia ought to be granted the right to intervene in the United States of America on grounds deemed acceptable within Islam or by Serbian public opinion.

Real action has to be feasible. Logistics, material resources, and trained humans have to be prepared by the time the need arrives. Doctors have to be trained before you become ill to help you, and not after you become ill. Appropriate rapid reaction may stop ethnic cleansing, but this reaction might mean a massive military engagement that includes all branches of armed forces. Half-baked solutions could sow the seeds of new conflicts without securing a liberal solution of the original conflict. Ethnic cleansing can be carried out by forcible expulsion of an *ethnie,* by killing off the majority of its members, by forcible change of ethnic composition of an area, or by any combination of these methods. Air raids might not be sufficient to stop ethnic cleansing that is carried out by government encouraged irregulars. Once cleansing has been achieved, other countries will have to decide how to drive the victors out of the cleansed territory and bring the refugees back and solve the security and democratization transitions by making mass murderers and relatives of their victims to start living together as friends and sharers of joint public interest.

A recent study by Charles-Philippe David of peacekeeping dilemmas in contested situations has concluded that the liberal blueprint might be inapplicable in cases in which at least one of the contestants wants victory more than it wants peace.[48] We have to assume qualitative differences between human societies: values, goals, behavioral standards, and their systems may be partially or wholly incompatible or incommensurable.[49] Barry R. Posen has pointed out that humanitarian intervention to deal with mass refugee flows usually means war.[50] War is never gentle. War is also a realm of strategy, tactics, logistics, and forces.

Institutions make real collective actions feasible. In addition to feasibility, they make actions legitimate or nonlegitimate. To avoid charges of colonialism, actions have to be legitimized by appropriate institutions. This reclassifies the actions as law enforcement, etc. Rapid reaction to genocide, ethnic cleansing, and gross violations of human rights in general by governance institutions that are democratically legitimate presumes supportive public majority opinion about permissibility and even obligatoriness of feasible interventions. There are time limits for deliberation in rapid reaction circumstances. Therefore, democratic decision making about interventions involves decisions about legitimate kinds of situations that justify use of violence as means of enforcement of legitimate aims. This majority decision about situations that justify the legitimate use of violence usually preexists decisions about the defense of a country. It might not preexist about committing massive units of ground troops to prevent citizens of another country from killing each other. It has to preexist if we want to move on effectively from mere pious talk.

The United Nations is not a government. It has democratic and authoritarian, Christian, secular and Islamic, communist and free market (capitalist) member states. Apart from being a clearing house and neutral negotiation forum, it has a limited governance role for the multicultural world. It legitimizes some wars for some participants (defensive wars, peace enforcement between states and sometimes in no-state territories such as Bosnia during the breakup of the former Yugoslavia). It has no brief to reclassify enforcement for the purposes of setup and operation of religious states, particular political regimes, or other specific purposes as intervention. It could be used to legitimize the prevention of genocide, but it failed to do this in the case of Rwanda.

The Vietnamese government was right to intervene against the Red Khmers, although it was a government of another country. It is not aggression for NATO to intervene against genocide, for the latter must be prevented or stopped. Globalization of communications provides sufficient means for evidencing genocide. We can reasonably overcome suspicions of colonialist arbitrariness in cases of genocide at present and in the (near) foreseeable future. In cases other than genocide, the absence of appropriate governance institutions weighs against undertaking actions that might constitute interventions.

Remarks and Observations

Individual states will survive during the first half of the twenty-first century.[51] Therefore, state nationalism(s) will continue to exist and to be used in political arguments. Alongside the survival of states, sovereignty will survive. Marxism might be wrong, but strong states are known to have used their power to gain advantage for their own commercial firms from governments of weaker states. Sovereignty provides some protection from flagrant misuses of economic power. Raino Malnes has argued emphatically that national sovereignty is just another side of freedom.[52] Collective decision making is free insofar as there is no higher authority to issue orders to the collectivity. Malnes used this argument for moral justification of the right of national defense for the case the aggressor wants to make the state *B* a colony of state *A*, but will not kill any of its inhabitants. It follows from Malnes's standpoint that erosion of sovereignty will be erosion of liberty, unless expressly and freely willed by the political community.

Sovereignty overrides are, therefore, not to be treated lightly. Otherwise, anything goes, and the Hobbesian state of nature between sovereign entities becomes a normative duty. Therefore, it would be a duty of a sovereign religious state to implement its religion within other states by intervention or by full-scale war. Crusades and jihads would be politically obligatory.[53] This is a dangerous road.

There are similarities between Estonians and Japanese. At present, both societies are influenced by male chauvinism and both are democratic. Nevertheless, there are also some cultural differences. Ethnicity will also survive into the first half of the twenty-first century. This does not necessarily mean it will have disastrous consequences. Anthony D. Smith has even argued that nations and nationalism remain the only realistic basis for the free society of states.[54] Michael Walzer noted that the crucial commonality of humanity is its particularism.[55] Therefore, an attempt to exclude all kinds of nationalism from rational and reasonable political discourse is both doomed to failure and dangerous. On Gellnerian theory nationalism is a corollary of the industrial society that needs universal literacy and numeracy.[56] This predicts that nationalisms will strengthen in less developed parts of the world. The problem is really how to manage nationalism. Ernest Gellner thought, of course, that the cultural variety has been advantageous for humankind.[57]

Many nationalisms provide reasons against engagement in crusades and jihads. Some nationalisms are compatible with genocide overrides. Therefore, all nationalisms are not necessarily moral or political evils. Knives are quite useful for eating, as humanity has known from the earliest times of its existence. They are also dangerous. In a cheap Soviet restaurant, you were issued a knife on the discretion of the staff, if you really begged for it (in any case, the knife was often too blunt to be of much use). Liberalism and democracy can be misused, but the misuse does not mean we have to condemn them out of hand.

Reasons for justification or legitimation of actions are important. They delineate the border between the permissible and nonpermissible. Locke's idea of the social contract provided a criterion for distinguishing legitimate and nonlegitimate governments on the basis of something other than just approval for a particular policy of a particular government. Without reasoning, there would be arbitrary government and legalization of aggressive war. Sovereignty and some forms of nationalisms supply reasons for not starting actions that would result in wars. If they are compatible or even support genocide overrides on justifiability of interventions, then they can certainly be part of rational and reasonable political thought and provide reinforcement for a rule-governed international regime, as distinct from a purely Hobbesian world.[58]

Notes

1. Nazism was accepted by a substantial majority of Germans between 1935 and 1945 as a proper (legitimate) way of running a particular country (Germany).

2. Paul M. Sniderman, Joseph F. Fletcher, Peter H. Russell, Philip E. Tetlock, *The Clash of Rights: Liberty, Equality and Legitimacy in Pluralist Democracies* (New Haven and London: Yale University Press, 1997).

3. Ian Black, "China Hand," *CAM* (Easter Term 1997).

4. There are also somewhat overrated possibilities of economic actions by private firms for the purpose of changing the policies of other countries without the help of their source countries.

5. A culture might distinguish between severing a hand cruelly or neatly (as a punishment, for example, for theft).

6. That is, within public (or published) discourse.

7. Michael Walzer, *Just and Unjust Wars: A Moral Argument with Historical Illustrations* (New York: Basic Books, 1977).

8. H. L. A. Hart, *The Concept of Law* (Oxford: Clarendon Press, 1994), 220-37.

9. Stephen D. Krasner, "Compromising Westfalia," *International Security* 20, no. 3 (1995/96): 115-51.

10. Christopher K. Ansell, and Steven Weber, "Organizing International Politics: Sovereignty and Open Systems," *International Political Science Review* 20, no. 1 (1999): 73-93.

11. Change of borders is a change of an entity.

12. Walzer, *Just and Unjust Wars*; Noam J. Zohar, "Can a War Be Morally Optional?" *The Journal of Political Philosophy* 4, no. 3 (1996): 229-41.

13. "Protectorate" is another name for a colony.

14. The opening of Japan by Commodore Perry is another example of interstate coercion. In the case of Turkey, threats both to use armed force and to impose financial sanctions were on the list of means used to produce compliance.

15. In Estonian, the word *"natsionalism"* has a negative meaning, while there is a native word, *"rahvuslus"* [*rahvus* = nation], which does not ordinarily carry negative connotations. In Sovietese, "natsionalizm" meant dissident activity by non-Russians.

16. The concept of persuasive definitions was elaborated in Charles L. Stevenson, *Ethics and Language* (New Haven, Conn.: Yale University Press, 1960).

17. Roger Scruton, *A Dictionary of Political Thought* (London: Pan Books-The Macmillan Press, 1982), 315-16.

18. Ernest Gellner, *Nations and Nationalism* (Oxford and Cambridge, Mass.: Blackwell 1983).

19. The distinction between units and regimes was underlined in David Easton, *A Systems Analysis of Political Life* (New York: John Wiley, 1965). Regime is analogous to an operating system, it provides for a possibility of various policy sets and policies (applications and inputs). A detailed discussion of nationalist legitimacy criteria for the setup of states is available in Eero Loone, "Rational and Reasonable Justifiability of States: Ethnic Pluralism and the Concept of Nation," in *The Constitutional and Political Regulation of Ethnic Relations and Conflicts,* ed. Mitja Zagar, Boris Jesih, Romana Bester (Ljubljana: Institute for Ethnic Studies, 1999), 37-51.

20. Thus, the right of self-determination will be accorded to the ethnic unit as a whole

and not to any of its parts. This is also probably the present doctrine in international law as set up in the Aland Islands case by the League of Nations.

21. Market forces will not always provide for films to be subtitled in native languages of large majorities of viewers in some small countries. There is no Estonian-language version of Windows because the market does not justify the cost (but there is a manual and a spell-checker; these were sufficient to drive WordPerfect out of the Estonian market and create a practical monopoly for MS Office).

22. Zohar, "Can a War Be Morally Optional?"

23. In theory, Russian communism was a version of Marxism. The relation became purely ritualistic by the beginning of the 1970s.

24. The assertion that cultural variety is valuable and that a particular culture may be valuable for its members does not mean that any culture is rationally a positive value. Nazi culture is not.

25. Obviously, any argument can have more than one premise. The wrongness of war and of colonialism are examples of some other premises of this chapter.

26. Benjamin Barber, *The Conquest of Politics: Liberal Philosophy in Democratic Times* (Princeton, N. J.: Princeton University Press 1988), 192-211.

27. R. A. Dahl, *Democracy and Its Critics* (New Haven, Conn.: Yale University Press, 1989), 193-209.

28. The government of Pol Pot might have been a client of the Chinese People's Republic, although I doubt whether Red Khmers were really no more than a native administration of a foreign colonial power. Even if they had been, this will not affect our argument.

29. Statement (3) within the present text must not be construed as being material to discussions about abortion ("pro-life" is to my mind a misleading and dishonest rhetorical label for a position I hold to be wrong, but making sense).

30. Many human beings are religious and believe in rational and reasonable beings (or one being) who are superior to humans. There are also some humans who do not believe that beings of this kind exist. A rational consensus argument has to be acceptable to atheists and religious persons.

31. The standardized version of rights as claims is available in Joel Feinberg, *Social Philosophy* (Englewood Cliffs, N.J.: Prentice Hall, 1973), ch. 4-6, and William K. Frankena, *Ethics* (Englewood Cliffs, N.J.: Prentice Hall. 1963), 45. Feinberg includes an introductory discussion of difficulties in grounding rights. Michael Freeman has recently argued in "The Philosophical Foundations of Human Rights," *Human Rights Quarterly* 16, no. 3 (1994): 491-514 that there are still no uncontested philosophical foundations of human rights. Therefore, the received version is still relevant. The approach used in this chapter is compatible with contingency and constructedness of human rights as well as with some kinds of foundationalism.

32. Zohar, "Can a War Be Morally Optional?"

33. The example constructs a situation with no revolt or civil war in Ruritania. In both these cases, Walzerian rules about just war would apply and actions against slavery in other countries would be perfectly justified, while intervention to preserve slavery would not be justifiable.

34. The nature of the case precludes statistics; half a million is a journalistic exaggeration, but a thousand is very much an understatement. Probably, the problem is less acute now than it was in the mid 1990s.

35. There are also important differences between humans and other animate entities.

36. Gladstone campaigned against Turkish atrocities committed against Christian Bulgarians. This comes under genocide (religion was the supposed reason for genocide, but genocide is wrong, whatever the reasons).

37. I am using the word to refer to the kind of regime that is named "democracy" in contemporary Western (somewhat fuzzy) usage. Differences between the Westminster

model and, for example, the Dutch model will not matter for this usage.

38. Jack Snyder and Karen Ballantine, "Nationalism in the Marketplace of Ideas," *International Security* 21, no. 2 (1996): 5-40.

39. The failure of Somalia intervention can have analogous explanation.

40. This idea is present in Krishna Kumar, *Rebuilding Societies after Civil War: Critical Roles for International Assistance* (Boulder, Colo.: Lynne Rienner, 1997) and has been advanced in an editorial, "The Limits of Nation-Building" *New York Times,* 11 December 1997, A26.

41. Thomas Pogge, "Moral Progress," in *Problems of International Justice*, ed. Steven Luper-Foy (Boulder, CO and London: Westview Press, 1988), 283-304.

42. Some Russian politicians in Estonia have argued that a law requiring members of the Estonian parliament to understand Estonian in a country where the language of legislation is Estonian, amounts to genocide. This seems to me a Zhirinovsky kind of thinking (or that of the Brezhnev doctrine). It is another matter whether this kind of law is liberal, democratic, authoritarian, justified or not justified.

43. J. Bryan Hehir, "Intervention: From Theories to Cases," in *Ethics and International Affairs* 9 (1995): 1-13.

44. Miles Copeland, *The Game Player: Confessions of the CIA's Original Political Operative* (London: Aurum Press, 1989), 178.

45. Philip Darby, *Three Faces of Imperialism: British and American Approaches to Asia and Africa 1870-1970* (New Haven and London: Yale University Press 1987).

46. George Modelski, "The International Relations of Internal War," in *International Aspects of Civil Strife*, ed. James N. Rosenau (Princeton, N. J.: Princeton University Press, 1964), 14-44.

47. Manfred Halpern, "The Morality and Politics of Intervention," in *International Aspects of Civil Strife*, ed. James N. Rosenau, 249-88.

48. Charles-Philippe David, "Does Peacebuilding Build Peace? Liberal (Mis)steps in the Peace Process," *Security Dialogue* 30, no. 1 (1999): 25-41.

49. Eero Loone, "'They Were Not Quite Like Us': The Presumption of Qualitative Difference in Historical Writing," in *Developments in Modern Historiography*, ed. Henry Kozicki (Houndsmills and London: Macmillan, 1998), 164-81. Shared classification of kinds does not necessarily mean shared assignment of incidents to kinds. Killing an opponent in a duel was not considered murder a century or two ago in some Western societies. An account of dueling and its moral obligatoriness in the Austro-Hungarian army is available in István Deák, *Beyond Nationalism: A Social and Political History of the Habsburg Officer Corps, 1848-1918* (New York, Oxford: Oxford University Press, 1990), 128-38.

50. Barry R. Posen, "Military Responses to Refugee Disasters," *International Security* 21, no. 1 (1996): 72-111.

51. This is actually a probability statement, but I consider the probabilities to be rather high.

52. Raino Malnes, *National Interests, Morality and International Law* (Oslo: Scandinavian University Press, 1994).

53. In their original medieval meaning, both were armed enterprises. Islam, of course, contains an additional rule that a religion must not be forced on a person.

54. Anthony D. Smith, *Nations and Nationalism in a Global Era* (Cambridge: Polity, 1995).

55. Michael Walzer, *Thick and Thin: Moral Arguments at Home and Abroad* (Notre Dame, Ind.: University of Notre Dame Press, 1994).

56. Ernest Gellner, *Nations and Nationalism*; "An Alternative Vision," in *Encounters with Nationalism* (Oxford and Cambridge, Mass.: Blackwell, 1993), 182-200.

57. Ernest Gellner, "From the Ruins of the Great Contest: Civil Society, Nationalism, and Islam," in *Encounters with Nationalism*, 170-81.

58. Kratochwil discussed the importance of rules in his critique of primitive realism: Friedrich V. Kratochwil, *Rules, Norms, and Decisions: On the Conditions of Practical and Legal Reasoning in International Relations and Domestic Affairs* (Cambridge: Cambridge University Press, 1989).

Chapter 11

Thinking Globalization, Rethinking Toleration

Teresa López de la Vieja

Introduction

"Drawing the lines," according to R. Nozick, is one of the most salient functions of principles because it establishes some guidelines for action.[1] Normative political theories are seeking a consensus of priorities, and therefore discuss some principles for public action. Those principles are usually guidelines like justice, liberty, equality, and toleration. On the one hand, egalitarian liberalism and Kantian republicanism show a wide interest in what has been called the good polity.[2] On the other hand, theories such as communitarianism, civic republicanism, and feminism are reluctant about this entanglement of abstract prospects, basic consensus, and political subjects. For instance, B. Barber remarks that politics is a way of living—it requires then the citizen's commitment to it.[3] In P. C. Schmitter and T. L. Karl's opinion, every consensus becomes contingent.[4] Therefore principles have to be prudently balanced with rules for action. To summarize: the main problem here is that normative theories could be too ample, or too thin to have clear success in very demanding situations. Since they deal basically with general norms and with procedures, or "politics," and practically banish the question of institutions, or "policies,"[5] they seem more fragile than fallible theories.

There are many nuances, such as F. Michelman's argument about the participation of citizens in the public sphere and the positive role of normative grounds.[6] However, the normative approaches would probably not stand the burden of proof. Moreover, they could not offer any plan to provide better opportunities for citizens, for real citizens in real democracies.[7] Instead of assuming that burden of proof, some normative theories just go the opposite way, putting all their emphasis on values, as does J. Habermas, arguing that the level of facts in the first place reveals constraining traditions and disasters.[8] Predemocratic descriptions of political membership, and mainly a kind of narrow nationalism have always caused harm to citizens. Lastly, post-nationalism and cosmopolitanism do not have any consistent proof to support the wide prospect of human rights for citizens, where every difference would be tolerated, and even valued. Hence they should be balanced with the "baseline" of social experiences.[9] Even if their horizon is too wide, do the criteria get bogged down by their non-realistic descriptions? F. R. Dallmayr explains that political terms, such as nation-state or rule by the people, depend on discursive articulations, which nowadays are multiple and diverse.[10]

In spite of reasonable criticism of the strictest normative theories, in spite of actual institutions (yet too weak to support demands at the global level), this chapter would suggest that principled politics are not to be put aside, since a basic consensus could be the core of politics in a global scene. For instance, the principle of toleration would be a reasonable guideline now, in a world-as-a-whole. Why just now? Let us expand here on a dilemma, or better yet, an argument *ad ignorantiam*.[11]

Arguing for Principles

Globalization is expanding the public sphere. Global and local frameworks could improve participation for citizenship beyond borders, eroding then the former link between basic rights and national membership, in both levels, *ius solis* and *ius sanguinis*. Recent analysis on the impact of the world-as-a-whole and well-known arguments, such as H. Arendt's remarks about human rights and about national membership,[12] run definitively in the same direction, in favor of a post-national and cosmopolitan citizenship. J. Habermas points to the European Union as the best example to improve the rule of law over frontiers and to defend a more inclusive notion of citizenship.[13]

Non exclusion is not *inclusion*, though. For instance, F. W. Schapf casts doubt on this cosmopolitan model of democracy because there is no European *demos*.[14] Indeed human rights and modern principles are drawing the basic framework, no more and no less. Meanwhile global and local trends are producing fragmentation and a kind of clash among cultural identities.[15] Besides, the global sphere carries a number of cruel conflicts among countries, agencies, and citizens. Because of that, a reasonable politics has obviously to be improved with specific policies, including a more accurate attention to difference. The better outcomes are up to political actors and to institutions, needless to say. At least, cosmopolitan citizenship traces the basic lines for the public sphere, balances also the political agenda with critical arguments, and calls to the political scene modern principles, such as toleration. For example, how to produce special rights for the sake of minorities and groups, warranting at the same time basic rights for every citizen?[16] With all due respect to difference; but which one? (In northern Spain, some young Islamic women immigrants are now claiming the protection of Spanish institutions because they are rejecting the tradition of arranged marriages).

To become more *tolerant citizens*, we the people have to accept blurred lines between "us and them," avoiding practices outside the line of human rights. The aforementioned normative theory conveniently draws the guidelines of post-nationalism and cosmopolitanism. The actual opening of frontiers, cultures, and more tolerant attitudes could not come only through these criteria. We are involved in institutional facts as well, thereby we have to reflect with more accuracy upon every topic, the global and local world, opening of borders, consensus, citizenship, sovereignty, and cosmopolitanism. We have to take account also of the plural discursive articulations in the political sphere, according to F. R. Dallmayr, [17] and of liberal principles, such as toleration. Lastly, the normative point of view would not include finished descriptions of post-national policies (for instance, it could not foresee how to harmonize Islamic traditions and a liberal way of life, but it could establish priorities for the sake of individuals, whatever happens in communities). Nevertheless, more realistic theories—here the argument—could *not* persuade us now, in a global world, to go back, and to explore again a veritable cul-de-sac, the narrowest form of nationalism.

Globalization

The world-as-a-whole offers the best occasion to rethink citizenship, sovereignty, rights, and democracy over frontiers. What does this mean? *Globalization* could be a good argument to get normative consensus on these subjects. It is an ambivalent argument or dilemma, it would avoid some disasters, but no theory could describe the strategy to produce the best outcomes. Let us come closer to this ambivalent subject. For some years now, the topic of globalization has become the focus of attention in many fields, such as sociology and moral and political philosophy. It has even caught the eye of the general public. What does it mean? Globalization is synonymous with well-integrated systems and with intensified relationships; it is also characterized by quick social change, especially by changes in economic production, the rise of more homogeneous cultural spaces, limitless circulation of goods, ideas, patterns, etc. However the global systems are paradoxically producing fragmentation and local frameworks, [18] including a kind of small-minded nationalism. According to B. Barber, they produce even strong antagonism between integration and tribalism.[19] Indeed, some communities are fighting against open frameworks, such as that of the European Union. Radical nationalism has something to do with the darkest side of the global culture since it is excluding citizens—the Other— and refreshing old borders inside the world-as-a-whole.[20] Therefore, the global systems produce many paradoxes since they provide new opportunities while, on the other hand, they take a lot of risks.[21]

To begin with, globalization seems a good argument for *post-nationalism*. From normative political theory, global dynamics gives the appropriate framework for more intense and more complex relationships, building supranational institutions, and therefore institutions beyond political borders.[22] Here, the problem is that we still stay in national frameworks, while the institutions and supranational agencies seem weak or very ineffective. For this reason, we have to consider at the same time both aspects of the topic: politics and policies.[23] Above all, coherent principles take part in the discursive articulation of democracy and of pluralism, for the sake of reasonable citizens with very different ways of life and for the sake of more tolerant political systems. To summarize: the new global context seems to confirm the theses of contemporary political theory in favor of the universal approach, post-national identity, cosmopolitan citizenship, and, especially, human rights warranting political legitimacy.[24]

However, we have to see the other aspect of the topic—namely, the fragmentation of identities and the assertion of differences. On the whole, globalization is coming close to modernization.[25] Now then, the world-as-a-whole could mean deep changes for democratic systems,[26] including the weakness of the nation-state and more complexity in the political arena, which involves many risks like the resurgence of tribalism.[27] This global process is *ambivalent*, as it increases also differences and local frameworks.[28] Their impact, a double impact therefore, is expanding relationships, institutions, and even the notion of citizenship.[29] Considering this ambivalent surface of the global process ("McWorld and Jihad," according to Barber), do the politics of difference invalidate post-nationalism?

Nothing is certain in this sphere. But the new emphasis on local elements could not invalidate the principles of the *supranational culture*,[30] as long as the line between social experiences and political ideals would last. Moreover, global processes invite us to map out modern principles, such as freedom and equality, with a kind of solidarity among strangers,[31] and with toleration in the public sphere.[32] This is because we expected that post-nationalism and cosmopolitanism would avoid some disasters.

After Disasters

How to learn from disasters? In recent works, summing up events of the twentieth century, Habermas mentions the cruelty that in 1945 public opinion became aware of—genocide, concentration camps, terrorism, refugees—as a no return point.[33] To think nowadays about political development means also to learn from past experiences, to be able to analyze new problems. His thesis is as follows: there is no way out. The politics of environment shows that risks are global. Globalization means also inequality. After the end of the Cold War, the end of colonialism and its uncertain consequences, the welfare state in crisis, etc., liberal societies are partially losing their capability to act. Why? Inside, there are problems of integration; outside, the loss of competitiveness in a global economy. Habermas stresses that the new openness of borders shows the growing necessity of wider political units for politics beyond the nation-state. In fact, governments intensify international agreements, and nationalities face up to the new challenges of market acting beyond frontiers. Although there is no global government yet, we have to think in terms of supranational politics, even though the international relationships are asymmetric relationships among countries, as Habermas remarks.

For example, the case of the European Union confirms that globalization could be the starting point to achieve new forms of political development. Through transnational markets, denationalization and the prospect of cosmopolitan solidarity are bringing us to a paradoxical situation. Not only because they make demands on abstract solidarity, Habermas admits, but also because there are side-effects, coming with the decline of the nation-state, such as uncertain identity, sovereignty in question, or lack of warrants concerning human rights. Thus, according to Habermas, the European Union is beginning to show what supranational politics could be, beyond the actual globalization of markets: post-national democracy, universal equality, community of rights for citizens, solidarity among strangers, and cosmopolitanism. The global process promotes an idea of citizenship, whose rights would not depend on context, and their validity would not be restricted to location.[34] In sum, openness of frontiers.

In addition, human rights as basic consensus or as guidelines support the notion of supranational or post-national politics since they are working in favor of the horizontal relationship among citizens. As a comment, it must be said that it is true that the cosmopolitan or post-national program is more attractive than unopened nationalism. There are political questions to solve yet, including the transfer of some functions from the nation-state to the global and post-national arena. In addition, how to define in political terms the solidarity among strangers, how to change the narrowest frameworks, and how to guarantee the principle of non exclusion for every citizen. Not the whole inclusion, though. In sum, beyond nationality the democratic systems would survive, only if they would give up the relative homogeneity of *demos*. Habermas identifies this as "constitutional patriotism."

Rethinking Citizenship

B. S. Turner explains that citizenship is more a process than a practice.[35] But the global flow is supporting both right and wrong practices. For instance, many Asian industries are creating new jobs for women,[36] a very good outcome at first sight. But in many countries low wages and intensive production are also eroding the fragile soil of women's rights. Hence the ambivalence of the global and local outcomes would reinforce the structure *ad ignorantiam* of some theoretical prospects. Although we disagree with the most limited form of nation-state, we are not able to produce a better framework either. Citizenship concerns the relationship between individuals and the state; but now, which state? How to get a public sphere from different cultures and identities? And how to get an overlapping membership in plural societies, divided by cleavages?[37] The cosmopolitan model does not work very well at the micro-level, but it takes advantage of the fluidity of the global sphere, the macro-level. Let us see how.

In post-national politics citizens have rights and obligations inside and outside defined territories. This type of citizenship is a "formal" one.[38] Could it mean membership or "substantive citizenship"? Liberal societies prefer the legal definition, giving priority to individual rights. What happens then at the societal level, with groups and identities? Habermas argues here that the universal point of view does not mean insensibility in the face of worthy differences.[39] In spite of that, communitarianism, feminism, and republicanism consider that territories, cultures, and communities are still relevant.[40] Moreover, liberal patterns are limited in defining policies for citizens. A suitable answer is that the public sphere would no longer remain within national limits.[41] Here the global focus could persuade us to define political subjects in nontraditional terms, even in post-national terms. The problem is the control of such disparate and peripheral powers.[42] Since the time of universality has not yet come, nothing guarantees that globalization would be as open as the term "supra-nationality" now suggests.

Immigration problems are demonstrating that social and political integration is quite insufficient.[43] For instance, the European Union has still to achieve an integrated public sphere from several different cultures and nationalities.[44] Indeed, globalization does not proceed in one way only, the cosmopolitan one, because it has contradictory effects. On the one hand, the world-as-a-whole is producing a kind of civil transnational society—for the first time, a democratic system over territories has good foundations. On the other hand, the cosmopolitan pattern, inclusion and solidarity, demand international structures, supranational institutions. Again, the case of the European Union shows what could produce an overlapping political sphere,[45] local, regional, and supranational.[46]

Recalling the Difference

Since globalization includes differences, since it is an ambivalent process, homogeneous and fragmentary at once,[47] it produces a many-sided and multi-form world. Why not a multilevel citizenship? Before, we saw a dilemma, even an argument *ad ignorantiam*; now let us see the analogy between an overlapping political sphere and a multinational citizenship. Global processes weaken the nation-state, alter local politics, and at the same time expand activities, producing a thick web of relationships.[48] The weakness of the territoriality principle has also a positive side, which erodes the former lines between center and margins.[49] Moreover, this decline of the nation-state offers the best argument in favor of multinationality.[50] Nevertheless, the global world produces a strong resistance; in the global arena the risks of "jihad" and of nationalism come together with this trend to blur frontiers.[51] Let us consider the dilemma, whether the isles or the sea, so to say, whether to localize citizens in territories and cultures, within national rights, or take seriously the idea that everyone could become a foreigner in the global flow.

First, the tension between heterogeneity and homogeneity has a positive function, assuring particularity and complexity in global experiences.[52] The cosmopolitan integration would go beyond nationalities and, at the same time, would maintain plurality and diversity.[53] Being cosmopolitan means participating in several worlds; but how? Democratic systems have to be defined better, within international networks, overlapping spaces and local, regional, and international relationships. Why not segmented authorities?[54] Better definitions of global systems could lead to the rejection of fundamentalism, even the dogmatic fighting for national identity. In the end, the world-as-a-whole provides new opportunities for citizens, even the opportunity to leave the narrow space of radical nationalism.[55] But, how wide could a political system be?

Second, every citizen could be a foreigner in the global world. Markets are showing how to act at local and global level; why not citizens participating on several levels, too? But, do we do that at the cost of substantive contents in civic culture?[56] While basic rights assure mutual recognition, specific practices and substantive values mean the unavoidability of conflicts.[57] Hence we have to seek another form of claiming local identities, without exclusions and without strong emotional background. While the segmented frameworks contribute to development, producing dynamism and competitiveness at a global level,[58] some traditions and some emotions usually dim the lines in the political sphere. Here the only problem is exclusion at global and local levels; not how worthy the local framework could be (we are talking about rights, not about feelings).

Among Strangers

Exclusion and marginality are acquiring new dimensions after the world-wide migratory movements.[59] Meanwhile pluralistic democracies produce weak integration, and the institutions are far at the back of global prospects. The public sphere, whatever its real dimension is local, regional, or international (as in the European Union),[60] and whatever the situation of the territorial principle would be, this sphere tends to separate "us and them." We have no cogent argument to avoid the exclusion trend, but we have principles, such as responsibility and mutual respect, to foresee better political outcomes for citizens from different cultures. Moreover, toleration draws an ample space, inside and outside the nation-state. To sum up: supranational institutions and principles, like toleration, would put forward relationships among strangers.

The *supranational model* has been defined in terms of community of laws, constitutional patriotism, and abstract solidarity.[61] This kind of community separately considers political processes and social activity;[62] does this universal point of view interfere with sensibility toward concrete necessities and toward disadvantaged situations? Quite the reverse, because the globalization of living necessities, food, health, and a good environment, reveals that to obtain results and to be efficient we have to organize solidarity, beyond our own borders or beyond our own way of life. That means also solidarity "among strangers."[63] For these reasons, human rights offer the framework for responsible action, and for the sake of citizens who have rights, not duties, in an asymmetrical situation. We are not talking about differences of opinion or about different points of view,[64] but about what has been called "global justice."[65]

The *drawing of lines* introduces some moral principles (equality, solidarity, respect, and toleration) in political discourse. For instance, the relationship among citizens without frontiers does not claim equal treatment,[66] but a kind of horizontal support;[67] that means rights, without regard for our own good and the good for strangers. The argument of difference seems relevant for democratic politics; according to M. Walzer, in unequal relationships we have to tolerate differences.[68] Rights warrant nonexclusion for strangers, as members of our own community. According to G. Frankenberg, solidarity could offer a secular groundwork for mutual support.[69] And toleration could organize a more suitable public sphere, because inequalities and differences are relevant at cultural and social levels. Toleration supposes heterogeneity, social contest, and inequalities; as a matter of fact, we need mutual respect just because we have to negotiate, to establish real commitments, and to respect actual differences.

Toleration in a Post-National World

"Drawing the lines" means criticism against intolerant and excluding practices. Normative theories usually argue for inclusion, fluidity of borders (post-nationalism), and a civil society, accepting and supporting worthy differences (toleration). But to tolerate is more than to bear something or someone. We have "to see" real identities,[70] taking into account minorities in unfavorable positions.[71] Therefore, we have to modify the institutions, acting somehow to balance positions.[72] For these reasons, toleration as a kind of recognition and respect for singularities[73] becomes a starting point to achieve equality, [74] fairness, and justice in plural societies. Liberalism has always defended such ideals. But ideals, such as solidarity and toleration, have been built for concrete communities, especially inside a nation-state. How to expand them in the global world?

Toleration is a moral ideal and a virtue in individuals and in institutions. As a kind of "disagreement with acceptance,"[75] it has a "weak" and a "strong" version, so to say. It means endurance and, besides, strict respect for difference.[76] Liberal societies encourage tolerant attitudes among individuals in a private sphere, without the least hint of partiality in the public sphere. Speaking about participation, and about "strong" political systems,[77] the conclusion could be that the democratic system has to reinforce the role of political actors in the public arena. It has, by all means, to avoid partiality, but it has to cross somehow the strict line between the private and the public sphere because many citizens have been excluded from actual participation, at local and at global levels. Toleration in the public sphere would mean, for instance, the improving of basic rights with special policies. So respect for difference could be related to positive actions (R. Dworkin analyzes the *De Funis* case), [78] for the sake of minorities or of individuals, who usually have been expelled from public affairs (History teaches us quickly about which groups are affected by political exclusion). Indeed, the overlapping global sphere produces many conflicts; but tolerant practices inside one's own culture show by analogy how to share the political global sphere with "strangers."

Cosmopolitan citizenship involves rights beyond territories, expanding the community of "we the people" (a more tolerant people). Liberalism stresses that rights concern individuals.[79] So the public sphere, now a global sphere, could improve the participation of every citizen. "Could" does not mean "have to." Since participation is a right, it is up to the citizens. And these citizens still stand on the dividing line between nationalism from the past and the prospective of post-nationalism. In theory, there exists no hitch in the global sphere to achieve this; since democratic systems are more complex, sometimes they are really open and plural. Citizens would some day accept new loyalties, respecting differences. In practice, the institutions seem too weak to expand the "good" politics beyond frontiers. Indeed, the nation-state is still warranting entitlements for citizens.

Hence, looking for the best understanding of politics means redefining nationality.[80] Citizenship usually means rights, rights inside a particular nation-state. Where are the ultimate borders now?

Globalization is partly reshaping this public scene, disentangling citizenship, nationality, and rights. It produces some reactions, such as reluctance to the world-as-a whole because the global flow has still to be fine-tuned to preserve some traditions, identities, and differences. Balancing arguments for and against the new political sphere, global and local, we could conclude that, on the one hand, many difficulties burden cosmopolitanism and post-nationalism, but they make room for citizens' sovereignty, to replace the sovereignty limited by nationalities; and that, on the other hand, the rule by the people could not be better if the nation-state were completely divided if the borders became smaller and smaller for "we the people." Quite the reverse, since citizens' rights, as basic rights, cannot depend either on their content or on their application of national frontiers, traditions, cultures, and ethnicity.

Concluding Remarks

Human rights are the core of some normative political theories. They intend to produce a basic consensus, arguing for justice, equality, solidarity, and toleration in the public sphere. They deal rather with "principled politics," not with policy, nor with polity.[81] Therefore post-traditions and post-nationalities belong to the same conceptual level as universal rights do (human rights for citizenship, not only citizens rights, according to Arendt). Does the nation-state give the best conditions for a global public sphere? The *global* world shows that citizens and "strangers" claim the same right to participate, to take decisions, and to shape public arenas beyond borders (openness). The *local* experience reveals that citizens value differences; but they reject whatever community or tradition threatens their basic rights (closure). Therefore, post-nationalism and cosmopolitanism set a basic agenda, relatively well defined, to improve supranational communities, transnational politics, solidarity among strangers, and toleration for citizens crossing frontiers.

Cosmopolitan citizenship within a global framework would mean, for instance, equal rights and, at the same time, different policies. Even if citizenship is always a difficult topic for political theories,[82] globalization becomes the perfect occasion to remove the former explanations and to draw the guidelines for a complex citizenship beyond borders and beyond parochial traditions. *Modern principles* could be the starting point to reshape the political scene, expand horizons, and trace straight lines for action. However, it is up to us, "we the people" in an ample sense, to achieve this open prospect, being citizens in the world-as-a-whole, or to go back to closure, and even to tribalism. Global arenas demand more than good foundations, of course. They also require institutions that would not collapse under global pressures, for the sake of a plural and multisided public sphere. At least, the goals and prospects have been set. Principles, especially toleration, work in favor of openness, for general cooperation without putting aside worthy differences. Do they belong to the "intellectual ex periments"?[83] As models, they have no real power, they could only have *some* influence—no more, and no less.[84]

Furthermore, realistic theories are closer to actual practices, taking account of citizens' demands and of the fragility in the public sphere. Only the commitment of real actors would sustain democracy (or not), as a sum of practices.[85] Let us suppose a more realistic argument, just to realize that the world-as-a-whole is an overwhelming experience in which we could hardly find out the best alternatives to improve justice, autonomy, liberty, equality, and toleration for citizens. Nevertheless, the darkest horizon cannot justify the return of intolerant nationalism, whose consequences are definitively predictable.

Notes

1. R. Nozick, *The Nature of Rationality* (Princeton: Princeton University Press, 1993), 3-40.
2. A. Hamlin and P. Pettit, "Preface," in *The Good Polity*, ed. A. Hamlin and P. Pettit. (London: Blackwell, 1991), 7-8,
3. B. R. Barber, *Strong Democracy* (Berkeley: University of California Press, 1984), 117-31, 261-311; and *The Conquest of Politics* (Princeton: Princeton University Press, 1988), 193-211.
4. P. C. Schmitter and T. L. Karl, "What Democracy Is . . . and Is Not," in *The Global Resurgence of Democracy*, ed. D. L. Diamond and M. Plattner (Baltimore: Johns Hopkins University Press, 1996), 49-65.
5. "Politics" puts emphasis on the procedures, "polity" on the institutions. For the terminology, among other authors, see U. Von Alemann and E. Forndran, *Methodik der Politikwissenschaft* (Stuttgart: Kohlhammer, 1995), 32-45.
6. F. Michelman relates citizens' participation with normative consensus in his "Law's Republic," *Yale Law Journal* 97 (1988): 1493-1537.
7. Numerous studies on political participation mention the tenuous relationship between normative theories and citizens' practice. The argument in favor of the practical dimension of civic politics is expanded by J. M. Rosales in "Ciudadanía en democracia: condiciones para una política cívica," *Sistema* 122 (September 1994): 5-23; and "Liberal Reformism and Democratic Citizenship," *Citizenship Studies* 2, no. 2 (July 1998): 257-72.
8. J. Habermas takes a position toward the internal relationship between social facts and values: *Faktizität und Geltung* (Frankfurt: Suhrkamp, 1992), 52-55.
9. C. Sunstein refers to the *status quo*; the social and political framework can be used to explain the existing forms of rights, their non-neutrality, even de facto discriminatory effects of law. See *The Partial Constitution* (Cambridge: Harvard University Press, 1993), 1-14, 79.
10. F. R. Dallmayr provides an excellent explanation of plural discursive articu-

lations, "Postmetaphysics and Democracy," *Political Theory* 21 (1993): 101-27.

11. According to C. Perelman, this kind of argument "tire sa force essentiellement de l'urgence, car il exclut un délai de réflexion . . . Par là, cet argument, pour être utilisable, place les interlocuteurs dans un cadre limité qui rappelle celui du dilemme": C. Perelman and L. Olbrechts-Tyteca, *Traité de l'argumentation. La nouvelle Rhétorique* (Brussels: Université de Bruxelles, 1989), 321.

12. H. Arendt developed her critical arguments in "Aporie der Menschenrechte," in *Elemente und Ursprünge totaler Herrschaft* (Frankfurt: Europäische Verlagsanstalt, 1955), 434-52.

13. J. Habermas is clearly on the side of encouraging cosmopolitanism in the global framework. See *Die postnationale Konstellation* (Frankfurt: Suhrkamp, 1998), 91-167.

14. F. W. Schapf, "Demokratie in der transnationalen Politik," in *Politik der Globalisierung*, ed. U. Beck (Frankfurt: Suhrkamp, 1998), 228-53.

15. S. P. Huntington, "The Clash of Civilizations?" *Foreign Affairs* 72, (Summer 1993): 22-49.

16. U. Haksar argues for special rights of groups, compatible with the priority of individual rights in "Collective Rights and the Value of Groups," *Inquiry* 41 (1998): 21-43.

17. Dallmayr, "Postmetaphysics and Democracy," 101.

18. J. Friedmann, "Being in the World: Globalization and Localization," in *Global Culture*, ed. M. Featherstone (London: Sage, 1990), 311-28; *Cultural Identity and Global Process* (London: Sage, 1995), 102-16.

19. Some dilemmas of globalization have been explained by B. Barber, "La cultura global de McWorld," in *La democracia de los ciudadanos*, ed. J. Rubio-Carracedo and J. M. Rosales (Supplement 1 of *Contrastes. Revista Interdisciplinar de Filosofía*, 1996): 31-48.

20. R. Robertson stresses the two sides of the same process, the global and the local one in "Mapping the Global Condition: Globalization as the Central Concept," *Theory, Culture & Society* 5 (1990): 15-30.

21. U. Beck, *Risikogesellschaft* (Frankfurt: Suhrkamp, 1986), 25-66; J. Bohman, "The Globalization of the Public Sphere: Cosmopolitanism, Publicity and Cultural Pluralism," *The Modern Schoolman* 75 (1998): 101-17.

22. For the role of democratic systems in the global process, see D. Held, "Democracy, the Nation-State and the Global System," in *Political Theory Today*, ed. D. Held (Cambridge: Polity Press, 1991), 197-235.

23. R. M. Dworkin, *A Matter of Principle* (Cambridge, Mass.: Harvard University Press, 1985), 72-103.

24. J. Habermas, "Human Rights and Popular Sovereignty: The Liberal and Republican Versions," *Ratio Juris* 7 (1994): 1-13; *Die Einbeziehung des Anderen* (Frankfurt: Suhrkamp, 1996), 192-236; "Remarks on Legitimation through Human Rights," *The Modern Schoolman*, LXXV (1998): 87-100.

25. For globalization as synonymous with modernization, see M. Waters, *Globalization* (London: Routledge, 1995), 1-10. For the ambivalence of the global process, see S. Benhabib, "Das demokratische Projekt im Zeitalter der Globalisierung," in *Philosophie und Politik*, ed. J. Nida-Rümelin and W. Thierse (Essen: Klartext, 1997), 48-62.

26. D. Held, *Democracy and the Global Order* (Cambridge: Polity Press, 1996), 3-27.

27. See Z. Baumann, "Globalisierung oder was für die einen Globalisierung, ist für die anderen Lokalisierung," *Das Argument* 217 (1996): 653-64; J. Bohman, "The Globalization of the Public Sphere: Cosmopolitanism, Publicity and Cultural Pluralism," 101-17; and "Schwache Staaten. Die Globalisierung und die Spaltung der Weltgesellschaft," in *Kinder der Freiheit*, ed. U. Beck (Frankfurt: Suhrkamp, 1997), 315-32.

28. Friedman, "Being in the World: Globalization and Localization," 311-28.
29. Against the obsolescence of the national approach, see E. Hobsbawm,"The Nation and Globalization," *Constellations* 5, no. 1 (April 1998): 1-9; M. Toscano, "¿Democracia de los ciudadanos o democracia de las nacionalidades?," in J. Rubio-Carracedo, J. M. Rosales, and M. Toscano, *Ciudadanía, nacionalismo y derechos humanos* (Madrid: Trotta, 2000), 87-115.
30. Habermas, *Die postnationale Konstellation*, 91-167.
31. The terminology has been used by H. Shue, "Solidarity among Strangers and the Right to Food," in *World, Hunger and Morality*, ed. W. Aiken and H. La Follette (Englewood Cliffs, N. J.: Prentice Hall, 1996), 113-32; H. Brukhorst, *Solidarität unter Fremden* (Frankfurt: Fischer, 1997), 39-94.
32. U. Beck, *Was ist Globalisierung?* (Frankfurt: Suhrkamp, 1997), 115-49; M. Walzer, ed., *Toward a Global Civil Society* (Oxford: Bergham Books, 1995), 7-27; "The Politics of Difference: Statehood and Toleration in a Multicultural World," *Ratio Juris* 10 (1997): 165-76; *On Toleration* (New Haven, Conn.: Yale University Press, 1997), 8-13; A. E. Galeotti, "Contemporary Pluralism and Toleration," *Ratio Juris* 10 (1997): 223-35; E. Garzón-Valdés, "Some Remarks on the Concept of Toleration," *Ratio Juris* 10 (1997): 127-38.
33. J. Habermas, "Learning by Disasters? A Diagnostic Look Back on the Short 20th Century," *Constellations* 5 (1998): 307-20; *Die postnationale Konstellation*, 47-61.
34. Habermas, "Remarks on Legitimation through Human Rights," 90-91; *Die Einbeziehung des Anderen,* 221-36.
35. B. S. Turner, *Citizenship and Social Theory* (London: Sage, 1993), 1-18.
36. A critical approach of global processes concerning women workers is argued by C. Wichterlich, "Von der Feminisierung der Beschäftigung," *Frankfurter Rundschau* 115 (18 May 1996): 5.
37. A. Lijphart considers how plurality would be responsible for instability and the breakdown in democracies, *Democracy in Plural Societies* (New Haven, Conn.: Yale University Press, 1977), 1-24.
38. A survey of citizenship, spheres, and conceptualizations in T. Janoski, *Citizenship and Civil Society* (Cambridge: Cambridge University Press, 1998), 9-17.
39. Habermas, *Faktizität und Geltung*, 468-537; *Die Einbeziehung des Anderen*, 237-76.
40. A. Gutmann, "Introduction," in *Multiculturalism*, ed A. Gutmann (Princeton: Princeton University Press, 1994), 3-23; S. Mendus, "Liberal Man," *Philosophy* 26 (1990): 45-57; C. Sunstein, "Introduction: Notes on Feminist Political Thought," *Ethics* 99 (1989): 219-28; U. Narayan, "Towards a Feminist Vision of Citizenship: Rethinking the Implications of Dignity, Political Participation, and Nationality," in *Reconstructing Political Theory*, ed. M. L. Shanley and U. Narayan (Cambridge: Polity Press, 1997), 48-67.
41. J. Bohman, "The Globalization of the Public Sphere: Cosmopolitanism Publicity and Cultural Pluralism," 101-17; M. P. Smith, "Democratic Deficit or Deficit of Democracy? European Integration and Privileged Institutional Position in Domestic Politics," in *Democracy: The Challenges Ahead*, ed. Y. Shain and A. Klieman (London: Macmillan, 1997), 161-83.
42. Z. Baumann, "Globalisierung oder was für die einen Globalisierung, ist für die anderen Lokalisierung," 653-64; M. Zürn, "Das Projekt 'Komplexes Weltregieren,'" in *Wozu Politkwissenschaft?* ed. C. Leggewie (Darmstadt: Wissenschaftliche Buchgesellschaft, 1994), 77-88.
43. G. Frankenberg, "Civil Society and Social Justice," in *Toward a Global Civil Society*, ed. M. Walzer, 195-99; F. Michelman, "Foreword: Traces of Self-Government," 33; T. H. Marshall and T. Bottomore, *Cititzenship and Social Class* (London: Pluto Press, 1992), 53-93.
44. Bohman, "The Globalization of the Public Sphere: Cosmopolitanism Publicity

194   *Teresa López de la Vieja*

and Cultural Pluralism," 101-17.

45. Hobsbawm, "The Nation and Globalization," 1-9.

46. The argument in favor of two-level citizenship (transnational institutions, national minorities) has been developed by W. Kymlicka and W. Norman. "Return to Citizen: A Survey of Recent Work on Cititzenship Theory," *Ethics* 104, no. 2 (1994): 352-81, and by Kymlicka and C. Straehle, "Cosmopolitanism, Nation-States, and Minority Nationalism," *European Journal of Philosophy* 7 (1999): 65-84.

47. Featherstone, "Being in the World: Globalization and Localization," 311-28.

48. Held, *Democracy and the Global Order*.

49. Bauman, "Schwache Staaten. Die Globalisierung und die Spaltung der Weltgesellschaft," 315-32.

50. Held, *Democracy and the Global Order*, 221-38.

51. J. P. Arnason, "Nationalism, Globalization, and Modernity," in *Global Culture*, ed. M. Featherstone (London: Sage, 1990), 207-3.

52. A. Appadurai points to the role of difference: "Dijuncture and Difference in the Global Cultural Economy," in *Global Culture*, ed. M. Featherstone, 295-310.

53. The typology of "locals" and "cosmopolitans" comes from U. Hannerz, "Cosmopolitans and Locals in World Culture," in *Global Culture*, ed. M. Featherstone, 237-51.

54. Waters, *Globalization*, 27-28. For cosmopolitanism within social practices, see B. Ackerman, "Rooted Cosmopolitanism," *Ethics* 104 (1994): 516-35.

55. Benhabib, "Das demokratische Projekt im Zeitalter der Globalisierung," 54-56; R. Bauböck, "Sharing History and Future?" *Constellations* 4, no. 3 (January 1998): 320-45.

56. G. A. Almond, "The Intellectual History of the Civic Culture Concept," in *The Civic Culture Revisited*, ed. G. A. Almond and S. Verba (Newbury Park, Calif.: Sage, 1984), 1-36; C. Pateman, "The Civic Culture: A Philosophic Critique," in *The Civic Culture Revisited*, ed. G. A. Almond and S. Verba, 57-102.

57. J. Kekes, *The Morality of Pluralism* (Princeton: Princeton University Press, 1993), 53-75.

58. A. Ingþórsson, "Democracy and Bureaucracy and the Marginalization of the State," *ARSP* 61 (1995): 106-13.

59. E. Hobsbawm, "Ethnicity, Migration, and the Validity of the Nation-State," in *Toward a Global Civil Society*, ed. M. Walzer, 235-40.

60. B. Barry, "Spherical Justice and Global Injustice," in *Pluralism, Justice, and Equality*, ed. D. Miller and M. Walzer (Oxford: Oxford University Press, 1995), 67-80.

61. Habermas, *Die Einbeziehung des Anderen*, 237-76; "Struggles for Recognition in the Democratic Constitutional State," in *Multiculturalism*, ed. A. Gutmann, 107-48.

62. S. Hicks, "Citizenship and the Modern Legal Theory of the State," *ARSP* 59 (1995): 139-45.

63. Shue, "Solidarity among Strangers and the Right to Food," 113-32.

64. A. Hügli and P. Lübcke, *Philosophielexikon* (Hamburg: Rowohlt, 1997), 629.

65. J. P. Sterba, "Global Justice," in *World, Hunger and Morality*, ed. W. Aiken, and H. La Follette, 133-52; A. Gutmann, "Justice across the Spheres," in *Pluralism, Justice, and Equality*, ed. D. Miller and M. Walzer, 99-119.

66. T. Baldwin, "Toleration and the Right to Freedom," in *Aspects on Toleration*, ed. J. Horton and S. Mendus (London: Methuen, 1985), 36-52.

67. Frankenberg,"Civil Society and Social Justice," 195-99.

68. Walzer, *On Toleration*, 52-82.

69. Frankenberg, "Civil Society and Social Justice."

70. A. E. Galeotti mentions the question of "invisible" minorities and disadvantaged groups in liberal societies in his "Contemporary Pluralism and Toleration," 223-35; see also her "Tólerance et justice sociale," in *Pluralisme et Equité*, ed. J. Affichard and J. B.

Foucauld (Paris: Esprit, 1995), 104-19.

71. S. Lukes, "Toleration and Recognition," *Ratio Juris* 10 (1997): 213-22.

72. M. López de la Vieja, "Tolerancia y cuotas de representacion femenina," *Derechos y libertades* 3 (1995): 253-61.

73. J. de Lucas, "Para dejar de hablar de la tolerancia," *Doxa* (1992): 117-26; J. R. de Páramo, *Tolerancia y Liberalismo* (Madrid: Centro de Estudios Constitucionales, 1993), 29-44.

74. L. Prieto Sanchís, *Tolerancia y minorias* (Cuenca: Ediciones de la Universidad de Castilla La Mancha, 1996), 27-66.

75. De Páramo, *Tolerancia y Liberalismo*, 24.

76. M. T. López de la Vieja, *Principios morales y casos practicos* (Madrid: Tecnos, 1999) 234-73.

77. Barber, *Strong Democracy*, 117-38.

78. R. Dworkin, *Taking Rights Seriously* (Cambridge, Mass.: Harvard University Press, 1977), 223-39.

79. R. Alexy, *Recht, Vernunft, Diskurs* (Frankfurt: Suhrkamp, 1995), 232-61; C. Lefort, *L'invention démocratique* (Paris: Fayard, 1994), 45-83.

80. U. Beck, "Neonationalismus oder das Europa der Invididuen," in *Riskante Freiheiten*, ed. U. Beck and E. Beck-Gernsheim (Frankfurt: Suhrkamp,1994), 466-81.

81. For a survey of literature and of the divergent use of these terms, see A. J. Heidenheimer, "Politics, Policy and Policey as Concepts in English and Continental Languages: An Attempt to Explain Divergences," *The Review of Politics*, 48 (1986): 3-30.

82. Janoski, *Citizenship and Civil Society*, 9.

83. A. McGrew argues for a global democracy, analyzing three models, or a kind of "Gedankenexperimente" in liberalism, cosmopolitanism, and communitarianism: "Demokratie ohne Grenzen?" in *Politik der Globalisierung*, ed. U. Beck, 374-422.

84. For instance, C. Closa considers the paradigmatic case of the European Union. He argues in favor of the normative basis without forgetting the empirical difficulties, such as the lack of a European public sphere; "International Limits to National Claims in EU Constitutional Negotiations: The Spanish Government and the Asylum Right for EU Citizens," *International Negotiation* 3 (1998): 389-411; "Supranational Citizenship and Democracy: Normative and Empirical Dimensions," in *European Citizenship: An Institutional Challenge*, ed. M. La Torre (Amsterdam: Kluwer, 1998), 415-33; "Some Foundations for the Normative Discussion on Supranational Citizenship and Democracy" in *European Citizenship, Multiculturalism, and the State*, ed. U. Preuss and F. Requejo (Baden-Baden: Nomos Verlag, 1998), 105-24.

85. J. M. Rosales, *Politica cívica: La experiencia de la ciudadanía en la democracia liberal* (Madrid: Centro de Estudios Políticos y Constitucionales, 1998), 25-43; and "Liberal Reformism and Democratic Citizenship," 265-70.

Part III

Citizenship in a Global World

Chapter 12

National Identities and Cosmopolitan Virtues: Citizenship in a Global Age

Bryan S. Turner

Introduction: On Virtue and Violence

There is an important historical relationship between citizenship, national identity, and masculinity, especially in a world that is subject both to powerful forces of global integration and to political fragmentation. If citizenship has in the past attempted to define a civic culture, then we need to identify, if we are to talk about global citizenship at all, [1] a corresponding set of cosmopolitan obligations, which in this discussion I shall call "cosmopolitan virtues." In fact, cosmopolitan virtue can be treated as the obligation side of human rights, where cosmopolitan rights and obligations form a normative framework for political action and responsibility. Cosmopolitanism is a normative standard of public conduct, but empirically the social order is breaking down into antagonistic ethnic, regional, and national identities.

In the traditional terminology of sociology, citizenship building is also and necessarily a process of nation-building. The creation of Marshallian institutions of citizenship in legal, political, and social terms was also the construction of a national framework of membership within the nation-state—a process that dominated domestic politics in Europe and North America through much of the late eighteenth and nineteenth centuries. The production of an institutional framework of national citizenship created a national "personality" that transcended indigenous and local identities. We might in fact speak of citizenship as an institutional framework within which national character is created. Citizenship identities during the rise of the European cities had been urban and local, despite the cultural context that was provided by secular humanism. With the rise of nationalism, urban citizenship became increasingly connected with strong nationalistic cultures that sought greater domestic coherence and simultaneously organized negative images of outsiders.[2] Nationalism does not automatically assume an illiberal and intolerant form, but in the eighteenth and nineteenth centuries nationalism, when mixed with Orientalism, produced a potent brew of racism.

Now the narratives of nationalism are typically masculine. They chart the heroic rise of the nation against internal and external enemies through a pattern of civil conflict, warfare, and liberation. If the struggle for self-government by the Founding Fathers established the foundations for Jeffersonian democracy, the naval victories of Nelson cemented early nineteenth-century society around the triumphant figure of Britannia against Bonapartism. The national mythologies of a society cement the individual biographies of men and the collective biographies of generations with the history of a nation-state and its people. It does not follow that women are excluded from nation-building. On the contrary, they are crucial for family formation and reproduction that in turn reproduce society. However, women's voices in the grand narratives of nationalism tend to be muted and marginalized by a warrior ethos, Epic poetry, tragic romances, and national mythologies combine collective emotions and sentiments with the stories of nation-building. James Joyce and modern national Irish mythology is one example.[3] Defining culture in *Culture and Anarchy* in 1869 as the best that can be thought in a society, Matthew Arnold was able to assume the moral authority of English high culture and the role of intellectual as its defender.[4] Arnold could also assume that a strong national culture required a powerful state to impose its hegemonic force at home and abroad. The fragmentation of modern cultures and the growing hybridity of national traditions have reinforced the feeling among public intellectuals not only that there are no final vocabularies but that multiculturalism imposes a certain detachment from one's own culture.

In modern times, films have replaced epic poetry as a carrier of myth. It would, for example, be difficult to think of the contemporary rebirth of Scottish nationalism at a popular level without Mel Gibson's *Braveheart*. Australian nationalism is periodically stimulated by film productions of the tragic wastage of Australian manhood at Gallipoli. The point of these examples is to suggest that modern masculine identity is forged and sustained by nationalism and that national identity is built around and sustained by the institutions of citizenship, which are national institutions of exclusionary entitlement. The nation-state presupposed a continuing pattern of patriarchy and patriotism as a legacy of monarchy and state building. However, the modern matrix of nation, citizenship and masculinity is beginning to unravel and the erosion of national-citizenship identity on the basis of national sovereignty provides opportunities for both global liberal cosmopolitanism virtue and reactive nationalism, ethnic violence, and male aggression. Against masculinist conceptions of civil virtue, it is possible to construct a feminist perspective of care and cosmopolitan culture that is compatible with the stoical tradition of Montaigne.

Rights and Relativism

Claims about the universality of knowledge and in particular the universality of rights have become distinctly unfashionable among social scientists, at least since the publication of J.-F. Lyotard's *Postmodern Condition*.[5] The assumption that there might be Truth to which our beliefs about society could be measured has been criticized from a variety of positions. For philosophers like Richard Rorty,[6] we should embrace pragmatism to ask, not whether a belief system is true, but whether it serve some useful purpose. Any notion that one could speak confidently about shared moral codes has also been increasingly regarded as obsolete.

There is an important alliance that has evolved in the last two decades between anthropological relativism and postmodern critiques of the universalistic assumptions of traditional moral discourse. Of course, anthropology, given its commitment to ethnographic detail, has probably been relativistic through most of the twentieth century, but it has in recent years found additional support from postmodernists, the literature on decolonization and subaltern studies. The erosion of the literary canon has also done much to reinforce this relativistic tendency. Intellectuals have therefore moved a long way from Kant's cosmopolitan ideal and his aspirations for a perpetual peace.[7]

While cultural and moral relativism are generally shared views of intellectuals, we also live in a period when theories of globalization are widely entertained by social scientists. Of course, an assumption that the modern world is subject to global pressures in economics, politics, and culture does not necessarily mean that there is any corresponding set of assumptions that the social world is becoming more uniform. A global age does not automatically result in McDonaldization because there can be equally powerful pressures toward localism, on the one hand, and hybridity, on the other. Nevertheless, there is a widespread view in sociology that there are powerful pressures toward the experience of a global village. The rise of global tourism, world sport, global communication networks, global agencies like WHO and UNESCO, and the global experience of common medical crises in AIDS and HIV are features of globalism that result in a common experience of social change.

Unfortunately cultural relativism and an optimistic version of globalization theory can induce an emotional response to modernity that is both comforting and dangerous. We need to recognize that the patterns of post-communist globalization and decolonization have produced more rather than less ethnic, political, and religious conflict. The so-called Middle East peace process, Iran-Iraq tensions, the Balkan crisis, the ethnic divisions within the former Soviet Union, genocide in Africa and more generally the ideological conflicts between Islam and Western cultures point to a much darker picture of the global village than McLuhan's benign picture of frictionless communication.

Cultural relativism has a much longer history obviously than nineteenth-century anthropology. We can approach the question of cosmopolitanism and cultural relativism from the point of view of Western Orientalism from the end of the sixteenth-century when Europe was divided by religious wars and Islam (in the shape of the Ottoman Empire) was a powerful and real threat to European political autonomy. In order to give this discussion some shape, it is valuable to examine the cosmopolitan scepticism of Michel Montaigne whose moral views were shaped by religious conflicts between Huguenots and Catholics. Montaigne appears to be a relativist, but in fact his relativism was a rhetorical smoke screen. In terms of relativism, Montaigne asserted that "what we call barbarism is simply what others do," but his *Essays* actually challenge that argument because he recognized that questions of justice cannot be easily discussed if relativism is accepted naively.[8]

Optimistic globalization theory may lull us into a false vision of the world as culturally integrated, or at least capable of such integration. Cultural relativism precludes any serious debate about justice and suffers paradoxically from the same dilemma as liberalism. What does a liberal do in a world that is inhabited by people who do not accept liberalism? A liberal has problems with fascism, when fascists do not accept norms about freedom of speech. Cultural relativists have similar problems when fundamentalists regarded relativism as an aspect of the disease of secularism. These questions of cultural relativism can be tackled through a commentary on Montaigne in order to defend "cosmopolitan virtue" as a necessary adjunct to the possibilities of global citizenship.

Orientalism and Montaigne's Cannibals

Living in the context of the French religious wars, Montaigne wanted to achieve a moral reform of the French nobility whose warlike ethic prevented political compromise and compassion. Montaigne, who in this respect could be seen in sociological terms as a theorist of civilizational processes, argued that the violent ethos of noble life had resulted in the destruction of French society. His question was simply: what is appropriate behavior for a noble class if we are ever to restore peace and civilization?

Montaigne presents an argument that gives priority to *humanité* as the basis for mercy and sympathy because *humanité* moderates vengence and resentment.

He was shocked by the cruelty and violence of his own times. Men have become like beasts; they delight in the torture of others. How can this be regarded as truly noble? Hunting as the principal past-time of the nobility prepares them for a warrior calling in which they will inflict terrible violence on human beings. He drew a parallel between refractory French noblemen, intransigent religious zealots, Roman gladiators and Brazilian cannibals. In many respects they all exhibit the virtues of Stoicism, which Montaigne argues have negative consequences. The unyielding behavior of the Stoic warrior rules out compromise and cooperation, and therefore Montaigne embraced the softer (feminine) values of mercy, compassion and tenderness.

Montaigne's interest in the Brazilian cannibals was a device for analyzing the violence of his own society. His version of Orientalism is used as a literary device to study his own society. This attitude was in fact an important part of the humanistic goal of understanding one's own society through the study of other societies. Montaigne's ethics—yielding, forgiveness, clemency, talking it out rather than fighting it through, adopting feminine virtues rather than masculine Stoicism—can make men behave more humanely to one another, perhaps lead his country men out of their civil war, and restore conditions of justice. Montaigne's ethical position ends in a tension between sympathy and understanding towards the other and the quest for justice.

While the modern discussion about Western views of the Orient are a product of postwar global conflicts, the controversy about other cultures can be traced back historically to the ancient encounter between the Abrahamic religions. The fundamental issue is that Islam, Christianity, and Judaism are variations of a generic religion (of Abraham), but they have been differentiated in order for the West to be categorically distinguished from the East. In historical and cultural terms, the Abrahamic faiths cannot be neatly and definitely assigned to specific geographical locations and destinations, but for political reasons such a desig-nation has to take place. These religions share the tradition of a high god, a sacred book, a religious teleology, and a lineage of charismatic prophets. While the modern equation of Christendom and Europe may be unproblematic, Christianity is a religion whose theological roots are in the prophetic tradition of Jewish radical monotheism and whose geographical origins are Near Eastern. In this respect, Orientalism is a family feud and hence the Otherness of the other religions is both inevitable and curious. The East appears in Western imagination as the forbidden Other, which is simultaneously repulsive, seductive, and attractive. Like the veil, the East is both secluded and inviting. From the eighteenth century, the Orient has existed within a literary and visual tradition that is romantic and fantastic.

In the geography of the imagination, the Orient is that part of the intellectual map by which the West has historically and negatively oriented itself.[9] The noun "Orient," which defines a geographical arena, is also a verb "to orient," that is, Orientalism offers a political and psychological positioning that constitutes social identities in a condition of antagonism. Orientalism as a textual practice divided the world into friends and strangers whose endless struggles define "the political." The Orient has been the negative Other that defines the edges and boundaries of the civilized world, and it thus patrols the transgressive possibilities of culture. The Occident was part of the ethical cartography of the West; it celebrated the Puritan consciousness in terms of a set of principles about moral responsibility and probity.

Geographic Otherness also defines our subjective inwardness; our being is articulated in a terrain of negativities that are oppositional and, according to Said, permanent and ineluctable. In *Culture and Imperialism* Said claims that the modern identity of the West has been defined by its colonies, but these colonies are not merely physical places in a political geography; they also organize the boundaries and borders of our consciousness by defining our attitudes toward, for example, sexuality and race. [10] Within the paradigm of the Protestant Ethic thesis, the aboriginal is defined as somebody who is not only poor and traditional but also licentious and lazy. Colonial policy and ideology produced a wide range of national types based on the myth of the lazy native.

For example, in the evolution of Orientalism, the plays of Shakespeare present a valuable insight into the characterology of such Oriental figures. The story of *The Tempest* was based on seventeenth-century naval records describing shipwrecks, and Caliban, who is probably modeled on early encounters with the indigenous peoples of the West Indies, is treacherous and dangerous. He stands as a contrasting negative mirror image of Miranda, who is perfect, naive, and beautiful. Caliban's sexual desire for "admir'd Miranda" forms part of the moral struggle of the play under the careful scrutiny of the island's patriarch. It is Prospero's rational interventions that master both storms and characters. It is in this respect the foundation of the literary analysis of modern colonialism because the magical island offered Shakespeare an ideal context for representing the struggles between European reason and its colonial subjects as a confrontation between magic and anarchy on the one hand and reason and statecraft on the other. It was Prospero's neglect of statesmanship that resulted in his original downfall and his careful management of the sexuality of his island subjects that eventually restores peace and good order to the land. While Prospero's original neglect of his princely responsibilities resulted in political despotism, his island kingdom is a model of patriarchal control. Gonzalo's description of a political Utopia—"I'th' commonwealth I would by contraries/Execute all things. For no kind of traffic/Would I admit, no name of magistrate . . . No sovereignty"—is taken directly from Montaigne's essay on cannibalism.

The study of Orientalism must also include an analysis of anti-Semitism. There is a general anti-Semitism in Europe, in which antagonism to Jews has often accompanied hostility to Muslims. Generally speaking, the critique of Orientalism has not noticed the ironic connection between two forms of racism, namely, against Arabs and against Jews. In his "Introduction to Orientalism," Said writes that in "addition, and by an almost inescapable logic, I have found myself writing the history of a strange, secret sharer of Western anti-Semitism. That anti-Semitism and Orientalism resemble each other very closely is a historical, cultural and political truth that needs only be mentioned to an Arab Palestinian for its irony to be perfectly understood."[11] In a reply to his critics, Said also noted the parallels between what he calls "Islamophobia" and anti-Semitism. There are in fact two discourses of Orientalism for Semites, one relating to Islam and the other to Judaism. Within Orientalism, there are two related discourses for Semites, namely, an Islamic discourse of absence and the Judaic discourse of contradictions.[12] While Islam had been defined by its absences (of rationality, cities, asceticism, and so forth), Judaism had been defined by the contradictory nature of its religious injunctions in which, for example, its dietary laws transferred the quest for personal salvation into a set of ritualistic prescriptions that inhibited the full expression of its monotheistic rationalism according to Weber's analysis in *Ancient Judaism*.[13] For Weber, the rationality of Jewish monotheistic prophecy was undermined by a ritualistic dietary scheme.

The West oriented its identity between two poles—the lazy, sensual Arab and the untrustworthy, greedy Jew. While Weber criticized the Islamic paradise as merely a sensual reward for warriors, he controversially described Jewish communities as a "pariah status group," because their social and geographical migrations were seen to be politically dangerous. Throughout the medieval and modern periods, Jews disturbed the consciousness of the Christian West. During the Protestant Reformation, there emerged a millenarian heresy that the Jews, after being restored to Palestine, would fight the Turks and thereby assist Christianity in its struggle against Islam. In the seventeenth century, British Puritans enthusiastically received the news of a messianic Jewish leader Sabbatai Sevi who had inflicted significant military defeats on the Turks. Their eschatological hopes were of course disappointed and in 1666 news of Sevi's conversion to Islam was circulating in London. He was subsequently denounced as an imposter who had misled his followers.

The experience of Diaspora and ethnic hatred meant that displaced Jews were defined as cosmopolitan and strange; the notion of the "wandering Jew" pinpoints the idea that their commitment to the nation-state could not be taken for granted. In the twentieth century, Hitler's hatred of Viennese Jews arose from the encounter with what he took to be a seething mass of unfriendly and strange faces. While Jews were strange, they were also guilty, according to New Testament theology, of religious treachery. These anti-Semitic stereotypes have been culturally crucial, because Christianity as the foundation of Western values has traditionally attempted to maintain its difference from other Abrahamic faiths. Precisely because Judaism and Islam shared so much in common (monotheism, prophetic and charismatic revelation, the religion of the Book, and a radical eschatology), they had to be separated culturally by a discourse of ethnic and moral difference from the Christian tradition. Jewish separate identity raised significant questions about the character of civilization processes in Europe. [14]

European fears about Ottoman expansion began to decline toward the end of the seventeenth century. In 1683, the Ottoman army was defeated outside Vienna and the Treaty of Karlowitz in 1699 recognized at least implicitly the military decline of the Ottoman empire through ceding territory to Austria, Poland, and Venice. The reform of the English navy was an important foundation for the growth of trade and the ability of English governments to impose treaties and trading arrangements. Dutch control over the East Indies was matched by British expansion in the Malaya Peninsula, Australia, and New Zealand. More significantly, the European nations began to look toward the New World as a market for goods and resources. Western technological supremacy, military dominance, and the expansion of trade were obvious consequences of the growth of industrial capitalism. Islam ceased to be a real threat to the economic and political dominance of Europe and became instead an object of scholarly curiosity. The growth of interest in Islam from around the middle of the eighteenth century was fueled by an academic interest in (dead) languages, translations, and the creation of catalogues and oriental libraries. With the decline of military power, Islam, along with Rome and the classical world, entered into the European story of the rise and fall of empires. In the eighteenth and nineteenth centuries, the Islamic lands became appropriate sites for European travel tales and exotic fiction.

Citizenship and Nation Building

Nation-state citizenship has been in the modern world a powerful agency for creating individual identities. It is primarily a political and juridical category relating to individuation and individualism; the juridical identity of citizens has evolved according to the larger political context because citizenship has been necessarily housed within a definite political community, namely, the nation-state. Of course, citizenship was originally a product of Renaissance humanism in which the ascending order of the state and the horizontal ordering of citizenship contrasted with the descending theme of the Church and its hierarchical order of institutionalized charisma. [15] This tradition of citizenship became linked to the norms of civility, civil society, and citizenship. The rise of nation-state citizenship somewhat replaced the tradition of humanism and urban cosmopolitanism with an exclusionary national ethic. Now the problem for the development of contemporary forms of citizenship is twofold: global society is not (as yet) a definite political community to which cosmopolitanism could be attached and nationalistic citizenship necessarily constrains the possibilities of global identity.

The development of these juridical identities is not, therefore, an evolutionary process. There was a transformation of the Enlightenment and revolutionary ambitions for cosmopolitanism (in for example Kant's notion of world history) into exclusionary nationalist paradigms of citizenship with the development of the nation-state. International socialism in opposition to capitalist rivalries suffered at least two major historical reversals in the First and Second World Wars, and it never fully recovered as a platform for international working-class solidarities. Friedrich Meinecke's notion of cosmopolitanism as a critique of Prussian militarism expressed the ambitions of a liberal bourgeois class in rejection of the spread of aggressive nationalism. His analysis of the Prussian state in *Weltbürgertum und Nationalstaat* clearly recognized the decline of cosmopolitan values from Goethe to Bismarck.[16]

This historical sketch of nationalism is partly motivated by the sociological concept of the civilizing process. In Alfred Weber's analysis of civilizational change,[17] feudalism required certain formations of warrior identity that were relevant to the militarized pattern of land settlement in the Middle Ages. With the development of court society, aristocratic identities were forged around the role of the court, in which ritualized manners exercised control over strong and violent emotions. The rise of the bourgeoisie represented yet a further development of civilized identities; bourgeois educational institutions became key elements in this social and psychological transition. We can map out a further possibility—the emergence of a global citizen whose lifestyle requires a new pattern of social restraint and self-formation, namely, cosmopolitan virtue. To be more specific, we need to identify the intellectual as a carrier of cosmopolitan values. This cosmopolitan value system is defined by irony, emotional distance, skepticism, secularity, and an ethic of stewardship.

In bringing together a debate about identities and ethics, on the one hand, and the political history of citizenship and liberalism, on the other hand, I am drawing attention to the obvious historical and etymological connections between the concepts of civil society and citizenship, civility and civilization, the city and the citizen. The concept of "civil society" (*bürgerliche Gesellschaft*) owes its origin to a particular pattern of historical development. A *Burger* was originally a person who defended a castle (*Burg*) and from around the twelfth century it referred simply to a town dweller. It has also retained its association with the French *bourgeois* (from *bourg* or *borough*), Hegel used *citoyen* to indicate the citizen of a state. Thus in *bürgerliche Gesellschaft*, we have a combination of "civic" and "bourgeois." Now *Gesellschaft* is from *Geselle* or somebody who shares a dwelling place as one's companion. This civil society is not a *Gemeinschaft* (community) but an association of citizens. For Hegel, civil society is a distinctive area of ethical life that stands between the family and the state.[18]

This connection between civil society and citizenship is retained in many European languages, such as in the Dutch *Burgermaatschappij* and the Hungarian *allampolgar*. Only in Russia, where the walled city did not fully evolve as a center of urban immunities, did the concept of citizen diverge significantly. The Russian *grazhdanin* indicates that the citizen belongs to the state, not the city. In this European tradition, the cultured citizen is somebody whose lifestyle and mentality has been cultivated by a process of discipline and education, because, in addition to being constituted around a juridical identity, the citizen is also somebody whose personality has been, in ideal terms, molded by a civil culture or "virtue." These virtues of the citizen are typically described within a framework of obligations and duties, which stand alongside the rights and immunities which are enjoyed by the citizen. Within a republican tradition for example, the "good citizen" is somebody who undertakes certain duties and responsibilities, not because they have a market value, but because they contribute to the common good.

The Marshallian Legacy of Social Citizenship

This introduction to an analysis of citizenship identities in the postmodern, global city provides an overview of the contemporary debate on culture and citizenship. My purpose is to reshape the Marshallian legacy as an analysis of identities, entitlements, and citizenship in the modern city. It is thus in part an extended commentary on the legacy of T. H. Marshall, although I argue that an adequate understanding of the issues surrounding citizenship in modern societies must go well beyond the Marshallian framework.[19] Citizenship is a particular case of social rights in which there are tensions between social and human rights. Marshall (1950) developed a theory of postwar societies through an analysis of the relationships between social class, welfare, and citizenship;[20] his approach to the citizenship debate proved to be seminal, but the Marshallian tradition is particularly deficient as a perspective on ethnically diverse societies.

Citizenship is a set of rights and obligations that give individuals a formal legal identity; these legal rights and obligations have been put together historically as sets of social institutions, such as the jury system, parliament, and welfare state. Citizenship has traditionally been a fundamental topic of philosophy and politics, but, from a sociological point of view, we are interested in those institutions in society that give expression to the formal rights and obligations of individuals as members of a political community. This approach may be regarded as "sociological," because political models of citizenship typically have a sharper focus on political rights, the state, and the individual. From a sociological point of view, we are interested in how citizenship shapes identity and how it functions to influence the distribution of resources in a society.

It is analytically useful to think of three types of resources: economic, cultural, and political.[21] Alongside these resources, we typically find three forms of rights: economic rights that are related to basic needs for goods and services such as food and shelter; cultural rights that include language and educational rights; and finally, political rights such as individual freedoms and rights to expression through political means such as parliaments. These rights may be collectively referred to as "social" rights as distinct from human rights, because they typically presuppose membership of a nation-state. At a more fundamental level, cultural resources include the special identities that people enjoy as citizens.

Citizenship regulates access to the scarce resources of society and hence its allocative function is the basis of a profound conflict in modern societies over citizenship membership criteria. The process of and conditions for naturalization and de-naturalization tell us a great deal about the character of democracy in society because these processes relate fundamentally to the basic values of inclusion and exclusion. French colonialism typically involved a notion of a *mission civilisatrice* in which the metropolitan culture attempted to impose a uniform identity on its dependent regions and, in the nineteenth century, colonization required cultural assimilation; but these inclusive and exclusionary processes are obviously not merely about cultural identity.

In this account of the transformation of modern politics, I want to consider an ancient problem of cultural diversity and political power. The word "ancient" is used advisedly, since it can be argued that fear of diversity in classical Greece was in fact the condition that produced political theory in the first instance.[22] Although this problem of cultural diversity within the framework of the city-state has a long history in political thought, there are some new ingredients within the contemporary context. The essence of these new circumstances are the globalization of economic and cultural relationships and the postmodernization of cultural phenomena. In reality, these are the same issues, because the postmodernization of culture is closely related to the development of hybridization and hybridity is a function of cultural globalism. The question then is: how can one be a citizen in such a context of staggering diversity? How can citizens be committed to some political community (the city or the state) when social and cultural fragmentation makes the possibility of solidarity unlikely? Generally speaking the response to this circumstance has been somewhat apologetic and typically nostalgic. The point of this chapter is to try to celebrate diversity and to do so through the development of a notion of cosmopolitan virtue. Here again, the ancients and the moderns cannot be kept apart, because it was after all the Stoics who, in response to the anxieties of diversity, created the notions of cosmopolitanism and universal order as a suitable ethic for the imperial city.[23]

Citizenship confers, in addition to a legal status, a particular cultural identity on individuals and groups. The notion of the "politics of identity" indicates an important change in the nature of contemporary politics. Whereas much of the struggle over citizenship in the early stages of industrialization was about class membership and class struggle in the labor market, citizenship struggles in late twentieth-century society are more commonly about claims to cultural identity and cultural history. These struggles have been primarily about ethnic identity, sexual rights, and aboriginality. Most debates about citizenship in contemporary political theory are as a result about the question of contested collective identity in a context of radical pluralization. Citizenship is not simply about access to scarce economic and political resources; it is concerned ultimately with questions about identity in civil society, and, as I argue shortly, it is principally about male identity in relation to the nation-state.

In formal political philosophy, the idea of citizenship contains a clear notion of the civic virtues that are regarded as necessary for the functioning of a democracy. The word "citizenship" (*citélzein*) itself indicates a connection with the rise of bourgeois society and in particular with the tradition of civil society (*die bürgerliche Gesellschaft*). For the Scottish political economists such as Adam Smith and Adam Ferguson, civil society was contrasted with the barbarism of primitive society; citizenship was seen to be connected with *civilitas*. In Germany, the idealists merged the idea of the Greek *polis* with the tradition of independent German towns with their distinctive educational cultures (in the virtues of the Bildungs tradition) to produce a defense of individual rights against both the militarized aristocracy and proletarian vulgarity.

The high point of this tradition is found in Fichte's Kantian statement of the intersubjectivity of rights. The values of citizenship were merged with those of civilization and hence Weber was to argue that citizenship as a uniquely Western institution had its origin in the peculiar structures of the Occidental city. However, for Weber the basis of "democratization is everywhere purely military in character; it lies in the rise of disciplined infantry."[24] The decline of the noble cavalry marks the rise of the urban militia, the autonomous city, civil society, and citizenship. The status of citizenship was part of the process of civilization wherein the virtues of the knight-at-arms were transferred to the arena of the royal court with its effeminate courtiers and its ideology of courtesy and later to the disciplined asceticism of the bourgeois household. These social conditions also indicate the rootedness of the concept of obligation as the cornerstone of bourgeois responsibility (to family and occupation), bourgeois morality with respect to the public/private division, and bourgeois versions of civil republicanism.

This politico-moral configuration was also the origin of Marx's hostility to the "possessive individualism" of the English utilitarians such as Bentham and Mill, and to the narrow, unidemensional development of the "political" in classical liberalism. With the rise of economic rationalism in the twentieth century, interest has once more returned to the analysis of the market in relation to egotistic individualism, indifference to strangers, and hostility to welfare-dependency among the economically marginalized. Citizenship and civic virtues are once more seen to be an essential ingredient of a civilized and pluralistic democracy. This concern for the political threat to civic culture in a market society has been associated with a reappraisal of Mill's liberalism, the importance of pluralism, and the role of voluntary associations in democracy. The cultural dimension of citizenship is now an essential component of citizenship studies, especially in a context in which there is political ambiguity around the analysis of cultural fragmentation and simulation brought about by postmodernization.

In this sociological model of citizenship, the idea of a political community serves as the basis of citizenship; this political community is typically the nation-state. When individuals become citizens, they not only enter into a set of institutions that confer upon them rights and obligations, they not only acquire an identity, they are not only socialized into civic virtues, but they also become members of a political community with a particular territory and history. In order to have citizenship one has to be, at least in most modern societies, a bona fide member of a political community. Generally speaking, it would be highly unusual for people to acquire citizenship if they are not a national member of a political community, that is, a nation-state.

One should notice here an important difference between human rights and citizenship. Human rights are typically conferred upon people as humans irrespective of whether they are Australian, British, Chinese, Indonesian, or whatever, but, because human rights legislation has been accepted by the nations of the world, people can claim human rights, even when they are stateless people or dispossessed refugees. In general, citizenship is a set of rights and obligations that attach to members of formally recognized nation-states within the system of nations and hence citizenship corresponds to legal membership of a nation-state. Citizenship identities and citizenship cultures are national identities and national cultures. Since nations are, following Benedict Anderson,[25] "imagined communities," the communal basis of citizenship has to be constantly renewed within the collective memory by nostalgic festivals, public ceremonies of national struggle, and effervescent collective experience. National culture has all the characteristics of a patriarchal civil religion.

The growth of urban citizenship required the extension of the nation-state as its political shell, and it also involved either the destruction of local, traditional, tribal cultures, or their pacification and inclusion. National citizenship developed on the basis of ethnic standardization. The marginalization and exclusion of the "Celtic fringe" in the United Kingdom is historically a classic example of the growing dominance of the Westminster model of citizenship founded on an assumption of ethnic and religious homogeneity. Citizenship is necessarily a contradictory force because it creates an internal space of social rights and solidarity, and thus an external, exclusionary force of non-membership. This inclusion/exclusion dynamic is one explanation of continuing ethnic violence in Central Africa where the modern boundaries of nationalistic states do not correspond with ancient boundaries between such ethnic communities as the

Tutsis and Hutus. One mechanism for the genocidal conflict has been the fact that the Banyarwanda have been stripped of citizenship by the government of Zaire.

Although he was not particularly interested in the question of political identity, Marshall's analysis of citizenship still provides a useful route into the discussion of political identity and contemporary citizenship. [26] Marshall's silence on this issue is, however, instructive, because it points to a period in British history in which, at least in public debate, the problem of identity politics had not fully emerged. Marshall claimed that citizenship evolved through three stages of legal, political, and social rights from around the middle of the seventeenth century to the creation of the welfare state in the middle of the twentieth century. This evolution of citizenship has to be seen against the background of the emergence of antagonistic social classes in the context of industrial capitalism. The growth of capitalist markets was accompanied by the emergence of class-based urban communities characterized by a high level of class consciousness and class conflict. Traditional sources of solidarity and legitimacy in rural communities, which had been partly held together by Christian rituals and beliefs, were challenged by the class-based ideologies of the working-class movement, namely, by socialist ideas of working-class cooperation. Old status relations were being replaced by the solidarities of class. Class, which in traditional political economy was an impersonal association of individuals with the same relationship to economic relations of ownership, began to assume characteristics normally associated with community or gemeinschaft. The stratification of modern societies has been orchestrated around the dynamic relationship between economic class, cultural status, and citizenship entitlement.

National Citizenship: Rights and Obligations

The formation of modern citizenship in the nineteenth and twentieth centuries was primarily associated with the growth of nation-states and with nationalism as the principal political ideology of nation-state building. The modern concept of citizenship was primarily a modern political notion, namely, a concept of political relations that dated from the American and French revolutions. [27] It charts the history of the growth of bourgeois civil society, that is, a public space of opinion formation in relation to democratic institutions. Any use of the concept with respect to the ancient city is misleading, because the concept assumes the absence of slavery, aristocracy, and feudalism. I do not wish to depart radically form that view, except to note here that the Treaty of Westphalia recognised a necessary precondition for such a development, namely, the creation of an international system of nation-states.

The Treaty of Westphalia in 1648 launched the modern system of nation-states as the principal actors within the world system. National identity and citizenship identity became fused in the late nineteenth century around the growth of nation-states characterized by the dominant ideology of nationalism. In many societies this juridic identity was given strong racist characteristics in the creation of such notions as "the British people" or "the German folk." The growth of national citizenship was associated with Occidentalism (as a necessary adjunct of Orientalism) creating strong notions of Otherness as the boundary between the inside and outside world. In this setting national citizenship became crucial to the building of loyalties and commitments around the nation-state.

Citizenship in this framework is both an inclusive mechanism for the allocation of entitlements and an exclusionary process for building solidarity and creating identity. National citizenship is constructed around exclusionary practices because it blocks outsiders from access to entitlements characteristically on the basis of a racial or national identity. The creation of the nation-state based upon citizenship involved various levels and degrees of "ethnic cleansing" because the exclusionary principle of citizenship was structured around a juridical and racial identity. As nation-states were challenged from within by class division and from without by warfare and imperial struggle, there was an enhanced requirement for a strong basis of loyalty in the national community.

In addition to membership of a political community, citizenship determines the allocation of resources between and across generations. Effective entitlements are not automatic and are normally tied to various patterns of service to the state. These entitlements are themselves organized around a number of dimensions that describe the specific types of contributions that individuals have made to society, such as war service or reproduction or work. For example people can achieve entitlements by the formation of households and families that become the sites for the reproduction of society in terms of the birth and maintenance of children. These services to the state via the family provide entitlements to both men and women as parents, that is, as reproducers of the nation-state. [28] These entitlements form the basis for family security systems, various forms of support to mothers and health, and educational provision for children. Questions of justice as a result become closely tied to principles of cross-generational responsibilities for the management and conservation of environment and society. [29]

Second, entitlements can be achieved through the production of goods and services, namely, through work that has been the most significant basis for the provision of superannuation and pension rights, but these entitlements also include rights to safety at work, insurance schemes relating to health and employment, and various provisions for retirement. It is for this reason obviously that the entitlements of men have been more significant than entitlements for women in societies where values relating to work form the core of the general value system.

Finally, service to the state through warfare generates a third range of entitlements for the soldier-citizen. Wartime service typically leads to various pension rights, health provisions, housing, and other entitlements for returning servicemen. There is an important, but somewhat neglected argument, that warfare is a fundamental force in the modern creation of national citizenship. Richard M. Titmuss argued that war had contributed significantly to the creation of social security schemes.[30] Perhaps the point to stress, however, is that warfare also creates a cultural identity in which the individual fortunes of servicemen and servicewomen are tied to the self-image of the nation-state as an historical actor. Here again the entitlements of men dominate entitlements for women, who may be able to claim rights indirectly as war widows. These routes to entitlement (family, work, and war) also generate particular types of identity, such as the soldier citizen, the working citizen, and the parent-citizen.

Within the Marshallian framework, these are the basic structures of effective or substantive entitlement but perhaps we can identify a fourth figure—the citizen as national intellectual. In many historical patterns of the formation of a national culture of citizenship, the intellectual has played an important part in shaping national consciousness, often through their contribution to the protection of a national language or a national system of mythology. Again these intellectual contrubutions to nation building typically involve masculine creation tales about national salvation. The cases that come to mind include Hugh MacDiarmid's contribution to Scottish national consciousness through his poetry (such as "Scotland, My Scotland"), the writings of W. B. Yeats in the construction of Irish historical consciousness, the cultural functions of intellectuals in the production of dictionaries of the Dutch language in the struggle against the dominance of French and German, or the role of ethnographers in the maintenance of Finnish identity through the work of The Finnish Literature Society of 1831 and the recovery of the ancient rune culture of the Finnish-Karelian tradition. It is possible to argue that the intellectuals enjoyed an entitlement by virtue of their contributions to the shaping of national culture and national identity.

The Marshallian model of citizenship has been eroded by the decline of a Fordist economy within which citizens find full-time and continuous employment. There has been a "corrosion of character"[31] with the decline of continuous employment in the same production unit, the casualization of work, and the growth of flexible employment. It is clear that in the postwar period there has also been a decline in mass warfare as a condition of effective entitlement. Finally, there has also been an erosion of the nuclear family as a typical unit of reproduction. These changes have transformed the traditional tripartite basis of effective entitlement. It is no longer clear upon what basis modern national citizenship might be based. This erosion of Fordist citizenship has created a space within which alternative (cosmopolitan) aspects of citizenship might be developed, especially a form of citizenship that is not tied immediately to the nation-state.

Postmodernizing Identity

We can think of two dimensions (political loyalty to the state and social solidarity) in terms of a fourfold property space defined by the notion of hot/cool loyalty, which indicates the level of commitment to the polity, and thick/thin solidarity, which indicates the depth and strength of the forms of inclusion. This fourfold property space enables us to develop an ironic theory of loyalty and solidarity in modern society.[32] Thick solidarities very well describe the type of social involvement of, for example, the Arunta tribe in Emile Durkheim's analysis of mechanical solidarity in his sociology of religion.[33] The Arunta world of the Arunta tribes of central Australia involved the closed communities of a quasi-nomadic life of hunter-gatherer tribalism. Their social relations were largely permanent, emotional, and solid, and their belief systems were not challenged by external cultures or by secularization. By contrast, modern societies are organized around the market place of anonymous strangers, in which these stangers are mobile and disconnected. The distinction between hot/cool loyalties is taken from an analysis of modern communication; for example, the telephone offers a unidimensional communication with high definition. It is a cool medium, where the tribal mode of communication of tradition by oral and ritualistic means is hot. This distinction in Marshall McLuhan's theory of the media is redeployed here in order to talk about modes of loyalty in the modern state.[34]

Postmodern or cosmopolitan citizenship will be characterized by cool loyalties and thin patterns of solidarity. Indeed we could argue that the characteristic mode or orientation of the cosmopolitan citizen would in fact be one of (Socratic) disloyalty and ironic distance. In Richard Rorty's terms, an *ironist* always holds her views about the social worlds in doubt, because they are always subject to revision and reformulation.[35] Her picture of society is always provisional and she is skeptical about grand narratives because her own "final vocabulary" is always open to further inspection and correction. Her ironic views of the world are always "for the time being." If the cosmopolitan mentality is cool, the social relationships of the ironist will be thin; indeed, e-mail friendships and electronic networks constitute the new patterns of friendship in a postmodern globe.

These postmodern cool loyalties will be characteristic of the global elite of symbolic analysts who are geographically and socially mobile, finding employment in different global corporations in different parts of the world. The mobile symbolic analyst is quite likely to enjoy multiple citizenships, several economic identities, and various status positions within a number of blended families. They are inclined toward reflexivity because they get the point of hermeneutic anthropology—namely, that the world is a site of contested loyalties and interpretations. The postmodern citizen is only moving on. By contrast, those sections of the population that are relatively immobile and located in traditional employment patterns (the working class, ethnic minorities, and the under classes) may continue in fact to have hot loyalties and thick patterns of solidarity. In a world of mounting unemployment and ethnic tensions, the working class and the inhabitants of areas of rural depopulation may well be recruited to nationalist and reactionary parties. Their worldview, rather than being ironic, becomes associated with reactionary nationalism. The third possibility would be characteristic of the liberal middle classes and professional groups who have relatively cool loyalties to the nation-state, but who are involved in a dense network of voluntary associations and other institutional links within society and therefore have thick solidarity. These ethnic patriots resemble the neo-tribalism described by Michel Maffesoli as a subterranean gemeinschaft in contemporary societies.[36] Their affective world will revolve around social spectacle, particularly the gladiatorial struggles between national football teams.

Conclusion: Irony, Stewardship, and Cosmopolitan Virtue

My final problem is that, given the complexity and the hybridization of modern society, there is no convenient place for real or hot emotions.[37] Intercultural sensitivities and the need to interact constantly with strangers promote irony as a possible orientation toward multicultural diversity, social differentiation, and hybrid cultures. Irony is sensitive to the simulation that is necessary for interaction in multicultural societies.[38] In such a world, ironic distance is functionally compatible with globalized hybridity because we have all become strangers in the Simmelian City. Hot emotions and thick solidarities are dysfunctional to social intercourse, which has to take place on a purely superficial and artificial plane. Although there has been much criticism of the emotional barrenness of the simulated or artificial City, postemotionalism may be functionally necessary for modern society to exist.[39] In a global village, hot emotions and thick loyalties create conditions for violent conflict.

By cosmopolitan virtue, I do not intend simply to mean moral indifference. My picture of ironic citizenship is taken from Søren Kierkegaard's vision of the tragic irony of Socrates and Christ, namely as a constructive moral principle. By describing the intellectual as ironic, it may be taken to mean that the intellectual is indifferent to ethical issues. We often think of the intellectual as the cultural hero, who is passionately committed to social and political causes. However, care for other cultures might be conceptualized in terms of an ideal doctor-patient relationship, in which the person giving care (the nurse, psychoanalyst, or general practitioner) must practice a certain type of emotional neutrality and distance to be effective. Moral responses to pain may not require passion but rather care as a controlled emotional engagement. One could imagine that cosmopolitan (feminist) virtue could take on a careful engagement with cultural issues such as the protection of so-called primitive cultures and aboriginal communities that are clearly threatened by globalization, and responsibility for advocacy in a world of collapsing environments and endangered languages.

Perhaps it is not too fanciful to believe that, precisely because of their exposure to global concerns and global issues, the ironist might, in recognizing the ubiquity of hybridization, reject all claims to cultural superiority and cultural dominance. Precisely because we are exposed to global forces of postmodernization, the ironist should welcome a stance that supports postcolonial cultures and celebrates the teaming diversity of human cultures. In their awareness of the tensions between local cultures and global processes, cosmopolitan virtue might come to recognize a stewardship over cultures that are precarious. The ironist, being convinced of the evolutionary importance of bio-diversity would be equally careful in their support of cultural heterogeneity.

In recognizing this historically close relationship between the development of the institutions of citizenship and the growth of urban culture, I am indicating the possibility that the growth of the global city may provide that definite political community that is a necessary adjunct of citizenship. There has to be a political agency that is able to deliver the rights and immunities to which citizens are entitled, and to anticipate the obligations, duties, and loyalties which underpin these rights. In short, citizenship has to correspond to some definite form of sovereignty and this political shell is also the arena within which certain mentalities, identities, and cultures are housed.

Earlier sociologists have argued that the plural and cosmopolitan cities of Europe in the late and early twentieth century produced, in the terminology of Georg Simmel, new identities or mentalities that were characterized by the blasé attitude of the stranger or the lifestyle of the flaneur in the work of Walter Benjamin. I have suggested that cosmopolitan virtue is dominated by the orientation of irony. There is an elective affinity between postemotional distance, cosmopolitan irony, and the multicultural tensions of global city cultures. Now traditionally expressions like "blasé attitude," or "the urban flaneur" or "ironic criticism" carry a certain negative quality, but in this conclusion I wish to argue that these cosmopolitan characteristics should be developed as the virtues of a global city. The real importance of this argument is that cosmopolitanism recognizes the continuity and existence of ethnic and national identities rather than their erosion by globalization. It implies recognition of and respect for ethnic identity and national character. Globalization will not necessarily bring about a McDonaldization or standardization of identity, and skeptical cosmopolitanism can happily respect the authenticity of national culture and national tradition. However, cosmopolitanism is an essentially liberal code of behavior and thus it is not compatible with hot or reactionary nationalism. In normative terms, cosmopolitan virtue is the necessary cultural envelope for the cultivation of transnational obligations of care and respect.

Notes

1. D. Held, A. McGrew, D. Goldblatt, and J. Perraton, *Global Transformations* (Cambridge: Polity Press, 1999).

2. M. Weber, *The City* (New York: Free Press, 1958).

3. T. C. Hofheinz, *Joyce and the Invention of Irish History* (Cambridge: Cambridge University Press, 1995).

4. M. Arnold, *Culture and Anarchy* (Cambridge: Cambridge University Press, 1969).

5. J.-F. Lyotard, *The Postmodern Condition: A Report on Knowledge* (Manchester: University of Manchester Press, 1984).

6. R. Rorty, *Contingency, Irony and Solidarity* (Cambridge: Cambridge University Press, 1989).

7. J. Bohman and Lutz-Bachmann, eds., *Perpetual Peace: Essays on Kant's Cosmopolitan Ideal* (Cambridge, Mass.: The MIT Press, 1997).

8. See D. Quint, *Montaigne and the Quality of Mercy: Ethical and Political Themes in the Essais* (Princeton, N.J.: Princeton University Press, 1998).

9. B. S. Turner, *Orientalism, Postmodernism and Globalism* (London: Routledge, 1994).

10. E. W. Said, *Orientalism* (Harmondsworth: Penguin, 1978).

11. Said, *Orientalism*, 27-28.

12. B. S. Turner, *Religion and Social Theory* (London: Heinemann, 1983), 29.

13. M. Weber, *Ancient Judaism* (Glencoe, Ill.: Free Press, 1952).

14. See S. Russell, *Jewish Identity and Civilizing Processes* (London: Macmillan, 1996), 83.

15. See W. Ullmann, *Medieval Foundations of Renaissance Humanism* (London: Paul Elek, 1977).

16. F. Meinecke, *Cosmopolitanism and the Nation State* (Princeton: Princeton University Press, 1970).

17. A. Weber, *Kultur-Geschichte als Kultur-Soziologie* (Munich: R. Piper and Co., 1950).

18. See M. Inwood, ed., *A Hegel Dictionary* (Oxford: Blackwell, 1992), 53.

19. B. S. Turner, "Outline of a Theory of Citizenship," *Sociology* 24, no. 2 (1990): 189-217.

20. T. H. Marshall, *Class, Citizenship and Social Development* (Chicago: University of Chicago Press, 1964).

21. B. S. Turner, "Citizenship Studies: A General Theory," *Citizenship Studies* 1, no. 1 (February 1997): 5-18.

22. As pointed out by A. W. Saxonhouse, *Fear of Diversity: The Birth of Political Science in Ancient Greek Thought* (Chicago and London: University of Chicago Press, 1992).

23. See S. S. Wolin, *Politics and Vision: Continuity and Innovation in Western Political Thought* (London: George Allen & Unwin, 1961).

24. M. Weber, *The City* (New York: Free Press, 1958), 324.

25. B. Anderson, *Imagined Communities: Reflections on the Origin and Spread of Nationalism* (London: Verso, 1983).

26. Marshall, *Class, Citizenship and Social Development.*

27. B. S. Turner, *Citizenship and Capitalism: The Debate over Reformism* (London: Allen & Unwin, 1986).

28. N. Yuval-Davis, *Gender & Nation* (London: Sage, 1997).

29. See B. M. Barry, "Justice between Generations," in *Law Morality and Society: Essays in Honour of H. L. A. Hart*, ed. P. M. S. Hacker and J. Raz (Oxford: Clarendon, 1977), 268-84.

30. R. A. Titmuss, *Essays on the Welfare State* (London: Unwin University Books, 1963).

31. R. Sennett, *The Corrosion of Character* (New York: Norton, 1998).

32. B. S. Turner, "Postmodernisation of Political Identities: Solidarity and Loyalty in Contemporary Society," in *Sociology and Social Transformation* , ed. Bo Isenberg (Lund University, Research Report, 1998), 65-79.

33. E. Durkheim, *The Elementary Forms of the Religious Life* (London: Allen & Unwin, 1954).

34. M. McLuhan, *Understanding the Media: The Extension of Man* (Toronto: McGraw-Hill, 1964).

35. Rorty, *Contingency, Irony and Solidarity*.

36. M. Maffesoli, *The Time of the Tribes: The Decline of Individualism in Mass Society* (London: Sage, 1996).

37. Turner, "Postmodernisation of Political Identities: Solidarity and Loyalty in Contemporary Society."

38. Rorty, *Contingency, Irony and Solidarity*.

39. S. G. Mestrovic, *Postemotional Society* (London: Sage, 1997).

Chapter 13

Multiculturalism, Differentiated Citizenship, and the Problem of Self-Determination

Matteo Gianni

Although multiculturalism cannot be considered a new phenomenon, its political relevance in Western democracies seems to be increasing.[1] The problems created by immigration, the resurgence of nationalist movements, or the mobilization of disadvantaged social groups probably represent "the greatest challenge facing democracies today."[2] Multiculturalism raises a very large range of political questions, in particular regarding the ways liberal states address claims to recognition of cultural differences. In this chapter I analyze this question, namely, the theoretical relationships between multiculturalism and citizenship in the light of the question of national minorities' claims to political recognition. In particular, I will examine whether differentiated citizenship is a satisfactory answer to national cultures' claims to self-determination.

Several authors have already emphasized that differentiating the rights of liberal citizenship is the only way to realize social and political justice in multicultural societies. It is interesting to remark that differentiated citizenship has been defended by authors belonging to different normative paradigms, such as—just to mention the most popular ones—Kymlicka from a liberal perspective, Taylor from a communitarian perspective, and Young from a postmodern one. Thus, it is not really surprising that, even if the idea of differentiated citizenship is becoming increasingly influential, there are still many disagreements among its defenders regarding its purposes, its normative limits and the modalities of its political institutionalization.

Basically, the conception of differentiated citizenship that I support in this chapter relies on the principle of political equality. In my perspective, through differentiated citizenship, liberal states should ideally aim, first, to improve the political resources of the members of discriminated groups; second, to endow with a symbolic recognition of stigmatized or presumed abnormal cultural differences, providing them political respect and visibility; finally, to reinforce, through democratic integration, the legitimacy of representative democracy.[3] Such a model of differentiated citizenship is based on a political understanding of multiculturalism. This means that the standard for assessing the validity of a claim to recognition should not be the intrinsic quality of a particular culture, but the fact that individuals or groups do not have equal political power in the public realm due to their cultural difference.

Now, is this conception of differentiated citizenship useful as a possible way to settle multinational disputes? In order to address this question, I will discuss some of the points that have been made by recent liberal nationalists regarding the importance, for liberal justice and liberal democracy, of the recognition of national cultures. My argument follows three steps: first, I provide an analytical discussion of multiculturalism. From a sociological standpoint, I present two main conceptualizations of multiculturalism, which I call respectively broad and narrow conceptions. I show that these views of multiculturalism are based on different anthropological and normative interpretations of culture. Generally speaking, liberals and communitarians share an institutional view of culture, whereas postmodern scholars refer to a relational conception of it.

Second, I show that these two conceptions of multiculturalism entail very different normative implications regarding the way of settling multicultural conflicts. More specifically, the normative solutions to nationalist conflicts principally depend on the moral, political, and social relevance that it is conferred on national culture. I will basically focus on two main normative arguments: first, the anthropological argument, based on the idea that national culture is necessary to people to live a just life or to follow their own conception of the good and thus that it should be secured by political recognition. Second, the instrumental argument, based on the idea that a common culture is a fundamental precondition for the existence of a stable and democratic polity. I will show that these arguments rely on sweeping anthropological and empirical arguments and that they cannot ground specific forms of political recognition based on the "superiority" of national culture. Therefore, in the last part of the chapter, I suggest that differentiated citizenship might be a solution to settle multinational conflicts, but only under the condition that it is not the specificity of national culture that should be recognized, but the existence of a gap between formal and actual rights of citizenship for people belonging to a national minority.

"Egalitarian" and "Differentialist" Claims to Recognition

Gutmann defines multiculturalism as "the state of a society or the world containing many cultures that interact in some significant ways with each other."[4] This is a very broad definition, which must be specified to be operational. The question is to know what is the kind of "significative" interactions that characterize multicultural societies. In my view, the more important sociological and political characteristics of multiculturalism is the existence of conflicts of recognition between cultural groups and political institutions. As many scholars have shown, the national state has imposed its power through a strong normalizing process of reduction of internal cultural differences.[5] Indeed, multiculturalism can hardly be considered a new phenomenon. What is relatively new is not multiculturalism in itself, but its salience and visibility as a political problem. In the last century, the capacity of social actors to bring their identities and interests into the public sphere has considerably increased.[6]

As Phillips points out, the relevance of multiculturalism "cannot be understood just in terms of an absolute or growing difference. . . . It reflects a shift in political culture and claims, where people who may be significantly less different than in some point in the past come to assert a stronger sense of themselves and their identities."[7] The rise of the politics of identity illustrates such a situation very well. Groups whose members decades ago fought for their equal political and social integration now claim recognition of their cultural particularity.

According to Kymlicka and Norman,[8] there are three types of social and cultural actors claiming recognition of their difference: (a) national minorities, claiming for self-determination rights; (b) immigrant and religious groups, claiming for polyethnic rights; (c) disadvantaged groups, claiming for representation rights. Besides the differences between the kinds of rights that are advocated, the existence of conflicts of recognition shows that citizenship is and has been called into question by social actors as the medium to realize political equality. In other words, the political mobilization of all these very different cultural groups expresses a common feature, namely, the idea that liberal citizenship rights are no more considered a sufficient condition to realize an effective political integration. In fact, within democratic multicultural societies, the likelihood that social actors' identities conflict with the values of citizenship is very high. For different reasons, these actors view their cultural loyalties as very thick, that is, as a set of values they cannot give up without losing their authenticity.[9]

This leads to a process of "negotiation" of citizenship, which no longer represents the main referent of political identity, but just one identity among others. This trend can weaken the nature of political integration on which liberal democracy should be built.[10] The rhetoric of authenticity inherent in the "differentialist" claim to recognition "proposes not only that I have a way of being that is all my own, but that in developing it I must fight against the family, organized religions, society, the school, the state—all the forces of convention."[11] Considered in this perspective, such "differentialist" claims to recognition virtually lead to the destruction of citizenship as a way to construct political equality. Nationalist claims (in its more dramatic expressions) can lead to the formation of strong identities, which threaten the bonds of citizenship and political integration in a given society.

Nevertheless, it would be wrong to reduce claims to recognition to the only goal of the expression of cultural difference. In other words, conflicts of recognition do not necessarily arise because of the social actors' willingness to promote and affirm their cultural identity (or authenticity). This differentialist view of recognition is only one side of the coin. Claims to recognition also stem from the actors' perception that their identity (or cultural specificity) is not recognized by the state and that this lack of recognition does not allow them to be treated fairly in the public space. I call "egalitarian" claim to recognition the claim that the state should politically recognize a cultural group in order to realize better forms of equality. Therefore, if the differentialist view of recognition aims to strengthen the differences between the cultural groups, the egalitarian view aims to promote a better form of political and social equality between groups.

Translated into political terms, Taylor's concept of "deep diversity" expresses the idea that what is at stake in multicultural societies is not only the problem of accommodating the diversity of cultural groups but also the diversity of political and social positions that the members of these groups occupy in the democratic system.[12] Therefore, it is not cultural difference in itself that creates conflict, but the political effects of being culturally different in a given political community. Despite their formal rights of citizenship, members of cultural groups suffering from ascriptive humiliation[13] or political invisibility (Galeotti),[14] are not treated as equal in liberal polities.[15] This calls for an empirical criticism of the idea that liberal citizenship is a sufficient condition to guarantee political integration.

Considered in the light of liberal citizenship, both conceptions of recognition entail a differential treatment of cultural groups. To quote Taylor, they both imply that "we give acknowledgement and status to something that is not universally shared."[16] In fact, differentiated citizenship—as it is based on collective or group rights—attributes to the members of cultural groups rights that are not universally distributed among citizens. Hence, it counters the basic liberal principle that all should be treated equally, which in liberal terms often means "in the same way."[17] In this sense, the differentialist and egalitarian claims to recognition call into question the (presumed) universal foundations of liberal citizenship. In other words, both dynamics cast doubts on the liberal ideal of citizenship as the neutral space in which a culturally differentiated society can be unified through the attribution of a common legal status. Having said this, it is also important to notice that the normative and political aims underlying the two kinds of recognition are very different.

On the one hand, the egalitarian conception is based on the assumption that, to reach equality, cultural groups must be politically recognized. In other words, the members of such groups should benefit from a differential treatment in order to increase their political resources and hence their political integration. This claim is based on the idea that differential treatment is necessary to fulfill the egalitarian aims of liberal citizenship. Therefore, the main goal of the groups claiming such recognition is their integration in the polity and society.[18]

On the other hand, the differentialist conception is based on the assumption that the recognition of cultural differences is necessary to provide to cultural communities the opportunity to live according to their conception of the good. Because community's values are constitutive of the member's conceptions of the good, then the members of the cultural community need the political power to preserve them. The denial of such power is understood as a form of cultural imperialism or cultural domination, phenomena that lead to the political mobilization of cultural groups. Here the purpose is not to realize better forms of equality, but to have the possibility to fully express its difference. In this case, it is not equality between groups that is at stake, but the liberty for the members of the group to live according to its cultural values.

Egalitarian and differentialist claims to recognition should be seen as two ideal-typical categories. The empirical reality is much more complex and contradictory than what these two types might suggest. For example, the identity of the group can be positive, in the sense that the group affirms the value of its own subculture, or negative, as the by-product of an external categorization and stigma inflicted on the members of one group.[19] Positive and negative identities are strongly connected to each other. The politics of identity can be seen as the result of the mobilization of social movements that aim to transform a negative identity into a positive one. For example, the black nationalist movement in the United States constitutes a powerful process of transformation of a stigmatized identity into a positive affirmation of a specific cultural heritage. The projection of an external identity defines the conditions of existence experienced by the members of these cultural minorities. As Honneth puts it, "we are dealing here with a practical process in which individual experiences of disrespect are read as typical for an entire group, and in such a way that they can motivate collective demands for expanded relations of recognition."[20] The search for better forms of equality or the expression of difference are two possible strategies to overcome this lack of social and political resources.

The distinction between the egalitarian and differentialist dimensions provides an analytical tool in order to empirically apprehend cultural groups' claims to recognition. From a normative level, nevertheless, the main question is:

do differentialist and egalitarian claims to recognition have the same normative weight according to the liberal theory of citizenship? The two kinds of claims cannot be treated in the same way because they raise very different normative implications. More specifically, from a liberal perspective, there is an enormous difference between these two statements: "groups should be politically recognized to be able to express their difference" and "groups should be politically recognized to reach better forms of political equality." These two claims imply very different views of political recognition. In order to assess the specificity of these two kinds of claims, it is crucial to define why a cultural group should be recognized. To do this, it is necessary to point out the reasons that are supposed to give to cultural membership the moral power that legitimize its recognition. As we will see below, the way we understand and construct culture determine substantially the normative weight of culture and the political modalities of recognition.

Conceptions of Multiculturalism and National Identity

If we go through the existing literature, it is possible to distinguish between two main analytical conceptions of the sociological meaning of multiculturalism. I will name them broad and narrow conceptions. Even if it cannot be considered as logically exhaustive, I believe that this distinction can help elucidate part of the complex relationships between multiculturalism, citizenship, and the politics of recognition. The most important opposition between the two conceptions regards the different understandings of culture. The narrow conception refers to an anthropologically thick view of culture. This idea is well captured by what Kymlicka calls a "societal culture," namely a "culture which provides its members with meaningful ways of life across the full range of human activities, including social, educational, religious, recreational, and economic life, encompassing both public and private spheres. These cultures tend to be territorially concentrated, and based on a shared language."[21] Thus, for the adherents to the narrow conception of multiculturalism, multicultural states are marked by the presence of strong cultural affiliations and identities. National minorities are the cultural groups of reference of such approach.[22] Therefore, this view excludes from the multicultural dynamics several groups that do not constitute a societal culture, such as gays, disabled, women, and, to a degree, immigrant or ethnic groups.

In contrast, the broad conception of multiculturalism takes into account groups that do not form a societal culture but whose members are supposed to share some characteristics that define them as different from the members of majority culture(s) with respect to values, lifestyles, and interests. These symbolic elements are embodied in social and political institutions, and this is precisely the reason why cultural difference affects the political resources of these individuals. The notion of culture is here defined in a sociological perspective, that is, in a relational and pragmatic way. [23] What is at stake is not—such as in the narrow conception—to start from a formal definition of culture and then to find the groups that fit with it, but to focus more directly on what is socially and politically done by individuals having different cultural loyalties and particularities. [24]

Considered in this perspective, multiculturalism not only concerns the relations between members of diverse societal cultures but also the relations between the members of subcultures in a given societal culture. Therefore, if the narrow conception focuses mainly on national minorities, the broad one considers also differences, such as sex, sexual orientation, or disability and even age, class, family, street gangs, crime, and popular cultures as part of the multicultural dynamics. [25] The members of these groups share an identity that is considered "significant" with regard to the construction of their autonomy, preferences, choices, and conceptions of the good.

The distinction between broad and narrow understandings of multiculturalism entails important methodological and normative consequences. To put it straightly, scholars who adopt a narrow conception of multiculturalism start from the assumption that national culture is morally relevant and hence it should occupy an important place in a liberal conception of democracy. [26] In contrast, scholars working with a broad understanding of multiculturalism basically consider national identity as one identity among others. This does not mean that they do not consider it as important, but they do not reduce the analysis of multiculturalism to the question of multinational states and multinational conflicts. Moreover, they tend to approach the question of nationalist claims to recognition within a broader normative framework that should be able to address also the claims to recognition articulated by other cultural minorities. In other words, to adopt a narrow conception of culture often entails a differentiation of the normative solutions supported to settle multicultural disputes, whereas adopting a broad conception often leads to the search for solutions that can address the conditions experienced by very different cultural groups. The reflection on the "particularity" or "superiority" of national cultures is therefore strongly dependent on the conception of multiculturalism one adopts.

The Normative Relevance of National Identity

According to the dominant theoretical and empirical analysis—inspired by a narrow conception of multiculturalism—national identities are considered as thicker than other forms of collective identities. In other words, they are supposed to have a greater symbolic and political weight than other kinds of identity. This is probably one of the results of the symbolic and ideological strength of the national-state model. Now, in order to decide about the legitimacy of policies of cultural preservation or protection of national communities, the validity of the argument of the intrinsic value of national identities must be assessed. [27] To put it differently, the justification of the superiority of national communities over other kinds of minorities is necessary to normatively ground self-determination as a specific form of political recognition. The "superiority thesis" relies basically on three main arguments:

> 1. The empirical argument (it is true that people consider their national identity as more important than other forms of identity).
> 2. The philosophical-anthropological argument (national identity is the precondition for social actors to live a good life or to make autonomous choices; outside the frame provided by a national culture, individuals are not able to autonomously determine their conception of the good).
> 3. The instrumental argument (in liberal polities, some forms of pre-political attachments are necessary to sustain political stability, solidarity, and civic participation). [28]

Several political theorists have recently endorsed these three arguments. For example, national culture is viewed as the precondition for autonomy, [29] for a healthy self-identity and good life, [30] and for the implementation of a liberal and republican polity. [31] Despite their differences, all these authors maintain that national culture establishes the symbolic structure necessary for the realization of liberal ideals. Thus, in some ways, national cultures ought to be protected by liberal states. Now, in order to justify the political recognition of national communities, we need to ascertain the validity of the three kinds of arguments mentioned above. This task is crucial because its result entails important methodological implications. In fact, if we fail to justify the normative and anthropological superiority of national cultures over other kinds of social identities, the argument according to which we need to determine specific forms of political recognition that suit particular cultural groups crumbles. [32]

In other words, if it is not possible to demonstrate that there are differences in the anthropological and political importance between national cultures, ethnic cultures, and social disadvantaged groups' cultures, the idea that the claims of these groups should be considered through different normative lenses would be hard to sustain. Obviously, this does not mean that all these groups should be provided with the same rights or forms of recognition: given the differences existing between the conditions experienced by all these groups, such a conclusion would be meaningless. What is at stake is the determination of the principle grounding the politics of recognition. If we fail to demonstrate that national cultures have a moral superiority given by their specificity, then it becomes compelling to determine another grounding principle for the politics of recognition—a principle that might address the claims of other kinds of cultural groups. Before discussing such a principle, let us look more precisely to the question of the specificity of national cultures. To assess their normative relevance, I am going to focus mainly on the second and third arguments.

The Anthropological Functions of National Identity

With regards to the anthropological perspective, I consider two kinds of justifications, namely, the liberal autonomy thesis and the communitarian social thesis. Several authors have emphasized that the realization of liberal autonomy presupposes a wide range of cultural options: "cultures are valuable, not in and of themselves, but because it is only through having access to a societal culture that people have access to a range of meaningful options."[33] Options are provided by culture, which gives them a meaning.

Kymlicka, for example, argues that a secure cultural context of choice is necessary for the autonomy of individuals. In his view, a secure cultural context of choice is provided by a societal culture. Kymlicka is not clear about the meaning of the expression "to have a secure cultural context of choice." For him "[A] cultural community continues to exist even when its members are free to modify the character of the culture, should they find its traditional ways of life no longer worth while."[34] The problem inherent in this statement is the following: if a cultural community is just a structure, why should its preservation serve as a necessary condition for the realization of autonomy? Does an individual who is not embedded in a cultural structure exist? Where there is human life, there is a cultural structure.

Therefore, to be consistent with his anthropological assumptions, Kymlicka should state that liberal states should protect a particular cultural structure, characterized by a particular symbolic content, and not any kind of cultural structure.[35] Moreover, Kymlicka should explain how membership in societal cultures that do not value autonomy would allow individuals to become autonomous. The danger faced by Kymlicka is to fall into a circular argument, namely, that only societal cultures that value autonomy are suited to the realization of their members' autonomy. But then, it is not only a general cultural structure that should be protected but a specific cultural structure, namely, the one in which autonomy is a central value.

In addition, Kymlicka does not provide adequate arguments to support the thesis that only societal cultures are able to provide the social and anthropological conditions for autonomy.[36] Other forms of identity, built around sexual or gender differences, also contribute in creating the options necessary to individuals to be autonomous. In addiction to national communities, other cultural groups provide a context in which members can obtain mutual recognition, gaining self-respect and mutual respect. Self-respect and mutual respect are very important preconditions for autonomy. To be respected—that is, to be treated as an autonomous moral being—implies the opportunity to choose freely between different options regarding one's own life. In contrast, a lack of self-respect or of mutual respect leads to a situation in which the autonomous action of individuals is limited by the attitudes and perceptions of others.[37] It is not clear then why national communities should be the only cultural groups providing mutual respect to its members. In this sense, Kymlicka (and liberal nationalists in general), fails to show that nations are "special" in some ways.[38] His anthropological argument cannot support the idea that political recognition of national cultures has priority over the recognition of other cultural groups.

From a communitarian perspective, Taylor argues that nations have a moral character that should be preserved by the liberal state. The argument is the following: the "embeddedness" of individuals in national cultures allows them to define and pursue their conception of the good. Thus, the liberal states should protect the values that are constitutive of the identity of the community's members. As Taylor puts it, "living within such strongly qualified horizons is constitutive of human agency, [while] stepping outside these limits would be tantamount to stepping outside what we would recognize as integral, that is, undamaged human personhood."[39]

In other words, taking Taylor literally, to step outside a national culture means to damage its own human personhood. Shared meanings and values provide the standards to determine individual options. But these options are not the result of the self-reflexivity of social actors; they are the cultural and cognitive basis structuring individual preferences and self-reflexivity. Thus, in this perspective, ends are given but people can find different ways to reach them. In this sense, the protection and reproduction of national culture is the prerequisite for implementing a politics of the common good. Political institutions ought not to be neutral regarding cultural values, but they should defend them against the threat of excessive internal cultural differences. Self-determination is probably the most powerful way to reach such a goal, but this implies a threat for other minorities to be fully integrated into the new polity.[40]

The communitarian anthropological thesis is highly problematic. For example, it is not clear why the moral development in a homogeneous national community would be more effective than the moral development in a heterogeneous culture.[41] Moreover, the anthropological thesis according to which ceasing to belong to his own original national community entails disastrous effects on one's identity is "surely false."[42] From an empirical perspective, Taylor does not take into account the internal differences of national communities and thus he does not fully consider the potentiality of "hybridity" for autonomy and self-reflexivity about conceptions of the good. Taylor's approach ultimately relies on a hierarchy among significant cultural attachments. But, as for Kymlicka, he does not provide convincing arguments to support the thesis that national culture is special enough to deserve a moral right to recognition. Even if we accept the idea that to belong to one cultural group is an important feature for individuals to live a good life, this does not mean that only national identity can accomplish this anthropological function.

The Instrumental Functions of National Identity

The instrumental thesis is based on political rather than anthropological considerations. The general argument rests on the idea that the preservation of national culture is instrumental to democratic governance, social solidarity, and citizenship. According to Miller, for example, "a common sense of nationality is an essential background" to republican politics.[43] Thus, "nationality must be something more than de facto citizenship. It must amount to a common identity that grounds citizenship."[44] Republican citizenship is demanding because it requires citizens to act responsibly: "they have not merely to get involved in public decision-making, but they have to try to promote the common good."[45]

Perfectionist liberals, as for example Galston or Macedo, claim that liberal states ought not to be neutral regarding the conception of the good. [46] Because it is a form of community, the state should foster the civic virtues necessary for the preservation of liberal values and liberal community. This implies that individuals have an emotional identification with the state and with its members. [47] Thus, according to this argument, the state must promote some forms of liberal nationalism to protect liberal community and to provide individuals with the social and political means for their flourishing as liberal citizens.

Hence, some forms of nationalist policies are seen as worthy for the stability of liberal political systems. The idea is that participation, solidarity, and trust in political institutions arise from a community within which co-nationals share a common history and common values. Although plausible, this point is difficult to assess from an empirical perspective. For example, according to some empirical research on the European Union, it is not possible to demonstrate that there has been a significant decline in the public's trust toward institutions during the 1980s. [48] Given the supranational status of the European Union, this empirical result supports the idea that liberal democracy can be secured in the absence of a shared national identity.[49]

But, besides empirical considerations, the question remains: is national culture the only kind of symbolic framework allowing members to develop positive attitudes and trust toward democratic institutions? If, with Newton, we consider that "trust involves the belief that others will, so far as they can, look after our interests, and not take advantage of us,"[50] it is possible to maintain that it is easier to trust (and to be trusted by) members of associations such a gays, women, ethnic minority groups, etc. than co-nationals. In the absence of actual social interactions, the representation of a co-national remains at an abstract level. But the representation of a fellow member of a, say, gay community is more real, because of the regular interactions in the community (or association). It is social proximity that makes trust, not the formal belonging to a national community. Therefore, according to this argument, to foster trust and democratic participation, the liberal states should not strengthen national identity, but find ways to increase associative democracy[51] and to make civil society stronger.[52]

This argument does not entail a denial of all the plausibility of the instrumental thesis. In fact, nationality is an identity that is more broadly shared than other kinds of more specific identities. Moreover, the strong normative link between nationality and citizenship (that underlies almost all the naturalization's policies) makes national identity a very important referent. Nonetheless, it seems to me that this thesis is not strong enough to be the normative justification for liberal nationalist policies. Putting it differently, there is not enough evidence to support the idea that only national communities deserve political recognition because of their moral, anthropological, and instrumental superiority over other kinds of identities. This means that it is not possible to support the idea that political recognition of national cultures has priority over the recognition of other cultural groups. In my view, this aspect shows the epistemological and normative limits of the narrow conception of multiculturalism and of its model of recognition: it is not able to address much of the demands claimed by the members of groups that face cultural discrimination in liberal polities.

In other words, solutions to conflicts of recognition taken on the basis of a narrow conception of culture and aiming to preserve a shared national culture will inevitably lead to other forms of conflicts of recognition with those internal minorities of the community that have been recognized. For these reasons, I believe that to ground differentiated citizenship on anthropological or instrumental arguments about national culture does not lead to adequate policies to settle multicultural conflicts. This argument does not entail that the broad conception of multiculturalism does not give rise to important problems.

As I explained before, this conception of multiculturalism is concerned with the realization of better forms of equality in liberal democratic polities. Due to its relational and pragmatic conception of culture, it considers a larger range of cultural groups as being part of the multicultural reality. The problems with this framework are opposite to the ones raised by the narrow conception. Whereas the latter assumes a too much restrictive understanding of culture, the former virtually expands culture to all forms of collective meaning and agency. [53] Then, scholars working with the broad conception are confronted with the task of defining precise criteria necessary to assess which cultural groups should be politically recognized and which should not.

Self-Determination and Differentiated Citizenship

The fact that national communities are not superior to other kinds of identity does not entail that they cannot be politically recognized. It just means that we should ground such recognition on a different principle from the moral superiority of national cultures. I suggest this principle to be political equality. Therefore, I argue that it is mainly egalitarian claims to recognition that should be taken into account by liberal states. In other words, differentialist positions ought to be considered only if the recognition of difference is meant to promote better forms of political equality. The balance between the search for equality and the right to the expression of difference is inherent in any form of differentiated citizenship. Nevertheless, some normative and political limits shall be established in order to keep the dynamics of expression of difference compatible with citizenship and democracy. I believe that, in order to move a step further in the discussion of differentiated citizenship, it is also important to focus on the aspect represented by citizenship and not only on difference. In other words, thinking about differentiated citizenship, we should not only conceive ways to reinforce the expression of difference but also devise procedures to strengthen citizenship.

As I explained above, both egalitarian and differentialist claims to recognition imply a differential treatment of cultural groups, namely, that some sorts of collective rights should be attributed to the group in order to rectify a situation of injustice. To be considered as liberal, differentiated citizenship should entail an enrichment of rights for the members of some disadvantaged groups, but never a diminution of individual rights because of membership in a cultural group. In the Rawlsian terminology, there should be a lexical priority of the individual universal rights of citizenship over the rights attributed to a collective subject, namely, the cultural group. In this sense, differentiated citizenship should not promote the possibility of increasing the "internal restrictions" regarding the liberty of the members of a cultural group,[54] because this would mean that what is at stake is not the purpose of their better integration, but the protection of given forms of culture. Differentiated citizenship does not concern cultures, but rather the empowerment of the members of disadvantaged cultural groups.[55]

There is a huge difference between providing the members of a cultural group with the political instruments that might enable them to preserve their culture and protecting a culture by administrative decisions.[56] Considered as a mean to promote better forms of political equality, differentiated citizenship is based on the assumption that one of the risks that members of liberal societies must assume is the fact that some cultural identities might disappear or become so highly "hybrid" that they might substantially change their character.

This view of differentiated citizenship contrasts with the one supported by Taylor, Raz and—in part—Kymlicka. The conceptions of differentiated citizenship that—explicitly or implicitly—arise from their narrow approach to multiculturalism focus too much on the preservation of national culture as a precondition for individual autonomy or the common good. In other words, the politics of recognition they support relies too much on sweeping anthropological assumptions regarding the functions of national culture. With regards to the instrumental thesis, it is plausible to think that a polity whose members can mutually recognize each other as fellows is more stable and peaceful than a polity marked by deep conflicts of recognition.

Nevertheless, as Mason points out, there is a difference between "belonging to a polity" and "belonging together."[57] The idea of belonging together involves a shared culture and a shared history. What is at stake, here, is the mechanism of horizontal recognition, that is, the whole processes fostering mutual social recognition. The notion of belonging to a polity refers to vertical recognition, that is, mutual recognition between political institutions and citizens. In other words, belonging together refers to a pre-political identity, while belonging to a polity defines a kind of political identity. The claim to self-determination is often based on the attempt to create a conjunction between these two sorts of belonging: it is because we belong together that we must create a new polity that will enable us to protect and preserve our common cultural and political belonging.

If we consider that one of the main tasks of liberal states is to protect the citizenship rights of individuals and not to interfere in the private liberties of individuals, then the priority of the state should be to strengthen the "belonging to a polity" rather than the "belonging together." This does not mean that the dimension of belonging together is not normatively important; it means that belonging to a polity is the precondition for individuals to obtain the resources that would allow them to find out ways to perpetuate their belonging together. The fact is that, in multicultural polities, the members of some cultural groups lack the social and political resources to fully realize their belonging to the polity. In other words, the members of some cultural groups, despite their formal rights of citizenship, are not fully integrated into the political system. This means that, for them, actual political equality has not been successfully realized. This power asymmetry stems in part from economic and social factors, but it also depends on the cultural bias of liberal states.

Communitarians, postmoderns, and (some) liberals have rightly stressed the empirical impossibility for the liberal state to be neutral regarding cultural values. Even if, according to liberal philosophy, it ought not to be, the liberal state is a fundamental actor in the symbolic and cultural sphere. Through public policies, it can actively promote or modify cultural values and shared meanings. Therefore, a polity is not culturally neutral. To belong to a polity means to be confronted with a given set of cultural values embedded in political institutions.[58] However, the analytical distinction between "belonging to a polity" and "belonging together" is not so clear: belonging to a polity entails a certain symbolic construction of a belonging together. Such cultural overdetermination of belonging to a polity leads to two problems for the members of cultural minorities: first, they can be confronted with cultural discrimination or marginalization due to the gap between their values and the polity's values; second, because of their discrimination, they do not have the political resources enabling them to modify this situation.

As we already mentioned, self-determination (through secession, namely, the creation of an autonomous state) or political autonomy (for example, through a federalist state) are the forms of recognition claimed by national communities to preserve and secure their cultural identity. Such recognition would lead to the modification of the borders of citizenship and to the implementation of new public policies aimed at the protection of the community's cultural values. In this sense, following the conceptual categories discussed above, as a product of secession, self-determination consists in the realization of a differentialist claim to recognition. In the case of secession, the result is not differentiated citizenship, but the creation of new citizenship rights, whereas in the case of federalism of partial autonomy, the result is a form of differentiated citizenship.

This means that secession does not necessarily lead to better political equality. All depends on the way authorities will deal with the subcultures that are part of the new political entity. Federalism might be the easiest institutional way to settle multinational disputes, but the success of this solution depends on the real power that the different political entities have to secure their national culture. In other words, it is not possible, without the reference to a specific political and cultural context, to determine an institutional solution to national claims to self-determination that is by definition successful.[59]

For example, theoretically speaking, it is also possible to conceive self-determination as the ultima ratio through which a cultural community can develop better forms of equality. Political autonomy would give cultural minorities the opportunity to establish forms of equality that could not be implemented in a situation characterized by the subordination of the cultural majority to the political will. Therefore, self-determination might be in this case a possible solution, but the standard of political equality will put some limits to the policies of cultural reproduction implemented by the new national authorities. This means that real political equality is the criteria on the basis of which oppressive and assimilationist policies that re-create the phenomena of discrimination, which claims to self-determination wanted to avoid, might be assessed and criticized.

Solutions to conflict of recognition taken on the basis of a narrow conception of culture and aiming at the preservation of a shared national culture will inevitably lead to other form of conflicts of recognition with the internal minorities of the community that has become independent. To ground differentiated citizenship on anthropological or instrumental arguments concerning the "superiority" of national culture will not allow determination of the adequate policies to settle conflicts between other kinds of cultural minorities. There is an unavoidable tension in the very idea of liberal nationalism. An excessive emphasis on the protection of national cultures risks overwhelming important liberal principles. In certain cases, the framework of differentiated citizenship can provide an answer to nationalist claims to recognition. But this holds only if it is the particular cultural situation of citizens that is politically recognized, and not the anthropological depth of cultures. Then, I believe that differentiated citizenship should be based on a broad understanding of the dynamics of creation of identity and creation of difference that characterize any polity.[60]

The evaluation of the claims to recognition should be inspired by political considerations, and not by cultural or instrumental arguments. I believe that the only way to fruitfully approach multicultural conflicts is to adopt a political perspective. This means to transfer the discussion from the anthropological (and eternally controversial) questions: "What is a culture?" or "Which culture does deserve to be recognized?" to the more political ones: "What are the effects of cultural membership on citizenship rights?" and "Could a political recognition of the group improve the integration of their members into citizenship, providing the political resources that allow them to participate actively and successfully in the determination of common values?"[61] In this perspective, the fulfillment of citizenship rights, and not the intrinsic value of a given culture, should be taken as the standard to assess claims to recognition. Such an approach does allow the determination of the result of the recognition process and can contribute to defining a criteria on the basis of which liberal states can assess the validity of demands raised by the members of minority groups.

It would be misleading to conceive differentiated citizenship as a final solution to conflicts of recognition. Post-structuralist authors have emphasized the impossibility of finding a final solution to conflicts of identity simply with political or legal decisions.[62] Even if I am not convinced about the validity of their normative conclusions,[63] I think that these scholars have made good arguments about conceiving politics as a never-ending conflicting process rather than as a way to constantly pacify, through specific procedures, the "mess" of society. This does not mean that politicians and theorists should not try to think about decisions and procedures that might regulate the worst effects of political and social disruption. What is at stake here is the difference between differentiated citizenship as an institutional solution and differentiated citizenship as a social and political process.

In my view, differentiated citizenship should not be considered only as a set of extra-rights, but also—and above all—as a process that, even if sometimes contradictory or unstable, aims to achieve a progressive political and social integration of cultural groups into the polity. We should not conceive solutions to conflicts of recognition as institutional zero-sum games in which what is obtained by some actors (as, for example, rights) is necessarily lost by others. Taken as a process, through the recognition of political disadvantages due to cultural reasons, differentiated citizenship is a way to promote a dynamic that might allow the members of cultural groups not only to benefit from new entitlements but also to actively participate in the determination of new political and legal values that might challenge the causes of their marginalization.[64] National claims to self-determination should be assessed within this general framework. Considered in this way, they can be compatible with a version of liberalism that is based on the idea that the state is legitimate if it gives to individuals the best possible opportunities to be politically equal in the political community.

Notes

1. I wish to thank Marco Giugni for his help and linguistic improvements.
2. Will Kymlicka, *Multicultural Citizenship* (Oxford: Oxford University, 1995), 1.
3. For a more in-depth discussion of differentiated citizenship, see Matteo Gianni, *Multiculturalisme et intégration politique: La citoyenneté entre reconnaissance de la différence et reconnaissance de l'égalité* (Paris: L'Harmattan, 2000).
4. Amy Gutmann, "The Challenge of Multiculturalism in Political Ethics," *Philosophy and Public Affairs* 22, no. 3 (1993): 171.
5. Ernest Gellner, *Nations et Nationalisme* (Paris: Payot, 1989).
6. See Craig Calhoun, *Critical Social Theory* (Cambridge, Mass.: Blackwell, 1995); Todd Gitlin, *The Twilight of Common Dreams* (New York: Metropolitan Books, 1995); Alberto Melucci, *Challenging Codes* (Cambridge: Cambridge University Press, 1996).
7. Anne Phillips, *The Politics of Presence* (Oxford: Oxford University Press, 1995), 12.
8. Will Kymlicka and Wayne Norman, "Return of the Citizen: A Survey of Recent Work on Citizenship Theory," *Ethics* 104, no. 2 (1994): 352-81.
9. See Charles Taylor, *The Ethics of Authenticity* (Cambridge, Mass.: Harvard University Press, 1991).
10. See Arthur Schlesinger, *The Disuniting of America* (New York: Norton, 1992); and *Theorizing Citizenship,* ed. Ronald Beiner (Albany: State University of New York, 1995).
11. Kwame Anthony Appiah, "Identity, Authenticity, Survival: Multicultural Societies and Social Reproduction," in *Multiculturalism: Examining the Politics of Recognition,* ed. Amy Gutmann (Princeton: Princeton University Press, 1994), 154.
12. Taylor, quoted by Kymlicka, *Multicultural Citizenship*, 189.
13. Steven Lukes, "Humiliation and the Politics of Identity," *Social Research* 64, no. 1 (1996): 36-51.
14. Anna-Elisabetta Galeotti, *La tolleranza. Una proposta pluralista* (Napoli: Liguori Editore, 1994).
15. In his "The Politics of Recognition", Charles Taylor argues that "equal recognition is not just the appropriate mode for a healthy democratic society. Its refusal can inflict damage on those who are denied it. . . . The projection of an inferior or demeaning image on another can actually distort and oppress, to the extent that the image is internalized." See Taylor et al., *Multiculturalism: Examining the Politics of Recognition* , ed. Amy Gutmann (Princeton: Princeton University Press, 1994), 36.
16. Taylor, "The Politics of Recognition," 39.
17. Iris Marion Young, *Justice and the Politics of Difference* (Princeton: Princeton University Press, 1990).

18. For Kymlicka (*Multicultural Citizenship*, 176ff), claims to recognition often express a demand for inclusion, and not for differentiation. In the same perspective, for Minow "the willingness of a minority group to use the language of rights . . . constitutes in a profound sense a willingness to join the dominant community." Martha Minow, "Rights and Cultural Difference," in *Identities, Politics and Rights*, ed. A. Sarat and T. Kearns (Ann Arbor: University of Michigan Press, 1997), 355.

19. See Erving Goffman, *Stigma* (New York: Simon and Schuster, 1964); and Louk Hagendoorn, "Ethnic Categorization and Outgroup Exclusion: Cultural Values and Social Stereotypes in the Construction of Ethnic Hierarchies," *Ethnic and Racial Studies* 16, no. 1 (1993): 26-51.

20. Axel Honneth, *The Struggle for Recognition* (Cambridge: Polity Press, 1995), 162.

21. Kymlicka, *Multicultural Citizenship*, 76.

22. See Charles Taylor et al., *Multiculturalism: Examining the Politics of Recognition*; Joseph Raz, *Ethics in the Public Domain* (Oxford: Clarendon Press, 1994); Michael Walzer, "Multiculturalism and Individualism," *Dissent* (Spring 1994): 185-91; Avishai Margalit and Joseph Raz, "National Self-Determination," in *The Rights of Minority Cultures*, ed. Will Kymlicka (Oxford: Oxford University Press, 1995), 79-92.

23. For Young, for example, "a group exists and is defined as a specific group only in social and interactive relation to others. Group identity is not a set of objective facts, but the product of experienced meanings." For her, culture "refers to all aspects of social life from the point of view of their linguistic, symbolic, affective, and embodied norms and practices. Culture includes the background and medium of action, the unconscious habits, desires, meanings, gestures and so on that people grow into and bring to their interactions" (Iris Marion Young, "Together in Difference: Transforming the Logic of Group Political Conflict," in *The Rights of Minority Cultures*, ed. Will Kymlicka, 161 and 86, respectively).

24. Tully employs a similar perspective on culture when he writes that "the diverse ways in which citizens think about, speak, act and relate to others in participating in a constitutional association (both the abilities they exercise and the practices in which they exercise them), whether they are making, following or going against the rules and conventions in any instance, are always to some extent the expression of their different cultures," in James Tully, *Strange Multiplicity. Constitutionalism in an Age of Diversity* (Cambridge: Cambridge University Press, 1995), 5.

25. Young (*Justice and the Politics of Difference*, 40) proposes a long list of oppressed groups in the U. S. such as "women, Blacks, Chicanos, Puerto Ricans and other Spanish-speaking Americans, American Indians, Jews, lesbians, gay men, Arabs, Asian, old people, working-class people, and the physically and mentally disabled." See also Thomas Dumm ("Strangers and Liberals," *Political Theory* 22, no. 1 (1994): 172), who considers "African American Nationalism, the problem of street gangs and urban disintegration, gender inequality, gender identity, and queer politics, Latino identity, and the role of popular culture in the transformation and dissemination of culture" as part of the problematic of multiculturalism. See also Bennet M. Berger, *An Essay on Culture* (Berkeley: University of California Press, 1995), 26-28.

26. This interpretation seems to be corroborated in the recent works of several authors, as for example the above cited works by Taylor, Raz, and Kymlicka, as well as Yael Tamir, *Liberal Nationalism* (Princeton: Princeton University Press, 1993); David Miller, *On Nationality* (Oxford: Clarendon Press, 1995).

27. As Margalit and Raz ("National Self-Determination", 79) correctly write, "the justification of the law rests ultimately on moral considerations, and therefore those considerations should also help shape the contours of legal principles."

28. I owe the concept of "instrumental argument" to Margaret Moore, "Liberal-nationalism, Nation-Building and National Self-Determination" (paper presented at the

APSA meeting, Boston, September 1998).

29. Kymlicka, *Multicultural Citizenship*.

30. Charles Taylor, *Sources of the Self: The Making of the Modern Identity* (Cambridge: Cambridge University Press, 1989); Joseph Raz, *Ethics in the Public Domain*; Avishai Margalit and Joseph Raz, "National Self-Determination."

31. Tamir, *Liberal Nationalism*; Miller, *On Nationality*.

32. See for example, Kymlicka, *Multicultural Citizenship*, 19.

33. Kymlicka, *Multicultural Citizenship*, 83.

34. Will Kymlicka, *Liberalism, Community and Culture* (Oxford: Clarendon Press, 1991), 167.

35. Such a lack of clarity is well captured by Tomasi, for whom "cultural membership is a primary good only in the same uninteresting sense as is, say, oxygen: since (practically) no one is differentially advantaged with respect to that good, it generates no special rights." See John Tomasi, "Kymlicka, Liberalism, and Respect for Cultural Minorities," *Ethics* 105, no. 1 (1995): 589.

36. See Daniel Weinstock, "Droits collectifs et libéralisme: Une synthèse?," in *Pluralisme, citoyenneté et éducation*, ed. F. Gagnon, F. McAndrew, and M. Pagé (Paris-Montréal: L'Harmattan, 1996), 53-80.

37. As Margalit and Raz put it, "individual dignity and self-respect require that the groups, membership of which contributes to one's sense of identity, be generally respected and not be made a subject of ridicule, hatred, discrimination, or persecution" (Avishai Margalit and Joseph Raz, "National Self-Determination," 87.) I agree with this statement. Nevertheless, it seems to me that it does not only concern national minorities but also other sorts of minority groups.

38. Moore, "Liberal-nationalism, Nation-Building and National Self-Determination," 5.

39. Taylor, *Sources of the Self: The Making of the Modern Identity*, 27.

40. Donald Horowitz, "Self-Determination; Politics, Philosophy and Law," in *Ethnicity and Group Rights*, ed. Ian Shapiro and Will Kymlicka, 421-63.

41. For a criticism of this thesis, see Waldron, for whom "meaningful options may come to us as items or fragments from a variety of cultural sources" (Jeremy Waldron, "Minority Cultures and the Cosmopolitan Alternative," in *The Rights of Minority Cultures*, ed. Will Kymlicka, 106).

42. Michael Hartney, "Some Confusions Concerning Collective Rights," in *The Rights of Minority Cultures*, ed. Will Kymlicka, 206.

43. David Miller, "Citizenship and Pluralism," *Political Studies* 43 (1995): 450.

44. David Miller, "The Ethical Significance of Nationality," *Ethics* 98, no. 4 (1988): 657. In a quite similar perspective, even if he does not explicitly refer to nationality, Barber emphasizes the importance of "common consciousness" to realize a republican polity (which he calls strong democracy): "without loyalty, fraternity, patriotism, neighborliness, bonding, traditional mutual affection, and common belief, participatory democracy is reduced to crass proceduralism." In Benjamin Barber, *Strong Democracy* (Berkeley: University of California Press, 1984), 216-17 and 242, respectively.

45. Miller, *On Nationality*, 8.

46. See William A. Galston, *Liberal Virtues: Goods, Virtues, and Diversity in The Liberal State* (Cambridge: Cambridge University Press, 1991); and Stephen Macedo, *Liberal Virtues: Citizenship, Virtue and Community in Liberal Constitutionnalism* (Oxford: Clarendon Press, 1991).

47. Moore, "Liberal-nationalism, Nation-Building and National Self-Determination," 9.

48. See Listhaug and Wiberg, "Confidence in Political and Private Institutions," in *Citizens and the State*, ed. H. Klingemann and D. Fuchs (Oxford: Oxford University Press, 1995), 298-322.

49. Andrew Mason, "Political Community, Liberal-Nationalism, and the Ethics of Assimilation," *Ethics* 109, no. 1 (1999): 261-86.

50. K. Newton, "Social and Political Trust" (paper presented at the Conference on *Confidence in Democratic Institutions: America in Comparative Perspective*, held at Washington, D. C., 25-27 August 1997), 3.

51. Paul Hirst, *Associative Democracy* (Cambridge: Polity Press, 1994).

52. See Percy Lehning, "Towards a Multicultural Civil Society: The Role of Social Capital and Democratic Citizenship," *Government and Opposition* 33, no. 2 (1998): 221-42; and Benjamin Barber, *A Place for Us* (New York: Hill and Wang, 1998).

53. In some respects, Kymlicka is right when he maintains that "[Young's] list of 'oppressed groups' in the United States would seem to include 80 percent of the population . . . In short, everyone but relatively well-off, relatively young, able-bodied, heterosexual white males" (Kymlicka, *Multicultural Ctizenship*, 145).

54. Kymlicka, *Multicultural Citizenship*.

55. Young defines empowerment as the "participation of an agent in decision-making through an *effective* voice and vote. Justice requires that each person should have the institutionalized means to participate *effectively* in the decisions that affect her or his action and the conditions of that action" (Young, *Justice and the Politics of Difference*, 251). Phillips' conception of the "politics of presence" is similar to this perspective.

56. See also Jürgen Habermas, "Struggles for Recognition in the Democratic Constitutional State," in *Multiculturalism: Examining the Politics of Recognition,* ed. Amy Gutmann (Princeton: Princeton University Press, 1994), 107-48.

57. Mason, "Political Community, Liberal-Nationalism, and the Ethics of Assimilation."

58. Bhikhu Parekh, "The Cultural Particularity of Liberal Democracy," *Political Studies* 40 (1992): 160-75.

59. For instance, one case is to consider that of the French-speaking minority in Canada, another to think about the situation of the Kurds, whose "nation" is located on the territory of several states.

60. William Connolly, *Identity/Difference: Democratic Negotiations of Political Paradox* (Ithaca, N. Y.: Cornell University Press, 1991).

61. See Matteo Gianni, "Taking Multiculturalism Seriously: Political Claims for a Differentiated Citizenship," in *Citizenship after Liberalism*, ed. K. Slawner and M. Denham (New York: Peter Lang, 1998), 33-55.

62. Bonnie Honig, "Difference, Dilemmas, and the Politics of Home," *Social Research* 61, no. 3 (1994): 563-97.

63. Basically, it is strange to notice that, if we consider the works of Mouffe, Connolly, and even Young, the normative solutions proposed are often very close to traditional liberal positions. In my view, it exists a gap between the epistemological assumptions of the post-structuralist model of citizenship or democracy and the normative conclusions that are suggested. For a more detailed discussion of this aspect, see Matteo Gianni, "Multiculturalism and Political Integration: The Need for a Differentiated Citizenship?" in *Rethinking Nationalism and Ethnicity*, ed. Hans-Rudolph Wicker (Oxford: Berg, 1997), 127-42.

64. I completely agree with Phillips that "when policies are worked out *for* rather than *with* a politically excluded constituency, they are unlikely to engage with all relevant concerns" (Phillips, *The Politics of Presence*, 13). In the same perspective, for Young "ensuring the representation of multiple perspectives gives voice to distinctive experiences in the society and relativizes the dominant perspectives which are assumed as normal and neutral" (Young, *Justice and the Politics of Difference,* 370).

Chapter 14

Multiculturalism and Constitutional Patriotism in Eastern Europe

Judit Hell and Ferenc L. Lendvai

The aim of this chapter is to show that, first, there are two types of multiculturalism, a modern and a traditional one, and that its decisive role can be associated in Hungary and in Eastern Europe with the latter one; that, second, due to the formation of Western countries, the nation-state and the constitutional patriotism associated with it became dominant; and, finally, that in Eastern Europe the concept of *Kulturnation* (culture nation) is dominant, which leads to the resurrection of nationalism. A proper solution, it will be argued, can only be reached through a Western-type development.

Two Types of Multiculturalism

It is appropriate to distinguish between two types of multicultural societies: the traditional and the modern. In traditional societies, several ethnic groups may have lived together, which, despite their differences, basically belonged to the same civilization. In countries that belong in the European civilization, for instance, English and Scots, French and Bretons have lived together; in the territory of historical Hungary, Hungarians, Slovaks, Romanians, Croats, Serbs, and Germans lived side by side for centuries. Even though their cultures were different from one another, all these peoples shared in the same Christian culture; the non-Christian exceptions among them were the Jews and the gypsies—the latter having been formally Christian. In modern societies, a new version of multiculturalism has evolved, which results from a break predominantly through immigration in a largely homogeneous society. In the first phase of the process, the immigrants mainly seek to be assimilated; in the second, they generally do not wish to be absorbed into the majority ethnic communities. On the contrary, they endeavor to preserve their language, traditions, and identity and wish to be recognized as a minority, their culture to be maintained and supported as such (see Latin Americans in the USA, Africans in Britain, Turks in Germany, Arabs in France).[1]

Modern Multiculturalism in the Western Societies

Handling multiculturalism in modern liberal democracies presents itself both as a theoretical (political, philosophical, and ethical) issue and a specific practical problem, since there are many multicultural societies in the modern sense of the word; moreover, the decisive majority of the countries of the world have multinational, culturally plural societies, and enmity between the various cultural groups is quite common. One fundamental theoretical problem that inevitably arises is how liberalism and multiculturalism can be connected; how, on the basis of individualist-centered classical liberalism, can the collective cultural rights of a minority be formulated in the interest of preserving the community and maintaining their culture when (a) all kinds of communities, traditions, and allegiances to traditions present lesser or greater restrictions on the individual liberties of its members; (b) the state should remain culturally neutral, that is, it should not resort to discrimination (not even positive discrimination) among ethnic groups, religions, ways of life, or cultures.[2]

Claiming that the individual is always defined in opposition to community ties, the community-centered (conservative, socialist, communitarian) ideas, on the basis of their reading of the liberal ideal of man, dispute the capability of liberalism to recognize the collective rights of minorities in the interest of maintaining their culture. John Rawls and Ronald Dworkin offer an elegant solution to this problem. Both recognize ways in which collective rights can be accorded as additional to, and without infringing on, individual rights. Both follow the same logical pattern. Collective qualities, they argue, can be acknowledged as values that can be chosen freely by individuals in a society built on the plurality of values. Rawls avers that an individual life plan is carried out by way of making free choices between alternatives, one of these alternatives being the potential presented by a particular cultural community. Dworkin suggests that in the free world of culture a free individual can freely choose between objectives (cultural objectives) and responsibilities (communal responsibilities).

In this light, collective cultural rights may be ensured on a liberal footing by way of widening individual choice, meanwhile supposing that the different cultures embody values (self-value) of their own. According to liberal multiculturalism, no repression of any hue, including repressive culture, is to be tolerated. (Rawls and Dworkin also suggest that only liberal cultures should be supported on moral imperative.) One should also reckon that a number of cultures that repress their own members become even more repressive in a multicultural context—especially when their survival is uncertain among the new circumstances. They may force their members to turn inwards and to break ties with the outer world. The practice of binding the individual to a group may strengthen the conservative elements in a culture and may lead to generational conflicts. Emphasizing in general the significance of collectivity, liberal multiculturalism respects also nonliberal communal cultures, cherishes their language, literature, music, and dances, meanwhile insisting on the defense of individual liberty in opposition to communal repression.[3]

It may happen that a particular practice within a culture is said to be repressive among multicultural circumstances. A certain attitude toward women may be seen in a homogeneous culture in an entirely different light from a multicultural one, which is especially sensitive to discrimination between sexes. The younger generations will presumably rebel against old practices, and the acceptance in their ranks by members of the majority culture is imperative. To sum it up: respect shown by liberal multiculturalism toward other cultures is conditional to the appreciation shown by the given community toward values (liberty, human dignity) that are heteronomous to their own value system. Sexual discrimination is a fundamental tradition in a number of non-European (Islam, gypsy) cultures. In some Arab and Middle East countries where Islamic fundamentalism prevails, equality of women and general human rights that are also due to women will hardly be granted. Women are often denied education and labor, they are not allowed to walk in the streets unless escorted by a man, or to drive a car; they cannot divorce yet can at any time be dismissed by their husband; women's testimony is taken less seriously than men's, and so on. Female members of this culture probably cannot even make much of the statement "sexual discrimination is wrong," for it reflects the value system of a culture alien to them.

The important question arises here whether equal human dignity can a priori be postulated when the female members of some homogeneous Islamic society accept and submit themselves to the practice of strong sexual discrimination amid the circumstances of multiculturalism, whereas, from a liberal angle, the practice of repressive cultures, whether it is directed against women, individuals, or anybody, is not to be tolerated. The circumcision of women, for instance, practiced in some immigrant African communities, has caused outrage and shock in the majority culture in France and other European countries (less an Islamic than an African tradition, it probably goes back to the age of the Pharaohs.) Protests in the name of humaneness, civil liberties, and human rights need no explanation, and it is unlikely that the female members of the minority group undertake such traditions willingly. Recognizing the inhuman character of the practice in a new multicultural medium, sooner or later they themselves will probably protest against it; for them, especially for the young who have been socialized in the new medium, the possibility of abandoning it, which the majority culture grants them, could be an attractive alternative.

Traditional Multiculturalism in Hungary and Eastern Europe

In Hungary, owing above all to a moderate presence of non-European cultures, the problem of multiculturalism presents itself far less acutely than in the United States or Western Europe. One sizable community (500,000 to one million) who wish to preserve their identity is that of the gypsies (Romanies). They have lived in the country side by side with Hungarians for centuries; owing to their mobility they are found practically in all settlements, yet predominantly dwell in backward regions in segregated, ghetto-like settlements. Their educational standards are low; there are few with qualifications among them. An interesting example, which is specific to women, occurs at physical education classes at school.

In the value system of those Romany groups, which are non-assimilated, gypsies who have kept their own mother tongue, and also of some Hungarian gypsy communities, the traditional relationship between the sexes is violated at school when adolescent Romany girls are required to wear gym clothes. According to Romany custom, girls aged 13 or 14 are regarded as women and are not allowed to reveal their body. Girls of this age are not to wear shorts or short skirts. At physical education (PE) classes, however, they are confronted with the alternatives of either to undress or to face comments by their teachers and classmates. Even though the Law on Public Education ensures the right of students that their religion, worldview, or other beliefs and their national or ethnic identity be respected, this is not always done in practice. Teachers justify their intolerance of the cultural otherness of gypsy girls by saying that allowing them not to change into gym outfits at PE class would constitute a discriminative act of sorts.

Another example is the question of whether a thirteen-year-old Romany girl who cohabits with a young man of the same ethnicity is to be accorded legal protection. In the Romany value system, juvenile cohabitation occupies the same rank as matrimony, and is practiced quite frequently too. However, Hungarian criminal law stipulates that sexual intercourse with a person under fourteen qualifies as a criminal act of perversion and is to be punished with detention from one to five years. The Criminal Code contains general norms that apply to all citizens.[4]

In East European countries, however, it is frequently taken to be usual that ethnic and religious groups are to be measured by their own scales. In a traditional society of the states each estate has its own rights, that is, its privileges: citizens did not share freedom or universal rights, but each estate had its own "freedom" (meaning privileges). Not only nobles, bourgeois, or peasants occupied a special position but foreigners (in Hungary mostly Germans, Jews, or gypsies) as well. Therefore, in East European societies, various ethnic and religious groups claim to have collective rights and not merely in the ordinary sense of having the possibility of practicing, individually or collectively, the universal rights of citizens, but in the sense of having a role as a "state-constituent" community. Thus the pursuit of autonomy in Eastern Europe does not mean a pursuit of territorial or regional autonomy, but an endeavor to achieve linguistic-cultural autonomy. This correlates with the following situation: most East European people lost their independence after the end of the Middle Ages and had been integrated into multicultural empires: in the modern age the common culture, instead of historical development, became the symbol of national integrity.

Modern State and Modern Nation

The empires still existing or just being formed in early modern times, including several ethnic groups (the Germanic-Roman Empire, the Ottoman Empire, and the Russian Empire), became unstable and finally broke up. It was actually in Switzerland that a federal structure was constituted and proved able to relieve the ethnic pressures in the public consciousness of the citizens. Growing from the centralized monarchies, the territorial states became the basis for the European state system. Later, after the French Revolution, and as a result of democratic development, these territorial states became "nations" or national states.[5]

The Nation-State

But what does the term "nation-state" mean in this context? Originally, in Roman times the meaning of the word *natio* was equal to *gens* or *populus* and unlike the word *civitas* it strictly referred to ethnic groups. This meaning was preserved throughout the Middle Ages. What is more, even Immanuel Kant used the terms *natio* and *gens* in the same sense. However, structures leading to the later semantic change of the word could be found in the late Roman society as well as in the system of estates in the Middle Ages. The word *romanus* was not used with reference to a person of Latin origin but rather to an individual having Roman civil rights. The Apostle Paul was a Jew only from an ethnical point of view but concerning his political position he was a Roman. By the end of the late Roman Age the meaning of this word was confirmed in such a way that after the fall of the western-Roman Empire the Hellenic and Hellenized inhabitants of the "second" and "new" Rome, i.e., Byzantium always called themselves *rhomaios*, that is, Roman. A similar phenomenon can be observed in the case of the feudal states: from an ethnic point of view a "hungarus" or a "polonus" was not definitely a Hungarian or a Pole, but he might as well be a Slovak or a Ruthenian, etc.[6]

However "nation," the new meaning of the word *natio* originated from these events of feudalism. According to the new ideas of state developing in modern times, such as theories of contracts, it is the sum total of the estates that represents or means the "nation" as opposed to the ruler and the nation conveying state sovereignty. This idea is modified by abbot Sièyes in his famous slogan: "What is meant by the third estate? Everything!" This expresses exactly the following state of affairs: The nation is identified as a politically organized unit of people. From this time on the meaning of *gens* and that of *natio* separates. Although nationalism, the ideology of the modern nation-state, considers belonging to a certain state of primary importance, it also attempts to bring about unity between ethnos and demos. (Let us consider Saint Simon's famous theory that states that French nobility are the descendants of the conquering Franks, while the French people are the descendants of the Gallic vassals.) This ideology necessarily led to the limitation of the rights of national minorities. It means that their living space was forced to the peripheries and they were expected to identify with the national culture as a sign of identification with the nation and their own cultural tradition was only tolerated as a part of interesting folklore.

On the other hand, the existence of ethnic groups outside the framework of the nation-state raises or at least can raise the problem of irredentism. In the case of France such an irredentist demand was represented by Savoy, and later Valais and the Walloon territory, but after the second Bonapartist period these intentions manifested themselves in a kind of coherence between the ethnic groups speaking Swiss- or Belgic-French and there was an expectation on the other side that they would cohere in this way. It is evident that in Western Europe the particular concept of nation that gained victory was the one we have to qualify as characteristic of the modern age, that is, the one regarding the nation as a political-communal formation that, even if not completely independent, is becoming more and more independent of ethnic origin, but in its tendency it is completely independent.

Constitutional Patriotism

Jürgen Habermas, referring to the type of ideal represented not only by Switzerland but also by the United States, comes to the following conclusion, which is the last consequence of this development: "It is only the common denominator of *Verfassungspatriotismus* (constitutional patriotism) that a liberal political culture can bring about simultaneously an inclination to the multiplicity and integrity of the different, co-existent ways of life typical of a multicultural society." Thus a democratic national status is not grounded in a kind of national identity, but in the socialization of each citizen in a common political culture.

In the stormy debate (so-called *Historikerstreit*) among German historians *Verfassungspatriotismus* was also present in a hidden form. In one of the articles that actually started the debate and was originally published in the weekly *Die Zeit* Habermas remarked: "Constitutional patriotism is the only kind of patriotism that does not alienate us from the West," and it is here that Habermas sets himself strongly against the German illusion of a kind of Central Europe [*Mitteleuropa*].[7] In other words: the only nation belonging to the West is the one that shares this kind of patriotism, since any other thought makes us return to the premodern system of relations, to the ideology of the nation existing before the modern political nation, that is, the ideology of gens. (The Hungarian historian Jenő Szűcs called it "gentilism.")[8] In German relations it goes back to the concept of *Sonderweg*, separated from the West, as well as the so-called *Blut und Boden* ideology.

Habermas is of the opinion that if it is possible for each cultural way of life existing side by side to unfold, sooner or later they will overlap in a common political culture. Thus, this gives rise to the possibility and reality of a unified democratic national status. As he points out, it will be determinative for a world state turning from utopia into reality: "The way for a cosmopolitan state [*Weltbürgerstatus*] can only be paved by a democratic national status that does not withdraw into itself in a particular way. . . ." It is not accidental that the word reminds us of the famous and classical writing by Immanuel Kant; it is Habermas himself who refers to this connection. But, whereas in the time of Kant world publicity was given only in theory, nowadays mass communication throughout the world as established by the electronic media makes real "communicational" relations and participation possible.[9]

The Situation in Eastern Europe

In what way does West European "facticity" apply to our East European reality? The most striking difference manifests itself with respect to the political, versus the culture nation. In the majority of cases public opinion in East European countries is convinced that the nature of nation consists of its common origin, language, and culture. This fact is amplified by the intellectual strata strongly attached to traditions. That is why Eastern Europe is full of *Volksungaren*, *Volkskroaten*, *Volksserben*, and *Volksalbanen*, living outside the borders of the nation-state. The milder form of what consequence this leads to can also be observed in the Carpathian basin and in a more radical form in Bosnia or Kosovo. It might be said that Western Europe is the terrain of political nations, while Eastern Europe is that of the culture nations. But this statement is false. There are no separate globes, one being the eastern and the other the western, nor are there at least two separate hemispheres in the North. (We do not intend to deal with the non-European relations of Afro-Asia in the South.) Anyway, what sense is there in supposing that such an idea exists when, from Devin to Vladivostok everybody wants to catch up with Europe (that is, the West)?

The Idea of Culture Nation

But let us examine the notion of culture nation more closely. As in the ancient world the notional antecedent of the nation-state was the Roman statehood (first *res publica,* later *imperium*), in the case of the culture nation the antecedent was the disunited *polis* -world of the Hellenics, the unity of which was guaranteed by a common culture (a more or less common language and a common religion) but mainly by the institutions connected to it and recognized to be common, such as the sanctuary in Delos, the oracle in Delphi, and the Olympic Games. That is, originally the culture nation also demanded a kind of institutionalized system, which cannot simply be qualified as a kind of ethnic gentilism. It is only later that the latter becomes popular: at the time when the Jews as an ethnic group with a special religion gain autonomy in the framework of the successive Persian, Hellenistic, and Roman Empires, and the same events happen to the Greeks and other Balkan people within the Ottoman Empire. Since there was a lack of political and legal possibilities, a system of institutions was guaranteed by church organizations, first by monasteries. That is why churches played a basic role in the national movement of independence in each Balkan nation, and that is why the ideology of the Roman nationalistic-fascist Iron Guard originally had a religious basis (Legion of Archangel Saint Michael). [10]

In modern times the concept of culture nation is related to the German development. The modern concept of the nation-state established by the French and the notion of a *nation française* united not only the southern French (*langue d'oc*) after a thousand years of opposition, but also the Bretons, the Alsatians, the Corsicans, and the inhabitants of Savoy and Nizza, what is more, mostly all these non-French, with the Northern French (*langue d'oïl*). In the same way the German national consciuosness was obliged to find some other basis lacking a collective revolution and wars fought together but mainly lacking a common state. In this way, the common culture became the vehicle of the national character for many larger or smaller German states. Moreover, the Germans had common political institutions, even if symbolic in many respects. Earlier there was the "Holy Roman Empire of the German Nation" (which meant that the Roman Empire was represented by the German feudal nation), then there was the Rhine Alliance and in the end the German Alliance. The operation of these alliances was not entirely symbolic but operated in certain legal areas and it was more than symbolic in enabling people to express their unity. [11]

It was only much later, that is, only after losing the First World War, that the notion of *Volkstum,* originally expressing democratic mindedness, acquired an ethnic-gentilist, what is more, a racial content. War was thought to be a fair case and its loss was considered to be a national catastrophe by German public opinion, since the concept of the bourgeois-democratic nation-state failed (a forceful hindrance of *Anschluss* by the Western Powers). The loss of the war and the nationalistic and ultimately national socialist reaction to the anti-national foreign policy of the Weimar Republic unanimously made Germany turn away from the West and move in the direction of the East. The Oriental-Balkan ideology of Hitlerism banished the notion of the "nation" completely—in a logical way—and replaced it by the notion of "race." Thus, the ethnic common consciousness of "gentilism" does not definitely mean racism, but its possibility and danger always exists in a hidden way. This ideology is oriental and bears the characteristics of the Middle Ages, with anti-Semitism as a typical concomitant (let us refer to the roots again: by the Athens Law of 451 B.C. civil rights were guaranteed only to those of "pure" Attica origin).

Thus those who wish to constitute a culture nation (in which, let us say, at least fifteen million Hungarians constitute one "spiritual" nation), identify the notion of *gens* with that of *natio* in such a way as in the Middle Ages. The fact that this idea has no sense at all can be demonstrated by asking the question: what is the difference between the theorem "each x living in the world belongs to x culture" and the theorem "each x living in the world belongs to x culture nation"? From a logical or a rational point-of-view evidently nothing, but exclusively (and very dangerously) the difference lies in the irrational and overwrought emotional excess. However, as we can see, the real concept of the culture nation not only builds on the consciousness of ethnic-gentilist origin but also has always needed a certain system of institutions, which, in turn, creates a dangerous transition (or its possibility) to the concept of the nation-state. Of course, this may create a real surplus in the interpretation, which evokes the danger of irredentism causing suspicious protests even tacitly. The expression of belonging to a nation (even with symbols) is quite unlike the obvious and unrestricted system of relations between ethnic groups living in different countries but sharing a common culture.

Nationalisms in Eastern Europe

The continous relevance of the idea of culture nation is in connection with the late development of a modern civil society because national markets and bourgeois classes were underdeveloped. Thus the bonds within the community were frequently manifested in common historical nostalgia: every nation had glorious historical periods in which its national greatness came to the surface. Therefore Eastern European nationalisms usually looked for a kind of historicist background. In Hungary the nationalist nostalgia felt toward the historical "Great

Hungary" is a typical feature. This state contained contemporary Hungary ("Lower Hungary"), Slovakia ("Upper Hungary"), Transylvania, Burgenland, Carpathian Ukraine, Vojvodina, and Croatia was a so-called "associated country." Once upon a time, these areas together were called "the Countries of the Hungarian Holy Crown."

Conservative nationalists urged that the "Holy Crown" be placed at the top of the arms of Hungary (which is an absurdity from the perspective of heraldry), and even today conservatives and neoconservatives tend to give a constitutional role to it. (According to their position, the crown is not "holy" in any ordinary sense, but it is holy in a magical or sacral sense given that it was sent, by the pope, to the first Hungarian king who was subsequently canonized: and this is merely a legend, since the original crown was lost and was later replaced.) For them the "Holy Crown" expresses the integrity of the Hungarian nation, and the Hungarian nation as a "cultural nation" involves every Hungarian national in all countries of the world. Correspondingly Hungarians living in Slovakia, Transylvania, etc. are citizens of Slovakia, Romania, etc. but they belong to the Hungarian nation (and not merely to the Hungarian ethnic or culture). Meanwhile, gypsies and sometimes Jews who are Hungarian citizens, and those who do not think in a national but a cosmopolitan way are to be expelled from the Hungarian nation represented by the "Holy Crown."

It is usually mentioned as a counterargument that the frameworks of the nation-state were established artificially and these states did not succeed in uniting their ethnic groups of different origin, language, and culture in a homogeneous nation having a really unified political culture and world of experience. This is really true. The situation is this: in this respect (as in many other respects) in Eastern Europe there have been premodern relations even up to recent times, which were either formations with the characteristics of empires, differing from the one-time Ottoman or Russian Empires only having smaller territories, or there were *gentes*.

Such a "small empire" was the late Yugoslavia. In principle it would have been possible for this country to become a Swiss-type of federation had it not been hindered by the conditions of premodern "gentilism" hiding under the surface and if it had not started quite a different process, which has not come to a conclusion yet. Luckily, the similar problem of the late Czechoslovakia where conditions were more favorable was accomplished advantageously.

As regards the future, Romania, a country with a seemingly different structure, may manifest surprises, but not because of nationality problems. That is, the structure of the country of Romania would have the characteristics of an empire even if the country had not even one non-Roman inhabitant. The actual Romania includes Transylvania, a geographically closed unit as well as half the country called Moldova, the other half of which is an independent country. Unambiguous as the basically Roman character of the whole region is and strong as the cementing force of the enthusiastic national sentiments is, sooner or later this gentilistic nationalism has to transform into modern patriotism (constitutional patriotism) and we have to count on the manifold conflicts of different traditions and interests. We hope the outcome will be peaceful and democratic.

We can only hope—and perhaps it is possible to hope today—that in the near future, after the burst of "gentilism" in Eastern Europe, the area will start to move toward modernization and in this respect it will lead to the formation of modern national consciousness, that is, constitutional patriotism. And the situation will be the same in connection with regional autonomies. In the United States we can find not only American and not only ethnic consciousness, but also a regional one (Michigan, Connecticut, etc.). Each canton, half-canton, town, and village in Switzerland is proud to bear its own emblem. (In Eastern Europe the coat-of-arms of the state are displayed everywhere.) The community at each level has territorial and local-government character due to the existence of the community and autonomy of the citizens.

Besides this, the existence of the ethnocultural consciousness of identity is also quite natural. At the same time it is not necessary for the constitutional patriotism to definitely manifest itself in a sterile and abstract manner. To experience the traditions of the cultural community or the values of the cultural areas formed by generations and reflecting objective traditions does not mean a kind of *Blut und Boden* ideology. (Undoubtedly Habermas himself does not emphasize this fact as required.) And even if East European countries, including Hungary, are not threatened very much with absorption into a structure existing above the nation, the necessary subordination to such structures will, in turn, manifest itself. Thus, constitutional patriotism (of course, not nationalism) may play a role in defending the interests of the democratic organizations being formed. Obviously, in that case such democratic organizations will truly be formed.[12]

Notes

1. See Judit Hell, "Frauenfrage und Multikulturalismus," Ferenc L. Lendvai, "Alte und moderne Multikulturalität im Westen und im Osten," in *Multikulturalismus. Studien - Multiculturalism. Studies*, ed. Judit Hell (Miskolc: Miskolci Egyetemi Kiadó, 1998), 55-71, 35-43.

2. See Jürgen Gebhardt, "Norms of Citizenship and Conceptions of Community," Fred R. Dallmayr, "Democracy and Multiculturalism," in *Multikulturalismus - Multiculturalism*, 105-13, 115-36.

3. See the well-known work of John Rawls, *A Theory of Justice* (Cambridge, Mass.: Harvard University Press, 1971), chs. 1-2, and the book by Ronald Dworkin, *Talking Rights Seriously* (Cambridge, Mass.: Harvard University Press, 1985); see as well Will Kymlicka, *Liberalism, Community, and Culture* (Oxford: Clarendon, 1991) and Joseph

Raz, *The Morality of Freedom* (Oxford: Oxford University Press, 1986), chs. 5-6.

4. Angus Fraser, *The Gypsies* (Oxford: Blackwell, 1995), chs. 5 and 9; Zoltan Barany, "Living in the Edge: The East European Roma," *Slavic Review* 53, no. 2 (Summer 1994): 321-44; and David Crowe, "The Gypsies in Hungary," in *The Gypsies of Eastern Europe*, ed. D. Crowe and J. Koltsi (Armonk, N. Y.: M. E. Sharpe, 1991), 117-32.

5. See Oscar Halecki, *The Millennium of Europe* (Notre Dame, Indiana: University of Notre Dame Press, 1963), chs. 22-23; Paul Kennedy, *The Rise and Fall of the Great Powers* (New York: Fontana Press, 1989), chs. 2-3.

6. Oskar Halecki, *Borderlands of Western Civilization. A History of East Central Europe* (New York: Ronald Press, 1952), chs. 6-7.

7. See Jürgen Habermas, *Staatsbürgerschaft und nationale Identität* (St. Gallen: Erker, 1991), also published in Habermas, *Faktizität und Geltung. Beiträge zur Diskurstheorie des Rechts und des demokratischen Rechtsstaats* (Frankfurt: Suhrkamp, 1992), 632-60; and Habermas, "Eine Art Schadensabwicklung. Die apologetischen Tendenzen in der deutschen Zeitgeschichtsschreibung," *Die Zeit*, 11 July 1986, also published in *"Historikerstreit". Die Dokumentation der Kontroverse um die Einzigartigkeit der nationalsozialistischen Judenvernichtung* (München-Zürich: Piper, 1987), 62-76.

8. Jenõ Szûcs, "'Gentilizmus.' A barbár etnikai tudat kérdése" ['Gentilism.' The problem of the barbaric ethnic consciousness], in Szûcs, *A magyar nemzeti tudat kialakulása* [The formation of the Hungarian national consciousness] (Budapest-Szeged: Balassi-JATE-Osiris, 1997), 7-295 [manuscript finished in 1970].

9. The famous work of Immanuel Kant, "Idee zu einer allgemeinen Geschichte in weltbürgerlicher Absicht" has many editions, first published by the author in the *Berlinische Monatsschrift*, November 1784.

10. William Totok, "Die Generation von Mircea Eliade im Bann des rumänischen Faschismus," *Halbjahresschrift für osteuropäische Geschichte, Literatur und Politik* 7, no. 1 (1995): 42-55.

11. See Helmuth Plessner, *Die verspätete Nation. Über die politische Verführbarkeit bürgerlichen Geistes* (Stuttgart-Berlin-Köln-Mainz: W. Kohlhammer, 1959), chs. 2-3.

12. See *Berliner Osteuropa Info* 13 (1999): "Osteuropa zehn Jahre nach dem Umbruch. Aktuelle Forschungsbilanzen und Zukunftsperspektiven."

Chapter 15

Justice and Immigration: An Argument against Nationality as "Cement" of Citizenship

Ricard Zapata-Barrero

Historically political theorists have more or less ignored the whole question of immigrants' accommodation, largely because they have seen it as politically irrelevant. This situation today is different. It is widely recognized that immigrants' demands are pressing states. This has put several novel questions on the political agenda, which broadly fall into two leading interrelated focuses.

The institutional focus starts from the persuasion that we are entering a new phase, that, instead of seeing immigrants as outsiders who would eventually return as potential citizens, accepts that they are here to stay and that they also wish to retain and transmit their ways of life. The question surrounding the debate is now how to accommodate immigrants in a country that is monoculturally structured? Does a policy of accommodating immigrants necessarily mean overhauling the traditional structure of institutions, and, if so, what guiding principles should be followed in implementing institutional changes?

The second focus, related to the previous one in terms of consequences, is that these practical problems are directly connected with the political key concepts of our traditional thinking: the state, democracy, nationality, citizenship, and justice. That is, immigration, as a political problem, is forcing political theory to revise the main conceptual categories that have been used in the past to describe and explain Western political societies. From this point of view, immigration is perceived as a challenge in terms of cultural pluralism.[1] The rationale of this normative focus can be described as follows: in the process of theorizing modern societies, there has been a biased tendency to unforeseen multicultural societies, that is, the possibility of coexistence within a shared territory of different cultures and traditions.[2] This historical assumption, once it is uncovered, leads to questions such as: are the bases of liberal democracy capable of managing these challenges or ought they to be changed? How should liberal democracy respond to claims for accommodation?

These institutional and normative challenges reveal that what is beyond doubt is the fact that today the changing composition of societies through immigration and the resulting increase in diversity has become a focal point for political controversy.[3] Some states have begun to change their policy oriented by this fact, while others show some reluctance to do it. In this new stage the issue I would like to put under consideration is that nowadays there are contextual elements that give us reasons to detach the strong, historical link between state, nationality, and citizenship, especially when we introduce the relationship between justice and immigration in this threefold traditional relationship. More concretely, I will defend the argument that a politics of accommodation is more just when residence instead of immigrants' nationality is used as a guiding principle.

However, it is not my intention to say that substituting nationality for residence from accommodation policies automatically renders the latter just. Clearly, there are other issues that have to be taken into account in making such a judgement. Matters concerning the relationship are far from being short and simple.[4] I will examine just one aspect of this complexity and consider the possibilities of following up this line of research.

The chapter is divided into three sections. In the first, reviewing Walzer's arguments, I will defend the need to introduce a language of justice to explore the phenomenon of immigration and point to some of the issues arising from the current debate. In the second section, I will propose some non-negotiable basic requirements in constructing an evaluation benchmark. My argument here will be that the basic principle of justice is the principle of equality. It can be defined in negative terms as the principle of non-discrimination against foreigners' national origin. In the third section, I will briefly examine two scenarios of the practical impact of these requirements: one at the state level, the other at the European Union level. Both of them require that nationality be divorced from the accommodation policy.

A Language of Justice Applied to Immigrants' Accommodation

M. Walzer is one of the first scholars who have detected the practical problems for political theorists when they try to place immigration issues within the framework of a theory of justice. Walzer leaves us the task of drawing up some aspects of political theory in order to reorient its practice. Advancing some of the arguments defended by Kymlicka,[5] the main practical problem of traditional theories of justice is that they have assumed the cultural homogeneity of the political communities under consideration.[6] This assumption raises the implicit relationship between nationality and politics, and it leads the discussion on the need to separate them.

Historically speaking, nationality either stemmed from political considerations or political decisions were taken based on nationality. A plural cultural context renders this historical relationship outdated. In other words, the acquisition of citizenship, understood as a political process of embracing social diversity, does not necessarily imply cultural assimilation.[7] This line of thought thus expresses an explicit rejection of ethnic policies, which amount to institutional racism.[8]

Walzer proposes several ways in which institutions can recognize the multicultural basis of the societies they serve. These include: state defense of collective rights; a policy of celebrating non-state cultural identities; providing ethnic communities with funds for bilingual and bicultural education and group-oriented welfare services; and a right to some sort of representation in state agencies with responsibilities in these spheres.[9] The state, faced with the problem of cultural pluralism, can intervene in two basic ways to restructure group life: it can apply an autonomist or an integrationist strategy. In the first case, the state can encourage groups to organize themselves, assigning them a political role in the state apparatus, thus institutionalizing cultural differences. In the second case, the state acts to reduce differences among groups by establishing symmetrical achievement standards for their members. The latter, if applied generally, tends to repress every sort of cultural specificity, turning ethnic identity into an administrative classification, regulated by the principle of loyalty to state institutions.[10]

These arguments reveal how the practical problems of cultural pluralism challenge political theory to seriously reconsider the traditional institutional structures. This problem receives special treatment in one of the first chapters of *Spheres of Justice*.[11] The initial argument could be formulated as follows: when we think about distributive justice, we have in mind independent states capable of arranging their own just or unjust patterns of division and exchange. We assume an established group and a fixed population, and so we miss the first and most important distributive question: how is that group constituted? (SJ, 31). Nowadays the issue that cultural pluralism poses is whether it is just for nation-states to run their economies with the help of people excluded from holding citizenship (SJ, 55).[12] In other words, can one justify states depriving people from making life choices simply because of their nationality? (SJ, 54). The conventional nature (without natural or religious foundations of legitimization) of citizenship implies that it is a primary good regulated in the same way as any other state-distributed good, i.e., through determinate criteria. In this respect it is difficult not to agree with Walzer that the criteria of accommodation used traditionally is far from being just.

To sum up Walzer's arguments, the principle of political justice is this: that the process of self-determination through which a just state shapes its internal life must be equally open to all those who live in the country, work in the local economy, and are subject to local law. When accommodation is closed, the political economy collapses into a world of members and outsiders, with no political boundaries between the two. No just state can tolerate the establishment of a fixed status between citizens and immigrants. A sound just policy has to make a choice: if it opts to admit people, it must treat them equally, without discriminating on the basis of nationality and, once admitted, must accept their full accommodation in the body politic.

This is the responsible choice that states must make. This means doing away with nationality as a policy guideline. One might go so far as to say that this structural problem of liberal democracies is what makes them work since the system would soon fail without denial of political rights and the ever-present threat of deportation. This kind of tacit political consensus is not legitimated by any theory of justice (SJ, 58).[13]

Hence the appeal to construct a theory of justice taking the accommodation of immigrants as its starting point. Efforts have been made in this direction during the 1990s given the need to adapt notions of citizenship to a New World order.[14] With regard to the link between justice and immigration, we can say that the problem lies with the use of nationality as a guiding criterion (used indistinctly as culture, in a broader sense, to include race, ethnicity, religion, national origin, and even language).[15] This way of legitimization lies at the root of a way of defining "foreignness" as a vehicle for cultural values at odds with the host nationality. This cultural dimension to design an accommodation politics forces states to redefine their responsibilities and to modify their basic institutional structure for accommodating immigrants.

These assumptions have to do with what J. Elster calls the "cement of society."[16] The main question is about the connection between nationality and immigration. If a state decides to admit immigrants, may it take nationality into account in the selection process? Liberal democratic states are, by definition, committed to individual freedom and autonomy, and thus to the pluralism that follows from individuals' right to pursue their own conceptions of right and wrong. Unfortunately, liberal democracy simply has no conceptual tools to formulate coherent answers when whole groups adopt differing value systems. In a strong liberal democratic state borders should be open to all, since there are no theoretical principles that legitimate limitations to access.[17] Even if limits can be justified, once immigrants live in a country, there are no political justifications for limiting public identity and action to a part of the population.

As this brief preliminary examination reveals, the language of justice in connection with accommodating immigrants is anything but straightforward. This link ultimately mirrors some of the most fundamental questions of the limits to state policy. In the following section, I will argue that these problems of matching theory and practice could at least be partially solved if we were to dispense with the principle of nationality in legitimizing the practice of states toward immigrants at the level of coexistence. To what extent is it legitimate for states to pursue interests, and to what extent ought they concern themselves with the interest of immigrants? Is it a question of "anything goes" or are there bounds to liberal democratic state practices? If so, where do these limits lie? Once we have mapped them, how do we give them institutional expression? My contribution here is to introduce this discourse and to venture some answers to these questions.

Justice and Foreigners: Basic Non-Negotiable Requirements to Construct a Critical Standard for Evaluation

When I speak of justice, the language I use is the language of final moral judgments. Justice establishes the morally legitimate parameters of public policy.[18] Justice is based on the principle of equality, which depends on the public foundation.[19] I will suggest that a rigorous application of this principle requires that national origin be dropped as a plank of accommodation policy.

At the level of coexistence, once immigrants have been admitted, I will discuss the reasons invoked by the state for legitimating restrictions of the equality principle to a significant part of the residing population. Taking this approach as a starting point, there are at least two opposed theoretical positions: one that invokes cosmopolitan reasons for eliminating these restrictions, and another that defends the need for them on grounds of "realism."[20] To distinguish between them we can ask which interest is more just. Realists would answer the state's interests; those of a cosmopolitan persuasion would say the immigrants' interests. Let me briefly examine their respective moral arguments.

Realists argue that justice presupposes the determination of citizenship, and not the other way round. The specific character of citizenship is naturally exclusive.[21] Following this line of reasoning, posing the relationship between justice and immigrants as a problem is simply to put the cart before the horse. They would therefore consider the problem to be based on false premises. Nowadays, resident immigrants without citizenship, or "denizens,"[22] possess almost all citizen's rights outside the political sphere. In these circumstances, it is reasonable for citizens to retain the few privileges that have no economic, social, and, even, psychological impact for immigrants living in a strange land.

This frontal attack against those who implicitly present their arguments as if they were a panacea is well directed. However, there is also evidence that some basic principles of justice are threatened when a number of adults fully capable of acting in the public sphere are subject to a political authority that leaves them no opportunity to fully express their cultural identities. This is the point of departure for those in the opposing camp.

The basis of the cosmopolitan argument is that all resident aliens have the moral right to give their cultural values public expression. A state that restricts this possibility is acting against a basic principle of justice: equality for all.[23] The justification of this position is that a just immigration policy must permit every long-term non-national resident to exercise the moral right to participate in the public sphere, since political authority must be based solely on the consent of its population. Permanent resident aliens belong to this population, consequently their rights to act in the public sphere have to be guaranteed.

As I stated above, this application of the principle of equality has a public foundation. This foundation can be read in two ways: on the one hand, it insists on the context in which the relationship between citizenship and the state takes place. Citizens can express their identities in the public sphere. On the other hand, it stresses the difficulty in delimiting what any theory of justice needs to establish: the public good. Let me examine each one reading them separately.

The problem the first reading poses is that even though the activity of citizens is functionally determinant as an instrument of inclusion, it is also implicitly exclusive for those groups that cannot express their distinguishing traits in a publicly recognized form.[24] This public activity thus entails cultural assimilation (in the sense of sameness or likeness) or cultural uniformity,[25] and therefore excludes differences that are what really concerns individuals. This is why the public sphere, as the distinctive sphere of citizenship activity, is considered homogeneous. The problem therefore lies in determining conditions that make it possible to establish a communication between citizenship and the state if only one part of the person is represented, namely, the one matching the identity represented within the public sphere.

In this respect, recent literature poses the problem in terms of the relationship between the universality and homogeneity that supposedly applies to citizenship and the public sphere on the one hand, and the cultural or identity differences that remain within the private sphere on the other. The political question that an accommodation policy has to answer is thus: how should one manage differences within a sphere that has always tended to reduce them and treat them as politically irrelevant?

The second reading of the public foundation starts from the premise that the public good and the national good are one and the same. This is not new. Traditionally, the public good has been considered as the exclusive good of the citizens, not the population. Here the public foundation reveals another facet. While the first reading was approached in terms of access to the public sphere, this second reading deals with the exclusive goods conferred by citizenship.

This sense of "public good" implies that an accommodation policy has to manage the interests of immigrants and to justify why they are not treated as citizens. Realists would argue the need for this double standard on the basis that the interests of immigrants simply do not represent the public good. Moreover, the fulfilment of the interests of immigrants is not politically cost-effective from an electoral point of view.[26] Cosmopolitans, however, would consider that resident aliens, once their status is regularized, should benefit from most of the public goods distributed to citizens, such as education, health services and almost all universal welfare services, but they would criticize the fact that they cannot participate in determining their distribution. This reading stresses the fact that the public good does not mean the good of the whole population (as has traditionally been supposed), but only the public good of citizenship (understood in democratic theory as the "demos").[27]

Concluding Remarks: Two Scenarios Requiring a Language of Justice for Accommodating Immigrants

The language of justice sketched above needs to be introduced in at least two different practical situations encountered by immigrants: one within state frontiers and another at the European Union level. These scenarios can be viewed as producing strains that go to the heart of the reorientation process taking place in the liberal democratic tradition since the beginning of the 1990s.[28]

My analysis takes this process on board. I start from the premise that liberal democracy will only triumph if it can show itself institutionally capable of managing these new tensions in a flexible fashion. These scenarios often run into serious difficulties in introducing a coherent language of justice when faced with the empirical evidence of the increasing movement of people beyond state borders.[29]

Scenario 1: Accommodation Politics within State Frontiers

In this context, at least three different positions try to tackle the tensions between group customs and standard practices in the host country, while combining unity and diversity in the terms of justice.[30] We can sketch the guidelines adopted by each of these models of justice (or accommodating immigrants into host societies) by using two key indicators. These are participation in political decision making as well as management of diverse nationalities, and the national character of the public sphere. These cover claims for assimilation, integration, and autonomy, respectively. I will now examine the foundations that legitimize state treatment of immigrants.

The assimilationist model of justice is founded on a defense of a cultural laissez-faire.[31] It has historically been one of the first reactions of states trying to manage increasing cultural diversity produced by the presence of immigrants. This model considers any change in the national contents and limits enshrined in the public sphere unnecessary, despite their eminently monocultural origin. Evidently, it does not foster immigrants' participation in political management of cultural difference—an issue that remains the exclusive preserve of citizens. The diversity of different nationalities is seen from a competitive point of view, thus the nationality disposing of greater resources will be able to marshal more support within the public sphere. In terms of the two indicators, assimilation could be defined as handing policy decisions regarding cultural differences over to citizens acting within a nationally homogeneous public sphere.

Consequently, immigrants who want to gain access to this public sphere will have to relegate their cultural practices likely to produce tensions to the private sphere and embrace those that have already been institutionalized and publicly recognized. This model of accommodation is strictly guided by the principle of national discrimination, and only calls for state intervention when the native nationality is seen to be threatened by those considered as "cultural invaders." This model treats immigrants as outsiders who would eventually return to their country of origin. Therefore, the politics of accommodation is viewed mainly as a politics of nationality. It is the model defended today by realists, even if the "return myth" has no empirical basis.

The integrationist model is the one that currently commands most support. It most characterizes Western liberal democracies and represents a stage in the state's treatment of immigrants, once it is realized they have abandoned any idea of returning to their homeland and have decided to build a life in their countries of residence. It is shaped by a perception of immigrants as outsiders, but who can freely gain institutional acceptance by a process of naturalization. The politics of accommodation is understood as a politics of citizenship. Immigrants are simply seen as potential citizens. Similar to the previous model, it defends the idea that the policy of managing cultural differences lies with citizens, but it accepts the need to vary some contents and national limits enshrined in the public sphere to permit recognition of some immigrant cultural practices. This institutional recognition is made in order to limit cultural conflict and ensure social stability. Advocates of this position can argue that the public sphere is pluricultural, even though its contents and limits are still the exclusive preserve of citizens. Those immigrants who manage to meet the acceptance criteria employed by citizens will find it easier to press their claims. [32] Nevertheless, citizens still have the last word on whether immigrants' cultural needs are met. In contrast with the previous model, the integrationist model of accommodation would mean that citizens are willing to change traditions in the public sphere, to "interculturalize" it, but reject any political say for immigrants in managing the process, whereas they have not yet encountered the acceptance criteria of belonging to the citizenry.

The autonomous model goes a step forward. Only five European countries (Sweden in 1975, Switzerland in 1975, Denmark in 1977, Norway in 1978, and The Netherlands in 1985) have entered this phase, albeit at the local level. [33] In common with the integrationist model, it accepts the need to create a public sphere that is sensitive to immigrants' cultural practices. It therefore supports state-led initiatives in accommodating them. But in contrast with both previous models, it incorporates a notion of justice in which immigrants play a part in determining the policies that affect them. Its participatory nature therefore lends itself to immigrants achieving political autonomy. In other words, immigrants can take part in political processes that determine the nature of the cultural contents and limits to the public sphere, just like any other citizen. In contrast with the previous two models, nationality discrimination, or a politics of citizenship, cannot guide an autonomous model of accommodating immigrants. The criterion to participate politically is not more nationality but residence. It is the only model that separates politics from nationality, and it is endorsed mainly by cosmopolitans.

Let me now pursue this line of reasoning in relation to the second scenario considered below. In passing, one should say it poses a serious challenge for political theorists interested in a multicultural theory of justice.

Scenario 2: The limits of a Political Europe

My contribution in this chapter has been to emphasize that the normative difficulties linking justice and immigration have at their core the strong historical tie between nationality and citizenship. I will conclude by generally reviewing the current European Union institutional structure and recommend some guidelines based on my central thesis: that nationality be replaced by residence as a criterion of orientation in the treatment of immigrants.

When we approach the process of construction of the European Union from the perspective of non-European Union immigrants (the Euro-foreigners) [34] the paradox is apparent. Euro-foreigners simply have no right to freedom of movement. They can maybe hold social rights if they attain permanent resident status (as denizens), but, because of the lack of freedom of movement, they are deprived of such rights in other EU countries. There are simply too many borders for immigrants in the EU. The Union, for them, is simply a closed system, built behind their backs and belonging to a "privileged" club from which they are excluded.

From the viewpoint of justice, there is a pressing need to start a theoretical and institutional debate on the accommodation model that the EU should adopt. If we want to speak of European citizenship in promoting political union in Europe, we ought to be able to speak of Euro-foreigners, something which is still impossible. [35] Similarly, if we want to speak of a political Europe, we ought to be able to speak of a single accommodation policy toward immigrants, not of fifteen policies. When these issues are addressed, they will need to be guided by the principles of justice sketched out above. Without a willingness to address them, future policy will undoubtedly get mired in specious new justifications for ignoring the democratic deficit in Europe. We cannot begin a discourse on justice unless we first face up to the asymmetrical situation experienced by immigrants in the EU.

This debate related to immigrants who are already inside a country and want public institutional recognition is what concerns me. At the moment, only European citizens benefit from this public recognition. In constructing European citizenship, a first step has been reached to detach citizenship from nationality, and hence a powerful argument to defend the autonomous model of accommodation for Euro-foreigners. For European citizenship the principle of nationality has disappeared and has been replaced by the principle of residence. Advocates of foreigners have now a strident institutional example to legitimize their claims. From a European Union point of view, there are no more justifications to maintain this situation.

Accordingly, the principle of residents' Europe rather than the more popular citizens' Europe should be used in designing a European accommodation policy. Three to five years of residence ought to be enough to allow Euro-immigrants to participate politically and ensure that they enjoy a degree of autonomy. Immigrants already living in Europe, whatever their national origins, should enjoy equal treatment and opportunities. Letting them participate in political decision making conforms to the principle that permanent immigrant residents (denizens) should not be deprived of opportunities for political accommodation.[36]

The second institutional change the EU should encounter is related to the pejorative connotation attributed to the immigrant's status, in spite of the efforts to use a new language in the recent Amsterdam Treaty.[37] Since the Maastricht Treaty, the situation is as follows: there is a formal institutionalization of European citizenship, which belongs to the first pillar, and is consequently a common policy and integration field. The opposite notion, "foreigner," "immigrant," in spite of its formal "communitarization" in the Amsterdam Treaty is still a subject of common interest and intergovernmental cooperation.

As these two leading issues show, the need for introducing a language of justice is compelling at the European Union level. To initiate a reflection on the topic, we have to face up to the asymmetrical situation experienced by immigrants in the EU. At the moment, in spite of the formal existence of European citizenship, an immigrant (for instance a Latin American) wanting to live in Spain enjoys a status quite distinct from what he would enjoy in Germany. In part, this is due to the variety of models in European states regarding the accommodation of immigrants and their concepts of nationality and citizenship. In any future European accommodation policy, clearly, application of nationality considerations can have no place.

Notes

1. The pluralism that particularly interests me is the one that questions the implicit "cultural cement" of society. Specifically, the cultural diversity expressed by the existence of territorially dispersed groups: see, among others, J. Raz, "Multiculturalism: A Liberal Perspective," *Dissent* (Winter 1994): 67-79; B. Parekh, "Cultural Diversity and Liberal Democracy," in *Defining and Measuring Democracy,* ed. D. Beetham (London: Sage, 1994), 199-221; W. Kymlicka, *Multicultural Citizenship* (Oxford: Clarendon Press, 1995); F. Requejo, "Pluralismo, democracia y federalismo: Una revisión de la ciudadanía democrática en estados plurinacionales," *Revista Internacional de Filosofía Política,* 7 (May 1996): 93-120; F. Requejo, *Zoom polític* (Barcelona: Proa, 1998).

2. D. Cohn-Bendit and T. H. Schmid, *Ciudadanos de Babel* (Madrid: Talasa, 1995), 45.

3. R. Bauböck, "Introduction," in *The Challenge of Diversity*, ed. R. Bauböck, A. Heller, and A. R. Zolberg (Aldershot: Avebury-European Center Vienna, 1996), 8.

4. W. F. Schwartz, ed., *Justice in Immigration* (Cambridge: Cambridge University Press, 1995).

5. W. Kymlicka, "Liberal Individualism and Liberal Neutrality," *Ethics* 99, (1989): 883-905; *Multicultural Citizenship* (Oxford: Clarendon Press, 1995).

6. In a recent work, Walzer emphasizes that social cultural homogeneity has never existed. When we speak in these terms we mean that "a single dominant group organises the common life in a way that reflects its own history and culture and, if things go as intended, carries the history forward and sustains the culture. . . . Among histories and cultures, the nation-State is not neutral; its political apparatus is an engine for national reproduction": M. Walzer, *On Toleration* (New Haven and London: Yale University Press, 1997), 25). In the last resort this justifies the efforts of the dominant cultural group to perpetuate its own survival, regardless of others and to legislate accordingly. See also, Walzer, "Exclusion, Injustice, and the Democratic State," *Dissent* 40 (1993): 55-64.

7. M. Walzer, "Pluralism in Political Perspective," in *The Politics of Ethnicity*, ed. M. Walzer et al. (Cambridge, Mass.: Harvard University Press, 1982): 12.

8. A. Dummet and A. Nicol, *Subjects, Citizens, Aliens and Others. Nationality and Immigration Law* (London: Weidenfeld and Nicholson, 1990); J. G. Kellas, *The Politics of Nationalism and Ethnicity* (London: MacMillan, 1991); M. Wieviorka, ed., *Une société fragmentée? Le multiculturalisme en débat* (Paris: La Découverte, 1997); *Le racisme, une introduction* (Paris: La Découverte, 1998).

9. See Walzer, "Pluralism in Political Perspective," 19-21.

10. Walzer, "Pluralism in Political Perspective," 24-27.

11. M. Walzer, *Spheres of Justice: A Defense of Pluralism and Equality* (New York: Basic Books, 1983). Hereafter, SJ.

12. See also J. F. Hollifield, *Immigrants, Markets, and States* (Cambridge, Mass.: Harvard University Press, 1992), and R. Zapata-Barrero, "Justicia para extranjeros: mercado e inmigración," *Revista Española de Investigaciones Sociológicas* 90 (2000): 159-81.

13. It is true that Walzer gives some arguments discriminating between foreigners at the access stage. However, he places insufficient stress on admission obligations. His rationale allows us to accept that these limits should be applied equally to everyone, independently of the nationality of the applicant, despite his defense of limits on admission. Walzer's most critical arguments address what happens once foreigners have been admitted. Here injustice is much more palpable. At this level, citizens unjustly rule over denizens with whom they share the territory.

14. Mainly under the pressure of globalization and multiculturalism in its two main dimensions: the plurality of national identities and immigration. See for instance R. Axtmann, *Liberal Democracy into the Twenty-First Century: Globalization, Integration and the Nation State* (Manchester: Manchester University Press, 1996). It is not possible to

cover the full complexity of this argument here. Accordingly, I will limit myself to opening up this line of research. I am, however, convinced that nationality is an artificial construct, which is employed in much the same way as religion was in the past and has more to do with outmoded notions of "loyalty" than the needs of modern states (see J. Habermas, *La inclusión del otro. Estudios de teoria política* (Barcelona: Paidós, 1999). This current system of allegiance is the core issue facing liberal democratic institutions today in accommodating immigrants. Institutions need to change as a result.

15. I broadly take the cultural definition of nation linked to Y. Tamir's project in *Liberal Nationalism* (Princeton, N.J.: Princeton University Press, 1993), 8-9.

16. J. Elster, *The Cement of Society* (Cambridge: Cambridge University Press, 1989).

17. This issue is being discussed from different viewpoints by, among others, J. H. Carens, "Aliens and Citizens: The Case for Open Borders," *The Review of Politics* 49, no. 2 (1987): 251-73, and "Liberalism and Culture," *Constellations* 4, no. 1 (1997): 35-47; J. Waldron, "Minority Cultures and the Cosmopolitan Alternative," *University of Michigan Journal of Law Reform*, 25, no. 3-4 (1992): 751-93; W. F. Schwartz, ed., *Justice in Immigration*; R. Axtmann, *Liberal Democracy into the Twenty-First Century: Globalization, Integration and the Nation State*; T. K. Oomen, *Citizenship, Nationality, and Ethnicity* (Cambridge: Polity Press, 1997); V. Bader, "Fairly Open Borders," in *Citizenship and Exclusion*, ed. V. Bader (London: MacMillan Press, 1997); J. M. Rosales, "Liberal Reformism and Democratic Citizenship," *Citizenship Studies* 2, no. 2 (July 1998): 257-72.

18. J. H. Carens, "Immigration, Welfare, and Justice," in *Justice in Immigration*, ed. W. F. Schwartz (Cambridge: Cambridge University Press, 1995), 10.

19. R. Zapata-Barrero, "Etica y política de inmigración," *Revista de Treball Social* 146 (1997): 68-87.

20. These two positions broadly correspond to what J. Hampton calls the consensual and the nonconsensual ideal-types of understanding membership. See her "Immigration, Identity, and Justice," in *Justice in Immigration*, ed. W. F. Schwartz (Cambridge: Cambridge University Press, 1995), 67-93.

21. K. Hailbronner, "Citizenship and Nationhood in Germany," in *Immigration and the Politics of Citizenship in Europe and North America,* ed. W. R. Brubaker (Lanham, Md.: University Press of America, 1989), 67-79.

22. According to T. Hammar, "State, Nation, and Dual Citizenship," in *Immigration and the Politics of Citizenship in Europe and North America,* ed. W. R. Brubaker, 81-95.

23. J. H. Carens, "Membership and Morality: Admission to Citizenship in Liberal Democratic States," in *Immigration and the Politics of Citizenship in Europe and North America,* ed. W. R. Brubaker, 31-37.

24. I. M. Young, *Justice and the Politics of Difference* (Princeton, N.J.: Princeton University Press, 1990).

25. B. Parekh, "British Citizenship and Cultural Difference," in *Citizenship*, ed. G. Andrews (London: Lawrence and Wishart, 1991), 183-204.

26. See M. J. Miller, "Political Participation and Representation of Noncitizens," in *Immigration and the Politics of Citizenship in Europe and North America,* ed. W. R. Brubaker, 129-43; Z. Layton-Henry, "The Challenge of Political Rights," in *The Political Rights of Migrant Workers in Western Europe* , ed. Z. Layton-Henry (London: Sage, 1990), 1-26, and "Citizenship or Denizenship for Migrant Workers?," in *The Political Rights of Migrant Workers in Western Europe*, 186-95; U. Andersen, "Consultative Institutions for Migrant Workers," in *The Political Rights of Migrant Workers in Western Europe*, 113-26; J. Rath, "Voting Rights," in *The Political Rights of Migrant Workers in Western Europe*, 127-57.

27. As defined by R. Dahl, *La democracia y sus críticos* (Barcelona: Paidós, 1992), 354.

28. R. Zapata-Barrero, "Estabilidad democrática y pluralismo cultural: ¿necesitamos

una nueva teoría de la ciudadanía?" *Revista Internacional de Filosofía Política* 13 (1999): 119-49; *Ciudadanía, democracia y pluralismo cultural: hacia un nuevo contrato social* (Barcelona: Editorial Proyecto A, 2000).

29. See R. E. Goodin, "If People Were Money . . .," in *Free Movement: Ethical Issues in the Transnational Migration of People and of Money*, ed. B. Barry and R. E. Goodin (College Park: Pennsylvania State University Press, 1992), 6-22; M. Weiner, *The Global Migration Crisis: Challenge to States and to Human Rights* (New York: HarperCollins, 1995); J. H. Carens, "Realistic and Idealistic Approaches to the Ethics of Migration" *International Migration Review* 30, no. 1 (1996): 156-70; D. Jacobson, *Rights across Borders: Immigration and the Decline of Citizenship* (London: Johns Hopkins University Press, 1996).

30. J. Rex, *Ethnic Minorities in the Modern Nation State* (London: MacMillan Press, 1996); R. Bauböck, A. Heller, and A. R. Zolberg, eds., *The Challenge of Diversity* (Aldershot: Avebury-European Center Vienna, 1996); B. Parekh, "Integrating Minorities in a Multicultural Society," in *Citizenship, Multiculturalism and the State*, ed. U. K. Preuß and F. Requejo (Baden-Baden: Nomos, 1998), 67-86.

31. J. Gray, "The Politics of Cultural Diversity," in *Post-Liberalism: Studies in Political Thought* (NewYork: Routledge, 1993), 253-71.

32. See C. Taylor, *Multiculturalism and "the Politics of Recognition,"* ed. A. Gutmann (Princeton: Princeton University Press, 1992).

33. D. Lapeyronnie, ed., *Immigrés en Europe: Politiques locales d'integration* (Paris: La Documentation Française, 1991).

34. R. Zapata-Barrero, "Thinking European Citizenship from the Perspective of an Eventual Euro-Foreigner," in *Citizenship, Multiculturalism and the State*, ed. U. K. Preuß and F. Requejo, 151-68; "El Euro-extranjero en una eventual Unión Política," *El País-Catalunya*, 10 June 1998, 6.

35. R. Zapata-Barrero, "Ciudadanía europea y extranjería," *Claves de Razón Práctica* 87 (1998): 29-35.

36. I am applying this principle to the city of Barcelona in an ongoing research funded by the *Fundació Jaume Bofill,* My framework is both normative (models of accommodation) and institutional (I interview the main actors involved in accommodation policies in various sectors, including health services, education, etc.).

37. Zapata-Barrero, "Ciutadania de la Unió i immigració: balanç institucional i desafiaments normatius."

Chapter 16

Globalization and Differentiality in Human Rights

José Rubio-Carracedo

Translated by José M. Rosales

Globalization is already a consolidated trend in the economy and telecommunications, and a growing trend in the political, cultural, and social realms. Indeed, as a structural phenomenon, it is unstoppable.

However, the direction of globalization is still undecided. To some extent, it proceeds like the industrial revolution: it was unstoppable where it was realizable, in spite of the resistence by physiocrats, socialists, and anarchists. Instead of fighting to regulate industrialization within humane and social margins, their reaction proved a failure. Especially the latter were unable to recognize the fact of industrial changes. Marx himself erroneously took the Industrial Revolution and capitalism to be identical, as Dahrendorf demostrated. [1] Hence, a notable part of his theory lost the point. At the end, Marx conceded the inevitability, given the appropriate conditions, of the Industrial Revolution. According to his theory of historical materialism, the industrial (capitalist) mode of production should overcome the feudal mode. And, subsequently, socialism would overcome the industrial mode of production.

A more reasonable aim and expectation would have been to give a socialist imprint to the process of industrialization. Furthermore, liberalism was frequently identified with capitalism, beyond the latter's clear incompatibility with the spirit of the liberal Revolutions. These errors and misconceptions, taken by their successors into different directions, stained with tragedy, instead of hope, the twentieth century.

Universalist Logic versus Differentialist Logic

The current debate in favor or against globalization may turn in the end to be useless, for reasons both of approach and of attitude. The debate itself evinces a dispute between universalists and differentialists, although, as I will argue, it reproduces a misleading antagonism between two logics: the universalist and the differentialist.

Advocates of the former, acritical heirs to the modernizing Enlightenment program, tend to identify globalization with the spread of neoliberalism (or, better, a post-liberal approach.) This trend aims to achieve an economic and cultural Westernization of the globe through a process of simple integration (by homogenization), induced or even imposed in extreme cases by the economic and political might of multinationals. Accordingly, globalization means Westernization of the economic, cultural, and political structures. Even the universalization of humans rights is taken frequently as a paternalist imposition of the liberal creed—somehow, a form of Western fundamentalism.

Another version of the universalist logic proves more critical toward the Enlightenment legacy. We may call it cosmopolitanism. It carefully distinguishes the spirit from the wording of the legacy, and it aims toward a free and contextualized universalization of human rights. These are taken as moral values of universal intent, though their current synthesis has been implemented by the liberal revolutions and the UN Declarations of 1948 (New York) and 1993 (Vienna). Thus, human rights constitute the moral standard for every State, recognized or not, a signatory or not of these universal declarations. The new International Law, especially after the Covenants of 1966, makes them binding documents for all the states.

Next we find the radical advocates of the differentialist logic, who tend to deny the legitimacy of globalization. Not only as an economic, political, and cultural trend, but also the critique affects the universalization of human rights, which are taken mainly as liberal, i.e., Western, rights. The extreme version opposes cosmopolitanism as groundless and illegitimate in its aspiration, incompatible as it is with cultural relativism. This position grounds the fundamentalist and neotribal versions of radical nationalism and of radical multiculturalism.

Other differentialist versions are more moderate and realistic, thus yielding to moderate, democratic nationalism and to moderate multiculturalism—encompassing both the dialectics of cultures under conditions of freedom and equality. My thesis in this chapter is that only the radicalized versions of both logics are really antagonistic, whereas their moderate versions are not only compatible but also complementary to each other. Actually, for the past decades the differentialist logic has radicalized its postulates, probably in response to Western globalization. But in the end it turns out to be an autonomous logic, oriented toward the protection and encouragement of differential features—differential indeed as opposed to common and shared features. The moderate approach also privileges the peculiar against the common, but it does not oppose the universal nor the cosmopolitan. I will argue that it is not contradictory to say "I am differential and cosmopolitan," at least with regard to the universal standards described by social anthropology for more than a century now. The same, likewise, can be applied to the sentence "I am cosmopolitan and differential." Only their extremist versions are exclusionary and unjustifiable by reflexive means.

Postmodernism and the "Bad Conscience" of the West

Ever since Alexander the Great, the West has obsessively pursued a colonizing expansion under integration patterns. But it has been during the past two centuries when we have experienced the reaction of non-Western civilizations to the expansionist trend of the West. Unfortunately, even human rights, the great Western legacy, have been taken as a part of global neoliberalism. Many writers, arguing under the umbrella of postmodernism, have adopted this critique, thus losing the point of the real humane improvement introduced by human rights—and silencing the Western tortuous process of recognition.

The origins of human rights can be traced back to two different legacies: the Stoic (under the project of cosmopolitan equality and fraternity) and the Christian (which is also a cosmopolitan synthesis of Eastern influences.) It is highly significant that the doctrine of human rights has an oriental influence, lately reformulated under Western, more rational patterns. Western culture has always been a syncretic culture, open to influences from all other cultures. To the extent that profound episodes of "bad conscience," provoking crisis, have reemerged from time to time, hence, Western culture, as Karl Popper observed, is the least ethnocentrist of all, precisely because its origins were so syncretic and favored a constant opening to other cultures.

An example of this attitude—not the most radical—is a recent essay by Giacomo Marramao. There, this representative of the postmodern left argues that the triple ideal of the liberal revolutions—liberty, equality, and fraternity—the ideals that legitimize Western universalism in virtue of its emancipatory legacy, "underlies *ab originibus* to a monocultural condition." This is so because it entails of its own "the logic of identity and of identification," so long as it is the "own mechanism of the western logos."[2] Aims to exorcize its "logo-fonocentrism" by appeals to the difference (from Herder to Nietzsche) have proved useless and illusory, since it is, according to Marramao, a closed logical model, unable to self-rectify. Its universalizing objective, therefore, becomes self-refuting. The consequence is clear: better for the rest of cultures to repel such a harmful colonization. Marramao, however, exaggerates the Western logocentrism. Indeed, the enlightened, homogenizing reason received serious corrections ever since Hume. The critiques by Rousseau are especially relevant, as his work inspires Romanticism and differentialism (Herder, Lessing, Schiller, and, more directly, Schopenhauer, Marx, Nietzsche, Freud) and whose reformulation of the Enlightenment ideals (through authors as different as Weber or Heidegger) reach to our postmoderns.

Another exaggeration is Marramao's judgment that the momentum reached by postmodernity and by communitarianism certify the breaking up of the West's cultural sphere.[3] The limits of its *discordia concors* have been far enough exceeded to the extent that Western culture has definitively fallen apart. This fact and the global "emergence of irreducible ethico-cultural differences" certify the failure of Western logocentrism. For more than two decades, instead of a presumed "universal homologation," the sign of the times shows a way "diametrically opposed to universalism." The internal critiques by communitarian and postmodern thinkers, who from different standpoints see that "the institutions of universalism represent the realm of Big Chill," confirm that Western universalism is dead and happily dead.[4]

Yet are we facing an irreversible rupture of the Western civilizing model and witnessing the failure of its universalist design? For lack of better arguments, we can think that the West is going through another, endemic crisis—an imbalance we need certainly to adjust. This two-centuries-old history points out that the Enlightenment's hegemony is far from definitive. The Western culture, on the contrary, keeps on dialectically receiving influences from the rest of the cultures.

Besides, Marramao is right when he denounces "the forgotten dimension," namely, fraternity.[5] Indeed the West has concentrated mainly on the conciliation of freedom and equality. He is also right when he characterizes this oversight as symptomatic: the early hegemony of liberalism (of capitalist liberalism) obscured fraternity's claims as a mere religious demand. Socialism, for its part, stressed the vindications of equality while placing on an imagined future the building of a fraternal world.

But that "bad conscience," justified as it is, can lead us neither to relativism nor to nihilism. The accusation of ethnocentrism is not always fair. I would rather propose the following criterion: the actions (economic, political, etc.) aimed directly or indirectly to privilege Western culture are ethnocentrist; instead, those aimed to protect from violation any human right, as long as it is objective and shares a reference to human dignity, are not ethnocentrist.

Indeed we are not fair. For example, all of us condemn, because of the violation of human rights, the Rushdie affair, although the "fatwa" belongs to his culture; and likewise, we condemn the brutal use of torture by numerous states; or the clitoris extirpation, so widely practiced in Africa, but also in the immigrants' Europe. However, we tend unjustifiably to tolerate the use of the veil in the European public school (imposed on Muslim girls by family or religious pressure) or the caste system—both being refined forms of oppression and hence of violation of human rights. Under this criterion of imposed homogenization we would be still living in the Inquisition days. So, any discriminatory practice based on cultural or religious claims should be rejected in light of basic human rights, whatever the authority conceded to those claims by the cultural or religious community. This is even more urgent when the violations happen within immigrant communities living in Western countries. I thus subscribe to John Rawls's criterion that human rights "set" the limits of recognition and pluralism "among peoples."[6]

The Myth of Cultural Incommensurability

Probably it was Herder who first launched the myth of cultural self-identity, which supported the incommensurability among cultures. Accordingly, each culture would be an autonomous dominion of meanings, a plain and inevitable autarchy: knowledge, techniques, values, rites, gestures, etc.—only fully intelligible within its global cultural frame. Intercultural influences would have an analogical or instrumental reach, precisely because cultures are incommensurable systems to each other.

Some anthropologists and sociologists (cultural relativists) have defended this myth. Yet even such a distinguished relativist as Herskovits recognized at the end the existence of "cultural universals": the family, kinship, rites, tabooes, or the "golden rule" of ethics.[7] Certainly those universals can be applied in different ways. The Inuit, for example, hold that the members of the community must honor and take care of their parents. Thus they think this precept favors certain forms of active euthanasia, while Westeners in contrast have established harsh forms of dystanasia with the same aim.

The commandment is, no doubt, the same for both cultures. Each one is an autonomous system, structured into functional subsystems, albeit strongly interrelated. However, no culture is a closed universe of its own, as implied by cultural relativists. On the contrary, every culture is open both to inner changes and to external influences. Needless to say, there are many degress of openness and of closure, but from this point of view Western culture is the most dynamic of all, due to its syncretic origins. Hence its ecclecticism and its incessant crisis.

Yet incommensurability is still a matter of discussion, though a groundless myth. The history of all civilizations demonstrates the real permeability among cultures, either under conditions of fair exchange or under conditions of oppression. So the cases of presumed incommensurability should be analyzed as independent, and not universal processes of inintelligible exchanges, caused by different reasons in each case.

The MacIntyre-Gewirth debate is very instructive in this respect, as it deals with issues such as moral epistemology, cultural relativism, the relation of virtues to rights, and—at least implicitly—the philosophical intercultural discourse. Furthermore, beneath the debate lies the old Western disjunction between teleology (Aristotle) and deontology (Stoicism, Kant). As it is well known, Alasdair MacIntyre criticizes Alan Gewirth's theory for being, according to MacIntyre, the highest example of a deontologist approach. [8] Indeed, Gewirth elaborates a theory of morality in terms of a theory of human rights, which he sums up in his revision of Kant's categorical imperative, now turned into the "principle of generic consistency." [9]

MacIntyre deems any rational-teleological approach inadequate to justify moral obligation. Such an approach should always assume the existence of previous social institutions. That would be like cashing a check without funds. For MacIntyre rights do not exist—the belief in rights being as illusory as the belief "in witches and unicorns." [10] Human rights, as MacIntyre points out, are not only "normative entities" counterfactually valid. They also have "empirical correlates" (which neither witches nor unicorns have). And, no doubt, violations of human rights are far from being fictions. These indubitable negative realities induce the social-rational justification of human rights, that way they are univer-sally recognized and legally guaranteed with no exception based on race, age, sex, etc. Gewirth himself has remarked that the lack of a similar concept in any culture would not justify the inference of the inexistence, or unreality, of human rights.[11]

Here we enter the logic of the historical and the contingent. The notion of human rights was relatively weak in the West until the liberal Revolutions of the 18th century. The Revolutions would have hardly succeeded, had those antecedents in despotic regimes never existed. This same process may be happening in different cultures from equivalent convictions, though they seem different in the first instance. As Gewirth argues, the individual's rights claims come logically prior to the social rules that legitimize them once they have been recognized. For a political community only legitimizes what it recognizes as rights, but rights already existed in logical-normative terms before their normative-institutional recognition.

Cultural relativism fails at both levels. According to cultural relativists, each culture is autarchic both symbolically and institutionally. Hence they affirm the uselessness of UN declarations and of international treaties demanding the respect of rights (meaning Western rights), because in practice any state will interpret them according to its cultural features. However, given the existence of cultural universals and the fact that every culture has a concept of human dignity, similar at least in the negative sense, it is possible to build upon that ground, through the intercultural dialectics, a certain universal code of human rights (we may remember how the application of torture under the Inquisition had its own code of "due process").

Certainly the task of translation and transcultural interpretation is immense and is subject to many errors and deviations. But to recognize its utility is not to deny its possibility. There are some issues in which the controversy will be especially long and hard: basically, the recognition of the individuals as the preferent subjects of rights, although the West should elaborate a concept of the individual that reflects their communitarian bonds—that is, the bonds of a complex citizenship.[12] But it is not difficult to get to an agreement on certain fundamental rights, like the rights to life, freedom (at least, as it opposes any form of imposed serfdom), basic guarantees of personal and collective security, due process, nondiscrimination based on race, sex, age, religion, etc., access to a family, house, work, basic health services, respect, and protection from torture and from emigration because of political persecution or subsistence reasons. Indeed, the agreements and legal recognitions of international justice, and also of international law, are ample enough. The remaining task points to their due implementation—but not only through humanitarian interventions.

The Universalizing Claim of Human Rights

I began this chapter with the assertion that globalization is a structural phenomenon, unstoppable as such, albeit its full realization is still at stake: either by imposing a Western assimilation or by facilitating an intercultural dialectics under conditions of freedom and equality. The market economy is bound to reign everywhere—and the same can be said of new technologies. For both cases the Western imprint is clear, but both realms need better (self)regulations to avoid distortions. In axiological terms, the universalizing claim of human rights is only analogous, as (in contrast with the economic-technological model, originating in the West) the original inspiration for human rights comes from the East, although lately inspirations were reformulated according to Western patterns, notably Stoic and Christian. So, it is fair to expect that the East contributes again strongly to the development of human rights, as their process of reformulation remains open and fully receptives to new influences.

To illustrate this, we may remember how the first generation of liberal rights (civil and political) was followed by a second generation of economic and social rights. The recognition of the second generation enforced the reformulation of some precedent rights, such the right to unlimited property. Now, a third generation of rights concerning solidarity and peoples, together with cultural rights, is coming, endorsed mainly by African peoples. But this recent process is provoking a reassessment of the very concept of individual rights.[13]

The outcomes of the crisis are uncertain but we can take it as a growth and readjustment crisis, which will imply a more careful differentiation between the profound moral core of human rights and their institutional covering. In the West, both were mixed due to the imperatives of its legal culture. But I see no reason to stop a further clarification of the Western concept of human rights. Hence the intercultural dialectics of human rights turns out to be not only possible but also necessary and fertile. We Westerners have still much to learn about human rights.

Some intercultural studies demonstrate this. Here I will focus briefly on the research by Chinese and Western scholars working within the framework of Confucianism—apparently unfitted to the culture of human rights. [14] Remarkable is the effort made by the Chinese scholars to retrieve and reconstruct the Confucian tradition, though with no intention of discovering antecedents to human rights. The humanist legacy of Confucianism is contained basically in the "mandate from Heaven" (*tianming*), according to which the emperor's authority has a vicar meaning—its exercise depends on the consent of the people. Different conditions include that political power in China has been clearly despotic and that the Confucian postulate of benevolent government has been interpreted in paternalistic terms with no real guarantees for the citizens.

However, it should be noted how the Confucian tradition that requires one to "behave like a human being" refers to "rites," instead of "rights," and how the attitude of "filial piety" is the hegemonic value. Confucianism moves in a particularistic *Weltanschauung*, with no pretension to universality. But we can confront this new challenge and check its degree of openness and flexibility.

On the other hand, for Confucianism the cardinal virtues are compassion, decency, modesty, and the sense of fairness-unfairness. So they are different axiological traditions that can be, however, more complementary than antagonistic to each other. Confucianism does not lead to any doctrine of human rights, though some scholars remind us that the Confucian virtues are more rights than obligations. But almost all the studies conclude that the Confucian tradition has since deviated from its origins, and even been perverted by modernization. The "Machiavellian" moment could be situated in the *Four Texts of the Yellow Emperor*, a book that legitimizes the supremacy of the emperor (although it warns of the abuses of power) and stresses the calculus of interests, as well as the material survival and a conservative observation of the laws. But the use of torture, so frequent and almost normalized in Chinese history, has never been theoretically legitimized. Surprisingly, it comes contextualized with the guarantist norm of the Confucian tradition that forces confession by the accused before conviction. (Also in the West the tribunal of the Inquisition made a systematic use of torture to get the confession of alleged culprits of heresy, under the same belief-excuse that the torment acted as a truth drug—hence the quasi-procedural rule of "torture the accused until confession.")

Indeed, these deviations have been persistently denounced by some reformists, radical or moderate, since the nineteenth century. The epilogue by one of the editors, Tu Weiming, is an interesting attempt to synthesize Confucian humanism, Kantian liberalism, and communitarianism; the result being a positive golden rule: "In order to establish ourselves, we must help others to establish themselves; in order to enlarge ourselves, we must help others to enlarge themselves." [15] It is also instructive to see how commentators of the Confucian tradition come closer to Gewirth than to MacIntyre as regards their dispute about the former's thesis on morality as a theory of human rights.

We have to take into account, nonetheless, that the requisite of universality is, and always will be, a complex discussion upon values or, more precisely, upon axiological codes. Then we have to consider insufficient and even simplistic the pretensions of a rational foundation for human rights, understandable and acceptable by all cultures, be it utilitarianist or neo-Kantian. Gewirth's justification is valid only for the West, and even here it raises disputes. Also, transcendental or quasi-transcendental approaches that take moral subjects as capable of acting according to universal, but ahistorical, principles should be abandoned, as claimed by Marramao. [16]

The failure of Rawls's *The Law of Peoples* becomes apparent. [17] The reason is that the conflicts of values cannot be reduced to mere questions of logical coherence or incoherence, as the neo-utilitarians think; nor can the starting point be an unreal rapprochement of liberal and hierarchical societies, as Rawls argues to the extreme that the outcome of both "original positions" would be equivalent, mean-ing a set of basic human rights acceptable by all, except by arbitrary regimes. We can also refer to the Habermasian model, grounded on assumptions almost entirely cognitivist, that reduce the value conflicts to logical-scientific discussions. According to this model, although only one proposal can be right, all of them must be compatible with each other and form a coherent ensemble. Today it is obvious that the consensus should be based on minimum standards. Beyond that, the axiological pluralism enters into force, above all in the interpretation and application of values.

But the critique of cognitivist abuses does not justify adopting an irrationalist stand and declaring, as Rorty does, that the solution lies in the education of sentiments. Rorty is right when he insists that we should abandon the old Natural Law assumption, still alive in the Western conscience, that has inspired the attempts to reach a universal consensus on human rights. The experience shows that every culture is spontaneously ethnocentrist and accordingly considers all other cultures inhumane to different degrees. From this consideration of inhumanity stems xenophobia and cultural domination. Hence Rorty assumes Eduardo Rabossi's thesis that "human rights foundationalism" is "outmoded and irrelevant." [18] For both authors the search for universal human rights had been already abandoned in the second half of the twentieth century—the current aspiration is not based on any philosophical theory but on the political will created in the West after the Holocaust.

This new vision of the problem is revealing, but also unilateral. As it is well known, the question remains open whether the true motor of the Western tradition of human rights is philosophy (the enlightenened doctrine of human rights sprung from a rationalist Natural Law doctrine) or the historical tradition of the Bills of Rights. What happened was that both sources converged around the liberal revolutions to bring about the French Declaration of the Rights of Man and of the citizen (1789). Certainly, the declaration soon fell into a latent state, but only in a latent sense did the UN Universal Declaration of Human Rights (1948) mean a refoundation of human rights. The UN Declaration entailed a recasting of the principles themselves, but above all, the implementation of a universalizing program, burdened, however, by the Western liberal view.

Rorty advances a new approach based upon the principle that Western foundationalism, of any type, should be abandoned in favor of our moral intuitions. These do not describe universal human nature, but guide us pragmatically in the task of achieving our life. Rorty assumes the epistemology of pragmatism, from Peirce to Dewey, that took beliefs as a guide for action and asserted that the only possible human progress should come from sentiments and not from institutions. The point is not to worry about the essence of man, "Kant's question," but to question "what sort of world can we prepare for our great-grandchildren?"[19] Here Rorty notably approaches MacIntyre: Kantian deontologism should be abandoned in favor of concrete virtues, that is, the education of sentiments (love, friendship, trust, solidarity). For Rorty "the goal of this manipulation of sentiment is to expand the reference of the terms 'our kind of people' and 'people like us.'"[20] To sum up, "producing generations of nice, tolerant, well-off, secure, other-respecting students of this sort in all parts of the world," argues Rorty, "is just what is needed—indeed *all* that is needed—to achieve an Enlightenment utopia."[21]

But Rorty does not seem to notice how he is attacking a unilateral standpoint from another unilaterial approach. Rationalism cannot be rectified simply by irrationalism. Only a balanced synthesis of both can produce a satisfactory result. His disjunction between sentiments and reason is neither possible nor real: "To rely on the suggestions of sentiment rather than on the commands of reason."[22] Obviously, the new cosmopolis cannot be built only upon rational arguments. The education of sentiments requires some deliberation not to become a mere manipulation. Also, it will be necessary to rely on institutions, as a complement to the narrativity of modelic examples.[23]

Reality and Fiction in the Globalization of Human Rights (The Vienna World Conference of 1993)

The conviction, widely shared, that the 1948 Declaration has a Western bias and that this should be rectified in order to open the conception toward a really universal horizon moved the UN General Assembly to convene in 1990 a World Conference on Human Rights. It was finally held in Vienna in June 1993. The preparatory proceedings included the organization of three regional meetings (convening states from Africa, Latin America and the Caribbean, and Asia and the Pacific). Afterward an Islamic Conference was convened. The four conferences issued their respective declations (Tunis, in November 1992; San José, in January 1993; Bangkok, in April 1993; and Cairo, in August 1993). All tried to underline their differential peculiarities (cultural, economic, and political). The first three conferences made partial corrections to the 1948 Declaration, while the fourth—the Cairo Declaration of Human Rights in Islam—entailed a thorough revision.[24] Also China held a remarkably critical position.[25]

The Vienna Conference was held between the 14th and the 25th of June 1993. The antecedents created by the four previous regional conferences paved the way for recasting the meanings of cultural relativism and of cultural differences within the framework of a universal conception of human rights. However, the final document, Declaration and Programme of Action of the Vienna World Conference on Human Rights, stressed the universality of human rights and recognized only minor exceptions concerning differentiality.[26] Probably the chance to proceed in the right direction was finally lost, but it proved that differentiated universality advances slowly—both in the intellectual community and in the official delegations.[27]

Indeed, the Vienna Declaration draws on the work done by the four regional conferences, as well as on claims advanced by intergovernmental and nongovernmental organizations. The Tunis Declaration recognizes that the character of human rights is "unquestionable." Consequently, it declares that all the states must protect and promote them, "regardless of their political, economic and cultural systems" (art. 2). But it also affirms that no single model can be universally promoted at the expense of the traditions, norms, and values of each people (art. 5). The Bangkok Declaration acknowledges the universal character of human rights. However, it recommends that they be interpreted inside the context of each culture, keeping in mind both the current importance of national and regional peculiarities and the different historical, cultural, and religious antecedents (art. 8). The San José Declaration is the least differentialist of all. The Cairo Islamic Conference, instead, contrasts the Islamic values with the UN Declaration. This raises the issue that in matters concerning the universalization of human rights, Islam is still a significant challenge.

On its part, the Vienna Declaration has four general aims: to "reaffirm" the universal character of human rights; to develop a "programme of action;" to endorse and introduce human rights of the third generation (rights of the peoples, rights of solidarity); to acknowledge the need to respect the value and the diversity of cultures and identities. The first two objectives are clear and well known; the third and fourth ones require a further analysis, as—to my knowledge—they have not been sufficiently characterized.

There is a major dispute concerning the meaning and reach of the so-called third generation human rights, advanced by the Banjul Chart of 1981, that constitute the most remarkable contribution of the Third World's moral sensibility. The rights are presented as collective rights (the rights of the peoples). This declaration proves almost unintelligible in Western legal terms and sounds strange in contrast to the liberal revolutions (primacy of the individual over the community.)[28] In the preamble, the document recognizes that all peoples have the right to self-determination, in virtue of which peoples freely determine their political condition and achieve their economic, social, and cultural development.

The recognition is generic, as it shows the preferential *locus* of application: peoples oppressed by colonial domination or other forms of foreign domination or occupation. However, it introduces an important condition when it points out that the recognition of this right neither authorizes nor endorses any action aimed at breaking or undermining, totally or partially, the territorial integrity or the political unity of sovereign and independent states with democratic systems and representative governments (art. 2). Next, the Banjul Chart recognizes the "right to development" and "to a healthy environment." Both include specifications on the right to enjoy scientific progress and its applications, which in turn leads to recommendations for alleviation of the developing countries' foreign debt, as well as adoption of efficient measures to avoid extreme poverty (arts. 10-14.)

Lastly, the Vienna Declaration confirms in energetic terms the condemnation of all forms of racism and xenophobia (art. 15), apartheid (art. 16); the acts, methods and terrorist practices of all forms and manifestations, as well as drug trafficking (art. 17); and the discrimination of women and sexual exploitation (art. 18). It also makes an explicit recognition of the rights of minorities to their own culture, to profess and practice their religion, to use their own language in public and private, freely and without interference and discrimination (art. 19). This right refers also to indigenous peoples (art. 20). Next, the Declaration acknowledges the specific rights of children (art. 21), disabled people (art. 22), refugees (art. 23), migrant workers (art. 24), and the poor and socially excluded (art. 25). The Declaration makes the states responsible for the efficient implementation of human rights and for the reparation of their violations (art. 28). Thus, it specifically mentions crimes against humanity (arts. 29-30) and advances a program to promote human rights through educative and institutional actions (arts. 31-37 and the whole second part of the Declaration).

Explicit mention is made of nongovernmental organizations. Their actions, the Declaration remarks, should not exonerate states from their responsibilities (art. 38). However, the Declaration does not address the necessary restructuring of the UN's mentality, which includes the abolition of the right to veto within the Security Council in order to improve its efficacy and credibility.

As regards the fourth aim, the Declaration reaffirms, almost obsessively, the universal character of human rights, which should be balanced with the explicit recognition of cultural differences. This has been already underlined, but it is worth noting how it declares that "*All human rights are universal, indivisible and interdependent and interrelated.*" Furthermore, it prescribes that "the international community must treat human rights globally in a fair and equal manner, *on the same footing, and with the same emphasis.*" Next, it warns that "While *the significance of national and regional particularities and various historical, cultural and religious backgrounds must be borne in mind*, it is the duty of States, regardless of their political, economic and cultural systems, to promote and protect all human rights and fundamental freedoms" (art. 5, my emphasis.).

The recognition of the importance of cultural differences is thus carefully contextualized: all human rights officially recognized must be accepted and cultural differences are relevant to their contexts of application. But they can neither be the source of new rights nor can they induce a recasting of the UN list of rights. The Declaration also establishes that "while development facilitates the enjoyment of all human rights, the lack of development may not be invoked to justify the abridgement of internationally recognized human rights". (art. 10). Lastly, the Declaration closely binds human rights and fundamental freedoms to democracy and development. Hence, it declares that these concepts are "interdependent and mutually reinforcing" (art. 8). This is obvious from a Western point of view, but not so for other cultures and sensibilities. The Declaration, therefore, constitutes an important landmark in the consolidation of the doctrine of human rights both universal and differential. The latter aspect is still insufficiently developed and the remarks made about their interdependent character and their irrevocable condition seem to be more a strategic argumentation than a reflexive justification.

Conclusion

Cosmopolitan universalism, embracing human rights under conditions of intercultural interpretation, is not only compatible with a moderate differentialism, but also with a reflexive pluralism. Both movements or logics complement each other inexorably: they combine the ideal of being cosmopolitan and pluralist differential. Cosmopolitanism is a Western conquest that cannot be waived. But the liberal revolutions that crystallized into human rights incorporated the influences of

Eastern cultures. Cosmopolitanism privileges the free and equal flourishing of individuals in a framework both communitarian and universalist. But the free and equal individuals are not only cosmopolitan citizens but also citizens of a specific culture and country, whose *humus* provides the groundwork and meaning for their initiatives. So, we should then pass from toleration to the recognition of the differential.

In this sense, the current booming of multiculturalism should be considered a positive reaction against the abuses of the *melting pot,* although it tends to reach the opposite extreme. Obviously, the cultural melting pot cannot be based on unequal or unfair exchange. But to overcome it in the direction of no melting pot at all is no logical response. Besides, it leads to a new tribalism that induces the subordination of the individuals to their community or state. As I said earlier: neither forced, one-dimensional homogenization nor defensive withdrawl toward one's own *ethnie* tribe, or clan, living in artificially closed enclaves. The recognition of the other is the first step. Then the logic of active toleration demands a step forward (concerning the recognition of the other's opinions, values, and institutions) to generate the transcultural dialectics.

What is now clear is that the future will be a common future for all, on the side of technological and economic globalization; but it will also be the future of a cosmopolitanism open to the relevant differences of the other.[29] To sum up: first, only if we appeal to moderate universalism or cosmopolitanism can we avoid a relapse into the new tribalism or radical nationalism; second, the Enlightenment universalism has forcefully imposed the model of Western civilization. Its antidote is neither multiculturalism nor radical differentialism, but reflexive pluralism and moderate nationalism, where cosmopolitans and reasonable differentialists combine.

Notes

1. Ralf Dahrendorf, *Class and Class Conflict in Industrial Society* (London: Routledge & Kegan Paul, 1959).

2. Giacomo Marramao, "Universalismo y políticas de la diferencia," in *Universalidad y diferencia*, ed. S. Giner and R. Scartezzini (Madrid: Alianza, 1996), 82.

3. Marramao, "Universalismo y políticas de la diferencia," 83-84.

4. Marramao, "Universalismo y políticas de la diferencia," 84-86.

5. Marramao, "Universalismo y políticas de la diferencia," 86ff.

6. John Rawls, "The Law of Peoples," in *On Human Rights*, ed. S. Shute and S. Hurley (New York: Basic Books, 1993), 71. For the final version of this monograph see John Rawls, *The Law of Peoples* (with "The Idea of Public Reason Revisited") (Cambridge, Mass.: Harvard University Press, 1999), 80. This enlarged version improves considerably his argumentation, although the content remains identical. I have analyzed it carefully in J. Rubio-Carracedo, "Justicia internacional y derechos humanos. Comentario al

último Rawls," in J. Rubio-Carracedo, J. M. Rosales, and M. Toscano, *Ciudadanía, nacionalismo y derechos humanos* (Madrid: Trotta, 2000), 189-215. In the same book I have also dealt with some ideas this chapter: "¿Derechos liberales o derechos humanos?" 153-70.

7. M. J. Herskovits, *Acculturation: The Study of Culture Contracts* (New York: Louis Valtey, 1936); *Man and His Works: The Science of Cultural Anthropology* (New York: McGraw-Hill, 1948).

8. See Alasdair MacIntyre, *After Virtue* (Notre Dame, Ind.: University of Notre Dame Press, 1981); and Alan Gewirth, *Reason and Morality* (Chicago: University of Chicago Press, 1978). A careful examination of the debate is made by G. J. Walters in his "MacIntyre or Gewirth? Virtue, Rights and the Problem of Moral Indeterminacy," in *Philosophical Perspectives on Human Rights*, ed. W. Sweet (Amsterdam: Rodopi, 1999).

9. The formulation reads as follows: "Act in accord with the generic rights of your recipients as well as of yourself." See Gewirth, *Reason and Morality*, 135.

10. MacIntyre, *After Virtue*, 67-69.

11. Alan Gewirth, *The Community of Rights* (Chicago: University of Chicago Press, 1996), 10-11.

12. José Rubio-Carracedo, "Ciudadanía compleja y democracia," in J. Rubio-Carracedo, J. M. Rosales, and M. Toscano, *Ciudadanía, nacionalismo y derechos humanos*, 21-45; a previous and abridged version is J. M. Rosales and J. Rubio-Carracedo, "To Govern Pluralism: Towards a Concept of Complex Citizenship," in *Rule of Law: Political and Legal Systems in Transition*, ed. W. Krawietz, E. Pattaro, and A. Erh-Soon Tay (Berlin: Duncker & Humblot, 1997), 305-11.

13. See Ignacio Ara Pinilla, *Las transformaciones de los derechos humanos* (Madrid: Tecnos, 1994) and A. E. Pérez-Luño, "Derechos humanos y constitucionalismo en la actualidad: ¿continuidad o cambio de paradigma?" in *Derechos humanos y constitucionalismo ante el tercer milenio*, ed. A. E. Pérez-Luño (Madrid: Marcial Pons, 1996), 11-52. I have addressed this issue in Rubio-Carracedo, "¿Derechos liberales o derechos humanos?"

14. W. T. de Bary and Tu Weiming, eds., *Confucianism and Human Rights* (New York: Columbia University Press, 1998). Another, less convincing study is E. P. Mendes and A.-M. Traeholt, *Human Rights: Chinese and Canadian Perspectives* (Ottawa: University of Ottawa Press, 1997).

15. Tu Weiming, "Epilogue," in *Confucianism and Human Rights*, ed. W. T. de Bary and Tu Weiming, 301.

16. Marramao, "Universalismo y políticas de la diferencia," 90.

17. See above note 6.

18. Quoted by Richard Rorty in "Human Rights, Rationality and Sentimentality," in *On Human Rights*, ed. S. Shute and S. Hurley, 115-16.

19. Rorty, "Human Rights, Rationality and Sentimentality," 122.

20. Rorty, "Human Rights, Rationality and Sentimentality," 123.

21. Rorty, "Human Rights, Rationality and Sentimentality," 127.

22. Rorty, "Human Rights, Rationality and Sentimentality," 130.

23. Rorty, "Human Rights, Rationality and Sentimentality," 134.

24. See Jesús González Amuchastegui, "Derechos humanos, universalidad y relativismo cultural," in *La Corte y el Sistema Interamericano de Derechos Humanos*, ed. R. Nieto Navia (San José, Costa Rica, 1994), 212-15. I am grateful to the author for facilitating me his paper and the texts of the four Declarations. A more detailed presentation is J. González Amuchastegui, "¿Son los derechos humanos universales?," *Anuario de Filosofía del Derecho* XV (1998): 49-78.

25. An official statement by the Information Office of the State Council had strongly remarked the differentiality of "Asian values" and the thesis that human rights were "always and inevitably" determined by the "historical, social, economic and cultural

conditions of the different nations:" *Human Rights in China* (Beijing: Foreign Languages Press, 1991), ii.

26. See the complete text of the Declaration at the United Nations website: <http://www.un.org/rights>. See also Kevin Boyle, "Stock-Taking on Human Rights: The World Conference on Human -rights, Vienna 1993," in *Politics and Human Rights*, ed. David Beetham (Oxford: Blackwell, 1995), 79-95.

27. See Antonio Cassese, *Human Rights in a Changing World* (Cambridge: Polity, 1990) and A. An-Na'im, ed., *Human Rights in Cross-Cultural Perspectives: A Quest for Consensus* (Philadelphia: University of Pennsylvania Press, 1992).

28. Rubio-Carracedo, "¿Derechos liberales o derechos humanos?"

29. González Amuchastegui cites in his "Derechos humanos, universalidad y relativismo cultural" the testimony by Aung San Suu Kyi, the Burmese Nobel Prize winner, who is surprised by, and even considers "insulting," the assumption that westeners tend to see easteners are "uncapable" to understand human rights as the expresion of the "inherent dignity and of the equal and inalienable rights of human beings," as if they might be "opposed to our own values."

Index

About the Contributors

Benjamin R. Barber is the Walt Whitman Professor of Political Science and director of the Whitman Center for the Culture and Politics of Democracy at Rutgers University. A political and educational consultant, writer for television and the theater, he is founder and honorary vice president of the IPSA Research Committee on Political Philosophy. Barber sits on the editorial boards of journals such as *Political Theory*, *The Responsive Community* or *CRISPP*, and is the author of *Jihad vs. McWorld* (1995), *A Place for Us: How to Make Society Civil and Democracy Strong* (1998), and *A Passion for Democracy: American Essays* (1998).

John Crowley is a research fellow at the Centre d'Études et Recherches Internationales of the French Council of Scientific Research. A corresponding editor of *CRISPP* and one of the vice presidents of the IPSA Research Committee on Political Philosophy, his research focuses principally on the theory of complex democracy, with particular reference to the interface between sociology and political theory. His recent publications include *Sans épines, la rose. Tony Blair: un modèle pour l'Europe?* (1999), and the essays "The Politics of Belonging: Some Theoretical Considerations" (1999), and "Some Thoughts on Theorizing European Citizenship" (1999).

Omar Dahbour is Assistant Professor of Philosophy at Hunter College, City University of New York. He is the editor of "Philosophical Perspectives on National Identity," a special issue of the *Philosophical Forum* (1996-97), coeditor of *The Nationalist Reader* (1995), and author of the essay "The Nation-State as a Political Community" (1998). Currently, he is finishing a book manuscript on national self-determination.

Fred R. Dallmayr is Packey J. Dee Professor of Political Theory at the University of Notre Dame. A vice president of the IPSA Research Committee on Political Philosophy, an Associate Editor of *The Review of Politics*, and a member of the editorial boards of journals such as *Human Studies*, *Constellations*, and *CRISPP*, Dallmayr is author of such recent books as *Hegel: Modernity and Politics* (1993), *The Other Heidegger* (1993), *Beyond Orientalism* (1996), and *Alternative Visions: Paths in the Global Village* (1998). He is also author of a forthcoming book titled *Achieving Our World* (2001).

Kennan Ferguson teaches in the Department of Government and International Affairs at the University of South Florida. He is the author of, along with a number of essays, the book *The Politics of Judgment: Aesthetics, Identity, and Political Theory* (1999).

Pedro Francés-Gómez is Assistant Professor of Moral and Political Philosophy at the Complutense University of Madrid. Currently working on economic approaches to general and applied ethics and political philosophy, he is the author of the essays "El contractualismo de mercado como modelo de legitimación política" (1997), "La alternativa contractualista" (1999), and the editor of the Spanish translation of David Gauthier's essays collected in *Egoísmo, moralidad y sociedad liberal* (1998).

Matteo Gianni teaches in the Department of Political Science at the University of Geneva. He is the author of the essays "Multiculturalism and Political Integration: The Need for a Differentiated Citizenship?" (1997), "Taking Multiculturalism Seriously: Political Claims for a Differentiated Citizenship" (1998), and the book *Multiculturalisme et intégration politique: La citoyenneté entre reconnaissance de la différence et reconnaissance de l'égalité* (2000).

Alan Gilbert is Professor in the Graduate School of International Studies at the University of Denver. A democratic activist since the 1960s, he is the author of *Marx's Politics: Communists and Citizens* (1981), *Democratic Individuality* (1990), and *Must Global Politics Constrain Democracy?* (1999). Currently he is finishing a book manuscript to be entitled *Emancipation and Independence: The American Revolution, Haiti, and Latin American Liberation*.

Judit Hell is Associate Professor and Deputy Chair of the Department of Philosophy at the University of Miskolc. Secretary of the Commission for Social Theory of the Hungarian Academy of Sciences in Northern Hungary, she is also president of the Condorcet Cercle in northern Hungary. She is the author of the essays "Ethische und juristische Annäherungen an den sanften Tod" (1996), "Die Stellung der Frauenforschung und Frauenbewegungen in Ungarn" (1999), and editor of the book *Multikulturalismus. Studien—Multiculturalism. Studies* (1998).

Ferenc L. Lendvai is Professor and Chair of the Department of Philosophy at the University of Miskolc. Member of the Doctor Council of the Hungarian Academy of Sciences and of the Philosophical Commission of the Hungarian Academy of Sciences, he is co-editor of the journal *Magyar Filozófiai Szemle*. He is the author, among other books, of *Közép-Európa koncepciók* (1997), and the essays "Religion, Kirche und Politik in Ost-Mitteleuropa" (1992) and "Alte und Moderne Multikulturalität im Westen und im Osten" (1998).

Eero Loone is Professor Emeritus at the Department of Philosophy, University of Tartu. Member of the Governing Body of the Estonian Union of Scientists, a free association set up at the time when Estonia started to regain its independence from the Soviet Union, he is the author of the book *Soviet Marxism and Analytical Philosophy of History* (1992) and the essays "'They Were Not Quite Like Us': The Presumption of Qualitative Difference in Historical Writing" (1998) and "Rational and Reasonable Justifiability of States: Ethnic Pluralism and the Concept of Nation" (1999).

Teresa López de la Vieja is Profesora Titular of Moral and Political Philosophy at the University of Salamanca. Currently working on feminism, ethics, and political philosophy, she is the editor of *Política de la vitalidad: "España invertebrada" de J. Ortega y Gasset* (1996), and author of the books *Etica: Procedimientos razonables* (1994) and *Principios morales y casos prácticos* (2000). She is also editor of the book *Feminismo: Del pasado al presente* (2000).

Tuija Pulkkinen is senior research fellow at the Academy of Finland at Christina Institute of Womens' Studies. Affiliated with the Department of Social and Moral Philosophy at the University of Helsinki, her current research focus on feminism and nationalism. She is the author of *Valtio ja vapaus* [The State and Liberty] (1989), *Postmoderni politiikan filosofia* (1998), and *The Postmodern and Political Agency* (2nd ed., 2000).

José María Rosales is Profesor Titular of Moral and Political Philosophy at the University of Málaga. Currently, one of the vice presidents of the IPSA Research Committee on Political Philosophy, he is the author of *Patriotismo, nacionalismo y ciudadanía: En defensa de un cosmopolitismo cívico* (1997), *Política cívica: La experiencia de la ciudadanía en la democracia liberal* (1998), and co-author, with J. Rubio-Carracedo and M. Toscano-Méndez, of *Ciudadanía, nacionalismo y derechos humanos* (2000).

José Rubio-Carracedo is Professor of Moral and Political Philosophy at the University of Málaga. Currently, president of the Spanish Association of Moral and Political Philosophy, he is the author of *¿Democracia o representación? Poder y legitimidad en Rousseau* (1990), *Educación moral, postmodernidad y democracia: Más allá del liberalismo y del comunitarismo* (2nd ed., 2000), and co-author, with J. M. Rosales and M. Toscano-Méndez, of *Ciudadanía, nacionalismo y derechos humanos* (2000). He is also editor, with J. M. Rosales and M. Toscano-Méndez, of the forthcoming book *Retos pendientes en ética y política* (2001).

Paul Thomas is Professor of Political Science at the University of California, Berkeley. Founder and secretary-treasurer of the IPSA Research Committee on Political Philosophy, he is the author of *Karl Marx and the Anarchists* (1985), *Alien Politics: Marxist State Theory Retrieved* (1994), and, with D. Lloyd, *Culture and the State* (1998). He is currently at work on a book manuscript to be entitled *Scientific Socialism: Career of a Concept*.

Manuel Toscano-Méndez is Profesor Titular of Moral and Political Philosophy at the University of Málaga. Currently working on pluralism, liberal theory, and nationalism, he is the author of the book *El nuevo universalismo de Maurice Merleau-Ponty y su significado para la filosofía práctica* (1994), the essay "La tolérance et le conflit des raisons" (2000), and co-author, with J. Rubio-Carracedo and J. M. Rosales, of *Ciudadanía, nacionalismo y derechos humanos* (2000). He is also editor, with J. Rubio-Carracedo and J. M. Rosales, of the forthcoming book *Retos pendientes en ética y política* (2001).

Bryan S. Turner is head of the Faculty of Social and Political Sciences at the University of Cambridge. Editor of the journal *Citizenship Studies*, and co-editor of *Body & Society* (with M. Featherstone) and of the *Journal of Classical Sociology* (with J. O'Neill), he is the author of *Classical Sociology* (1999), co-author, with K. Brown and S. Kenny, of *Rhetorics of Welfare* (2000), and editor of *The Blackwell Companion to Social Theory* (2000).

Iván Vitányi is Professor Emeritus of Sociology at the University of Budapest and former director of the Institute for Sociology of the Hungarian Academy of Sciences. A member of the Imre Nagy reform group during the 1950s, for the next three decades he has been involved in democratic resistance movements. A founder and secretary of the New March Front in 1988, since 1991 he has been a member of the leading board of the Resistance Association and spokesman for the Democratic Chart since 1993. A parliamentarian since 1990, he is the author of *A társadalom logikája* [The Logic of Society] (1997) and *The Social Democratic Vision of the Future* (1999).

Ricard Zapata-Barrero is Profesor Titular of Political Theory at the Pompeu Fabra University. Currently working on citizenship, democracy, justice, and immigration from the local to the European Union levels, he is the author of the essays "Thinking about European Citizenship from the Perspective of a Potential Euro-Foreigner" (1998), "The Limits of a Multinational Europe: Democracy and Immigration in the European Union" (2000), and the book *Ciudadanía, democracia y pluralismo cultural: Hacia un nuevo contrato social* (2000).